CHEAP ON CRIME

CHEAP ON CRIME

Recession-Era Politics and the
Transformation of American Punishment

Hadar Aviram

UNIVERSITY OF CALIFORNIA PRESS

University of California Press, one of the most distinguished university presses in the United States, enriches lives around the world by advancing scholarship in the humanities, social sciences, and natural sciences. Its activities are supported by the UC Press Foundation and by philanthropic contributions from individuals and institutions. For more information, visit www.ucpress.edu.

University of California Press
Oakland, California

Library of Congress Cataloging-in-Publication Data

Aviram, Hadar, author.
    Cheap on crime : recession-era politics and the transformation of American punishment / Hadar Aviram.
        pages cm
    Includes bibliographical references and index.
    ISBN 978-0-520-27730-4 (cloth : alk. paper)
    ISBN 978-0-520-27731-1 (pbk. : alk. paper)
    ISBN 978-0-520-96032-9 (ebook)
    1. Corrections—Economic aspects—United States.   2. Prisons—Economic aspects—United States.   I. Title.
    HV9471.A98   2015
    364.60973′090511—dc23

                                        2014027007

Manufactured in the United States of America

24   23   22   21   20   19   18   17   16   15
10   9   8   7   6   5   4   3   2   1

In keeping with a commitment to support environmentally responsible and sustainable printing practices, UC Press has printed this book on Natures Natural, a fiber that contains 30% post-consumer waste and meets the minimum requirements of ANSI/NISO Z39.48–1992 (R 1997) (*Permanence of Paper*).

To Chad, Spade, and Archer
for their unconditional, unwavering love
and in loving memory of my grandfather
Shmuel Katvan

CONTENTS

ILLUSTRATIONS

FIGURES

TABLES

ACKNOWLEDGMENTS

The seed for this book was planted in 2008, when several of my colleagues at UC Hastings College of the Law met to discuss the possibility of organizing a conference on the California correctional crisis. We were expecting a decision in *Plata v. Schwarzenegger* to be delivered later in the year, and as a newcomer to the American correctional scene, I decided to start a blog about corrections in California as a way to promote the conference, as well as a vehicle to learn and educate.

A few months after the blog came to life I started noticing cracks in the punitive facade of American punishment and identifying nonpunitive trends justified by cost arguments. I started collecting examples of these trends on the blog and thinking about them more deeply. The California Correctional Crisis conference of 2009 was an opportunity to start pondering the future of the criminal justice system, and it yielded my first publication on recession-era criminal justice policy. This book was already well under way when we held a sequel conference in 2013, "California Correctional Crisis: Realignment and Reform." My work on the blog and the conferences, and my involvement in advocacy and education in California, allowed me to engage with lawmakers, advocates, activists, families of victims and offenders, and formerly incarcerated people and discuss the main themes of this book.

During the course of the project, I received wonderful feedback and advice from many scholars and activists working on criminal justice and corrections. My mentor and friend, Malcolm Feeley, offered advice and asked excellent questions about privatization. Margo Schlanger and Sharon Dolovich organized an informative prison research workshop, during which I had an opportunity to think about the broad themes of the book. David Ball offered a money-savvy, pragmatic perspective on local government. Mona Lynch and Jonathan Simon sat with me for dinner in Ann Arbor, heard the first version of the thesis, and provided support and constructive feedback. David Greenberg sent numerous useful newspaper clippings. Selena Teji exchanged ideas and thoughts about the California Criminal Justice Realignment. Jeanne Woodford and Ana Zamora offered thoughts about the death penalty abolition campaign. Alessandro De Giorgi, Ben Fleury-Steiner, Paul Kaplan, Edi Kinney, Josh Page, Michelle Phelps, Keramet Reiter, Kimberly Richman, Ashley Rubin, and other members of the Punishment and Social Control collaborative research network met with me at conferences and enriched the creative process with their thoughts and perspectives. The good people at KALW, the *Daily Journal,* CBS-5, KTVU, the *San Francisco Bay Guardian,* and the *Recorder* gave me opportunities to speak with, and hear from, the public on current events. The excellent and dedicated lawyers at the Prison Law Office and at Rosen, Bien, Galvan and Grundfeld offered food for thought at every encounter. The Crime Group at Hebrew University, the Law and Society Forum at Haifa University, the law school at the University of Hong Kong, and the Law and Society research group at the University of Hawai'i at Mānoa graciously invited me for workshops and offered feedback that transcended the national context. Michael Munger, Barry Winegast, and Todd Zywicki taught me public choice economics and furnished me with enriching tools and vocabulary that came just at the right moment.

My colleagues at Hastings were invaluable in shaping my ideas and offered advice and resources. Special thanks go to Kate Bloch, George Bisharat, John Crawford, Heather Field, Caitlin Henry, Eumi Lee, Evan Lee, Rory Little, Aaron Rappaport, Dorit Reiss, Reuel Schiller, Darien Shanske, and David Takacs. Dean Frank Wu and Academic Deans Shauna Marshall and Beth Hillman provided me with institutional encouragement and support, as well as with the necessary resources, in the form of the Harry and Lillian Hastings Research Chair. All my students, and especially the members of the Criminal Law Society and the editorial board of the *Hastings Race and Poverty Law Journal,* inspired me to think more deeply and write better.

The book would never have come to life without the intelligent and thorough work of my phenomenal team of fact checkers and research assistants: Deanna Dyer, Alexandra Jacobs, Amanda Leaf, Ryan Newby, Lizabeth Pollack, Darah Protas, Rosie Reith, and S.C. Thomas. Chuck Marcus provided outstanding and knowledgeable library assistance.

The process of working on the book was pleasant, collaborative, and enriching thanks to everyone at the University of California Press, particularly Maura Roessner and Jack Young.

Any mistakes, omissions, and inaccuracies are, of course, my own.

Life, John Lennon said, is what happens to you while you're busy making other plans, and in the process of working on this book I suffered several medical and personal setbacks that made my work very difficult, including the prolonged illness and subsequent loss of my beloved grandfather Shmuel Katvan. Grandpa and I spoke on the phone every day during his long illness, and he frequently expressed interest in the project and asked great questions. My parents, Yael and Haim Aviram, offered immense love. Also in my circle of support were Dr. Xiao-Ping Cheng, Dr. Keely Kolmes, Karsten Gryziec, Brian Soo, the swimming community at the Sports Club L.A. and at USF Masters, the South End Rowing Club and the Marathon Swimmers Federation, Raeeka Shehabi-Yaghmai and all the singers at Taneen Voice Studio, and my cadre of brilliant and loving friends: Suzanne Atkinson, Eric Chase, Sharon Cowan, Heather Eloph, Inbal Etgar, Rosie Etis, Yael Finberg-Liebi, Shachar Fuman, Francisco Hulse, Cynthia Gómez, Amit Landau, Schachar Levin, Katie Morrison, Tal Niv, Jacqueline Omotalade, Annick Persinger, Yvonne Rathbone, and Robert Rubin.

The California inmates' hunger strike in protest of solitary confinement ended shortly before I completed the first draft of the manuscript. Their struggle for dignity and human rights has inspired me beyond measure. I was also deeply moved by the dialogue between victim families and death penalty abolition advocates in the aftermath of Proposition 34's failure in California. Their shared humanity was a reminder that, beyond the incessant chatter about dollars and cents, there is no "other" and we are all in this together. My heart goes out to all those who suffer and struggle in the trenches of the American mass incarceration project and believe in the possibility of transformation.

INTRODUCTION

At five-thirty on a San Francisco summer morning, Aquatic Park is still shrouded in menacing darkness. Figures in heavy coats and swim parkas slowly make their way toward a grassy patch overlooking the water, sipping hot beverages and donning their swim gear. Shortly before sunrise, as we listen to a briefing about this morning's currents and water temperature, we can already see it looming in the dark: Alcatraz Prison, standing proud and somber upon The Rock. Today is race day.

Even after many years of experience in open water races, including several successful Alcatraz crossings, the mile-and-a-half swim course from Alcatraz Island to Aquatic Park is a treacherous route. San Francisco Bay is characterized by ever-changing tides, uncomfortable temperatures, and murky waters hiding a surprising array of marine life, all of which require careful attention to the race director's instructions and will later demand resilience and good navigational skills. After the briefing, we all walk along a sleepy Fishermen's Wharf and board the ferry that will take us to The Rock.

Excitement on the ferry builds up as we prepare to jump. For security reasons, we jump about fifty feet away from the rocks of Alcatraz. The platform is a few feet high; some swimmers are already in the water, stroking quickly to avoid being hit by subsequent jumpers. As I await my turn to jump with a mix of excitement and dread, I enjoy listening to swimmers from all over the world engaging in excited chatter in a dazzling number of languages.

It's my turn to jump. The coldness of the water, its absolute darkness, stun me for a minute. Despite having jumped into the water in this very location numerous times, the initial shock can only be predicted, not prevented. A thought races through my head: Perhaps this is not my day. Perhaps today I shouldn't do this. It's so cold. It's so hard. It's so choppy. Another voice tells me: Swim faster, and it'll be over faster.

After a few hundreds of strokes I look back over my right shoulder. The Rock looms large, close, and threatening in the early morning light, dwarfing my progress. How frustrating this effort to escape must have felt to Alcatraz inmates trying to flee their terrifying place of confinement. Most attempts to escape Alcatraz were thwarted before the escapees managed to even enter the bay, but some inmates managed to go as far as to immerse themselves in the water.[1] On December 16, 1937, Theodore Cole and Ralph Roe escaped under the cover of fog, dove into the icy water, and were never seen again. On September 15, 1941, John Bayless eluded the guards while working his garbage detail; he jumped into the water, but the cold got the better of him and he quickly gave up. On April 14, 1943, James Boardman, Harold Brest, Floyd Hamilton, and Fred Hunter managed to overpower their guards and escape into the water; guards opened fire on them. Some of the bodies were never found. And Aaron Burgett's body was found two weeks after he jumped into the water on September 29, 1958. One escapee actually managed to make it to San Francisco: On December 16, 1962, John Paul Scott cut through the bars of a kitchen window using banjo strings and an improvised saw. He jumped to the water and swam to shore. With no fancy breakfast, race information on tides, wetsuits, or interval training with a masters team, Scott successfully swam to shore and made it to Fort Point, only to be found by teenagers in a state of severe hypothermia.

But the escapees that most engage my imagination are Frank Morris and the Anglin brothers—John and Clarence—who, on June 11, 1962, carried out what might well have been the only successful Alcatraz escape. Chiseling away concrete from the wall of a utility corridor, disguising the noise by working as accordions played during music hour, they dug an escape route through an air vent. Their bodies were never found. The lore among the open-water swimming community is that Morris and the Anglin brothers made it successfully to shore. I like to imagine them, now old men in berets and old-fashioned suits, sitting at Café Tosca in North Beach, quietly chuckling into the *San Francisco Chronicle* or the *Examiner*, congratulating themselves privately on their success.

It is precisely its natural isolation, the inhospitable waters that surround it, and the existing structures of the military prison that preceded it that made Alcatraz such an attractive venue for a maximum-security federal institution. And yet, as I swim toward the Ghirardelli towers and Fort Mason, I wonder: Had no one questioned the financial expenditure and the alternative attractive usages of the island? Tourists flock to Alcatraz to see the prison and hear stories of its most famous inhabitants but also to appreciate its natural beauty. In an alternate universe, in which the correctional project was less of a priority, Alcatraz could be home to beautiful picnic and hiking grounds, perhaps a nature reserve, perhaps a vacation resort. But even if institutions like Alcatraz were deemed necessary to incarcerate the "worst of the worst," our immense investment in the complex web of federal, state, and local institutions reflects our limited collective imagination. Many of the prisons nationwide occupy beautiful, scenic locations; San Quentin's location on the North Bay shore is a prime example. Other prisons are built amid small towns, where many residents come to accept their existence as an inevitable fact on the ground, assuming their essential role in the towns' economies and being surprisingly unaware of the thousands of lives lived within those walls, either in remote locations or in close proximity to the life outside. Our constant financial support of the gargantuan machinery and expenditure required by the American punitive project is rivaled by our willful blindness to the way our taxes and bonds are spent in its service.

China Mieville's *The City and the City*,[2] a noir-fantasy novel, tells of two European city-states that share the same geographic space but do not have mutual diplomatic relations. Each city's residents are socialized from infancy to "unsee" any person, building, landmark, or vehicle pertaining to the other city. Like the unseen city in the novel, the carceral machinery is largely invisible to the public that funds its operations. For the past forty years, the number of residents in the unseen city has risen astronomically, to 2.3 million, financed by a public that remains woefully uninformed about and uninterested in its existence. We have created incarceration policies that send eighty thousand people to rot in solitary confinement for twenty-two and a half hours a day. We have created a mind-boggling system of sentencing enhancements whose complicated mathematics have sent people to decades in prison, constructed upon previous offenses, circumstances of the offense, and other add-up factors. We have built back doors through which those who are released from prison may end up behind those invisible gates for technical parole violations, their short stints in our world between revolving door incarceration periods keeping us oblivious to their unseen lives. And we have spent many years paying for these intricate passages and hallways with considerable percentages of our state and local budgets. While we may be dismayed by our own impermeability to human rights concerns, to doubts about the power of deterrence and incapacitation, to the realization that our fellow citizens and residents are behind bars and most of them will return to us, it is particularly puzzling to me that, in a society obsessed with Keynesian cost-benefit calculations, in which questions of ideological values, social responsibility, and public priorities are so frequently framed as concerns about public spending, we have not, until recently, seriously questioned our collective investment in what many have come to call the prison industrial complex.

But recent developments in the correctional world suggest that the tables have begun to turn on four decades of financial support coupled with ignorance. For the first time in thirty-seven years, 2009 saw a decline in the overall numbers of prisoners in the United States. Traditionally punitive states have modified their correctional policies, closing down prisons and reducing their reliance on solitary confinement. In the past seven years, several states have abolished the death penalty or placed moratoria upon executions. Many states are increasingly open to early releases, geriatric and medical parole policies, and modifications of their contract with private prison service providers to allow for an overall smaller number of incarcerations. Conversations about drug legalization have led two states to legalize recreational marijuana use, and politicians of all stripes are seemingly less concerned about advocating such nonpunitive reforms and appearing "soft on crime."

This book attributes the increased political and public support for these transformations to the Great Recession of 2008. It should, however, be stressed at the onset that this book does not advance a hard causal connection between the recession and all changes in punishment. Some of the shift toward less punitive perspective preceded the crisis, and some of it can be attributed to a combination of factors, of which the crisis is only one. Nor does this book argue that current correctional policies represent a distinctive break from the philosophies that characterized corrections before the financial crisis. Quite the contrary: the economic events that have created political legitimacy and opportunity for these transformations have not generated a shift in our overall "tough on crime" mentality. We have not become more attuned to human rights concerns or more optimistic about rehabilitation. In many ways, we are still a society of risk, engaging in selective incapacitation of its underclass, perceiving their oppression and confinement through the same neoliberal frame of reference. And, while some things have gotten better, as this book argues, some things have gotten worse, and some things are doomed to remain the same for some time to come.

My argument, therefore, is that the advent of the financial crisis has given rise to a prominent new discourse of cost, frugality, and prudence, which has permeated our political and public conversations about corrections and has become a powerful rhetoric and motivator in political campaigns and administrative negotiations. I call this new discourse "humonetarianism," a term I chose because it draws attention to the cost-centered logic behind nonpunitive reforms. Humonetarian discourse is prioritized and prominently displayed at the forefront for traditionally polarizing public conversations, such as the question of death penalty abolition and the future of the war on drugs. An anatomy of campaigns, public statements, and policies shows that this discourse is utilized in a way that disarms the political impasse and allows politicians, policy makers, businesspeople, and taxpayers to find common ground and reach significant compromises in the penal field that were more difficult to achieve without the broad appeal of humonetarianism.

The expectation that periods of economic downturn might make a difference in the correctional realm is not new; opinions differ, however, as to the form such change might take. Chapter 1 lays out the theoretical framework for the book's argument. An increasing chorus of punishment scholars attributes the sorry state of the American penal landscape to the proliferation of neoliberal ideologies, and in particular to the free market materialist and instrumentalist rationality behind mass privatization of the state, including corrections. This increased reliance on market self-regulation and the decline of the public sphere also imply an erosion in the sense of social responsibility for the lower rungs of the socioeconomic ladder, manifest in a "new penology" with no lofty goals, just risk management, selective incapacitation, and administrative confinement. This approach may have transformed American punishment in the past two decades, but how might it be affected by a severe economic downturn? One approach relies on social historical accounts of the correlation between punishment and the economic structure, in the tradition of Rusche and Kirchheimer's *Punishment and Social Structure,* which sees punishment as an extension and expression of the mode of production. In the late 1930s, Rusche and Kirchheimer predicted that an increase in unemployment (one of the major markers of an economic downturn) would also generate harsher punishment, because of the punitive animus directed at a threateningly idle underclass. Quantitative studies in later decades have confirmed that unemployment tends, indeed, to generate harsher punishment across cultures, and scholars in the tradition of social history have noted that punitive animus under such circumstances tends to be directed at the weakest members of society. On the other hand, economists analyzing the costs of crime and justice, in the tradition of Gary Becker's work from the 1960s, have argued that a given society can only mete out as much punishment as it can afford, and recent econometric studies suggest that the correctional apparatus expands and contracts with the rise and fall of the economy. Both perspectives have immense merit, and as the rest of the book shows, both, to a great extent, are validated by the phenomena we are witnessing since the early days of the Great Recession: harsh economic conditions may generate a more punitive animus, and are therefore not the centerpiece for a humanitarian penal reform, but may also make the large correctional project ultimately unsustainable and prompt developments that affect its capacity.

With these perspectives in mind, chapter 2 sets out to test them by examining the financial history of mass incarceration. Beginning with the era of Prohibition and its repeal following the Great Depression, the book examines an era of penal parsimony and public nonpunitivism seldom covered by current mass incarceration scholars. The repeal of Prohibition is framed here in the context of public despair of the futile expenditures in the losing federal battle against organized crime. This trend proceeded through the New Deal years of economic recovery, leading to small federal expenditures in crime control justified by war investment and low crime rates. In the 1950s and 1960s, the advent of federal investment in state criminal justice was born of an ideological clash between the Warren Court's federalization of criminal procedure as a constitutional enterprise and the Nixon administration's federalization of policing as an enforcement and administration enterprise. Ironically, these politically polarized developments both led to a fundamental transformation of crime control, which, while still an overwhelmingly local enterprise, was now part of a broader, and more closely supervised, national phenomenon. While the pattern of federal funding pertained largely to the front end of the criminal process, the states mostly were left to their own devices with respect to its back end, namely, the need to find incarceration solutions for an increasing population of inmates resulting from the increased capacity to apprehend and convict. Different states had different traditions of incarceration, ranging from the massive California correctional apparatus to the Arizona and Texas "tough 'n' cheap" models, but all states experienced a considerable expansion of their punitive needs. As a result, states increasingly recurred to more intricate, and less transparent, financial instruments that facilitated funding for speedy prison construction and the privatization, if not of the institutions themselves, of their basic functions and services.

But these models of expenditure had to undergo considerable transformation when the financial crisis of 2008 threw the country into a deep recession. Chapter 3 offers a brief account of the advent of the crisis, followed by an analysis of its impact on state and local budget systems in general and on allocations for corrections in particular. Despite the considerable percentage of state budgets devoted to corrections, it was the financial crisis that drew public and professional awareness to the need to conform correctional practices to this new period of austerity. The chapter then presents the basic tenets of humonetarian discourse: far from a critical examination of punitivism, and even farther from an embrace of dignity and human rights, humonetarianism is the growing tendency to view criminal justice and correctional policies primarily through a prism of cost. Its emergence in an era of scarcity and desperate solutions means that this perspective seems, for the most part, shallow and focused on the short term. Humonetarian discourse is characterized by turning to former enemies—libertarians, old-school free market economists, and financially prudent politicians of all stripes—as new allies to create initiatives and alternatives that roll back years of punitive legislation. Humonetarianism is also characterized by a unique perspective on the prison population: the dying perception of inmates as wards of the state, which gave way to a neoliberal reclassification of inmates as burdensome consumers of precious resources, also led to a new focus on groups of inmates that received little attention prior to the crisis, such as the old and the infirm, whose incarceration tends to be particularly costly, as well as to inmates caught in a pattern of lengthy incarceration by habitual offender laws.

Chapters 4 through 7 discuss, respectively, the four main traits of humonetarianism. Chapter 4 uses the recent campaigns to abolish the death penalty as a case study for humonetarian rhetoric, its promise and its pitfalls. Since the onset of the financial crisis, six states have abolished the death penalty, and SAFE California—a proposition to put an end to the nation's largest death row at San Quentin—failed by the narrowest margin of support for the death penalty since the 1960s. A genealogy of anti–death penalty arguments shows how the abolitionist discussion increasingly gave up on depth (arguments pertaining to human rights and concerns about government overreach) in favor of arguments with broader public appeal, culminating in the current focus on cost and wrongful convictions. SAFE California is analyzed in depth as a quintessential example of humonetarian advocacy. Humonetarianism, however, may be a double-edged sword, as several states consider amending their death penalty statutes to streamline the process and eliminate costly postconviction remedies using the same logic as that of the new abolitionists.

Chapter 5 examines the way in which cost-centered rhetoric has freed politicians and stakeholders of all political stripes not only to discuss crime control in financial terms, but to collaborate across political divides in nonpunitive initiatives. The chapter shows how crime has gradually disappeared from the national agenda, from the days of Nixon's crime control platform and Reagan's war on drugs to the Obama administration's more conciliatory rhetoric. It follows up with a few examples of political players from across the political map—a liberal attorney general, a radical prison abolitionist organization, and a group of fiscally prudent conservative politicians—who, in different ways, have shifted their advocacy on penal and correctional reform from the once-obligatory "tough on crime" rhetoric to "smart on crime" or "right on crime." These perspectives converge on various issues, but their quintessential example is the decline of the war on drugs, particularly in the arena of marijuana legalization. The successful campaigns to legalize marijuana in Washington and Colorado are provided as examples of humonetarian discourse carefully crafted to appeal to mainstream voters and to create alliances for fiscally advantageous policies across the political spectrum.

Chapter 6 turns from political rhetoric to recession-era incarceration policies and shows the interaction of humonetarian discourse with the logic of the market in transforming state and local incarceration, creating an ever-changing landscape of privatization, out-of-state incarceration, jurisdictional and geographic shifts, and prison closures. The chapter begins by examining the changing business practices of private prison providers, and in particular the colossal Corrections Corporation of America, which has adapted to the humonetarian era by adopting a conciliatory, long-term approach to its contracts with states and localities while at the same time diversifying its investment in the correctional market toward even more marginalized populations such as undocumented immigrants and advocating punitive legislation for profit. I then examine recent trends in prison closures, the usage of good-time credits, the increasing openness to cheap alternatives to incarceration, and the recession-era transactions involved in out-of-state incarcerations, fluctuating with states' relative progress in balancing their correctional checkbooks. The effects of these changes on the overall welfare of the prison population, including overcrowding, health care, and access to rehabilitation programs, are discussed. Finally, I examine the California Criminal Justice Realignment, which shifted all nonserious, nonviolent, nonsexual offenders away from state prisons to county jails, thus holding counties financially accountable for their sentencing practices, as well as the ways in which the budgetary implications of this significant sentencing reform are used as pawns in the struggle between the state and federal courts.

Chapter 7 examines the ways in which the humonetarian perception of inmates is particularly conducive to the neoliberal tendency to see them less as wards of the state, the provision of whose basic needs is a taken-for-granted state obligation, and more as financially burdensome loci of consumer decision making and responsibilities. This represents a subtle but important shift from the decades-long practice of perceiving and classifying inmates according to risk toward an increasing incorporation of cost into the equation. The chapter shows how this powerful mechanism of classification operates in creating policies for previously invisible prison populations, such as the elderly and the infirm; how the expense involved in housing long-term inmates played a central role in the 2012 passage of California's Proposition 36, which reformed the Three Strikes Law; and how an increasing reluctance to shoulder the costs involved in incarceration has lent support to the pre-recession practice of rolling incarceration costs onto the inmates themselves, through "pay-to-stay" programs, self-financed GPS mechanisms, and the like.

Finally, chapter 8 assesses the future of humonetarianism and its potential to generate real, lasting change in America's penal ideology. Returning to the sociohistorical and economic perspectives presented earlier in the book, the chapter concludes that recession-era politics have supported a complex web of changes, some of which may have an unexpected benign and malignant impact on the correctional apparatus. Since the book does not aim to present a hard causal model, I pay attention to other factors, such as lower crime rates and more fundamental arguments against punitivism, and examine how these factors work in tandem with humonetarian discourse. I also tackle the thorny philosophical question of the moral and discursive price of an increasingly shallow public conversation, emptied of dignity, equality, and concern for human rights, and the ways in which reformers committed to ending mass incarceration can reframe the cost argument as a deeper, more inclusive perspective on the criminal process.

While this book highlights winds of change—some benign, some sinister—brought about by a sense of economic scarcity, the real challenge ahead lies in generating long-lasting change on a publicly acceptable platform. Chapter 8 offers some thoughts about the lasting effect of humonetarianism as the Great Recession comes to an end. While I am more optimistic about some humonetarian changes than others, I believe that, for activists and under certain conditions, the crisis presents a unique opportunity to refocus public discourse on important matters of priority and not simply to regress to the most punitive common ground.

After taking a conservative course along the barges stationed in the Bay, I push through the current and make it into the protected waters of Aquatic Park. I swim as far in to shore as I can before standing up. I stroke until my fingers start grazing the sand, then set one foot on the ground, then the other. Safely on shore, huddled in my swim parka and sipping hot tea, I look into the distance, seeing flocks of fellow athletes who have successfully escaped from Alcatraz this morning. May you, gentle reader, find this book a guide and a companion to you in our collective escape from an expensive and unsustainable system that has us all imprisoned, and may it raise your awareness of the potential and pitfalls of a serious economic crisis as a catalyst that may, under certain conditions, bring us all safely to better shores.

TALKING ABOUT MONEY
AND PUNISHMENT

This book maps and explores the impact of the financial crisis on the American correctional landscape and examines how scarcity and austerity, real and perceived, have changed the discourses and policies that characterized the past forty years of mass incarceration. The Great Recession catapulted financial scarcity to the top of the list of American concerns, yielding humonetarianism—a set of rhetorical arguments, political strategies, correctional policies, and cultural perceptions that focuses on cost-saving and financial prudence as its raison d'être. Assessing the extent to which this new discourse can achieve real and lasting change to the American penal system as its effects unfold is a challenging task and requires a deep theoretical understanding of large-scale predictions of economic conditions. I want to begin therefore by building on a rich body of literature examining the interaction between crime, punishment, and the economy. Much of this literature situates the American mass incarceration of the past forty years (and sometimes the events that preceded it) in the context of American neoliberal politics, attributing this punitive turn to privatization, alienation, increasing social gaps, and the retreat of the state from responsibilities to the lowest rungs in its social ladder. Against this backdrop, this chapter presents two theories that offer predictions regarding the impact of an economic downturn on punishment: Marxist social historical theories, which predict increased punitivism in eras of increased unemployment, and economic analysis of the criminal justice system, which predicts that the extent of punishment will conform to the ability to punish and therefore shrink during economic downturns.

NEOLIBERALISM, PUNITIVISM, AND THE PRISON
INDUSTRIAL COMPLEX

Recent years have produced an explosion of macro-level critical analyses of the emergence of mass incarceration in America, many of which point to economic factors. Some of these powerful works focus on the shift to political conservatism as the turning point in the journey toward punitivism, such as Katherine Beckett's *Making Crime Pay*[1] and Marie Gottschalk's *The Prison and the Gallows*.[2] In these national-level accounts, a retreat from welfarism often contributes to punitive policies: in Beckett's account, punitivism is a top-down backlash against the civil rights movement's gains in racial and social justice; in Gottschalk's account, progressive actors, such as women's rights groups, inmate's rights groups, and death penalty abolitionists remain relatively muted in a political structure that allows economic elites to capture the reins of the correctional project, sometimes co-opting these groups by funding punitive initiatives that suit their narrow interests. Economic factors matter for accounts of local punitivism as well. Vanessa Barker's *The Politics of Imprisonment*,[3] which compares criminal justice legislation in California, New York, and Washington, addresses the political differences between the three states to account for California's punitivism, New York's neutral stance, and Washington's parsimony. Her analysis of the political cultures of the three states takes into account their economic structure and history. Mona Lynch's *Sunbelt Justice*,[4] which addresses the growth of the correctional apparatus in Arizona, is attentive to the change in that state's economic responsibilities and its move from "tough 'n' cheap" politics through a brief period of positivism and welfarism to a culture of punishment based on libertarian ideology. Robert Perkinson's *Texas Tough* focuses on Texas's heritage of a slavery-based economy as the explanation for its punitiveness, aimed particularly toward people of color,[5] an explanation echoed (on the national level) by Michelle Alexander's *The New Jim Crow*.[6] While Lynch, Perkinson, and Alexander all highlight the important role of racism and xenophobia in shaping penal policies, they do not ignore the ways in which economic self-sufficiency and free market ideology have become proxies for racism and xenophobia. Ruth Gilmore's *Golden Gulag*,[7] which provides an anatomy of the explosion of mass incarceration in California, addresses the financial instruments and economic mechanisms by which prison construction is funded and local cooperation guaranteed for new correctional institutions.

Some works rely even more explicitly on broad economic transformations—namely, on the American turn to neoliberal politics and free market ideology—to explain mass incarceration on a larger scale. David Garland's *The Culture of Control* attributes much of the current emphasis on crime control, victim-oriented vindictiveness, and an expansion of the punitive infrastructure to the demise of the penal welfare state and the turn to consumer capitalism.[8] Garland observes that the two last decades of the welfare state, the 1950s and 1960s, were character-ized by economic growth and an improvement in living standards. As the oil crisis struck, leading to a rise in unemployment and to growing social stratification, social solidarity crumbled, manifested, among other ways, in "white flight" of the middle classes to the suburbs and in increased spatial segregation. The broad social conditions in late modernity, including increased inequality and increased opportunities and targets for crime, yielded an increase in crime rates, which was sensationalized in the media and generated an outcry against welfarist politics. Ironically, the welfare state was attacked by those who benefited most from the conditions it created. Coupled with an increasingly conservative political climate, the demise of the welfare state led to a government that is no longer perceived, by itself and by its subjects, as able to provide a holistic answer to the challenges of crime.

Another account of punitivism as the outcome of the collapse of the welfare state is Jonathan Simon's seminal *Governing through Crime.*[9] It examines the proc-ess by which crime and crime control have become the main metaphors for all social problems and government intervention, infecting areas of life as diverse as the home, the workplace, and schools and yielding a culture of fear and isolation. Simon attributes the rise of the "war on crime" metaphor to the decline of New Deal governance in the 1960s. While Simon's focus is mainly political, he also points out that the quintessential New Deal citizen was the industrial worker, and later the vulnerable consumer, whom the government sought to protect. These perceptions of the subject of legislation were supplanted, after the collapse of the New Deal, by a perception of the citizen as, first and foremost, a potential victim, yielding an increased focus on crime control as the primary mode of protection for the individual and creating discourses and policies that addressed a variety of social problems through the tools and techniques of crime control.

Perhaps the most explicit recent attribution of crime control policies to neolib-eral ideology can be found in Loic Wacquant's *Punishing the Poor*[10] and in Joe Soss, Richard Fording, and Sanford Schram's *Disciplining the Poor.*[11] Both works blame neoliberal politics for America's alienation from its weakest citizens, poor people of color, and situate crime control and punishment within this political and eco-nomic structure to argue that the criminal justice system is the primary mecha-nism through which discipline and punishment are administered against these populations. Wacquant argues that the retreat from welfarism and the punitive turn are two arms of the same phenomenon, namely, neoliberal governance. The increasingly privatized state shrinks its social and economic responsibilities to its less fortunate citizens but chooses to impose its full force against them, shifting its energetic, political, and financial investment from "workfare" to "prisonfare." The combination of a free, unregulated market ideology and a powerful, intrusive criminal justice apparatus is aimed directly at oppressing poor people of color.

Wacquant's argument, as some critics have observed, fails to acknowledge local nuances that contradict it.[12] Similarly, Soss, Fording, and Schram argue that the increased discipline and oppression, directed primarily at people of color, stem from the convergence of a neoliberal market ideology and the rise of paternalism. The combination of the loss of welfare responsibility and the push to incorporate vulnerable populations into the ungoverned market leads to greater oppression on the basis of race.

Wacquant and Soss, Fording, and Schram are hardly alone in observing the immense economic potential of the industries related to crime management. Indeed, many critical writings on mass incarceration refer to the profitability of the correctional industry as the "prison industrial complex"[13] and highlight the economic pressures that keep oppressive structures and policies in place.[14]

While privatization, the shrinking responsibility of the state to its weaker citizens, and the immense profiteering by the prison business explain the punitive turn and transformation of punishment in the past forty years, they are less helpful in predicting the relationship between punishment and the recession-era economy. The need exists to engage in a deeper investigation of the ways in which they affect each other. In an economic system governed by free markets, in which punishment is arguably the combined product of state toughness and corporate profiteering, how do fluctuations in the market influence crime rates and the scope of punishment? Do periods of plenty and of austerity give rise to different crime rates or to different punishment structures, or both? To what extent do the legislative, executive, and adjudicative institutions internalize economic pressures in decision making? How, and under which conditions, can periods of austerity and a call for fiscal responsibility counter the profitability of the prison industry? And if an economic downturn produces changes in our correctional policies, do they last when the market recovers?

An important theoretical caveat is appropriate. To the extent that the American correctional apparatus has undergone change since 2008 (and this book argues that it has), it would be simplistic to attribute it solely to fluctuations in the economy. Some of the patterns examined in this book preceded the recession, which only made them more salient or easier to implement. Moreover, several of the recession-era patterns highlighted here can be partly explained by noneconomic factors, such as a greater emphasis on racial justice,[15] more sensitivity to the question of innocence and wrongful convictions in the era of DNA exonerations,[16] and changing public attitudes toward various social phenomena, such as the prevalent use of marijuana.[17] However, the common mechanisms behind these changes—a new, cost-centered discourse; new political alliances based on fiscal rationales; new policies; and a new perception of inmates, focusing on the expense involved in warehousing and handling them—draw attention to the power of economic concerns to shift the seemingly established camps formed around criminal justice policy. Without this important explanatory component, any "history of the present,"[18] after the 2008 financial crisis, would have to rely on a deep ideological shift toward nonpunitive solutions to crime and humane treatment of inmates, when there are plenty of examples in the correctional universe that undermine such an explanation and suggest that American society has not undergone a seismic shift in its perception of crime and punishment. Tempting as it is to hope that we are in the process of developing a more progressive and empathetic political culture, this book shows how the roots of some policies, both benign and malignant, can be more thoroughly and clearly explained by the explicit references of policy makers to economic scarcity and the shrinking allure of mass incarceration for revenue enhancement and private profit.

In the context of a neoliberal economy, how might an economic downturn affect the criminal justice apparatus? Two bodies of literature offer very different insights into this inquiry: social historical studies and economic literature. These perspectives originate from very different political standpoints; social historians of punishment and the economy frequently examine the world under the assumption of social conflict, class struggle, and a considerable degree of determinism stemming from the mode of production, whereas economists of crime and public choice theorists, when not politically committed to law enforcement perspectives, tend to assume at least partial rationality and free choice on the part of the offenders and to overlook issues of class and power inequalities. But the questions these perspectives raise address similar questions, and both are pertinent for an examination of the impact of economic downturns on criminal justice policy.

HOW DOES THE ECONOMY IMPACT PUNISHMENT? SOCIOHISTORICAL STUDIES OF INCARCERATION AND THE ECONOMIC STRUCTURE

A large body of sociohistorical literature, mostly written within a Marxist tradition, examines the premise that the mode of production, which dictates the economic climate and conditions at a given time, has a profound impact on the methods of criminal justice and punishment practiced. The first large-scale exploration of this theme was Georg Rusche and Otto Kirchheimer's groundbreaking text, *Punishment and Social Structure.*[19] The book's examination of historical punishment methods is based on the premise that the prevalent forms and rates of criminal punishment are crafted to cater to the mode of production prevailing at the time, and particularly to the demand for labor. For Rusche and Kirchheimer, punishment as such has no ontological existence; it functions as one more form of controlling the lower classes and serving the interests of economic elites. They theorize that, since punishment tends to target the poor and underserved, the methods used can provide an index of the needs of the ruling class in any given historical period. Rusche and Kirchheimer divide their historical survey into three periods: the early Middle Ages, the late Middle Ages, and the rise of capitalism in the early modern period. In each of these periods, they argue, the preferred methods of punishment—fines and religious penance in the early Middle Ages, corporal punishment of various types in the late Middle Ages, and the birth of the prison with the advent of modern capitalism—corresponded to the prevalent mode of production. Corporal punishment was more prevalent in periods of surplus labor, whereas incarceration, with its accompanying forced labor aspects, became prevalent when working hands were necessary to the capitalist project. Given that criminal enforcement was, and still is, geared almost invariably to the poor, it served as a tool for managing surplus labor or providing access to forced working hands. The uniqueness of criminal law in serving this function lies in its dual role: not only does enforcement and punishment constitute an effective instrument of oppression, but they also come with seemingly class-neutral, moral, ideological justifications, thus giving legitimacy to the prevailing mode of production and quelling protest and uprising.

Rusche and Kirchheimer's work was rediscovered in the 1960s and beyond by critical criminologists and social historians and yielded a rich literature explaining trends in criminal justice as a function of the economic structure. Several macro-theorists have refined and analyzed the crime-labor relationship,[20] and some have examined it in particular historical contexts. William Chambliss's analysis of anti-vagrancy laws, for example, attributed their emergence to the demand for labor created by the decimation of the workforce by the Black Plague and their reemergence in the sixteenth century as a means to preempt property crime committed by the poor against wealthy merchants.[21] Similarly, E. P. Thompson's *Whigs and Hunters*[22] ascribed the emergence of the Black Act, a draconian criminal code administering the death penalty for a large number of petty offenses, to the need to protect the king's property. An interesting example of the law's dual role in oppressing the lower classes is presented in Douglas Hay's *Property, Authority and the Criminal Law*,[23] in which he argues that the administration of the death penalty in early modern England served as a means of domination and terror and at the same time, when applied against members of the ruling class and when dispensed with occasional mercy in the form of royal pardons, served to create the illusion of fairness and hope so as to quell rebellion. Looking at more recent history, Troy Duster's work on the emergence of drug prohibition demonstrates that the criminal stigma attached to some drugs but not to others was crafted to address economic xenophobia and concerns about labor scarcity prompted by the immigration of certain ethnic groups: marijuana to the Latino population, opium to the Chinese population, and cocaine to the African American population.[24] Other works, exploring the history of juvenile justice and incarceration,[25] the institution of probation,[26] and the growth of noncarceral sentencing alternatives that "widened the net" of criminal justice to capture people beyond those serving prison terms,[27] ranging from the benign[28] to the malignant,[29] all accept the premise that the focus on the poor and downtrodden is no coincidence and invariably serves the interests of the ruling class and the perpetuation of the economic status quo.

Rusche and Kirchheimer's analysis has also been the subject of serious critique. For example, it is difficult to accept the labor-punishment link without wholesale acceptance of a Marxian understanding of the world, which some perceive as a reduction of any nuanced perception of the political process as the function of multiple coalitions and conflicts. Ascribing so much explanatory power to economic factors, without examining alternative variables, has also been regarded as highly problematic.[30] Moreover, even within the universe of Marxist explanations, *Punishment and Social Structure* is a fairly extreme example. Rather than see law as having relative autonomy within the social structure, it is perceived as merely a tool in the hands of the elites for maintaining the capitalist status quo.[31] Indeed, for Rusche and Kirchheimer, "punishment as such [did] not exist; only concrete systems of punishment and specific criminal practices exist[ed]," making punishment merely one more variation on class domination. Some of these theoretical shortcomings were refined and addressed in later works.[32]

Moreover, over the years, as is often the case with macro-level sociological and criminological analyses, historians of punishment have found inaccuracies in Rusche and Kirchheimer's historical account, as well as particular settings in which their logic did not apply.[33] The same critique was leveled at some Marxist historians' studies of the 1960s that were inspired by their work; for example, Chambliss's account of the antivagrancy laws was criticized as being too general and as providing an inadequate explanation in some settings.[34]

The extent to which the link between economic conditions and punishment is valid largely depends on how one understands Rusche and Kirchheimer's thesis. In their metaanalysis of later works, Ted Chiricos and Miriam Delone provide three theoretical explanations for the linkage between labor surplus and harsher punishment.[35] The first suggests that labor surplus reduces the value of labor. As the profit obtained from prison labor decreases, the motivation and means to maintain reasonable work conditions in prison also decrease. As minimum wages for free labor outside prisons decline, the value and worth of forced labor need to fall beneath those minimal amounts. Also, harsher conditions of labor increase the motivation to commit crime, which in turn produces harsher punishment.[36] The second explanation suggests that harsher punishment is the reaction of the state apparatus to the threat and fear produced by a growing underclass and predicts that marginalized workers and lower-class people of color will more likely be the target of harsher punishment. And the third explanation, advanced by David Greenberg[37] and Steven Box and Chris Hale,[38] ascribes the higher levels of incarceration to the agency of judges and other criminal justice decision makers, who might be more likely to assume that unemployment causes more crime and thus to punish potentially unemployed defendants more harshly. Dario Melossi expands this third explanation to a social animus of concern and moral panic about scarcity-driven crime: "In periods of economic decline, a 'discursive chain' of punitiveness and severity spreads across society, linking the attitude of 'moral panic' expressed by business leaders and 'moral entrepreneurs' to the ways in which citizens, police, courts and correctional authorities perceive behavior as deviant and/or criminal."[39]

Chiricos and Delone's analysis of forty-four empirical studies of the relationship between labor and crime shows a robust "empirical plausibility" for the connection. Labor surplus was found to be consistently and significantly related to an increase in prison population, across methodologies and aggregation levels, even when controlling for crime rates. The findings suggest that jails, which were understudied, may be even more responsive to unemployment levels but notably and explicitly leave open the question whether the correlation between labor and punishment would hold under conditions in which periods of budgetary shortage prompt a shift toward noncarceral punishment options. And newer macro-level research also lends support to the thesis, improving our understanding of the relationship between economic cycles and punishment, particularly through careful operationalization. Raymond Michalowski and Susan Carlson conducted an analysis of the American economy from the 1930s to the 1990s, controlling for rates of violent crime, and found a strong correlation between unemployment and incarceration.[40] David Barlow, Melissa Barlow, and Ted Chiricos found linkages between long cycles of capitalist development and the historical formation of criminal justice policy in the United States.[41] In 1993, as Richard Freeman observed, the number of incarcerated men exceeded the number of unemployed men.[42] And as James Inverarity and Daniel McCarthy found, the relationship between demand for labor and level of imprisonment remains robust even when controlling for alternative explanations and persists across geographic and national settings.[43] One of the latest exceptional contributions to this literature, Alessandro de Giorgi's *Rethinking the Political Economy of Punishment*,[44] masterfully analyzes the impact of new trends in the capitalist economy in the post-Fordist era, arguing that the emergence of a flexible labor force constitutes a new system of production that has prompted nations to use their punitive apparatuses to control this new disenfranchised and fear-inducing population.

But beyond the fact that the linkage between surplus labor and harsher punishment is empirically plausible, Rusche and Kirchheimer's work raises some important questions that are highly pertinent to this inquiry into the recession's effect on criminal justice policy. Its novelty lies in the notion that punishment can be framed in the context of the economic universe and addressed as a product of market forces rather than as a detached phenomenon stemming solely from political and moral considerations. Specifically, economic conditions affect punishment irrespective of crime rates. This notion goes against the grain of the natural assumption that crime rates will provide explanatory power to the model because during economic downturns people commit more crimes, which in turn raises the incarceration tally.

Of course, regardless of whether crime rates affect punishment, it is not without importance that judges and parole boards believe they do; as Chiricos and Delone suggest in their metaanalysis, decision makers who believe in a link between unemployment and crime would be more likely to send defendants with bleak employment prospects to prison and less likely to parole them. However, that begs the question whether that assumption is empirically founded.

Research seeking to examine the impact of economic downturns and unemployment on crime rates has found a tenuous connection. In an analysis of crime rates during the Australian recession of the early 1990s, Don Weatherburn concluded that the short-term effects of economic downturns could not clearly predict an increase in crime rates and that a rise in crime shortly before the Australian recession could be explained by several intervening variables.[45] A recent United Nations report on the impact of the financial crisis on crime patterns, using police-recorded data for the crimes of intentional homicide, robbery, and motor vehicle theft from fifteen countries or cities across the world, found that, whether in times of economic crisis or noncrisis, economic factors played an important role in the evolution of crime trends. The report found that in twelve of the fifteen surveyed countries changes in the economy predicted at least one crime type, and in eight of those countries there were identifiable "peaks" of crime during the recession.[46] However, data from Britain suggest a continued decline in crime rates throughout the recession,[47] and data from the United States suggest a more anomalous pattern: despite grim predictions and proclamations from law enforcement officials,[48] FBI statistics from 2010 suggest an overall decline in crime.[49] Anthony Karmen's analysis of the decline in violent crime in New York found no clear correlation between crime rates and the economy.[50]

Another problem with studies examining the link between economic conditions and crime rates is the assumption that crime rates are a fixed and objective measure. In *Criminology and Political Theory*,[51] Anthony Amatrudo examines several strains in criminological literature that suggested that link, such as the Chicago school of criminology in the 1920s and 1930s[52] and Robert Merton's strain theory.[53] The Chicago school argued that crime stems from social disorganization in urban centers, the product of migration to the suburbs that leaves the poor population in the city center without proper social institutions. Merton's theory relied on the gap between the advertised goals of the American dream and the unavailability of means to reach these goals, arguing that different people find different ways to adapt to the gap, one of which could be turning to illegitimate means. Both theories, argues Amatrudo, did not account for the fact that crime is a socially constructed concept—an idea explored and analyzed in the works of Box and Hale, who have problematized the downturn–crime rates hypothesis in the context of Britain.[54]

As Beckett argues in *Making Crime Pay*,[55] while a rise in crime rates certainly fueled the turn to punitive policies, this was largely the product of top-down political campaign advertising rather than genuine public fear. Moreover, as Simon[56] and Barker[57] remind us, crime (and criminal justice) is experienced largely on the local level. Neighborhoods and communities that are already politically and economically disenfranchised tend to experience higher levels of crime and social control, and therefore the rise and fall of crime rates nationwide does not necessarily influence personal and community experiences.[58] Moreover, while incarceration rates rose, victimization rates dropped after the early 1980s.[59]

If crime rates did not fuel mass incarceration, has mass incarceration at least had a role in reducing them? In analyzing the incarceration boom in the United States, Bruce Western concludes that the decrease in crime rates in the 1990s is mostly the product of changes in the drug market and an increase in policing; incarceration explains only about 10 percent of this downward trend.[60] Moreover, in his analysis of the economic boom of the 1990s, Western disproves the assumption that periods of economic plenty necessarily lead to a decline in crime rates, as the population primarily targeted by law enforcement—young men of color—hardly benefited from the boom and in fact was economically hindered from accessing its benefits because of the serious disadvantages brought about by mass incarceration and the stigma associated with it. Western's work and similar conclusions reached by Zimring and Hawkins about the disconnect between mass incarceration and a decrease in crime[61] suggest that if economic cycles have an impact on law enforcement and criminal justice policies, that impact is not mitigated by crime rates.

The conclusion from the above studies is that the relationship between economic conditions and crime rates and the relationship between crime rates and punishment are tenuous. Without crime rates as the explanatory "middleman," we are left with the need to explain why periods of economic uncertainty, particularly pertaining to labor and unemployment, give rise to an increase in incarceration. One possible explanatory direction follows Emile Durkheim's concept of anomie.[62] During periods in which big societal shifts occur—for Durkheim, these were shifts in social solidarity—the feeling of uncertainty requires tightening social control so as to reaffirm and clarify boundaries. Building on this theme, Kai Erikson showed that during times of legitimacy crises—that is, times when governments felt insecure and were confronted with resistance—authorities in Puritan colonies tended to be more punitive.[63] In a study correlating methods and severity of punishment with governmental attributes, Martin Killias found that legitimacy crises gave rise to harsher punishment.[64] Alessandro de Giorgi's analysis of post-Fordist capitalism and punitivism suggests that economic uncertainty and transition might also produce harsher punishment, particularly aimed at the more vulnerable members of the labor force, such as immigrants.[65]

These powerful explanations would have us predict that as economic conditions worsen governments would tend to punish more severely. But, as this book argues, the 2008 financial crisis has not uniformly led to more punitivism. In fact, as the rhetorical devices, political alliances, and criminal justice policies presented in chapters 4–7 of this book argue, the effect of the financial crisis on penal and correctional policies in the United States has been more complex and nuanced. In some criminal justice sites the recession scaled down the punitive project, whereas in others it has led to tough policies. These mixed trends require an explanation in light of the literature suggesting that in times of austerity governments tend to recur to greater, not lesser, reliance on punishment and oppressive social control. The recent contraction of the criminal justice apparatus suggests that there are other important factors that might counter the reasons that social control is enhanced in times of austerity. One such factor might be a simple economic calculus: budget shortages might make mass incarceration on a grand scale financially unsustainable and thus require a scaling back of the punitive project or significant modifications, punitive or nonpunitive, that render it financially feasible. A fertile body of scholarship that addresses the costs of crime from an economic standpoint is helpful for addressing this issue.

WHAT IS THE PRICE OF PUNISHMENT? ECONOMIC ANALYSIS OF THE CRIMINAL JUSTICE SYSTEM

The recent literature on mass incarceration has left insights from economic analysis largely unexplored. While the point of departure of economists is highly debatable, the concept of cost-benefit analysis as it applies to the entire criminal justice system may provide additional insights as to the effect of limited resources on the landscape of punishment.

The pioneer of economic analysis of crime was Gary Becker, whose article "Crime and Punishment: An Economic Approach"[66] aimed at providing an inclusive analysis of the costs and benefits of crime and crime control. Becker's point of departure is the classic economic assumption of perfect rationality and perfect information, under which, as is the case for any other behavior, "a person commits an offense if the expected utility to him exceeds the utility he could get by using his time and other resources at other activities."[67] Rather than eliminate crime altogether, his model aimed at reaching an optimal level of deterrence that would make offenders internalize the costs of their own offenses and thus create equilibrium in terms of expenditures on reactions to crime. This calculus would allow economists to measure the effectiveness of public policy addressing crime. For that purpose, Becker suggested quantifying the damage caused to society by crime, the costs of apprehension and conviction, and the costs of punishment; notably, he included the possibility that each of these categories may generate gain, perhaps predicting the possibility of profit made from incarceration. Becker also included in the model private expenditures on crime prevention and harm reduction. He even warned against the effects of collusion, analogizing from market monopoly and emphasizing that organized crime could skew the cost-benefit analysis.

Becker was cautious to distinguish between the legal and sociological approaches to punishment and his own economic approach. His article addresses punishment in a cut-and-dry manner, without paying lip service to theories of crime that doubt free choice and rationality and without considering the impact of social policies, such as education and welfare, on crime levels. However, he acknowledged that different groups of offenders may respond differently to punishment and that the deterrence potential would be lessened for impulsive offenders. It is also important to note that Becker's political stance was not as diametrically opposed to that of critical and radical criminologists as scholars of both disciplines sometimes assume: while Becker's work inspired fiscally libertarian and socially conservative ideas of crime control,[68] his original analysis was not infused with punitive values and in fact made a strong case for the use of fines in lieu of imprisonment because of their lesser costs to society: "probation and institutionalization use up social resources, and fines do not, since the latter are basically just transfer payments, while the former use resources in the form of guards, supervisory personnel, probation officers, and the offenders' own time."[69] Moreover, Becker estimated that the elasticity of responses of offenses to changes in imprisonment would be more difficult to measure than their reactions to fines.

Becker's was not the first effort to assess the costs of crime. The 1931 Wickersham Commission was convened by President Herbert Hoover to assess the economic costs and benefits of prohibition, and its findings were material in the effort to repeal it.[70] While the report was not solely focused on costs and the reels of evidence presented to the committee reveal a focus on curbing misconduct in police interrogations and evidence collection proceedings,[71] a substantial part of its review was dedicated to an assessment of the expenditures on enforcement and imprisonment and the strong financial incentives to produce illegal liquor, concluding that the effort to enforce Prohibition cost two-thirds of the total amount the federal government spent on law enforcement. Since then, and after the publication of Becker's analysis, several presidential commissions and many governmental agencies as well as academics have tried to provide assessments of the costs of crime and criminal justice. Charles Gray's review of many of these efforts reveals that they differed in their assessment of harm, particularly in monetizing the public and private costs of protection and the costs of victimization.[72]

Following in the footsteps of Becker and other early law and economics scholars, public choice theorists have applied the rationales of microeconomics and macroeconomics in the private market to governmental decision making in criminal law and other arenas.[73] However, even with these economic tools, the project of finding an optimal level of criminal justice to address crime is exceedingly problematic. One primary difficulty is scant data; in 1967 the Task Force on Assessment of the President's Commission commented, "Crime in the United States today imposes a very heavy economic burden upon both the community as a whole and individual members of it. . . . [I]n view of the importance . . . it is surprising that the cost information . . . is as fragmentary as it is."[74] But there are other serious problems, and economists have been increasingly sensitive to the subjective nature of such calculations.

One major problem is estimating the costs of crime. In an effort to itemize these costs, Mark Cohen draws a distinction between costs directly caused by the crime (to the victim), costs involved in societal response to crime, and costs to the offender. Cohen notes that not all of these costs can be quantified using existing or collectable data, and some of them cannot be quantified at all.[75] Even costs that can be itemized using proxies, such as jury awards or drops in property prices,[76] raise disagreements in the field. A 1996 report assessed the costs of crime at $450 billion annually, factoring in medical spending, mental health care, violent crime, and reduction in quality of life, arguing that these were "conservative assessments." The report used jury awards of compensatory damages to estimate pain and suffering.[77] The criminologist Alfred Blumstein, remarking on the report for a *New York Times* story, criticized it for overassessment of pain and suffering.[78]

David Anderson's effort to provide a figure for nationwide costs of crime aimed at including factors left out of previous assessments, such as opportunity costs, prevention costs, and indirect costs.[79] He includes crime-induced production and production due to property loss.

Calculating the costs of criminal justice also proves a complex task. Information about different expenses at all stages of the process is decentralized and difficult to access.[80] Moreover, states themselves do not itemize all their correctional expenses properly in their budgets.[81] Costs to the offenders themselves are notoriously difficult to estimate, because there are "only sparse data" on prior earnings history that allows quantifiable calculation.[82] In this category, Cohen mentions lost freedom, which cannot be estimated; disruption of lives; hardening of people; and the higher rate of injury and death while in prison. Notably, he also considers overdeterrence and the impact of the system on lives beyond those touched by crime as one of the costs. One interesting way to estimate these costs, which offers a dimension of class awareness missing from the mainstream literature in economics, is to focus on the costs of imprisonment per neighborhood, which draws attention to the existence of "million dollar blocks" in which a substantial percentage of residents are incarcerated or subject to supervision.[83]

The challenges of deciding which costs and benefits to include in the calculus of optimal criminal justice produce serious controversy in the econometric literature. A review of studies evaluating the cost-effectiveness of various criminal justice policies revealed only ten studies, of a total of 154 studies reviewed, that encapsulated rigorous application of economic analysis to criminal justice interventions. Even those ten studies exhibited flaws in their methodological rigor.[84] Similar findings emerged in a review of cost-benefit analyses of sentencing, which found only three studies whose quality was not considered poor.[85] The problems are not merely with producing solid models, but with uncovering costs and benefits that seem pertinent to some and external to others. For example, in assessing the Illinois early release of 21,000 inmates between 1980 and 1983, James Austin found that even though victims suffered losses and costs from crimes committed by early release inmates, overall the reduced prison costs to taxpayers more than offset those associated with the slight increase in crime committed by recidivists.[86] Cohen, however, used the same figures and came to the opposite conclusion, because his assessment of the cost of crime to victims was significantly higher.[87] Drug treatment program assessments yield similar controversies. Andrew Rajkumar and Michael French found that the cost of treatment outweighs the benefit of the decline in crime;[88] however, a study of more recent drug treatment conducted by the U.S. Department of Health came to the opposite conclusion, citing additional benefits to treated drug abusers, such as reduced medical costs, increased employment, and reduced welfare benefits.[89] An additional source of confusion is that some policies, such as running one big prison in lieu of several smaller ones, may increase efficiency with regard to a certain function but be detrimental to other functions.[90]

Finally, it bears remembering that evaluation and optimization studies of criminal justice often assume rationality, not only on the part of offenders, but also on the part of law enforcement officers, prosecutors, judges, and parole boards. Studies in behavioral economics conducted by Daniel Kahneman, Amos Tversky, and others have revealed heuristics and biases that stand in the way of reaching equilibrium in criminal justice policy.[91] As Becker acknowledged, different offenders exhibit different levels of elasticity in responding to punishment; studies of deterrence show that severity of punishment has significantly less impact on behavior than the likelihood of apprehension.[92] Even if the effort to optimize criminal punishment to ensure public safety relies not on deterrence but on incapacitation, it is difficult to systematize releases based on risk; relying on judicial and parole decision making as a basis for systematic policy may be fallible, as studies have revealed that judges are prone to heuristics and biases in release decisions.[93]

Given that trained and capable economists find it difficult to generate solid, objectively acceptable cost-benefit equations for criminal justice policies, it is interesting to examine the way such costs factor into arguments made by lawmakers, elected officials, campaign managers, correctional officers, and the general public. One of the themes in the analysis of recession-era politics and rhetoric is the debate over the costs of punishment, made particularly salient by the general sense that the economic downturn has made resources scarce and precious. Questions of externalities are especially important, and, as the discussion in the next chapter illustrates, much of the controversy about policy changes has to do with how the accounting is conducted.

Social histories of the economy and punishment and econometric analyses of the costs of crime differ dramatically in style, audience, and scope. However, they share some important features that are pertinent to this project. First, both bodies of literature see crime and punishment as part of a larger governance project, which happens in the context of a given economic system and a given amount of resources. These issues cannot be neglected and need to be studied side by side with national and local politics, cultural norms, media presentation, and public animus. Second, identifying correlations and explanations—between changing labor markets and punishment, between changing policies and changing costs—is at the forefront of debates in the era of austerity. The following chapters pay attention not only to what governments say about crime and money but also to what they do, showing the ways in which presumed or calculated correlations and cost-related arguments are used to justify and implement a spectrum of policies, old and new, benign and malignant. And third, the different schools of thought show how people with radically different perceptions of human nature and the social order are contemplating very similar questions, albeit from different perspectives, another theme examined in the following chapters.

The next chapter grounds these theoretical insights in the history of American penal policy, by retelling the mass incarceration story through a financial lens, with emphasis on criminal justice funding trends during periods of plenty and scarcity.

2

A FISCAL HISTORY OF MASS
INCARCERATION

Various scholars have tried to pinpoint the events that made sentencing and corrections nationwide take a punitive turn. By now the story of increased punitiveness and the mass incarceration crisis has become received wisdom in the field for all but a few. In *Governing through Crime*,[1] Jonathan Simon relies on this literature to tell two complementary stories. The first story is one of top-down political initiatives sweeping federal and local legislatures, as well as the American public, toward punitive legislation, beginning with the Nixon election campaign and its backlash against the Warren Court and the civil rights movement and continuing with the Reagan-era war on drugs, supermax incarceration, determinate sentences, and punitive enhancements.[2] The second story is managerial-administrative in nature, and it involves the quiet adoption of warehousing and incapacitation as the main goal of incarceration by correctional officials and other actors in the system in the era of despair of utilitarian aims of punishment, shifting away from the project of eradicating or diminishing crime toward the modest goal of managing inmates according to the level of risk they posed.[3] Both stories are strongly supported by a neoliberal cultural ethos that encourages fear and increased control of a dangerous underclass.[4]

As the ideological and political roots of these perspectives are fairly well known, this chapter aims at highlighting the economic and fiscal aspects. By recounting this history from a fiscal perspective, I do not mean to advocate for crude historical materialism or argue that motivations and ideological trends do not matter. The political and managerial stories hold a great deal of truth; the financial story is an additional dimension of the growth of mass incarceration.

My intent in providing insight into the fiscal underbelly of the well-known punitivism story is threefold. First, it highlights an important point underlying several recent important works, namely, that crime and criminal justice are primarily experienced on a local level. Recent important works, such as Mona Lynch's *Sunbelt Justice,*[5] Robert Perkinson's *Texas Tough,*[6] and Franklin Zimring's *The City That Became Safe,*[7] examine trends in punitivism as they relate to the political, economic, and cultural conditions of specific localities. Vanessa Barker's *The Politics of Imprisonment*[8] compares the punitive turn in three states, arguing that political culture in different localities produced different penal outcomes. Lisa Miller's *The Perils of Federalism,*[9] which is especially pertinent to this chapter, argues that the punitive turn is largely the product of a federal hijacking of the criminal justice conversation from the hands of local organizations, which may have been more invested in rehabilitation and nonpunitive solutions. Since the local experience of crime and its solutions were felt less at the federal level, the macro-level solutions voted on were far more punitive than those that local stakeholders would likely support. As my account highlights, the financial machinations behind the increasing federal involvement in local criminal justice policies included federal decision making, but this intervention from above was particularly effective because it was accompanied by a stream of considerable funding made directly to states and municipalities. The trend of federalizing punitive policies by means of grants, loans, and deals localities cannot refuse persists to this day.

Second, while following the flow of funds is no substitute for the careful analysis of political rhetoric and cultural zeitgeist, it is arguably a manifestation of intent and thoughtfulness. Policies and reforms supported by funding are those that the government intends to see realized. In that sense, a fiscal account of reform is a way to bridge two types of analysis: a "depth" analysis of what is "true" in the correctional realm—that is, the actual growth in prison population, or the actual policies put in place to enable said growth—and a Foucauldian "surface" analysis of the rhetoric and discourse surrounding these policies. Third, the economic story is an opportunity to examine the two hypotheses posited in chapter 1— namely, whether economic difficulties and downturns produce a punitive animus or whether they imply a shrinking of the correctional apparatus.

The usual departure point for historical accounts of mass incarceration is the rise in crime rates and punitive advocacy during Richard Nixon's first presidential campaign. For the purposes of this book, however, it is more useful to start with the repeal of Prohibition and the Great Depression, which present important parallels to the 2008 recession-era narrow coalitions and cost-related antipunitive campaigns I am analyzing.

THE GREAT DEPRESSION AND PROHIBITION

Making economic arguments for criminalization or decriminalization is not a new phenomenon, and the campaigns for and against Prohibition were no exception.

Prohibition, ratified by the Eighteenth Amendment in 1919 and repealed by the Twenty-First Amendment in 1933, yielded an era of problematic and inefficient law enforcement fueled to a considerable extent by fiscal concerns. Criminalizing the sale of alcohol was, for the most part, the product of a coalition that framed drinking as a moral issue. While the Women's Christian Temperance Union is often credited with being at the forefront of the struggle for Prohibition, the constitutional success was the product of a massive but narrow coalition of factions whose motivations ranged from concern about prostitution and domestic violence to an association of alcohol with ethnic minorities.[10] In this climate, moral arguments were more productive than economic ones, but some supporters of Prohibition did bring up fiscal concerns. In his 1918 book, *Why Prohibition!*, Charles Stelzle advocated Prohibition as a means to yield a reduction in taxes; his opinion was that drinking fueled institutions funded by tax money, such as "police courts, jails, hospitals, almshouses, and insane asylums."[11] The counter-campaign mounted by liquor manufacturers used a variety of rhetorical devices but emphasized the importance of commerce in liquor and the devastating economic impact Prohibition would have on that segment of the economy. Public choice economists point out that while the narrow coalition supporting Prohibition did so for a variety of ideological reasons, Prohibition was made possible by issues of taxation. Prior to World War I, the federal government's main revenue source was customs duties and liquor taxes, accounting for more than 70 percent of revenue in most years. During the war, however, these sources were eclipsed by the newly instated income tax, which by the end of the war accounted for almost two-thirds of the federal government's revenue. In 1917, two months before the proposal of the Eighteenth Amendment, Congress passed legislation that would yield an enormous increase in income tax receipts.[12]

Prohibition itself, while initially popular, is largely regarded as having been a law enforcement disaster, and it lost popularity starting in the mid-1920s. The illusion of Prohibition covered up not only a large-scale illegal industry in trafficking in alcohol, accompanied by prostitution and gambling controlled by organized crime, but also an abundant number of legal exceptions for medical and other reasons, which legitimized a large share of alcohol consumption. The efforts to enforce Prohibition were concentrated at the federal level and against organized crime lords rather than on the local-level manufacturers and sellers.

In 1929 Herbert Hoover convened the Wickersham Commission, whose mandate was to investigate law enforcement. The commission's report,[13] released on January 7, 1931, focused on law enforcement against Prohibition violators, finding public opinion on Prohibition skepticalt, and highlighted the colossal failure of law enforcement (exposing police corruption and various coercive interrogation methods, among other phenomena) while remaining largely supportive of Prohibition and recommending more zealous enforcement.

The commission's report offered little data on the economic effects of Prohibition, which may be ascribed to the great differences of opinion among its members. However, one member of the Wickersham Commission, the economist Harry Anderson, pointed out the lack of economic logic in maintaining Prohibition and the faulty set of incentives it generated: "This would inevitably lead to social and political consequences more disastrous than the evils sought to be remedied. Even then, the force of social and economic laws would ultimately prevail. These laws cannot be destroyed by governments, but often in the course of human history governments have been destroyed by them."[14] This notion, according to which market forces made Prohibition lucrative for organized crime while depleting the legitimate national economy, was picked up by repeal advocates. Pauline Sabin, a wealthy Republican trying to rally members of the Republican Party to the cause of repeal, argued that the lax enforcement and rampant hypocrisy discouraged respect for the rule of law. Not finding support among the party, she managed to summon the support of the Democrats, who by then had regained control of the legislature and whose composition changed from "drys" to "wets." The main arguments made by liberal Democrats, such as Fiorello La Guardia and Franklin D. Roosevelt, were fiscal in nature: Prohibition was depriving the nation of much-needed tax revenue. Again, changes in governmental finance were seminal to this change. The Great Depression severely diminished individual and corporate incomes, and income tax revenues plummeted; in 1932 income tax receipts fell by more than a third from their level in 1931 and almost half their 1930 level. In 1933 income tax receipts were less than two-fifths of their 1930 level—the lowest since 1917. The framers of the 1932 Democratic platform, therefore, explicitly advocated for a repeal in order "to provide therefrom a proper and needed revenue." Jouett Shouse, president of the Association Against the Prohibition Amendment, predicted that a repeal would yield at least a billion dollars in tax revenues.[15] The need to increase the liquor tax and to create a demand for employment in alcohol manufacturing and sales were important factors in repeal. So was the interest of organized labor unions and industrialists, who sought to limit the expansion of income taxation by providing an alternative revenue source.[16] Eventually, in 1933, the Constitution was amended to give the states full control of their alcohol prohibition status. Repeal quickly delivered on its promise: liquor tax receipts, which constituted 2 percent of government revenue in 1933, increased to 13 percent by 1936. A side effect welcomed by many supporters of repeal was that the income tax rate fell considerably for all but the top earners.

Of course, the repeal of Prohibition did not occur in a cultural vacuum. Relatively low crime rates, as well as the focus on economic recovery, may account for the American public's lack of appetite for punitivism in the early 1930. Habitual offender laws were enacted throughout the 1920s in connection with the fight against organized crime, such as New York's Baumes Law,[17] as a result of the growing realization of the existence of a class of "career criminals."[18] But these laws, which bore a striking resemblance to their successors of the 1990s, were repealed because the public considered them overly punitive.[19]

THE NEW DEAL AND THE ERA OF PROSPERITY

The demise of Prohibition coincided with a concerted effort to improve the American economy through New Deal economic policies. In a nutshell, the New Deal consisted of Roosevelt's efforts to accomplish relief (of unemployment), recovery (from the Depression), and reform (to prevent another Depression.) The New Deal consolidated the Democratic Party's power for a decade after its demise.[20]

While these reforms were occurring in the economic arena in a way that centralized federal power and pushed the economy away from *Lochner*-era laissez-faire capitalism, crime enforcement was still decentralized. In the aftermath of Prohibition repeal and the failure of the federal enforcement machine, crime control was largely left to the states, which enjoyed a great deal of freedom to create substantive and procedural criminal law as they saw fit, including budgetary allocations for law enforcement and corrections. This state of things stood until the decade after World War II and was aided by the fact that crime rates were consistently low.

And, indeed, the fiscal structure of prisons between the 1930s and 1960s, as well as prison life for inmates, differed greatly across localities. Institutions distinguished by security levels with which we are familiar were largely unheard of. The shape correctional institutions took, and the fiscal structure that enabled them to function, changed from state to state and from county to county.

The reigning ideology, at least in some local settings, was that of rehabilitation, though the extent to which it was a truly benign and serious goal of punishment is debatable. Prisons in this era did not lack discipline, of course, but they were not all equally committed to the ideal of rehabilitation, and even those who engaged in rehabilitation did not do it well. In *Sunbelt Justice*,[21] Lynch examines the variation in correctional institutions, comparing the expensive and cumbersome California correctional apparatus, which was at least nominally committed to the idea of rehabilitation, with the Texas model of parsimonious prison farms fueled by inmate labor.

The importance of inmate labor as the economic engine of such prisons cannot be overestimated. With the ratification of the Thirteenth Amendment and the abolition of slavery in 1865 came explicit language excluding inmates from the prohibition of forced labor. Inmate labor had always been an unseen aspect of the economy, but it received an explicit, constitutional seal of approval. One of the rarely mentioned but difficult to watch scenes in David O. Selznick's *Gone With the Wind* sees Scarlett O'Hara, a wealthy businesswoman in the postbellum South, contracting with a local prison to obtain a chain gang to serve as employees in her lumber factory. The men—all of whom are white, a depiction that couldn't be further from the truth—are shown chained to each other and humiliated, while Ashley, Scarlett's business partner, tries to dissuade her from the contract. The scene says at least as much about 1950s prisons as it says about the period it purported to depict. Inmates in the South, predominantly African American as a result of enforcement efforts disproportionately directed at them, labored under conditions remarkably similar to slavery.[22] The racial injustices were compounded by the fact that prison guards were overwhelmingly white.[23] Even in urban areas, where prisons were not modeled as farms, it was not uncommon for wardens to do business with local factories and contractors, earning money for prison maintenance on the back of inmate labor and occasionally benefiting the warden personally.[24]

The horrors of law enforcement and corrections did not go unnoticed by the courts, and the 1960s were the start of an era of judicial intervention in correctional policy.[25] Prompted by the activism of inmates in Texas such as Fred Cruz,[26] *Ruiz v. Estelle* was decided.[27] It was the first recognition of inmate rights that brought the Texas correctional ogre to its knees and forced the system to engage in extensive reform, both in terms of providing inmates with resources for their litigation and in terms of physical conditions.

But judicial activism on behalf of criminal defendants exceeded the correctional realm and tackled policing as well, requiring the states to respect defendants' rights in ways that had a non-negligible impact on state budgeting. Under Earl Warren's leadership, the Supreme Court largely incorporated the constitutional provisions providing rights to criminal defendants against the states. The most prominent of these decisions were *Mapp v. Ohio* (1961),[28] which incorporated the exclusionary rule against the states, meaning that evidence collected in violation of the Fourth Amendment's guarantees against unreasonable searches and seizures would not be admissible in court; *Gideon v. Wainwright* (1963),[29] guaranteeing defendants the right to counsel in offenses that were not "petty" (this definition was later refined to include all offenses in which the defendant was at risk of at least a six-month imprisonment term); *Duncan v. Louisiana* (1968),[30] providing the right to jury in cases expected to yield a prison term; and *Miranda v. Arizona* (1966),[31] source of the eponymous warning to the subject informing him or her of the right to remain silent, the right to counsel, and the state's obligation to provide said counsel. Often set aside from this series of pro-defendant decisions is *Terry v. Ohio* (1967),[32] which authorized the police to conduct limited stops and frisks—short searches—in circumstances in which the police's suspicion, while more than a mere hunch, did not rise to the level of probable cause. At first glance, this decision appears to be pro-police,[33] but a more careful reading of Warren's opinion indicates that his intent was to bring police actions to light and regulate stops and frisks (which were already happening) through the mechanisms of the Fourth Amendment.[34]

At the time prosecutors and police officers at the federal and state level expressed serious concern and dismay over these criminal procedure innovations, fearing that they might lead to an alarming rise in acquittals of guilty people on "technicalities"; in *Gideon,* these concerns also revolved around federal interference not only in states' policies but also in their budgets, as the decision's implication would be that states would be unduly burdened by the need to bankroll the costs of defense.[35] The expenses involved in jury trials, expanded by *Duncan,* would be largely meaningless in a system that was already based on abundant plea bargaining and a small percentage of trials.[36] It is also important to recall the vast variation in local defense practices. Many states, for years prior to *Gideon,* already had public defender systems in place, providing not only felons but also misdemeanants with defense services of varying (and often questionable) quality.[37] It is therefore important to point out that during this era of relative prosperity the Warren Court decisions would not have a fiscal impact on all states similarly and would have relatively little impact on various states in which jury trials and government-funded defense attorneys were already routine.

While these reforms were occurring top-down on the constitutional level, policy makers started responding to the problem of rising crime rates. Public alarm over the rise in crime, and violent crime in particular, led President John F. Kennedy to appoint a task force on crime, which published a seven-volume report on criminal justice in the 1960s. The report's findings were summarized in *The Challenge of Crime in a Free Society.*[38]

The thorough report spends a mere four pages on the economics of crime and crime control.[39] Its slant on the issue is decidedly progressive and in line with Democratic policies and Warren Court jurisprudence. While the report starts by stating that harm to victims cannot be quantified, it proceeds to support a laissez-faire position on crime control and reject punitive ideas. The committee's sympathetic approach to the Warren Court's constitutional incorporation project is evident in its words, possibly aimed at states balking at the notion of offering criminal representation to indigents at the states' expense: "The poor, unemployed defendant in a minor criminal case is entitled to all the protections our constitutional system provides—without regard to monetary costs."

It is possible that the committee's lack of sympathy to the economic analysis of crime might also have stemmed from lack of data. The report candidly admitted that the committee did not have more data on the costs of crime than its predecessor, the Prohibition-era Wickersham Commission. It appears, however, that the committee's perception of economic incentives for criminal justice policy pointed away from punitive frameworks and toward a more conciliatory approach to crime. For example, in a comment remarkably ahead of its time, the committee points out that "even excluding value judgment about rehabilitative methods, the fact that an adult probationer costs 38 cents a day and an adult offender in prison costs $5.24 a day suggests the need for reexamining current budget allocations in correctional practice." The committee went on to assess the economic impact of different kinds of crime, concluding that the allocation of resources for law enforcement did not address their disparate economic harm. While noting that controlling violent crime was important regardless of the economic harm posed by it—homicide was the only violent crime said to have a significant economic impact—the commission highlighted the need to pursue law enforcement against organized crime and fraud rather than street crime—robbery, larceny, auto theft, and the narcotics trade. The committee also noted that crime control and correctional policy were a local matter fiscally. Public expenditures were estimated at more than $4 billion a year and were borne primarily by taxpayers at the state and local levels. Salary, rather than equipment and research, accounted for 85 to 90 percent of police costs. The commission showed more insight into the allocation of the correctional budget than do current commentators, who tend to romanticize the so-called rehabilitative era: it noted that only a small percentage of all correctional costs was spent "for the treatment—as opposed to custody—of institutionalized offenders."

Similar economic calculations occurred in the states. And in the District of Columbia, bail reform and a shift to a system mostly releasing offenders on their own recognizance was a direct response to cost concerns.[40]

THE NIXON ELECTION AND THE RISE IN CRIME RATES

The Warren Court pro-defendant decisions provided a convenient backdrop to Richard M. Nixon's campaign focus on rising crime rates and public safety concerns. Heavily quoted in election materials at the time was the concern that criminals would not be deterred from committing crime given the projected impotence of a law enforcement system bound by the Warren Court's limitations.

Crime rates did, indeed, rise in the 1960s. As Beckett explicates in *Making Crime Pay*,[41] the data quoted by Nixon campaign managers to alarm the public were not untrue.[42] However, the political turn to punitiveness and "tough on crime" stances was not an organic response to bottom-up public concerns about rising crime rates. Rather, public awareness of the rise in crime rates was brought about by a concerted top-down governmental effort to draw attention to those rates. The purported link between the Supreme Court decisions and a projected further rise in crime rates was emphasized in the campaign.

The impact of Nixon's election on political rhetoric in the next four decades cannot be underestimated. At both the federal and state levels, the new post-Nixonian playing field required actors to tout their toughness on crime. Being regarded as "soft on crime" became a political impossibility that transcended party affiliation. Today's framing of nonpunitive approaches and initiatives as "smart on crime" are a reflection of the enormous impact of the Nixonian focus on crime as a main feature of the election campaign on criminal justice discourse. But there was one more important element in this transformation: a growing involvement of the federal government in crime control and law enforcement at the state level. This represents a dramatic change from the days of federal enforcement against Prohibition; at the time, state and local enforcement in "wet" jurisdictions was lax. This would be the first time that federal-state collaboration would be part of a concerted presidential effort, complete with the budgetary transfers to back up this policy.

Ironically, Nixon did not invent federal involvement in state policies. It was his nemesis, the Warren Court, that did much of this federalization by enforcing its constitutional interpretation not only at the federal but also at the state level. Nixon's response was merely an executive willingness to play on the national arena, for which the Supreme Court had set the stage.[43] For example, Congress's direct response to *Miranda* was to enact the Omnibus Crime Control and Safe Streets Act of 1968,[44] which stated that confessions would be admissible regardless of whether the defendant received Miranda warnings and would only require application of a "totality of the circumstances" test.[45]

The big difference between the Warren Court's project and Nixon's project was, however, that the former focused on creating doctrinal justice, thinking of the creation of rules as the key to achieving justice.[46] The latter, being a project of the executive and legislative branches, would involve law enforcement strategies, more collaboration between federal and state agents, and, of course, more funds flowing from the federal government to the states to ensure collaboration. And, indeed, the 1968 act's less famous but more influential aspect was the deliberate creation of an office devoted to liaising with states and remunerating them for their efforts to improve and toughen up law enforcement. Parts B, C, and D of the act establish guidelines for the provision of federal grants to the states. Some of these grants were meant to assist the states in setting up "planning agencies" that would centralize law enforcement policies and fund up to 90 percent of the operational costs of these agencies. States with planning agencies would also be eligible to receive grants for law enforcement and crime prevention enterprises, including recruitment and training of personnel, construction of buildings, and implementation of programs; the federal government was prepared to cover 75 percent of the costs of these programs, though no more than a third of the allocated money could be spent on salaries. Provisions were made for special grants for research and training purposes as well. The allocations of funds were supposed to target municipal police forces addressing especially high levels of street crime and clearly targets some urban threats over others. Pamela Irving Jackson and Leo Carroll have found a strong correlation between racial composition of communities and black political activism and police funding.[47] The Nixon administration's focus on law enforcement was, therefore, not merely a piece of ideological electoral propaganda; it was a real program to combat crime rates, complete with budgetary allocations and increased federalization of law enforcement.

While the federal government focused on the front end of the process, the back end was left unaddressed. The growing academic interest in the sociology of prisons and corrections, starting with Erving Goffman's *Asylums*[48] and continuing with various contributions published in Johnston, Savitz, and Wolfgang's classic *The Sociology of Punishment and Correction,*[49] brought to the forefront of prison scholarship seminal concepts such as prisonization[50] and the pains of imprisonment.[51] But this scholarship, for the most part, remained within the realm of academic research and was not at the forefront of policy making. It was only in the mid-1970s that public and political attention was drawn to the correctional project and its discontents.

THE BACK END: DESPAIR OF PRISON REHABILITATION

As policing techniques became more efficient and aggressive, correctional institutions nationwide varied widely in their commitment to rehabilitation and in their interpretation of it; for many southern states, rehabilitation equaled prison labor, often conducted in harsh conditions. But there was one important factor that held constant across states: whatever version of rehabilitation or correction was advocated, inmates' release dates depended on it. True to the heritage of reformatories and penitentiaries of the nineteenth century, sentencing prior to the late 1970s was largely done under an indeterminate scheme. Under the federal and state sentencing laws of the time, judges almost invariably imposed broad ranges of sentences, frequently measured in years, not months. The ultimate gatekeeper, the parole board, had immense power over the release date, and the decisions were made on the basis of clinical assessment consisting of information about the inmate's time in prison, personal circumstances, and demeanor at an interview before the parole board. This release process was increasingly viewed with discontent by a growing number of critics during the 1960s and 1970s. Their critiques did not address the issue of costs directly, and some of the proposals made involved suggestions that critics themselves admitted would need to be tempered by a cost perspective. For example, J. Q. Wilson, who would become President Ronald Reagan's primary adviser on matters of crime, in an interview about his then-forthcoming (and later influential) book *Thinking about Crime,* quoted a study by "a professor at the City College of New York, and his son, which has concluded that the rate of crime in New York State would be only one-third of what it is today if every person convicted of a serious crime had been automatically imprisoned for three years." Advocating an approach based solely on incapacitation, without any utilitarian perspectives, he advised communities to experiment with such approaches "at acceptable costs."[52]

This despair was not merely a political diatribe; it reflected the shock of the community of correctional policy makers, practitioners, and academics at empirical data that refuted the efficacy of rehabilitation. In 1970 Doug Lipton, Robert Martinson, and Judith Wilks conducted a survey of rehabilitative projects in prison that had been systematically evaluated, in order to assess their impact on recidivism, prison adjustment, educational achievements, and other measures.[53] The study was published in full in 1975, but a year earlier, in 1974, Robert Martinson published a popularized version of the findings without his coauthors' approval in the conservative magazine the *Public Interest*.[54] The article, titled "What Works?," stated that "with few and isolated exceptions, the rehabilitative efforts that have been reported so far have had no appreciable effect on recidivism."[55] Moreover, Martinson concluded, "education . . . or psychotherapy at its best, cannot overcome, or even appreciably reduce, the powerful tendency for offenders to continue in criminal behaviour."[56]

The scientific publication in 1975 was more optimistic, acknowledging the possibility of some rehabilitative success; and even in the popular version of the article, Martinson refrained from announcing the complete demise of rehabilitation; he merely stated that the existing projects failed to show evidence of success. But the careful framing of the conclusions did not detract from its devastating effect on the rehabilitative ideal. Rather than conclude that more effort should be made to assess the efficacy of rehabilitative programs or that mass incarceration was futile—which was how Martinson himself, a former freedom rider arrested and incarcerated for left-wing political activism, hoped his results would be interpreted—readers understood the piece as a call to renounce what had been until then, albeit often in name only, the major ideology driving correctional practices.

A contemporary reading of "What Works?" reveals several flaws. The negative conclusions are selectively drawn from the more negative results. The assessment of rehabilitation is rather crude and does not examine reduction in crime as an index of rehabilitation. Moreover, the work does not distinguish between well-funded and underfunded projects and does not account for the criminogenic countereffect of imprisonment itself. Attentive to these flaws and others, a handful of vocal critics launched studies attempting to refute Martinson's sobering findings. Some of these works, published in the 1970s, used the original data.[57] Other research, conducted in the 1980s using analytic tools unavailable to the original research team, found more evidence of rehabilitation than the original study.[58] Most convincingly, a subsequent law review paper by Martinson himself, written in 1979, examined a plethora of studies and concluded, much more optimistically, that "some treatment programs do have an appreciable effect on recidivism."[59] Despite significant empirical evidence for his new claims, Martinson's 1979 piece failed to find a receptive audience; the message of the failure of rehabilitation had been fully heeded, and conservative commentators such as Wilson would not entertain Martinson's original prediction that the 1974 publication would lead to less, not more, imprisonment on account of its futility. Martinson committed suicide in 1980 by jumping out of the window of his Manhattan apartment; at that time, rehabilitation as an idea and a correctional practice was already dead.

The renunciation of rehabilitation was particularly hard for systems that spent resources and employed personnel with the explicit premise of providing rehabilitative programs, such as California. Correctional systems that relied on "tough 'n' cheap" models akin to antebellum plantations, like Texas and Arizona, were strengthened in their resolve to stay away from ambitious and ultimately fruitless rehabilitation projects.

Some critiques of the existing system came, surprisingly, from the judiciary itself. One of the most influential critics was a federal district judge, Marvin Frankel. In his 1973 book, *Criminal Sentences: Law without Order,*[60] Frankel focused on the wide sentencing disparities between judges. Written from the perspective of a federal judge operating with federal caseloads and a federal budget, the book was unconcerned with the expenses entailed in different sentencing systems. Rather, it appealed to a sense of justice shattered by the unfettered, and practically unreviewable, power of the trial judge, who had absolute discretion to set the sentence. While Frankel was willing to accept that indeterminate sentences were suitable for some categories of offenders, such as dangerous offenders, drug users, some sex offenders, and juvenile offenders, he advocated significant curtailment of judicial discretion by the legislature. Under his proposal, sentencing commissions would be entrusted with the task to create rules for sentencing, which would be subject to review by the legislature and the courts. Frankel did not foresee the punitive turn that structured sentencing might bring; on the contrary, he thought that sentencing commissions could protect sentencing from "tough on crime" politicians sensitive to public outcries for punitivism.[61]

Frankel may not have been entirely wrong in his prediction. Vanessa Barker's analysis of mass incarceration in California, Washington, and New York shows that California's neopopulism was a driving force behind its increasingly severe punishment system. By contrast, New York, whose elitist and professional governance involved little public engagement, saw a more moderate increase in punishment. But even in the federal system and in states where Frankel later said he was "pleased to report that the idea [of professional sentencing commissions] has been adopted,"[62] the resulting sentences were harsher.

Frankel was not alone in his critique; other academics and advocates had concerns about the injustices of indeterminate sentencing. In 1971 the American Friends Service Committee published *Struggle for Justice: A Report on Crime and Punishment in America.*[63] An enterprise in the Quaker tradition of involvement in criminal justice reform, *Struggle for Justice* bemoaned not just the arbitrariness of sentencing under an indeterminate regime but also the personal injustices propagated by it, especially against poor defendants and defendants of color. For that purpose, it marshaled evidence from prison riot studies and provided personal accounts of inmates. This was an important and influential publication. After all, since the dawn of incarceration in the United States, Quakers had played an important role in forming and shaping the early penitentiaries, in particular Eastern State Penitentiary in Philadelphia, constructed with an ideology of isolation and reflection in mind, and were considered authoritative commentators on correctional matters.[64] The report questioned the received wisdom of positivist criminology, according to which crime resulted from individual pathology, as well as the parole board's ability to predict recidivism in the course of deciding on an inmate's release date.

Struggle for Justice influenced two other important works that advocated structured sentencing: the report of the Twentieth Century Fund's Task Force on Criminal Sentencing, titled *Fair and Certain Punishment*,[65] and the report of the Committee for the Study of Incarceration, which was published as Andrew von Hirsch's *Doing Justice: The Choice of Punishments*.[66] While both works decried indeterminate sentencing and argued for sentencing structures that offered more predictability and uniformity, their approaches somewhat differed. In *Fair and Certain Punishment*, Task Force member Alan Dershowitz argued that legislatures should set specific penalties based on the severity of the offense and that judges would be obliged to impose the statutorily set penalty, which could be raised or lowered through the application of aggravating or mitigating factors by the court. Parole release would be available but limited. Von Hirsch, on the other hand, argued for a more radical shift, stemming from his sense that utilitarian aims of punishment—rehabilitation and deterrence—had failed. By contrast to Wilson, Von Hirsch did not approve of incapacitation either; rather he thought that an appropriately modest goal for the criminal justice system is merely providing fair and uniform retribution ("just desserts" or "commensurate desserts"). Individual factors pertaining to the defendant would not be taken into account; sentencing would be a function of the severity of the offense and, to a limited extent, prior criminal history. The two actors that had an immense amount of power in the indeterminate system would essentially be disenfranchised. Judicial sentencing would follow the determined sentence and deviate from it only on finding explicitly specified aggravating or mitigating circumstances present. The grid would enable judicial review of sentencing, which was practically impossible under the old system, and parole would be abolished.

Over the course of the late 1970s and early 1980s, almost all states and the federal system gradually structured their sentencing schemes. The resulting sentencing regimes fell into three main groups: voluntary or advisory sentencing guidelines, determinate sentencing, and presumptive sentencing guidelines. Guideline implementation, a slow and expensive process, was introduced to the states through the National Institute of Justice in a process that involved experimental testing and collaboration. On average, the Bureau of Justice Assistance (BJA) estimates that implementing guidelines requires two years of work and that the annual budgets for guideline commissions and support staff range from $250,000 to $500,000. The implementation requires detailed quantitative data on the existing system's sentencing patterns; moreover, after setting guidelines, considerable and continuous support is required to monitor and analyze compliance with guidelines and to project the impact of modifying guidelines. The most common format for guidelines relies on offense severity and prior criminal history. These guidelines were accompanied by "truth in sentencing" laws, requiring that convicts would not be eligible for parole until they finished serving the majority of their sentences. Most recently, the Supreme Court, in a surprising move emerging from a doctrinal-technical discussion of the right to jury trial, eliminated the mandatory quality of the federal sentencing guidelines, leading to a change in the status of not only the federal guidelines but those of guideline states as well. Guidelines are, at present, deemed advisory only, and studies show that judicial adherence to the guidelines has indeed declined. It is an indication of the perceived severity of the guidelines by the judiciary that most of the deviations are downward departures.[67]

Five states did not adopt guidelines but rather opted for a set of determinate sentences set in place by the legislature. The first state to adopt determinate sentencing—and one widely regarded as a bad example for sentence structuring—was California, in which the the Penal Code would specify the punishment for different offenses by providing judges with a "triad" of sentences established by the legislature.

One of the hoped-for effects of the transition—the elimination of sentencing disparities—was only partially achieved. Subsequent studies confirmed that guidelines helped reduce sentencing disparity but found that this reduction eroded over time, partly through judicial operationalization of permitted extralegal factors. However, the transformation did have two other important effects. One of them was an overall increase in severity of punishment. As pointed out earlier, save for Wilson's advocacy of incapacitating, lengthy prison sentences, none of the commentators who advocated for determinate sentencing had hoped for this.

The second change, which has been commented on often since determinate sentencing became ubiquitous, was a significant shift of power within the criminal justice system. The judges who formerly held immense discretion in meting out sentences based on the circumstances of the offense and the offender were now divested of this discretion by the constraining guidelines (in guideline states) and laws (in determinate sentencing states). And parole boards, which formerly had full discretion to assess the extent of rehabilitation and dangerousness of each individual, lost their power to truth in sentencing laws, their discretion now limited to inmates sentenced to life with the possibility of parole, the one area left under the auspices of the old regime. The new holders of punitive discretion were legislators and sentencing commissions, which created the constraints within which judges operated, and a newly empowered prosecutor, who could use the newly created formal grids as bargaining chips for negotiation purposes.[68]

It is impossible to understand the awesome prosecutorial power under determinate sentencing out of the context of plea bargaining. In a world of flexible sentencing, plea negotiations could rely on using the length of sentences as bargaining chips. But in a world of determinate sentencing, where the sentence would closely follow the charge, prosecutors would use the charge as a powerful bargaining chip. Under this system, the facts behind a given criminal offense would become divorced from the official charges brought against the defendant, which in more than 90 percent of the cases would be a function of plea bargaining. Thus the world described by David Sudnow in his classic 1965 article, "Normal Crimes,"[69] had become a realm in which facts and law drift further apart from each other.

The contribution of mandatory sentencing to the practice of plea bargaining has been widely commented on but is better understood when taking into account the fiscal context. Determinate sentencing, while pioneered by some states, was largely a federal project, marketed to the states with vast federal weight thrown behind it.[70] But contrary to the federal government, which could afford to adopt true-sentencing regimes and to guarantee broad enforcement because of the relatively small number of offenders it handled, states' fiscal condition and much greater criminal caseload require constant adjustment and compromises in enforcement. As pointed out above, setting up the initial framework to rationalize a sentencing system requires significant guidance and monetary investment; states are in need of federal stimulus money, and unlike the federal government, they are required to balance their budgets.[71] The states found themselves, therefore, adopting a regime that was far more fitting for the federal system, and handling the implications—longer sentences and more people behind bars—in a reality of limited budgets required some compromise. Since discretion was now unavailable at the judicial or correctional level, the sentencing suit burst at another seam, almost requiring that prosecutors and defense attorneys plea bargain the vast majority of cases, with judicial support.

While the bargains purported to offer defendants better deals than the ones offered by the guidelines or the penal codes, the legislative structure strongly supported the prosecutor's bargaining power, because the official charge was not the only bargaining chip in the prosecution's arsenal. Over the course of several decades, the rational, albeit increasingly severe, sentencing grid was gradually complicated, both in the federal and states system, by an ever expanding set of sentencing enhancements. In some states, these were the product of legislative activity. In other states, some of these resulted from voting initiatives.

Among the most pervasive enhancements were the new habitual offender laws. As mentioned earlier, New York had the Baumes Law, but the new generation of habitual offender laws offered judges less discretion than those proto-versions that had lost popularity during the era of Prohibition. By the 1990s public punitivism had increased, and voters embraced these laws with renewed enthusiasm; California's Three Strikes Law, the most sweeping version of a habitual offender law, was supported by 72 percent of voters.[72] Habitual offender laws often bore the names of children—a sad reminder of the heinous crimes that led victims to embrace these avenues to process their sorrows. The now-infamous California Three Strikes Law, for example, was adopted following the heinous murder of Polly Klaas. As Joshua Page writes in *The Toughest Beat,*[73] Three Strikes was the brainchild of the California Correctional Peace Officers' Association—the prison guards' union, a powerful political player in California—in conjunction with victim organizations initiated and puppeteered by the union. Voter pamphlets at the time provided fiscal information as to the projected costs of sentencing enhancements, but the public embraced them on the grounds that the prevention of serious risks would override the expense. What is less known is that police departments that successfully increase their budgets often capitalize on sensational crime, a strategy found to be consistently successful in a study of three hundred police departments nationwide.[74]

Often neglected in this discussion of habitual offender laws and other punitive legislation is the important effect of federalization on state law.[75] A Department of Justice report from 2000 found a large, and increasing, number of federal mandates that either bind the states or offer them significant monetary incentives for compliance. The project to federalize criminal law, initiated by the Warren Court, has therefore come full circle. Ironically, funds and efforts are not put in place to guarantee defendants' constitutional rights but instead to provide law enforcement with more authority and to impose harsher punishment.

One example of a federalized, and federally funded, criminal justice enterprise is Section 2(a) of the National Child Protection Act of 1993, which requires an authorized criminal justice agency in each state—usually, the state's criminal record keeper—to report arrests and convictions in child abuse cases to the FBI. The act sets a time line for states to create digital records of child abuse and authorizes appropriation of funds to allow for the implementation of the system in the states.

Similarly, a provision of the 1994 Violent Crime Control and Law Enforcement Act amends the 1968 Gun Control Act by prohibiting people convicted of some domestic violence offenses from purchasing firearms. A provision of the 1997 Omnibus Appropriations Act, otherwise known as the Lautenberg Amendment, creates a system of appropriations to fund the record-keeping practices necessary for compliance. More federally funded protection for victims of domestic violence or stalking is guaranteed by a provision of the 1994 Violent Crime Control and Law Enforcement Act, which allows that federal and state justice agencies that submit information for inclusion in the FBI's national crime databases may also submit court orders for the protection of persons from stalking or domestic violence. Orders issued by both criminal and civil courts may be entered into the FBI's National Protection Order File, which operates as a part of the National Crime Information Center (NCIC).

The enthusiasm for punitive laws backed by federal funding is perhaps greatest in the context of sex offenders, a group that probably enjoys the least amount of sympathy from American lawmakers. In *Sex Fiends, Perverts, and Pedophiles: Understanding Sex Crime Policy in America,*[76] Chrysanthi Leon documents the gradual change in the national (and particularly Californian) approach to sex offenders, which manifested in the gradual "unification" of the sex offender image as a monster, regardless of the type or severity of the offense. The perception of convicted sex offenders as dangerous, which stands in stark contrast to their low recidivism rates,[77] has resulted in abundant federal and local legislative energy spent not only to increase sentences for sex offenders but also to document and surveil them as they exit the system. What is often not highlighted in sex offender literature is the robust apparatus of federal legislation and funding that is binding on the states. The Jacob Wetterling Crimes Against Children and Sexually Violent Offender Registration Act required states to follow sex offenders by confirming their residence annually for ten years after release and for life if the crime was violent. The subsequent Megan's Law required states to release information about sex offenders to the public. The mechanism for doing so was established in the Pam Lychner Sexual Offender Tracking and Identification Act of 1996, which mandated that the U.S. Attorney General establish a national sex offender registry that provides abundant information on convicted sex offenders: their image, full name and aliases, physical description, and the offense for which they were convicted. Registration requirements by states were increased and expanded in the Jacob Wetterling Improvements Act, which also allowed the state to delegate its responsibilities of registration and notification, as well as to register offenders for offenses not federally requiring registration. Subsequent litigation in the late 1990s and early 2000s included the 2003 PROTECT Act, mandating that sex offender registration be easily accessible online as a condition for receiving federal funds,[78] and culminated in the 2006 Adam Walsh Child Protection and Safety Act, which further expanded registration requirements to jurisdictions that were not included in the original mandate and centralized the sentencing and monitoring of sex offenders in federal hands.[79] Sex offender legislation is therefore an excellent, though by no means the only, example of the federalization of criminal enforcement funding, leading to significant increases in sentencing and in postsentence burdens under the provenance of the states.

The fiscal mechanism allowing for federal control of the states consists primarily of two federal grant programs: the National Criminal History Improvement Program (NCHIP), administered by the Bureau of Justice Statistics (BJS), and the Five Percent Set-Aside Program, administered by the BJA. A third federal grant program, established by the Crime Identification Technology Act of 1998 (CITA), is designed to provide funding for an especially wide array of criminal justice information identification and communications initiatives. Eligibility requirements for CITA funds are tied to assurances that the state "has the capability to contribute pertinent information" to the National Instant Criminal Background Check System (NICS) and assurances that there is a "statewide strategy for information sharing."

The increasing fiscal and organizational intervention of federal authorities in state law enforcement raises doctrinal issues on the constitutional level, as such policies could be perceived (and have been attacked) as commandeering, in violation of the Tenth Amendment guarantee of state independence. But less ostensibly, they also raise the problem of insufficient federal funding to implement reforms in information gathering and management, as well as lax enforcement at the local level. A report by the BJA finds that these federal requirements have succeeded in garnering only partial state support and flow of information. States that did not have an apparatus for collecting information set up through the courts were not in compliance with federal requirements and were therefore not the recipients of federal assistance. Also, while police departments generally benefit from playing the federal grant game, studies of police budgeting warn police administrators about "feds bearing gifts," as some federally mandated law enforcement reforms require substantial expenditures on the part of the local agency, such as equipment repair and maintenance and technology training.[80]

The burdens of increased incarceration practices, especially when these emerge from mandatory sentencing schemes strongly supported and encouraged by the federal government, have to be borne locally, as the vast majority of inmates are housed in state and local institutions. And, indeed, over the course of implementing determinate sentencing, new punitive legislation, and aggressive enforcement of drug offenses, state and federal expenditures on corrections rose sharply.

In 2008 and 2009 the Pew Center on the States issued two alarming reports: "One in 100,"[81] the title of which is the incarceration rate in state institutions nationwide;[82] and "One in 31," which represents the rate of people under any form of carceral supervision, including probation and parole.[83] The statistics are much more distressing when broken down by gender, age, and race: one in nine African American men between the ages of eighteen and twenty-four is incarcerated. These large numbers of inmates are housed in a large number of institutions. The 2005 edition of the Census of State and Federal Facilities shows not only an increase in the overall number of facilities between 2000 and 2005 but also a transition away from community-based institutions to confinement-based ones.[84]

The costs were considerable as well. In 2003 states spent $39.2 billion on corrections and local governments spent $57.5 billion on policing. All expenditures on criminal justice rose across the board. Between 1982 and 2003 correctional expenditures increased 423 percent, from $40 to $209 per U.S. citizen; judicial and legal expenditures increased 321 percent, from $34 to $143; and police protection expenses increased 241 percent, from $84 to $286. Between 1977 and 2003 state and local expenditure for all justice functions increased 567 percent. The total number of state and federal inmates grew from 403,000 in 1982 to over 1.4 million in 2003. The number of local jail inmates more than tripled, from approximately 207,000 in 1982 to over 691,000 in 2003. Adults on probation increased from over 1.4 million to about 4.1 million persons. Overall, corrections employment more than doubled, from nearly 300,000 personnel to over 748,000 during this same period. Salaries for correctional personnel accounted for 50 percent of all expenditures on corrections.[85]

Punitiveness was considered to be a function of what Zimring and Hawkins referred to as "the correctional free lunch."[86] The problem they identify is that prosecution, adjudication, and sentencing takes place at the local level, whereas imprisonment occurs at the state level. A study comparing states whose courts were state-funded to states in which courts were locally funded found no differences in terms of funding on the dimensions of adequacy, stability, equity, and accountability. However, when courts were funded by the state there was more uniformity across counties in terms of administrative and substantive "best practices." Trial courts, especially in jurisdictions in which judges were elected, tended to have a local perspective when assessing the adequacy of funding and focused on their particular court's caseload.[87] Since then David Ball has advocated shifting most, if not all, responsibility for incarceration to the counties, so as to internalize the costs of harsh sentencing.[88] One possible way to mitigate these effects has been to educate judges about budgetary constraints or to structure judicial decision making in a way that requires them to take said constraints into account, a policy supported by data suggesting that judges are not oblivious to the budgetary impact of their decisions.[89]

FINANCING PRISONS AT THE STATE LEVEL

While federal grants and interventions addressed mostly the front end of the criminal justice process, state and local governments had to handle the back end themselves by finding financing mechanisms for prison construction. Rather than recur to taxes, states sought bonds; bonds are a loan to the government, which pays interest until the loan's maturity, at which point the principal is paid back.[90]

The dramatic increase of bond-funded prison building is a direct effect of determinate sentencing on mass incarceration. Until the 1980s, when correctional expenditures by the states were $9.6 billion, about 40 percent of state prison construction was financed by cash and current revenues (a system referred to as the pay-as-you-go method, as it does not result in accruing debt) and 50 percent by general obligation bonds, which are paid out of tax revenues and often require voter approval. Only 10 percent of prison building expenditures was financed through lease revenue bonds. However, by 1996 state correctional expenditures had risen to $22 billion, and general bonds lost popularity with voters troubled by dwindling local budget and tax rates. Funding structures had shifted, and in 1996 more than half of the debt issued to finance prisons was accrued through lease revenue bonds.[91] Lease revenue bonds are created to finance a specific project, built by an agency that later leases the right of use to the government. The bonds are repaid by rent or lease payments that are appropriated by the legislature and paid for by taxpayers, but the indirect collection method does not require voter approval, as is the casefor general bonds. While municipalities can theoretically stop making payments on the lease and thus not roll the expense onto taxpayers' backs, doing so would carry serious reputational and credit consequences. It is therefore a hidden method of funding specific projects, particularly suited for the financing of prisons, which at the time were often removed from the public eye and whose tax consequences went unnoticed.[92]

Other downsides of using lease revenue bonds are their higher price, stemming from the fact that they are not backed by the state's full faith and credit; the resulting need to back them up by insurance; the private negotiation on their sale, which means no competition from the market; and the many middlemen involved. But the most problematic aspect of this financial instrument is that it circumvents the need for disclosure and voter approval and thus becomes a hidden form of taxation. In the late 1970s many states shifted from a property tax base to one heavily dependent on personal taxes, such as income and sales tax.[93] This change resulted in making the tax base more vulnerable to market changes, which tend to affect income and expenditures more than property, which is a fact of immense importance in explaining the public aspects of the financial crisis. But another important implication is that in many states changes in taxation became subject to voter approval. Using the lease revenue bond to finance prisons essentially created a covert form of taxation, which did not need to be approved by the voters and whose burden would be shouldered by future generations.[94]

An additional wrinkle of the financing story relates to the construction of private prison industries. Private providers such as the Corrections Corporation of America (CCA) and the GEO Group were able to raise considerable capital for prison construction through private investors and banks, as well as by forming real estate investment trusts (REITs), which are publicly traded but do not pay corporate income taxes. In addition to these sources, private prison companies received government subsidies in the form of industrial revenue bonds, issued by local governments and bearing below-market interest rates. Gradually, a considerable number of private prison providers have come to rely on even less direct financing instruments: lease revenue bonds and certificates of participation. These instruments have the advantage of raising revenue less directly. The bonds are tax-exempt, and the project built with the bonds is leased to the correctional agency. The bonds are then repaid under the lease terms, and when the interest and principal are fully paid the government acquires the prison. Certificates of participation are a particularly risky form of lease revenue bonds that are sold to investors; these, in turn, receive the funds from the government and become shareholders in the prison. In theory, the government pays the debt via lease installments, and there is a rent abatement clause if the project is not utilized—which means that empty institutions do not have to be filled.[95] This is conducive to the business of private prison providers, who initially build institutions before they are populated and on occasion build prisons on speculation.[96]

The story of California, as told by Ruth Gilmore in *Golden Gulag*, is illustrative.[97] The transition to determinate sentencing in the late 1970s, which required additional facilities, occurred shortly before a political transition from a Democratic to a Republican state administration. The new administration green-lighted massive prison construction, successfully petitioning voters to approve $495 million in general obligation bonds so new prisons could guarantee public safety. While recurring to bonds, rather than taxes, circumvented the need to include these expenses in the budget, these bonds still required public approval. The early 1980s saw a bipartisan bloc of lawmakers partner with private underwriters to supplant the general obligation bond with lease revenue bonds, which did not pledge the government's full faith and credit and did not need to be placed before the voters in general elections. This new source of capital raised the debt for prison construction from $763 million to $4.9 billion, allowing fast construction of abundant prison cells. California once more recurred to risky financial instruments to fund more construction shortly before the financial crisis.[98]

Even with these swift mechanisms, prison budgets fail to account for the full cost of the carceral project. A 2012 report by the Vera Institute of Justice found that states differed dramatically in terms of prison costs not included in the corrections budget, such as employee benefits and taxes, pension contributions, statewide administrative costs, private prisons, hospital care funded outside the corrections department, and some educational and vocational programs.[99] The report estimated that the total taxpayer cost of prisons in the forty states that provided data was 13.9 percent higher than the costs represented by their combined corrections budgets and that the full cost of prisons to taxpayers was $39 billion.

Before the financial crisis of 2008, therefore, state prisons were overcrowded, supplied with inmates on a regular basis by harsh enforcement of drug laws, sentencing enhancement, and special punitive measures. Parole had lost its power, and faith in rehabilitation programs was fairly low. This system thrived on the following fiscal mechanisms: a constant federal flow of "strings-attached" grants to guarantee compliance with punitive programs that were more suitable to federal caseloads than to state and local needs; government bond structures allowing for the construction of more prisons; and an increasing private sector of prison companies that thrived on the states' inability to meet their incarceration needs with their own budgets. On the collapse of the financial system, and with it a shattering of state fiscal constructs, voters and policy makers woke up to a new reality. The next chapter examines the basics behind the collapse of the financial system, its impact on governmental budgets, and the creation of a discourse of scarcity.

3

THE FINANCIAL CRISIS OF 2007 AND
THE BIRTH OF HUMONETARIANISM

"Many Contra Costa Crooks Won't Be Prosecuted," read a *San Francisco Chronicle* headline in 2009.[1] The story proceeded as follows:

> District Attorney Robert Kochly also said that beginning May 4, his office will no longer prosecute felony drug cases involving smaller amounts of narcotics. That means anyone caught with less than a gram of methamphetamine or cocaine, less than 0.5 grams of heroin and fewer than five pills of ecstasy, OxyContin or Vicodin won't be charged.
>
> People who are suspected of misdemeanor drug crimes, break minor traffic laws, shoplift, trespass or commit misdemeanor vandalism will also be in the clear. Those crimes won't be prosecuted, either.
>
> "We had to make very, very difficult choices, and we had to try to prioritize things. There are no good choices to be made here," said Kochly, a 35-year veteran prosecutor. "It's trying to choose the lesser of certain evils in deciding what we can and cannot do." Barry Grove, a deputy district attorney who is president of the Contra Costa County District Attorneys Association, said, "There's no question that these kinds of crimes are going to drastically affect the quality of life for all the citizens of Contra Costa County."
>
> The decision not to go after any perpetrators of certain offenses, Grove said, amounts to "holding up a sign and advertising to the criminal element to come to Contra Costa County, because we're no longer going to prosecute you."
>
> Don't even bother submitting the cases, Kochly said Monday in a memo to the Contra Costa County Police Chiefs Association. "If they are submitted, they will be screened out by category by support staff and returned to your department without review by a deputy district attorney," he wrote.
>
> Kochly wrote that he had long taken pride in saying that his office could do "more with less."

"Unfortunately, we have now reached a point where we cannot maintain the status quo," he said. "We will definitely be doing 'less with less' as a prosecution agency."

"The changes are needed to help eliminate a $1.9 million budget deficit in the district attorney's office for this fiscal year. By month's end, six deputy district attorneys will be laid off, and 11 more will have to be let go by the end of the year," Kochly said.

Whether Kochly's announcement was a genuine expression of priorities or political posturing to lobby for a budget increase, it was hardly unique. Since the advent of the financial crisis, state and local governments responded by shrinking their correctional apparatuses and introducing nonpunitive reforms. This chapter explains the economic mechanisms behind this transformation, the effect of the financial crisis on state and local governments and particularly on their correctional budgets and expenditures, and the main features of humonetarian discourse, which is discussed further in the next chapters.

THE FINANCIAL CRISIS OF 2007: TRIGGERS AND VULNERABILITIES

There is considerable variation in economic and financial scholarship on the specific causes of the financial crisis[2] and their foreseeability,[3] but for our purposes it is useful to frame the crisis, as Ben Bernanke, chairman of the Federal Reserve, did in his remarks in 2009,[4] 2010,[5] and 2012,[6] as a convergence of triggers and vulnerabilities. The most significant trigger was the prospect of big losses on residential mortgage loans to subprime borrowers after the bubble in housing prices, fueled by unrealistic home owner expectations[7] and rising construction costs,[8] started unraveling.[9] The structured financial products that served as collateral for home purchase loans were difficult for banks to value, leading to an increased reliance on "originate to distribute" models by creating and packaging loans as products of further sale.[10] Underwriters' incentives became misaligned, rating agencies misrepresented the risk involved in structured financial products, and lending institutions lowered their lending standards accordingly. These lending difficulties created a rolling situation in which even banks whose portfolios relied only partially on subprime-related securities raised serious concerns and encountered difficulties securing funding. As investors around the world, who placed high value on safety and liquidity, withdrew their funds, sponsoring banks faced funding pressures. These problems converged with a "sudden stop" in syndicated lending to large, relatively risky corporate borrowers, and the resulting withdrawal from investment resulted in a "run on the bank"—a classic financial panic—which contributed to the collapse of financial markets.

These developments occurred against the backdrop of structural vulnerabilities in the financial system and in regulation and supervision. Various "shadow banks" and financial institutions had become increasingly dependent on short-term wholesale funding. Deficiencies in these institutions' risk management structure stemmed from considerable declines in underwriting standards for mortgages and an overreliance on credit agencies' inflated ratings of structured mortgage bundles. While the existence of collateralized financial instruments was not in itself a factor in the crisis,[11] credit ratings of these instruments were unlimited and created opacity about the risk they involved.[12] These deficiencies remained unaddressed by regulating mechanisms because of large statutory gaps and conflicts in the regulatory scheme in the public sector, which plagued not only private institutions but also government-sponsored Fannie Mae and Freddie Mac. The Federal Reserve, whose role as lender of last resort could not be wholly realized given the gaps in its authority and the inherent conflict between its lending function and its role as overseer of the market,[13] was slow to respond to noncompliance with the information requirement,[14] lulling high-risk firms into a false sense of security and the misapprehension that they were "too big to fail" and would be offered a helping hand by the government if necessary.[15]

Other commentators expand the lens to acknowledge the broader context of a culture of greed,[16] short-term calculus, lack of perspective,[17] and cynical exploitation of borrower ignorance.[18] And, finally, some commentators highlight the global aspect of the crisis, ascribing the housing bubble to increased capital flows, especially from China,[19] and predicting a decline in the financial importance of the United States vis-à-vis China and other emerging markets.[20]

Within weeks of the crash, several critical financial institutions failed under the weight of distressed mortgages. Activity in key financial markets—construction in particular—came to a halt. Unemployment rates rose sharply, household spending deeply declined, and the global economy entered a deep recession, from which it has been slow to recover,[21] partly because of the immense amount of debt left in the wake of the crisis.[22]

THE CRISIS HITS LOCAL GOVERNMENTS

The origins of the financial crisis can be traced geographically to the financial centers of the world but also to the urban and suburban sites from which the mortgages emerged.[23] Local geographies were involved at all phases of the crisis, and they have been the cause and the outcome of the recession that resulted. The relationship is best described as circular: the crisis was geographically constituted, in that local housing and mortgage bubbles became systemically linked into global financial institutions, but also geographically consequential, in that the main effects of the recession that resulted were felt on the local and municipal level— even in areas in which there had been no local housing bubble. The main effects hit manufacturing areas, especially those specializing in consumer durables, and local employment rates. In Michigan, for example, where subprime loans barely exceeded 5 percent of total lending, the effect of the crisis on an already weak economy yielded the highest unemployment rate of any state (23 percent).

Reversing a trend of 1.6 percent growth per annum, states cut spending by 3.8 percent in 2009 and an additional 5.7 percent in 2010. These cuts had a devastating impact on education and on the state workforce. They led to spending cuts by more than 28 percent per college student from 2008 to 2013, deeply affected after-school programs and class sizes, and eliminated 681,000 jobs in state and local government since 2008. They also minimized salaries, health and retirement plans, and the last vestige of security against unemployment, unemployment benefits.[24]

While the crisis is more easily observed on the national level, municipalities, which are the centers of economic wealth, were the source of the crisis, which started in urban and suburban areas.[25] Mortgage markets shifted from a locally originated and locally held arrangement to one that is globally distributed, and there is a strong link between local lending practices in some cities and the growth of the subprime mortgage market. Geographers observe that the current round of austerity is local in nature; cities are the resulting victims of economic restructuring because their fiscal tax base makes them particularly vulnerable to the effects of financial instability. The tax vulnerability, as well as the collapse of the welfare state in the post-Fordist era, also explains the difference in recession impact among cities; those that disregarded welfare in the early 2000s and instead prioritized faddish economic developments have experienced gross income inequalities and neighborhood segregation, as different neighborhoods felt the recession to different degrees. In San Francisco, for example, the median household income in 2010 was $71,416; however, income ranged from $37,431 in the poorest neighborhoods to $105,509 in the richest neighborhoods. Predictably, the income gaps had the worst effect on communities of color. In San Francisco the average income of white residents was $83,796, whereas that of African American residents was $30,840.

In *Fate of the States*,[26] Meredith Whitney explains the devastating impact of the crisis on state budgets. Whitney argues that many state and local governments were embroiled in the crisis because they made the same types of gambles on housing that banks and consumers had, assuming that home prices and property tax revenues would continue to rise and certainly would not decline beyond a temporary, small setback. This assumption shaped government borrowing and spending patterns. When the market crashed, the only coping mechanism available for state government was accruing more debt and hoping that revenues would rebound. This strategy proved counterproductive, as higher debt required higher taxes, which increased the indebtedness of taxpayers already struggling with personal debt. The resulting cuts in public services to decrease debt led to changes in the value of neighborhood real estate, pressured home prices, and eliminated the value of home equity as a financial safety net. The cuts also foreshortened the avenue of employment and stunted income growth, as unemployment rose in both the public and private sectors. Whitney predicted that states that had not prospered prior to the recession suffered less from the bust, due to the benign neglect of financial institutions, and therefore would recover more quickly than states like New York, Illinois, and California, whose lending bubble banks had supported and encouraged during the boom.

Some have criticized Whitney's predictions regarding the closing gap between have and have-not states, but strong evidence supports her insights into the impact of the private market crash on governmental budgets. Michael Lewis's interview with Whitney highlighted the fact that irresponsibility in pension plans was a big contributor to the crisis.[27] According to Whitney, whose assessments are in dispute in the financial community, from 2002 to 2008 states accumulated massive debts: their collective level of indebtedness had almost doubled, and state spending had grown by two-thirds. At the same time, states systematically underfunded their pension plans and other future liabilities by a total of nearly $1.5 trillion, and the amount of pension money invested in the stock market rose from 23 percent in 1980 to 60 percent in 2008. The pension crisis, combined with underfunded health care plans and significantly reduced federal assistance, left states with massive debts that only an increase in taxes (levied on individuals with fewer jobs and smaller personal revenues) could address. As Darien Shanske argues in the context of California, the pioneer in shifting the tax base from property tax to income and sales tax, the latter system tends to be more sensitive to economic cycles. A compounding factor is the fact that cuts in governmental services lead individuals to pursue some equivalent services privately, which is an additional burden on taxpayers.[28] While the change in California in the late 1970s was related to local political realities, several states followed its model[29] and suffered the consequences of an unstable tax base during the recession. Indeed, as of 2013 state revenues have remained constrained because collections from sales taxes, which increased by 0.9 percent in 2012, have been slow to rebound since the end of the recession.

The pension crisis contributed to a string of municipality bankruptcies, resulting in further cuts in services and job losses. The considerable gap between state spending and tax revenues, estimated at $192 billion, or 27 percent of the combined state budgets, in 2010, meant that municipalities would face their own budget crises. Municipalities generally received one-third of their revenues from the states and were therefore arguably the weakest link in the governmental budget chain. Whitney's grim prophecies that municipalities would default on bonds that their full faith and credit had backed up did not, however, materialize.[30]

There is some hope for improvement, but economic recovery has been slower than in previous recessions. Since 2012 states have seen a modest increase in tax revenue, both from income and from sales.[31] However, the unemployment rate remains high. Moreover, economists expect states to face expenditure pressures in areas that authorities cut back during the crisis. In 2013, the National Association of State Budget Officers (NASBO) predicted that most states would moderately increase spending in 2014, with general fund spending increasing to $728 billion, compared to $699.2 billion in 2013 and $672.4 billion in 2012. However, spending for the fifty states is still below prerecession levels and predicted to remain below the historical growth trend, indicating that state budgets are not growing quickly enough to compensate for the effects of the recession. Moreover, recovery is not even across the nation; nineteen states still have nominal general funds expenditure levels below prerecession highs. States were still struggling with significant budget gaps in 2013, albeit smaller ones than in 2012 and 2011, partly because the rise in demand for state services and spending began to decline. Budget balances have required dipping into emergency reserves. The recovery of general fund revenues is due to a combination of the slowing pace in increased spending and various gubernatorial initiatives to increase taxation.

Another important factor burdening state budgets is the decline in federal funds, partly as an effect of the 2013 sequestration and partly as a result of the expiration of the American Recovery and Reinvestment Act of 2009 (ARRA). Even in areas exempt from the effects of sequestration, such as Medicaid, federal fund rates have fallen. Indeed, expenditures on Medicaid are one of the biggest hurdles on states' path to economic recovery; in 2012 Medicaid comprised 19.6 of general fund spending, the second-largest spending category after K–12 education. States increased their spending on Medicaid by 9.6 percent in 2013, to compensate for prior years and to offset the decline in federal spending. Various strategies are under consideration to address a projected rise in Medicaid applications in coming years. State spending plans may not adequately counter large reductions in the levels of federal spending in 2014, particularly in the area of Medicaid matching rates. This projected gap may therefore temper the slow trend of improvement observed in 2012–14.

LESS WITH LESS: PRISON DE-CROWDING AND THE DECLINE IN FISCAL CAPACITY

Data collected since the advent of the financial crisis shows that 2009 was a turning point in state and local government expenditures on corrections. Prior to the financial crisis, the growth in prison population occurred primarily at the state and local levels. In fact, in 2007 the Pew Center on the States predicted, in the first study of its kind, that prison population and expenditure would continue to grow throughout 2011.[32] The report argued that this growth was avoidable, pointing out that "the central questions are ones of effectiveness and cost."[33] With the total national spending on corrections rising to more than $60 billion in 2007 from just $9 billion in 1980, the report recommended investing in recidivism reduction programs rather than in more incarceration. A subsequent report, "One in 100," highlighted the high incarceration rates and provided data on correctional expenditures per state.[34] In 2007 states spent an average of 6.8 percent of their general funds on corrections; figures for specific states varied from 3.8 percent in Hawaii and 4.0 percent in Wyoming to 9.3 percent in Florida, 8.8 percent in Colorado, and 8.6 percent in California and Texas. In 2007 an average state spent 60 cents on corrections for every dollar spent on education, compared to 32 cents in 1987. In 2009, before the more severe effects of the recession on local budgeting could be perceived, a Pew study found substantial correctional expenditure disparities among states.[35] It also pointed out that states spent seven times more money on prisons than on probation and parole, even though the vast majority of the 7.3 million people then under correctional supervision were not in prison. In 2009, one in 31 adults was under some form of correctional supervision, compared to one in 77 adults in 1982.[36]

Nevertheless, this trend, like many other spending items in the budget, would suffer a harsh setback with the recession. A 2013 Bureau of Justice Statistics report points out that local government expenditures on corrections started declining in 2009, from $28.4 billion to $26.4 in 2011. This decline was evident at the local municipal level as well, and it is especially evident when examining the expenditures for capital outlay of correctional institutions in real dollars.[37]

There are more direct indications of the impact of the financial crisis on the punitive capacity on the state and local levels. In his analysis of the micro and macro causes for the growth in prison population, John Pfaff found strong correlations between incarceration at the state level and the states' financial capacity.[38] Relying on state and local government data from the Bureau of Justice Statistics, Pfaff correlated governments' overall spending with their correctional spending. He found that correctional share in spending remained flat until the mid-1970s, grew steadily until the mid-1990s, and then fell and flattened into and throughout the 2000s. In 2008, just as the financial crisis occurred, Pfaff found, "corrections' share of the various measures of expenditure was 2.9% (up from 1.4% in 1952), 7.0% (up from 3.8% in 1952), and 9.8% (up from 5.0% in 1952), respectively. Thus, for many years, spending on corrections did grow somewhat faster than overall state fiscal capacity, but a few years into the crime decline corrections' share of the budget generally flattened or even fell."[39]

Pfaff concludes that at least since the mid-1990s government spending and correctional spending have been highly correlated. His conclusions dovetail with those of William Spellman,[40] who found that variations in state resources could explain up to 30 percent of the variation in state prison populations.[41] Further confirmation of this trend is the late 2000s increase in the number of states whose prison populations declined.

Since much of the prison growth until the crisis is attributable to charging policies, and therefore to prosecutorial activity, Pfaff astutely deduces from this trend that cost considerations drive prosecutors.

Note that the stability of corrections' share of the budget may explain the durability of a well-documented criminal justice moral hazard problem. Prosecutors are county officials, but the state pays to incarcerate the defendants they convict; we should thus expect prosecutors to "overuse" prison beds, since neither they nor their constituents bear the full cost. These results suggest that state-level officials may have been willing to tolerate these moral hazard costs because they were not particularly important— they do not appear to have crowded out spending on other programs. State-level politicians continued to adopt "tough-on-crime" positions without appearing to have to sacrifice other programs they favored. Tellingly, the onset of the financial crisis has seen state-level officials begin to rein in county-level actors. Many efforts have been blunt, such as gubernatorial furloughs and early releases. California, at least, is targeting the moral hazard problem more directly by attempting to require county jails to maintain custody of some drug offenders who previously would have gone to state prison.[42]

Pfaff found similar trends for county-level incarceration, concluding that lack of fiscal capacity contributes to a decline in prison growth.

Evidence of state and local governments' deliberate focus on cost reduction in corrections strongly supports Pfaff's large-scale analysis. Indeed, reports on state policies since the onset of the recession consistently indicated a trend of cost saving through a reduction in prison populations. A 2008 Pew report showed that Texas, known for its tough-on-crime policies, "changed direction" by introducing halfway houses and community corrections and closing prisons.[43] A 2009 report pointed out the increasing focus on high-risk individuals as subjects of incarceration while saving costs by incarcerating less low-risk offenders.[44] Other reports highlighted cost-cutting strategies in Arkansas,[45] South Carolina,[46] Kentucky,[47] Georgia,[48] and South Dakota.[49] Several states formed partnerships with business leaders to develop cost-saving correctional policies.[50] Indeed, 2012 was the third year in a row in which the number of inmates in state prisons declined, 2.1 percent during 2012. State imprisonment rates dropped by 2.6 percent, and while the federal prison population continued to grow, the rate of growth slowed, a trend attributed to state strategies for cost-effective correctional systems.[51]

What is interesting about these developments is not merely their occurrence, the reversal of a forty-year trend of growth in corrections, but also the common features behind them. An examination of recession-era correctional policies and practices identifies several common threads.

HUMONETARIANISM: THE NEW CORRECTIONAL DISCOURSE OF SCARCITY

The main feature of humonetarian discourse is, of course, the focus on cost in correctional policy. The cost argument can take several forms. Some campaigns and policies purport to divert wasteful money from the criminal justice system to other public goods, such as education and health care. But far more frequent are campaigns arguing for a shift in expenditure within the criminal justice system, away from correctional policies that yield low returns in risk and recidivism reduction and toward public safety measures such as incarcerating high-risk offenders and funding police work and violent crime solving rates. Another frequent argument, made especially in the context of the war on drugs, is the potential of making illegal substances into a vehicle for generating tax revenue. These arguments are remarkably neutral in nature, framed in a way that does not demonize or humanize offenders but merely addresses the expense in processing and incarceration. They also focus on short-term cost-saving solutions and therefore tend not to trigger rehabilitation and reentry programs that yield savings only in the long run.

The neutrality and political objectivity of humonetarian discourse also makes it an efficacious tool for creating alliances. Humonetarianism expands the limits of the sayable in a political universe that does not reward "soft on crime" stances from politicians regardless of their political stripe. Those who shape policy usually achieve this by recasting nonpunitive arguments as being "smart on crime" or "right on crime" and not implying leniency toward offenders.[52] As South Dakota governor Dennis Daugaard said, "We're a heavily Republican state, and I'm sure there were some who worried that the Republicans would be afraid to look soft on crime. So from the beginning, we had to be careful to point out that this approach was a way to be smart—not soft—on crime. We also had to emphasize the fiscal side of it. And we stressed that we're still holding people accountable, that they're not being mollycoddled. They're just being held accountable in a more effective and responsible way."

Using cost-centered arguments is also a tool for forging alliances and narrow coalitions around criminal justice issues. Death penalty abolition campaigns bring together ideological abolitionists, victim advocacy groups, law enforcement officials, and libertarians. As later chapters of this book show, marijuana legalization campaigns unite patient advocates, drug war protesters, Keynesian economists, and religious figures. These arguments create opportunities for bipartisan collaboration to support crime commissions, sentencing reforms, and early release programs.[53]

Humonetarian discourse brings with it a host of strategies for shrinking the correctional apparatus. Given the immense profit-making machinery of the prison industry, including private prison providers, state and local prison management, and utility providers, it is necessary to adapt to less lucrative circumstances. The recession exposes a focus on prison closures, repurposing and interstate barters, a stream of constant traffic of inmates across state lines and jurisdictions, and a continuing effort to diversify the private prison market and adapt it to the incarceration of new populations, such as undocumented immigrants.

Accompanying these changes and policies is the transformation in perceptions of the offender. The offender as ward of the state, whose basic needs the state should provide for as an inevitable cost of incarceration, is recast by the shrinkage of the correctional apparatus as an unnecessary burden, whose contribution to the tally of correctional costs the state can avoid if reliance on expensive incarceration declines. One implication of this change is consideration of previously invisible categories, for example, the old and infirm, as high-cost and low-risk inmates who can be the target of release and consolidation reforms. Far from an abandonment of actuarial penology, humonetarianism considers risk and cost as two parts of a calculus of "worthiness of incarceration."

Humonetarianism is often accompanied by older nonpunitive rationales like fairness and equality. But, because of the more general appeal of the cost argument, it enables more attention and salience to issues and policies that have not made headway since the the the 1970s. Finally, humonetarianism selectively focuses on certain types of offenders, estimating the costs of their incarceration to be worse than that of others while retrenching the view that other populations of offenders are worthy of correctional energy and expense.

The next four chapters discuss several important sites of correctional reform, showing this discourse in action.

THE NEW CORRECTIONAL DISCOURSE OF SCARCITY

From Ideals to Money on Death Row

In *Governing through Crime*,[1] Jonathan Simon speaks of the language of public safety adopted by politicians of all stripes who, regardless of party affiliation, tried to avoid appearing "soft on crime" like the plague. But recession-era politics have proven to be game changing, at least with respect to the sayable and permissible in political conversation. Lawmakers, politicians, judges, and activists across the political spectrum are willing to propose nonpunitive criminal justice policies and changes, deeming them politically viable when defended as a measure of fiscal prudence rather than humanitarian concern or belief in the rehabilitative ideal.

This chapter addresses the advent of humonetarian discourse and the ways in which it transforms political campaigning, focusing on the example of recent death penalty abolition campaigns. The death penalty makes a useful case study for a number of reasons. First, it has been a stubborn American tradition to break in the face of worldwide developments, to the point that it is routinely touted as an example of American exceptionalism.[2] Long after most European countries have abolished capital punishment, death sentences and capital postconviction litigation are still constant features of the American legal system.[3] Its stubbornness is enhanced by the fact that, contrary to the example of all other countries,[4] it returned to effect after four years of a Supreme Court–infused moratorium.[5] Second, in contrast to many other operations of the punitive project, the death penalty has always had a fairly visible public profile. The public has been consistently polled on its opinion about capital punishment,[6] and while there is a dearth of information about the minutiae of execution procedures or of postconviction litigation by death row inmates,[7] there has always been public debate about the moral

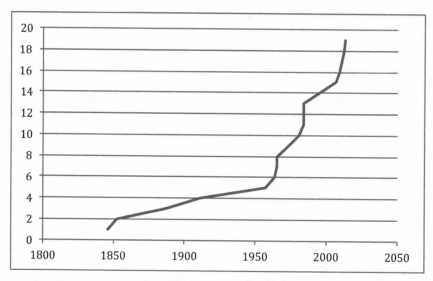

FIGURE 1. Number of states to have abolished the death penalty, by year.

merits of the death penalty. And third, the recent developments regarding capital punishment make it a convenient site for examining the impact of humonetarian discourse; since the financial crisis, the United States has witnessed several examples of legislative moves, voter initiatives, gubernatorial decisions, and stakeholders' changes in opinion that can only be explained by a fundamental change in the discourse. Eighteen states in total and the District of Columbia have abolished the death penalty; remarkably, six of them have done so since 2007. As shown in figure 1, this trend is a clear acceleration of the slow pace of abolition since the mid-nineteenth century.

As I argue in later chapters, the death penalty is not the only punitive policy to suffer a recession-era setback fueled by cost-saving arguments. But the nature of public debate about the death penalty allows for an examination of the changes in anti–death penalty discourse over time. This chapter begins, therefore, by tracing the genealogy of abolitionist arguments in the United States, from the early days to the financial crisis. The early ideological influence of the Enlightenment-era emphasis on rationality and limits on state power gradually gave way to econometric arguments about the deterrent effects of the death penalty. Later years, particularly in the aftermath of the Supreme Court's decision in *Gregg v. Georgia*, initially saw the rise of arguments claiming racial discrimination in the application of the death penalty.[8] The introduction of DNA testing techniques and the emergence of innocence projects prompted a focus on wrongful convictions and factual innocence. Finally, a recent line of litigation strategies is confined to what could be referred to, with apologies to Justice Harry Blackmun, as "tinkering with the machinery of death": debates over the relative humaneness and constitutionality of specific execution techniques. However, a newly introduced family of arguments—humonetarian discourse—highlights the costs and inefficiency of administering the modern death penalty. This new line of arguments is largely responsible for the revival of the abolitionist project and for several abolitions, moratoria, and initiatives that are marking a visible and encouraging trend. Austin Sarat has described a "new abolitionism" based on pragmatic concerns that allows mainstream politicians to oppose the death penalty without taking controversial moral stances.[9] Indeed, this new abolitionism may be currently understood in the context of the financial crisis; politicians and stakeholders can now safely argue for abolition as financially unsustainable, regardless of whether they are personally for or against capital punishment. The rest of this chapter analyzes several recent abolition campaigns, focusing on the failed 2012 campaign to abolish the death penalty in California, home to the nation's largest death row.[10] Campaign materials and exit poll information show the role played by the cost argument in reviving public debate about the death penalty and breaking through the political impasse surrounding it.

HUMAN RIGHTS DISCOURSE: MOVING AWAY
FROM THE BLOODY CODE

The intellectual herald of the European anti–death penalty discourse was Cesare Beccaria's 1764 seminal work, *On Crimes and Punishments*.[11] Committed to a rational, parsimonious criminal justice system, Beccaria rejected the notion that capital punishment was consistent with the idea of the social contract, in which citizens sacrifice some freedoms in exchange for the protection and benefits of living in society. He argued that no potential citizen would agree to such a serious and permanent deprivation of rights.

The European abolitionist project was, for the most part, the result of a top-down intellectual debate heavily influenced by Montesquieu and Beccaria. These notions were not confined to the Old World; Beccaria's book was a big success in the colonies,[12] and American colonial leaders like Thomas Jefferson expressed opposition to the broad application of the death penalty even before the American Revolution.[13] Colonial and revolutionary opponents to capital punishment also argued for the need to distinguish the new republic's penal regime from the punitive one of the British, the "Bloody Code," which gave a long list of offenses that merited capital punishment.[14] This rationale was advanced by patriots such as Benjamin Rush. According to Rush, "Every execution undermined the vitality and security of America by drawing the Republic back towards the monarchical institutions and away from republican virtue."[15] Rush further argued that not only did capital punishment fail to deter crime, but deterrence itself was an illegitimate goal of punishment, and that the proper aim was rehabilitation.

With most European states (and a few American states) abolishing the death penalty in the nineteenth century, the United States was left as the only retentionist nation in the West,[16] and it focused its humanitarian energy on developing more humane methods of execution. These efforts led to the invention of the first electric chair in 1889, followed by the gas chamber in the 1920s and lethal injection in the 1980s. These technologies, and the litigation that surrounded them, are described in greater detail below.

Another substantive family of arguments emerged during the twentieth century: concerns about due process in applying the death penalty. In the first half of the twentieth century, the use of the death penalty varied widely across states. In many southern states, for example, the list of capital offenses included not only homicide but also attempted homicide, robbery, and rape, though in practice non-homicide offenses were capital ones only for black defendants. Juries were often given leeway to apply punishments that ranged from a few years in prison (or no prison time at all) to death. Jurors received no guidelines for making their determination and were not required to explain their decisions. It was in this context that the Supreme Court decided *Furman v. Georgia* in 1972.[17] The three petitioners, including Furman, had been convicted and sentenced to die under wholly discretionary schemes. The Court found the schemes unconstitutional by virtue of their vulnerability to arbitrary application. This decision invalidated every death penalty statute in the United States except for Rhode Island's. That statute provided an automatic death penalty and was invalidated by *Gregg v. Georgia*.[18]

The abolitionist victory was short lived. In 1976 the Supreme Court approved Georgia's new capital punishment statute, which bifurcated guilt and punishment proceedings, limited application of the death penalty, and offered guidance in the form of "aggravating" and "mitigating" factors. In *Gregg v. Georgia*, the Court found that the death penalty was not cruel and unusual where the statute provided safeguards for basic principles of proportionality, fairness, and procedural reliability. The Court's favorable decision on Georgia's statute in *Gregg* provided the template for all death penalty statutes in the United States after 1976.

DETERRENCE: HOW MANY HOMICIDES DOES ONE EXECUTION PREVENT?

Some commentators attribute the Supreme Court's decision in *Gregg* in part to the 1975 publication of Isaac Ehrlich's article, "The Deterrent Effect of Capital Punishment: A Question of Life and Death."[19] Following the tradition of Gary Becker's economic approach to crime and punishment, Ehrlich provided an econometric analysis of capital punishment using the FBI's Uniform Crime Reporting data as the basis for regression. His conclusion that every execution deterred eight homicides was brought up in several Supreme Court cases in the interim[20] and received wide publicity, which may have contributed to the rising support for the death penalty in the mid-1970s.[21] The article was highly controversial and was soon followed by several pieces discrediting its analysis.[22]

The aftermath of the deterrence debate is an illustration of the lack of dialogue between the world of research methodology and the world of politics and policy making. The years since Ehrlich's article have not been kind to the deterrence argument in the public arena; several important stakeholders have concluded the death penalty has no deterrent effect, and activist pamphlets and policy documents often treat this conclusion as fact.[23] Most recently, a new report by the National Research Council has come to this conclusion:

> Research to date on the effect of capital punishment on homicide rates is not useful in determining whether the death penalty increases, decreases, or has no effect on these rates. The key question is whether capital punishment is less or more effective as a deterrent than alternative punishments, such as a life sentence without the possibility of parole. Yet none of the research that has been done accounted for the possible effect of noncapital punishments on homicide rates. The report recommends new avenues of research that may provide broader insight into any deterrent effects from both capital and noncapital punishments.[24]

In the world of scholarship, however, the deterrent effect of the death penalty has remained unsettled and is mostly relegated to the world of rigorous econometric methodological debate. Most recently, two teams of economists have examined data from the postretention era and have come to opposite conclusions. Hashem Dezhbakhsh, Paul Rubin, and Joanna Sheppard found support for Ehrlich's original findings, to the extent that their study was quoted as finding that "the death penalty deters scores of killings."[25] Using the same data but with reservations about the methodology (in particular, the inclusion of anomalous Texas data in the analysis), John Donohue and Justin Wolfers came to the conclusion that the death penalty is not a deterrent.[26] A recent confrontation of the two research teams centered on methodology and the ethics of data sharing rather than on the ideology surrounding the death penalty.[27] But the debate has failed to register in the arena of public opinion. The decline of interest in the deterrence argument may be due to an increased perception among the public, fueled by images of drug-related homicides in the heyday of the crack epidemic, that many such homicides were not premeditated, and therefore the response to the prospect of execution was inelastic.[28] While some abolitionists give a nod to arguments about the death penalty's lack of deterrent effect, they largely became a footnote to the more prominent arguments for abolition, namely, cost and innocence, but not before an interlude in the discourse devoted to the issue of racial discrimination.

RACIAL DISCRIMINATION: McCLESKY AND
THE LEGAL IMPERMEABILITY TO STATISTICAL
PROOF OF OVERREPRESENTATION

A new era of ideologically fueled abolitionism emerged in 1980 with the publication of David Baldus and James Cole's *Statistical Proof of Discrimination*.[29] Using panel data—two thousand murder cases in Georgia in the 1970s—Baldus and Cole found that the likelihood of a convicted murderer being sentenced to death was determined in large part by the race of the defendant and the race of the victim. When examining black and white offenders with black and white victims, black killers of white victims were the most likely to receive death sentences. The least likely recipients were black killers of black victims.[30]

Baldus and Cole's study gave fuel to arguments that, even after the post-Fuhrman reforms, death penalty statutes continued to produce racially discriminatory and arbitrary punishment. The petitioner in *McClesky v. Kemp* sought to attack Georgia's death penalty based on the disparate allocation of capital and noncapital sentences among black and white defendants.[31] The Supreme Court held that without evidence of specific racial animus directed at the petitioner himself, the study was insufficient to find a violation of either his Fourteenth or Eighth Amendment rights. The Court affirmed the district court's holding that "assumed the validity of the Baldus study but found the statistics insufficient to demonstrate unconstitutional discrimination in the Fourteenth Amendment context or to show irrationality, arbitrariness, and capriciousness under Eighth Amendment analysis."[32] McClesky claimed that the capital sentencing scheme in Georgia violated the Equal Protection clause, as well as the Eighth Amendment's prohibition on cruel and unusual punishment by virtue of the racially discriminatory application of the law. However, because there was no showing of racist intent on the part of the legislature and because the death penalty scheme was within the guidelines established by *Furman* for juror discretion, both of these claims were found to be without merit. To prevail on a claim of discrimination, said the Court, petitioners would have to demonstrate "evidence specific to [their] own case that would support an inference that racial considerations played a part in [their] sentence." Simply put, the "discriminatory purpose" requirement for showing racial discrimination in an Equal Protection claim shields a system in which the outcomes are racially skewed but the actors all disavow any overt racial considerations.

The effect of *McClesky v. Kemp* was to render racial discrimination a fruitless litigation strategy in the post-*Gregg* era.[33] Some efforts have been made in lower courts to use data on minority overrepresentation in a way that created a closer link to the particular facts of the case, with little success.[34] However, racial discrimination arguments are more frequently made outside courts, in the context of framing American punitivism as "the new Jim Crow,"[35] where they face the possible criticism that African Americans are overrepresented in the population of violent crime perpetrators and not only sentenced death row inmates.[36] Public efforts on behalf of death row inmates such as Mumia Abu Jamal[37] and Troy Davis[38] often cite racial discrimination and use it in an effort to galvanize a progressive critical mass of supporters.

THE RISE OF INNOCENCE

Concerns about the irreversibility of the death penalty and the potential for a mistake, while theoretically acknowledged for many decades, became more pronounced with the establishment of innocence projects in law schools in the 1990s,[39] followed by the emergence and rapid improvement of DNA technology for use in evaluating old evidence.[40] The obvious appeal of the innocence argument, which transcends political disagreements about public safety, was largely responsible for the growing disfavor of the death penalty with the American public in the mid-1990 after an all-time peak in support for it, as demonstrated in figure 2.[41] But these apolitical features are also the reason progressive activists are concerned about using innocence as the be-all, end-all argument for abolition.[42] The risk is that by caring solely about the innocent, the argument entrenches the legitimacy of the death penalty for the truly guilty, thus standing in the way of wholesale abolition and reform.

One of the risks involved in innocence advocacy against the death penalty has indeed come to pass. The 1990s started a flow of DNA-based exonerations, some of them after convicted defendants spent many years in prison.[43] However, actual innocence also became increasingly difficult to prove.[44] Supreme Court jurisprudence narrowed the possibility of successful habeas corpus petitions by disallowing arguments not pursued earlier in the proceedings (the "cause and prejudice" test), and federal legislation created a strict statute of limitations on habeas petitions. The only path bypassing the cause and prejudice test is an actual innocence argument, but the threshold for proving actual innocence is extremely high.[45]

Nonetheless, the apolitical nature of innocence arguments has had a tremendous effect in at least one state. In 2003 then Illinois governor George Ryan performed a mass commutation of inmates on the state's death row shortly before leaving office. Declaring that he was not an abolitionist, he gave as his reason the unacceptable level of risk of executing an innocent person due to flaws in the Illinois criminal justice system.[46] This act was arguably the most visible outcome of the "innocence revolution" in American capital punishment—a time when DNA exonerations and the failure of eyewitness identifications in rape and homicide cases undermined the widely held belief that the American criminal justice system was generally free of error. Suddenly false convictions weren't merely a bogeyman of the Old South and legal lynchings.[47] They were, instead, what happened to some seventeen men later freed from Illinois's death row in 2003 thanks to the work of

Are you in favor of the death penalty for a person convicted of murder?

———— % In favor - - - - - % Opposed

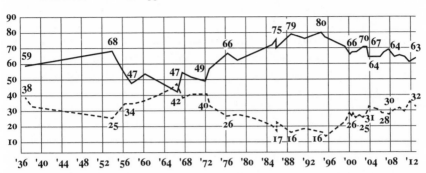

FIGURE 2. Public support of and opposition to the death penalty.

the Innocence Project and students in Northwestern University's journalism program.[48] Governor Ryan's mass pardon cleared the path for Illinois's subsequent abolition of the death penalty, which married innocence rationales to cost logic.

TINKERING WITH THE MACHINERY OF DEATH

In 1994 Justice Blackmun proclaimed his distaste for litigation regarding technical safeguards in the death penalty context.

> From this day forward, I no longer shall tinker with the machinery of death. For more than 20 years I have endeavored . . . to develop . . . rules that would lend more than the mere appearance of fairness to the death penalty endeavor. . . . Rather than continue to coddle the court's delusion that the desired level of fairness has been achieved . . . I feel . . . obligated simply to concede that the death penalty experiment has failed. It is virtually self-evident to me now that no combination of procedural rules or substantive regulations ever can save the death penalty from its inherent constitutional deficiencies. . . . Perhaps one day this court will develop procedural rules or verbal formulas that actually will provide consistency, fairness and reliability in a capital-sentencing scheme. I am not optimistic that such a day will come. I am more optimistic, though, that this court eventually will conclude that the effort to eliminate arbitrariness while preserving fairness "in the infliction of [death] is so plainly doomed to failure that it and the death penalty must be abandoned altogether." . . . I may not live to see that day, but I have faith that eventually it will arrive. The path the court has chosen lessens us all.[49]

"Tinkering with the machinery of death" has since then become a major capital punishment litigation avenue in the most technical way: assessing the relative humanenenss of different methods of execution. These litigation techniques stem from the immense difficulty of succeeding with general arguments about the constitutionality of the death penalty and follow the path forged by the nineteenth-century inventors of the electric chair.[50]

In recent years debating the minute details of execution methods has become the bread and butter of appellate litigation over the death penalty. The most current iteration of these strategies focuses on the constitutionality of lethal injection practices. In *Baze v. Rees,* the Supreme Court determined that petitioners, death row inmates in Kentucky, had failed to show sufficient evidence that the method Kentucky used violated their Eighth Amendment right to be free of cruel and unusual punishment.[51] Petitioners came to the Supreme Court challenging the three-drug cocktail method used by Kentucky as too prone to risk of improper administration. If the sedative is not effective, the paralytic administered second will prevent the executed from moving but will not prevent him from feeling the crushing pain of dying by simultaneous suffocation and cardiac arrest caused by the potassium chloride. The Court found that the standard urged by petitioners, in which the state should be required to adopt alternative procedures that could prevent such blunders, was too lax and would invite litigation. The Court held that "simply because an execution method may result in pain, either by accident or as an inescapable consequence of death, does not establish the sort of 'objectively intolerable risk of harm' that qualifies as cruel and unusual."

In 2010 the Court heard a challenge, brought in a 1983 suit against the planned Arizona execution of Jeffrey Landrigan by means of non-FDA-approved drugs.[52] The district court first invited, then ordered, the Arizona Department of Corrections to provide "the source of the drug, the drug's expiration date, the *efficacy of the drug* for its intended purpose . . . and all available documentation concerning the manufacturer and its process for producing sodium thiopental."[53] The defendants refused, on the grounds that Arizona law prohibited disclosure of the identity of executioners and that the Court's order improperly required the state to use only FDA-approved drugs. Three petitioners had previously challenged the three-drug cocktail used in Arizona, and their claim was denied at the federal district court based on a finding that the method was "substantially similar" to the one used by Kentucky in *Baze v. Rees.*[54] Landrigan was pursuing his suit on state law grounds; his claim was denied based in large part on the Supreme Court's decision in *Dickens,* which found Arizona's protocol sufficient under *Baze.*[55] Upon denial of Landrigan's claim, Arizona moved for a warrant of execution, which Landrigan opposed, raising for the first time the issue of the nationwide shortage of sodium thiopental and requesting the Arizona Supreme Court to stay its decision "until the State had demonstrated that it possessed or could legally obtain the drugs necessary to carry out his execution in a manner consistent with Arizona's protocol."[56]

Landrigan filed a motion to disclose a number of matters, including the source of the drug, the lot number, and the chain of custody of the specific drugs to be used in his execution. At oral argument "counsel for the State declined to reveal where ADOC obtained the sodium thiopental for Plaintiff's execution but acknowledged that it was not obtained from or manufactured by Hospira, Inc., which Plaintiff alleges is the only manufacturer of sodium thiopental approved by the Food and Drug Administration." The state further stated that the drug was "lawfully" obtained and was not expired. In his motion for an injunction, Landrigan argued that "because ADOC's supply of sodium thiopental lacks the appropriate safeguards, it could be 'contaminated with toxins that cause pain, as opposed to unconsciousness' or could fail to properly anesthetize him, thus resulting in excruciating pain when the second and third drugs are administered." The state, in response, contended that the protocol provided sufficient safeguards to ensure that the inmate is unconscious before the second and third drugs are administered, which eliminated any genuine risk that Landrigan might suffer pain during the course of his execution.[57]

The Supreme Court noted that Arizona behaved unusually in this case, refusing to give any evidence to undercut Landrigan's claim or support its position. Based in significant part on the use of non-FDA-approved drugs, the Court determined that it was unable to evaluate the risk to Landrigan and that the state's failure to give any evidence on the matter forced the Court to accept Landrigan's "factual showing that such drugs are more likely to contain harmful contaminants." The Court concluded:

> The issue is whether there is a sufficient level of confidence that the sodium thiopental Defendants plan on using to sedate Plaintiff does not create a substantial risk of harm. FDA approval is relevant in that drugs manufactured under FDA guidelines are likely to perform as expected; drugs manufactured by non-FDA approved sources might not benefit from such a presumption. Without the assurance of FDA approval, the Court is left to speculate whether the non-FDA approved drug will perform in the exact same manner as an FDA-approved drug and whether the non-FDA approved drug will cause pain and suffering. This is not a factual issue the Court can resolve by adopting Defendants' assurances that sodium thiopental "is simply a chemical compound" and the source of that compound is irrelevant.[58]

Despite this record, the Supreme Court, in a 5–4 vote, issued a one-paragraph decision granting the state's application to that body to vacate the district court's restraining order.

> The application to vacate the order by the district court granting a temporary restraining order, presented to Justice Kennedy and by him referred to the Court, is granted. There is no evidence in the record to suggest that the drug obtained from a foreign source is unsafe. The district court granted the restraining order because it

was left to speculate as to the risk of harm. But speculation cannot substitute for evidence that the use of the drug is "*sure or very likely* to cause serious illness and needless suffering.'" . . . There was no showing that the drug was unlawfully obtained, nor was there an offer of proof to that effect. The motion to file documents under seal is denied as moot.[59]

Because Landrigan did not present evidence of the harmfulness of the drugs the state was planning to use—evidence that was only within the state's power to produce and which it had been ordered to produce—his case was short-circuited. The restraining order was lifted on direct petition by the state, while the Ninth Circuit had affirmed the lower court's decision and denied rehearing. He was executed as scheduled on October 26, 2010, two days after the Supreme Court's ruling.

As illustrated by *Landrigan*, the controversy over lethal injection is not just about the order of operations in administering it but also about the ability of states to acquire the necessary drugs in the first place. In fact, there are a number of things that are logistically challenging about lethal injection that may also add to the risk of botched or excruciating executions. In 2009 Ohio death chamber technicians were unable to inject Romell Broom properly, and after sticking him over eighteen times with a needle, they put off the execution because they couldn't find a vein.[60] In 2009 Hospira, the sole U.S. producer of sodium thiopental, ceased production of the drug.[61] In 2011 that company announced they would not be resuming production of the drug at their plant in Italy, out of concern that doing so would subject the company to liability under Italian law if the drug was used in lethal injections.[62] The drug was never approved by the FDA for executions but had been used for that purpose as an "off-label" use—a common practice in medicine. However, it is a practice that should raise some interesting questions in the arena of capital punishment. The American Medical Association and state medical boards have taken the position that it is an ethical violation of a physician's professional duties to participate in an execution.

A physician, as a member of a profession dedicated to preserving life when there is hope of doing so, should not be a participant in a legally authorized execution. Physician participation in execution is defined generally as actions that would fall into one or more of the following categories: (1) an action that would directly cause the death of the condemned; (2) an action that would assist, supervise, or contribute to the ability of another individual to directly cause the death of the condemned; (3) an action that could automatically cause an execution to be carried out on a condemned prisoner.[63]

Among the actions deemed to constitute "participation" is prescribing agents or medications to be used in an execution. While a physician may certify that a condemned person has died, he or she may only do so after a nonphysician has declared death. In 2007 the North Carolina Medical Board (NCMB) issued a

Position Statement that forbade any physician licensed in North Carolina from participation in an execution that extended beyond mere presence or certification of death (retracted in 2011).[64] Following this statement, physicians refused to participate in North Carolina executions at all, halting executions. The state's corrections agency sought and obtained from the state supreme court an injunction against the NCMB prohibiting them from disciplining any doctor who participated in an execution based on the Position Statement's incompatibility with state law, which requires a physician to be present at all executions.[65]

THE RISE OF HUMONETARIANISM

The rise in cost-centered arguments against the death penalty in the late 2000s occurred, therefore, against a backdrop of failed approaches to abolition. At the advent of the financial crisis, this is how things stood. The deterrence argument faded from the public stage and became relegated to an insular academic debate among methodology-minded economists. The racial disparity argument, following its failure in the Supreme Court, was frequently mentioned in progressive circles but unpersuasive for political adversaries. The innocence argument, while successful in Illinois and successful in decreasing the gap between death penalty proponents and opponents in the general population, retrenched death penalty support for the guilty and was ineffectual in overturning standards to prove actual innocence in court. And death penalty litigation focused on increasingly technical arguments about humane execution methods and drug availability.

But winds of change had already begun to blow. By the mid-2000s public support for the death penalty had declined considerably. While in the 1992 Democratic primaries candidate and former Massachusetts governor Michael Dukakis famously flubbed his response to a reporter's question about what he would want if his own wife were raped and murdered,[66] political wisdom at the turn of the twenty-first century began to be more permissive regarding abolitionist stances. New Hampshire's legislature voted to end the death penalty in that state in 2000; the bill was then vetoed by Governor Jeanne Shaheen.[67] In that same year Governor Ryan of Illinois declared a moratorium on executions and, as mentioned above, in 2003 commuted the sentences of all Illinois death row inmates.[68] In 2005 New York's legislature declined to reinstate capital punishment when the appellate court struck down the existing statute;[69] in 2007 New Jersey abolished its death penalty;[70] and in 2009 New Mexico followed suit.[71] In 2011 Illinois[72] and Connecticut[73] repealed their death penalty statutes, and legislatures in Florida,[74] Kansas,[75] Maryland,[76] Ohio,[77] Pennsylvania,[78] and Texas[79] all considered bills to abolish the death penalty in those states. Such bills were also considered in California in 2012[80] and in Delaware in 2013.[81] Other states have considered and implemented moratoria on their death penalty practices, often citing costs.[82]

Arguing that the humonetarian discourse is the sole explanatory variable for these great strides toward death penalty abolition would be an exaggeration. An examination of advocacy materials provided by abolitionist and civil rights organizations reveals that websites and brochures frequently list myriad reasons for abolition. Among them are arbitrariness of the death penalty, racial disparities in its applications, due process failures resulting from geographic and class disparities in death penalty sentencing, and concerns about innocence.[83] Part of the distaste for capital punishment is also a function of its increasingly rare application in many counties. Supreme Court Justices such as Blackmun and John Paul Stevens have, as stated above, expressed their objection to the practice. Moreover, Justice Potter Stewart, hardly a liberal in his day and an opponent of abolition, famously wrote in *Furman* that the chance of a defendant being sentenced to die was less than the likelihood of being struck by lightning.[84] Governor Ryan's 2003 speech announcing his mass clemency, "I Must Act," lists a panoply of reasons that, taken together, compelled him to halt executions in his state. Among other reasons, he notes that in one of 1,000 homicides committed in 2002, only 2 percent of those cases, or twenty murderers, received a capital sentence.[85] Moreover, downstate defendants were much more likely to wind up in a death chamber than were defendants in Chicago. In California the death penalty is likewise an unlikely outcome of a homicide trial, and the vast majority of such sentences come from three counties in Southern California.[86] California Attorney General Kamala Harris is opposed to the death penalty.[87] San Francisco County has had a string of district attorneys opposed in general or in all cases to capital punishment. The newest San Francisco district attorney, George Gascón, committed to never seek the death penalty in San Francisco after initially drawing fire for saying he would keep the option open for the most heinous cases, such as the murder of a police officer.[88] Gascón has by turns expressed philosophical opposition to the death penalty and as opined that life without parole would be more economically viable for California.

Another consideration often combined with the discourse of cost is the fear of wrongful convictions, which is similar to the humonetarian discourse in that its universal appeal transcends the tough/soft on crime dichotomy. In 2011 the Illinois legislature voted to abolish the state death penalty, and Gov. Patrick Quinn signed the measure into law. Like Governor Ryan eight years before, lawmakers cited numerous reasons for their votes. The possibility, even likelihood, of executing an innocent person was among the top reasons. In *The New Abolitionism*, Sarat argues that pragmatic "universal" concerns, like the innocence argument, provide cover for mainstream political actors who may or may not also hold moral views opposing or supporting the death penalty.[89] For example, Sarat argues that Ryan's actions in Illinois and the grounds he listed in 2003 provided cover for the New Hampshire legislature's later attempt to ban the death penalty in that state.[90] While the New Hampshire governor eventually vetoed the legislature's abolition attempt, the fact that it was passed by both houses of the state legislature may have demonstrated a shift in the popular attitude to abolition.

Finally, the success of recent initiatives can be attributed in part to inertia. Death sentences and executions are not equally distributed nationwide. Texas leads the nation in number of executions,[91] and only 2 percent of the nation's counties account for the vast majority of death row inmates.[92] The corollary is that several states have not experienced frequent capital sentences and may have not experienced an execution in years, even without formal moratoria. In 2004 New Jersey became the first state to abolish the death penalty since 1976. Activists first achieved a moratorium in 2004 and convinced a legislature composed of an unusually high proportion of officials not seeking reelection to vote out the practice. Apparently key in both New Jersey's and New Hampshire's votes was the fact that neither state had executed an inmate since the nationwide moratorium ended following the *Gregg* decision.[93] By contrast, Illinois had an active execution chamber until Ryan's moratorium in 2000. However, the trauma of seeing convicted men released as innocent and the posthumous exonerations of several executed men likely had a lasting effect on at least some lawmakers in that state.

The power of humonetarianism as a contributor to abolitionist reform lies, therefore, not in its dominance as a causal explanation but in the fact that the climate of austerity has created the conditions that make it possible to succeed on arguments that have previously failed to make a difference. The perception that the financial crisis can facilitate bipartisan reform of the death penalty has been at the forefront of each of the campaigns in the new wave of abolitionist activism, and each of them has prominently featured the costs of the death penalty as its focal, albeit not sole, point.

The New Hampshire campaign, for example, features a "cost fact sheet,"[94] which estimates the costs of the conviction of Michael Addison, the first person condemned in in that state since 1938, at $2.3 million as of September 2013 and the defense effort at $2.6 million. Similarly, public hearings in New York prominently featured cost estimates, extensively citing Richard Dieter of the Death Penalty Information Center.

> [Mr. Dieter] believes the question of cost as it relates to the death penalty is a central issue. He argued that having the death penalty means sacrificing compensation for victims' families, funds for more police and even more prison space. Mr. Dieter noted that the Ryan Commission in Illinois made eighty-five recommendations, most of which, he said, would make the Illinois death penalty even more expensive. Mr. Dieter argued that most states have a symbolic death penalty. He said that in most jurisdictions, a significant majority of death sentences are overturned and life sentences are imposed instead. Thus, he asserted, most states that have the death penalty pay the significantly higher costs associated with trying a death penalty case, but frequently end up with a non-death sentence anyway. Mr. Dieter also argued that

expenses associated with the death penalty are "top heavy," meaning that most costs occur quickly during the trial and early appeals, rather than being spread out over a long period of time, as in the case of a person who is sentenced to a life term for murder. Special procedures, including the fact that capital trials have two phases, add to the costs. Mr. Dieter asserted that with so significant a portion of the cost of capital cases coming early in the representation, the cost[s] of death penalty cases quickly surpass those of non-death penalty cases, eclipsing even the costs associated with forty years or more of imprisonment for non-capital defendants.[95]

The Maryland death penalty repeal in 2013 also heavily relied on costs, which the governor's office cited as being three times as much as for noncapital cases.[96]

States in which the struggle to abolish the death penalty is still ongoing refer to the cost argument as a potentially revitalizing factor. The website for Floridians for Alternatives to the Death Penalty, which focuses on innocence factors, also features a video illustrating death penalty costs, arguing that these factors "rekindle the debate."[97] The Indiana campaign features a Web page that dispels "seven myths about the death penalty," the first one being that capital punishment is cheaper than life without parole.[98] The Kansas campaign held a 2013 conference featuring four workshops, one of them on death penalty costs.[99] Ohio's campaign relies on the support of Eve Stratton, former state supreme court justice, who stated that she now opposes the death penalty, among other issues, because of the "exorbitant costs."[100]

Even campaigns that prioritized substantive and moral arguments mentioned cost as a relevant consideration. Such was the case in the Illinois campaign, which was fueled by concerns about wrongful convictions and procedural violations.[101] In New Mexico, where the governor, Susana Martinez, explained repeal as a step to avoid wrongful convictions and racial discrimination, she pointed out that the cost of mounting a death penalty trial was more expensive than that of a noncapital trial. She stated, "We can put that money toward enhancing law enforcement, public works, you name it."[102].

But the quintessential example of a humonetarian campaign that relied primarily on costs was California's Proposition 34, which failed to pass by a narrow margin in the 2012 election. Despite its failure, the campaign is notable for making headway in a punitive, neopopulist state with the biggest death row in the nation. I want to turn now to an in-depth examination of Proposition 34, a classic example of a cost-centered campaign.

HUMONETARIAN ABOLITIONISM IN ACTION: CALIFORNIA'S FAILED PROPOSITION 34

California's Proposition 34, otherwise known as SAFE California, purported not to abolish the death penalty but to "replace" it with life without parole.[103] Earlier in

2012 an effort was made to introduce a death penalty abolition bill in the legislature, but the bill failed to garner sufficient support to pass.[104] A problematic legal construction, requiring a constitutional amendment, meant that the only way to achieve repeal would be through a voter initiative. And, indeed, a subsequent voter initiative managed to gather the required 750,000 signatures to be placed on the California ballot.[105]

Despite its eventual failure, 47 to 53 percent,[106] Prop 34 is of particular interest for several reasons. First, California's San Quentin prison has the nation's largest death row, housing 734 inmates.[107] The dilapidated facility has raised serious security and maintenance concerns.[108] Since 1976 only 13 of death row's inhabitants have been executed; during the same period, 85 have died of natural causes before they could be executed.[109] San Quentin and its death row have been the subject of numerous legislative and litigated battles, pertaining not only to the constitutionality of death row practices but also to the immense expense involved in renovating and maintaining death row at a constitutionally acceptable standard.[110] In addition, California's role as an early adopter of punitive reforms, such as mandatory sentencing and the Three Strikes Law, meant a high-stake battle for abolition.

The initiative's name, "SAFE California," was chosen for its humonetarian meaning: SAFE stood for Saving, Accountability, and Full Enforcement.[111] This choice of words was not coincidental. The Prop 34 campaign deliberately shied away from arguments of human rights and deterrence and focused on two factors: the cost inefficiency of the death penalty as it is practiced in California and the risk of executing innocent people. To dispel any concerns that the initiative might be "soft on crime," it explicitly created a fund that would have shifted $30 million of the projected budget savings into investigation of unsolved rape and murder cases. The fact sheet distributed at events and available on the website focused exclusively on the cost issue, providing a pie chart that illustrates the causes for high costs: trials and investigations, special housing (one person instead of two persons to a cell, with a heightened security level), and state and federal appeals. Proposition 34's focus on fiscal grounds was supported by the Legal Analyst Office's analysis of the bill, which estimated death penalty abolition would save $100 million annually.[112]

Volunteers for the SAFE California campaign who distributed flyers, worked phone banks, and organized fund-raising events, received a standard instruction sheet, which explicitly requested that they avoid using the words *abolition* and *barbaric*.[113] The sheet, and preevent instructions for volunteers, discouraged any human rights–oriented discussion of the death penalty. Instead, activists were prompted to discuss the fiscal viability of the death penalty as it is practiced in California. In public appearances, politicians and activists who endorsed the proposition often spoke about the harshness of life without parole as an alternative to the death penalty and about the fact that the small number of people who have been executed in the state since *Gregg* rendered the death penalty an expensive, inefficient method of punishment. At the 2010 gathering of the World Coalition Against the Death Penalty, which featured the would-be proponents of Proposition 34, Senator Mark Leno, a well-known supporter of progressive, nonpunitive criminal justice reform, was cheered by a full house when assuring the audience, which included victims' families and law enforcement agents, that convicted murderers would still be "locked down for the rest of their lives."[114] The message was one of fiscal responsibility, not of abolition.

The focus on costs was an important factor in garnering support for the initiative from a diverse group of stakeholders, including several unlikely supporters. Among the bill's endorsers were the lead proponent of California's 1978 death penalty initiative, the lawyer who wrote California's death penalty law,[115] four hundred murder victims' family members,[116] and numerous law enforcement officials.[117] The organization was spearheaded by Jeanne Woodford, former warden of San Quentin, who during her tenure there presided over four executions.[118] It is unlikely that these parties would have joined such a narrow coalition were it presented as a human rights–focused initiative. Instead, some of the people featured in Prop 34 ads were family members of victims of unsolved crimes, calling for better funding of police investigations.

One such ad starts with police car lights and a caption reading, "Each year more than 1000 homicides go unsolved in California." The caption continues, "More than half of all rapists walk the streets . . . because police don't have enough money to go after criminals." As crumpled dollar bills fall down the screen, former San Quentin warden and chair of the SAFE California campaign, Woodford, is heard saying, "We spent more than four billion dollars on the death penalty since 1978 . . . we carried out 13 executions." Another caption reads, "If voters replace the death penalty in California, the state will save a billion dollars over the next five years." Woodford presents the alternative, life without parole, "which would ensure that [the convicted] would die in prison," and a caption introduces the "many extra services" received by death row inmates. Woodford elaborates on the expense involved in legal teams and on the alternative use of the money: "putting more police on the streets and keeping our community center." A police siren is heard in the background, as Woodford discusses budget shortages for solving violent crime.[119]

Two weeks before the 2012 election, the *San Francisco Chronicle* reported on an informal poll soliciting reactions of death row inmates to Prop 34.[120] According to poll results, most inmates on San Quentin's death row were opposed to it. The reasons for this opposition were nuanced and telling. Given the rarity of executions, the report stated, inmates were willing to risk the chance of an execution in return for free litigation services for appeals and habeas corpus petitions, resources that are not available to the prison's general population.

The exit polls conducted by SAFE officials revealed the advantages and short-comings of relying primarily on cost as an argument.[121] Twenty-six percent of voters voted yes on Proposition 34, not because of their ideological objection to the death penalty, but solely because of the issue of costs. Anecdotal conversations I had with volunteers during the campaign revealed that not only voters but also active phone bank volunteers and those handing out flyers joined the campaign even though they were on the fence about the death penalty ideologically; the budgetary effect of replacing the death penalty with life without parole was attractive to them.

The exit poll results are particularly interesting in light of a 2009 survey, conducted by Craig Haney.[122] The survey showed that death penalty support rates had declined over the past two decades, from 79 percent to 66 percent, and attributed the decline to concerns about innocence. Moreover, the proportion of adult Californians who view themselves as "strong" supporters of the death penalty dropped from 50 percent in 1989 to 38 percent. Conversely, fewer than 9 percent were "strongly opposed" to capital punishment twenty years ago, compared to 21 percent at the time the survey was taken.[123] Haney's respondents also were found to erroneously believe that the death penalty was less expensive to taxpayers than life without parole. While the cost argument was clearly not responsible for the overall decline in support of the death penalty, its emergence against the backdrop of the financial crisis made a difference, albeit not enough to pass the initiative.

BROKEN BEYOND REPAIR? HUMONETARIAN LOGIC
AND STREAMLINING THE DEATH PENALTY

The failure of Proposition 34 by a narrower than ever margin is telling and important. The success of the campaign in bridging the gap of public opinion—at some point with a majority of poll takers in support of repeal[124]—is one more data point in a growing trend of abolitionist states. The change in discourse that has made this development possible is largely, though not exclusively, attributable to the introduction of cost-centered arguments into the abolition debate.

Humonetarian discourse on the death penalty, however, can be a double-edged sword. In a 2009 op-ed arguing for the abolition of the death penalty, Republican lawmaker Tom Harman touted his support of the death penalty, arguing that the real problem was not executions in themselves but rather the litigation surrounding capital punishment.

> Advocates on both sides of this debate can agree on one point—the death penalty system in California is broken and unworkable. As long as the citizens of California continue to support the death penalty, it is the job of the Legislature to fix this dysfunctional system. If lawmakers don't, then the citizens of California will do it themselves through the initiative process. As it stands now, justice isn't being served for anyone.[125]

This prophecy has come to pass in several states, much to the chagrin of anti–death penalty activists, in the form of legislation preserving capital punishment while making it cheaper. In June 2013 Florida governor Rick Scott signed a bill restricting postconviction remedies in Florida in an effort to streamline the death penalty and make executions cheaper.[126]

A similar effort to limit capital punishment remedies to one appeal in California, pushed by the Association of District Attorneys, was initially stopped in its tracks,[127] but it was followed by a ballot measure proposed for November 2014. Under the new initiative, which is supported by the former Democratic governor Gray Davis as well as former Republican governors Pete Wilson and George Deukmejian, the death penalty would be "fixed" and "streamlined" in a way that would "correct the flaws, reduce the cost and give both victims and defendants a quicker path to justice."[128]

But tough 'n' cheap rhetoric received a new blow in the form of a District Court decision by Judge Cormac Carney of Orange County, *Jones v. Chappell*.[129] In *Jones*, Judge Carney, a George W. Bush appointee, found the death penalty in California unconstitutional because of the delays in its application. The decision reviews the sources of execution delays on direct appeal and on collateral review, concluding that the promise of the death penalty

> is made to the citizens of the State, who are investing significant resources in furtherance of a punishment that they believe is necessary to achieving justice. It is made to jurors who, in exercise of their civic responsibility, are asked to hear about and see evidence of undeniably horrific crimes, and then participate in the agonizing deliberations over whether the perperators of those horrific crimes should be put to death. It is made to victims and their loved ones, for whom just punishment might provide some semblance of moral and emotional closure from an otherwise unimaginable loss. And it is made to the hundreds of individuals on Death Row, as a statement their crimes are so heinous they have forfeited their right to life.
>
> But for too long now, the promise has been an empty one. Inordinate and unpredictable delay has resulted in a death penalty system in which very few of the hundreds of individuals sentenced to death have been, or even will be, executed by the State. It has resulted in a system in which arbitrary factors, rather than legitimate ones like the nature of the crime or the date of the death sentence, determine whether an individual will actually be executed. And it has resulted in a system that serves no penological purpose. Such a system is unconstitutional.[130]

Judge Carney's decision to vacate Jones's death sentence is a classic humonetarian decision. It builds not on issues of individual rights but on the administrative dysfunction of the death penalty. To the extent that it addresses the impact of this dysfunction on death row inmates themselves, it does not focus on issues of humanity and barbarism but rather on a "promise" to "deliver" a just dessert. And it is clearly more concerned with the impact of the broken system on victims' families, jurors, and the California taxpayers.

As the California attorney general gears up for her appeal of Judge Carney's order,[131] the debate is likely to turn on the tough 'n' cheap issue: is it possible to streamline postconviction remedies in a way that speeds up executions and saves on litigation resources? Judge Carney answers in the negative, arguing that all efforts to reform and "fix" the death penalty have failed. But it would be odd, and deeply humonetarian, to move to a phase in which abolition rhetoric turns on the fact that the state is not killing the inmates fast enough.

It is also important to keep in mind an unspoken aspect of humonetarian rhetoric. The rejection of the death penalty on cost and efficiency grounds implies a cost comparison with its obvious alternative, life without parole. Ads like those aired on behalf of Prop 34 do not argue for rehabilitation or humane treatment. Instead, they rely on public safety arguments to differentiate between death row inmates and general population inmates, expressing no qualms about locking up the latter for the rest of their lives. This rhetoric may become a thorn in nonpunitive activists' sides if they hope for incremental reform, starting with abolition and continuing with long-term incarceration.

The risk of restoring the tough 'n' cheap approach also begs the question of the viability of abolitionist efforts in the long run. Will these pragmatic rationales for abolition hold up when the American economy improves? Death penalty scholarship, such as Franklin Zimring and David Johnson's *The Next Frontier: Death Penalty in Asia*,[132] points out that once a country abolishes the death penalty reinstating it is no longer on the table and the entire debate becomes a nonissue. While the return of the death penalty in *Gregg* after it was halted in *Furman* may suggest that American exceptionalism may operate differently here, the context of these two cases suggests that a wholesale abolition scheme may indeed be permanent, as in the rest of the Western world. While the recent achievements on this front are not solely attributable to the cost-centered argument, its contribution lies in creating the conditions that made it possible to transcend the traditional debates about the death penalty (human rights, deterrence, racial discrimination) and make abolition an appealing cost for voters across the political spectrum. The next chapter elaborates on the potential of humonetarianism to bridge the political divide in political rhetoric and in the context of the war on drugs.

5

THE NEW COALITIONS OF
FINANCIAL PRUDENCE

From Tough on Crime to the Drug Truce

The first marijuana legalization campaign advertisement broadcast in Washington State featured Kate Pippinger, a white woman described as a "Washington mom." Seated at a café, holding a mug, dressed in a cardigan, with a string of pearls at her neck and shoulder-length hair, Pippinger looks straight at the camera and says:

> I don't like it personally, but it's time for a conversation about legalizing marijuana. It's a multi-million-dollar industry in Washington State and we get no benefit. What if we regulate it, have background checks for retailers, stiff penalties for selling to minors?[1]

Grinning, Pippinger adds:

> We could tax it to fund schools and healthcare. Free up police to go after violent crime instead. And we would control the money, not the gangs.[2]

The ad is evocative of the new discourse highlighted in the previous chapter, which introduced revenue enhancement and austerity as the source of consensus on reform. But it is notable not only for the discourse. Pippinger's attire and demeanor, as well as the ad's location at a café, is aimed at a conservative audience, who, it is assumed, does not like "it"—legalization—personally. The powerful idea conveyed by the speaker's appearance, context, and words is that financial responsibility can, and should, be bipartisan or even nonpartisan, transcend political disagreement, and override the entrenched public debates about public safety and human rights.

The ad and the other phenomena surveyed in this chapter represent the second feature of humonetarianism: the power of cost-centered arguments to empower conservative lawmakers, politicians, and citizens to embrace arguments that would be unthinkable before the recession and to openly associate themselves with political adversaries in advocating nonpunitive, fiscally lean policies and reforms.

Many accounts of mass incarceration examine the transformation in electoral and political rhetoric that made "soft on crime" positions into political kryptonite regardless of party affiliation.[3] Espousing death penalty abolition, alternatives to incarceration, decriminalization, and legalization is a very risky choice for many politicians, certainly for conservative ones. By contrast, progressive politicians supporting "tough on crime" positions are protected from unfavorable public opinion because their progressive constituents will vote for them anyway and disenfranchised groups who are targeted by punitive policies do not have the political cachet and lobbying power to make a difference. This trend became even more pronounced during the 1990s, which might be referred to as the Decade of the Victim, when victim interest groups and advocates, for the most part representing the interests of white, middle-class victims of violent crime, became important political players.[4]

The political fear of espousing "soft on crime" opinions and policies has not subsided, but the financial crisis has created the opportunity to position oneself neutrally in the criminal justice realm without being penalized for not espousing punitive opinions. Republicans, Democrats, and others have participated in criminal justice campaigns that advocate scaling back the punitive project for financial reasons. The previous chapter highlighted some of the unexpected collaborators in the struggle to abolish the death penalty in California and other states. This chapter focuses on another area of criminal justice that has been particularly conducive to political neutralization and bipartisan policy making: the war on drugs. Drug policy is a poignant example of the bipartisanship and new alliances in criminal justice. As the examples provided here demonstrate, the recession-era Obama administration combines its commitment to racial equality with cost-centered, bipartisan humonetarian discourse to create a truce of sorts in the war on drugs. In doing so, it conveys the message that recession-era politicians can afford to advocate for drug policy reform without being penalized in the polls. This message has been adopted by politicians of all political persuasions, on both the federal and state levels. Here I want to examine several formulations of the cost-centered bipartisan political stance by looking at the career of a moderately progressive state official, an alliance of conservative lawmakers, and the rebranding of radical messages. I then return to the successful legalization campaigns in Washington and Colorado to show the potential of bipartisan humonetarian discourse to create change.

THE INCIDENT OF THE DOG IN THE NIGHTTIME:
A FEDERAL ADMINISTRATION UNCONCERNED WITH
THE WAR ON DRUGS?

As explained in chapter 2, drugs were made a polarizing, high-profile political issue in Richard Nixon's election campaign, and most of his successors in the White House made crime control a centerpiece of their platform. Gerald Ford, for example, espoused more mandatory sentencing for the purpose of protecting the victims: "Too many Americans had forgotten that the primary purpose of imprisonment was not to rehabilitate the convicted criminal so that he could return to society but to punish him and keep him off the streets. The certainty of having to spend a specified time behind bars after being convicted of a serious offense, was more important as a deterrent that almost anything else. . . . I do not seek vindictive punishment of the criminal but protection of the innocent victim."[5] He also sought to rationalize the way in which the death penalty is imposed.[6] Jimmy Carter, an outlier in a string of presidents espousing punitivism, a death penalty opponent, and a rehabilitation supporter, expressed the positivist belief that crime represented a societal illness: "Every time a person goes back to prison as a repeat offender, it is a sign that our prisons have failed. I believe we can reduce the percentage of failures and at the same time reduce the amount of crime. Presidential leadership can make a difference. We can make our existing crime-fighting programs more efficient and effective. We can have a stronger economy, and more jobs for our people, and that will lessen crime."[7] His campaign speeches highlighted social inequities and the need to focus on white-collar crime: "Poor people aren't the only ones to commit crimes, but they seem to be the only ones who go to prison."[8] Carter's successor, Ronald Reagan, is of course well known for making the war on drugs one of the focal points of his presidency; going well beyond Nancy Reagan's "Just Say No" campaign, her husband bolstered the FBI's drug investigation activity, created five hundred additional Drug Enforcement Administration positions, and established thirteen regional antidrugtask forces, all of which led to increases in drug arrests and convictions.[9] But it is also useful to keep in mind his support for the death penalty as a deterrent and an important institution for victims.[10] While Reagan is often remembered as having reduced California's prison population during his gubernatorial term,[11] his presidency saw the approval of three new prisons and a 6 percent growth in law enforcement.[12]

Also well remembered is George H. W. Bush's capitalization on the war on crime, notable during his campaign for the notorious Willie Horton ads that are theorized to have led to Michael Dukakis's defeat. Responding to later accusations that the ads were racially divisive, Bush highlighted the focus on crime: "I felt we did the right thing. It was definitely a crime issue. We got on Dukakis about having this lenient furlough program where he let people out of jail, and here was the best example—a man who was a convicted rapist who went out and raped again when he was on furlough."[13] Bush stated his commitment to the war on drugs in his inaugural address in 1989, in which he said that, despite his personal live-and-let-live approach, "there are few clear areas in which we as a society must rise up united and express our intolerance. The most obvious now is drugs. And when that first cocaine was smuggled in on a ship, it may as well have been a deadly bacteria, so much has it hurt the body, the soul of our country. And there is much to be done and to be said, but take my word for it: This scourge will stop."[14]

Punishment and punitiveness was a major aspect of President Bill Clinton's domestic policy as well—to the extent that Republican politicians felt that he was "carjacking" their traditional issues.[15] Prioritizing the war on drugs, he argued for more and tougher policing, complaining at the 1984 Democratic National Convention that Republicans were removing police officers from the streets.[16] Perhaps attempting to avoid Dukakis's political fate, Clinton publicly supported the death penalty and would approve the Arkansas execution of a mentally retarded man, Ricky Ray Rector, in the midst of his presidential campaign.[17]

The George W. Bush presidency is of course remembered mostly in terms of its reaction to the World Trade Center and Pentagon attacks on September 11, 2001, but the presidential campaign that preceded the attacks featured law enforcement and street crime as a central issue. The second presidential debate between Bush and Al Gore focused on police powers, racial profiling, and hate crime legislation.[18] Gore, not to be thought soft on crime, advocated a tough-on-crime stance relying on heavy drug testing.[19] Bush advocated an added expenditure of $2.8 billion on the war on drugs, funding both treatment and punishment and arguing that the Clinton-Gore drug policy was "one of the worst public policy failures of the '90s."[20] The debates between Bush and John Kerry did not take up crime as a major issue, save for questions about assault rifle bans and immigration policy.[21]

Against the backdrop of this presidential attention on crime in general and drugs in particular, the Obama administration represents an important departure. It is important to keep in mind that as late as 2009 the United States was still spending approximately $40 billion each year trying to eliminate the supply of drugs and arresting 1.5 million of its citizens each year for drug offenses, locking up half a million of them.[22] And yet in his presidential campaign Barack Obama avoided typical "war on drugs" rhetoric. As an Illinois lawmaker, Obama was a lead sponsor of criminal justice reform that included mandatory videotaping of all capital interrogations.[23] And throughout his presidential campaign, both in speeches and in brochures and materials, he advocated reentry vocational training as a way to "break the cycle of poverty and violence."[24] In a speech at a Chicago church, he highlighted poverty, addiction, and lack of support for families as causes of crime.[25] Campaign materials targeted racial profiling,[26] sentencing disparities, and lack of opportunities for minorities.[27] Obama has been particularly active voicing concern about mass incarceration of people of color,[28] highlighting his personal experience dabbling in drugs.[29] Even more notably, Obama's Republican adversaries, John McCain in 2008 and Mitt Romney in 2012, did not seek to discredit him for being soft on crime.[30] This is not to say that the presidential elections of 2008 and 2012 did not seek to influence voters through fear; the object of fear, however, was the crumbling economy, and the focus on the recession and its prognosis overshadowed the symbolic potential and political cachet of the war on crime.[31]

The Obama administration did not bring an end to the war on drugs, but the steps it took during both presidential terms could best be described as a "drug truce."[32] The main architect of these reforms, Attorney General Eric Holder, had come of age as an African American law enforcement professional at the height of the war on drugs and had always resented the stigmatizing effect of mass incarceration and its racial and class inequities. The changing political climate provided him with the opportunity to create reform.[33]

The first significant change occurred in 2010, when Obama signed the Fair Sentencing Act, an initiative to reform drug sentencing.[34] The new law repealed the five-year mandatory sentence for first-time offenders and for repeat offenders with less than 28 grams of cocaine (an increase from the previous sentencing scheme, which imposed a five-year minimum on possession of 5 grams). The change resulted in reducing the sentencing disparity between crack and powder cocaine from 100 to 1 to 18 to 1.[35] The change was fueled by, and publicly explained as, the administration's commitment to racial equality; the sentencing disparity between crack and powder cocaine had long been regarded as a proxy for racially discriminatory enforcement.[36] However, its passage was the outcome of a newfound willingness in Congress to sponsor bipartisan bills on drug reform. Prior to the financial crisis, similar propositions to modify drug laws, espoused, among others, by Republican senators Jeff Sessions and Orrin Hatch and Democratic representatives Sheila Jackson Lee and Charles Rangel, failed to pass.[37] By contrast, the Fair Sentencing Act received wide bipartisan support and was authored by Assistant Senate Majority Leader Dick Durbin, a Democrat, and cosponsored by Democratic senator Patrick Leahy and Sessions. The Congressional Budget Office's cost estimate predicted savings totaling $42 million between 2011 and 2015.[38]

Further reforms were enacted in Obama's second term. In 2014 an alliance was formed between Tea Party Republicans and Democrats in the Senate to make the 2010 Fair Sentencing Act retroactive, extending reductions and pardons to inmates serving sentences under prior drug laws, as well as to lower the minimum sentences for various drug offenders. Commentators estimated that, given the willingness of traditionally conservative states like Texas and Kentucky to experiment with drug sentencing reform as a cost-saving measure, the bill would also prevail in the Republican-dominated House of Representatives. However, President Obama and Attorney General Holder had already been using executive power to pardon inmates sentenced under the original crack statutes, and Obama's 2014 State of the Union speech indicated his intention to act on these measures whether or not he received congressional support.[39]

The Attorney General Office's explanation for these trends, as presented in remarks prepared by Deputy Attorney General James Cole to the New York State Bar, is a case in point, combining a sense of fairness and substantive reform with cost concerns.

> Over half of the federal prison population is there for drug offenses. Some are truly dangerous people, who threaten the safety of our communities and need to be taken off the streets for a long time. But others are lower level drug offenders, many with their own drug abuse issues, who fall into the all too common vicious cycle of drug abuse, crime, incarceration, release—and then the cycle repeats.
>
> In addition, there is a basic truth that dollars are finite. Every dollar we spend at the Department of Justice on prisons—and last year we spent about $6.5 billion on prisons—is a dollar we cannot spend supporting our prosecutors and law enforcement agents in their fight against violent crime, drug cartels, public corruption, financial fraud, human trafficking, and child exploitation, just to mention a few. In other words, if we don't find a solution to the federal prison population problem, public safety is going to suffer.[40]

The latest piece of drug reform legislation has been the bipartisan Smarter Sentencing Act, which would eliminate and liberalize mandatory minimums and allow inmates serving lengthy incarceration periods under the old law to appeal for resentencing. Asking Congress to pass the bipartisan law, Holder remarked:

> Today, I'm urging Congress to pass common-sense reforms like the bipartisan Smarter Sentencing Act, introduced by Senators Dick Durbin and Mike Lee—which would give judges more discretion in determining appropriate sentences for people convicted of certain federal drug crimes.
>
> This bill would also provide a new mechanism for some individuals—who were sentenced under outdated laws and guidelines—to petition judges for sentencing reductions that are consistent with the Fair Sentencing Act.
>
> Thanks to the leadership of Senators Durbin and Lee—along with Chairman Patrick Leahy and Senator Rand Paul—it's clear that these and similar proposals enjoy bipartisan support on Capitol Hill.
>
> These reforms would advance the goals of the Smart on Crime initiative—and other efforts that are currently underway—by fundamentally improving policies that exacerbate, rather than alleviate, key criminal justice challenges.
>
> And such legislation could ultimately save our country billions of dollars in prison costs while keeping us safe.[41]

Holder's remarks touch on the characteristic features of new alliances: bipartisan support, narrow coalitions that combine traditional motives with cost-saving rationales, and neutral language, presenting the reform as "smart" rather than "tough" or "soft." Notably, these considerations, and particularly the traditional notion of fairness, are the basis for the Department of Justice's most recent announcement: a presidential clemency initiative for drug offenders who cannot retroactively benefit from the recent sentencing reforms. The initiative, in the spirit of "redirecting some of the dollars we spend on prisons to prosecutors and law enforcement agents working to keep our streets safer,"[42] seeks to identify low-level, nonviolent offenders with a clean prison record and extend to them a benefit equivalent to what they would have received under the new federal legal scheme—a differentiation and classification mechanism present in all "drug truce" initiatives.

SMART ON CRIME, RIGHT ON CRIME: BEYOND "TOUGH" AND "SOFT"

Much of the research on the politics of imprisonment has focused on the reasons leftist politicians espouse punitive views, which arguably are at odds with their political agenda.[43] Some accounts point to the need to court centrist electoral potential while not losing the "captive audience" of the left.[44] Other accounts highlight the broader social and cultural changes, primarily the increasing shift to individualism and consumerism,[45] which leads voters of all stripes to perceive themselves as potential crime victims.[46] And others doubt that politicians' fears of appearing soft on crime stem from public opinion, using public surveys and time lines to show that the public does not necessarily espouse punitive views[47] and that political alarmist campaigns precede the public's fear of crime.[48]

A feature of humonetarian discourse has been the moving away from the tough/soft on crime dichotomy and the adoption of nonpunitive policies under milder monikers. Progressive politicians, experts, and consultants market nonpunitive policies—decriminalization, prevention of false confessions, use of forensic evidence to exclude the innocent, benign juvenile justice policy, death penalty abolition, and prison reform—as being "smart on crime" and saving resources. Conservative politicians advocate not dissimilar ideas—mainly in the area of curbing the war on drugs and mass imprisonment—as being "right on crime." There are some important differences between these two phenomena, but they share several features: the repackaging of the punitive project as devoid of traditional partisan ideology, the reliance on facts and figures to present the new policies as "evidence based," and the willingness to signal a new era in criminal justice and corrections through bipartisan collaborations previously thought impossible.

"Smart on crime," which has become code for nonpunitive policies in the name of parsimony and responsibility, is best explained by two initiatives: the Smart on Crime Coalition and its reports to Congress[49] and Kamala Harris's 2009 book, *Smart on Crime: A Career Prosecutor's Plan to Make Us Safer,*[50] published during her campaign for the position of California attorney general.

The Smart on Crime Coalition, whose first report to the government was published in 2008, comprised forty individuals and organizations. Membership is rather diverse, including civil rights groups, libertarian institutes, private law firms, restorative justice specialists, and inmate rights organizations. Not all groups endorse the report in its entirety, but one idea seems to have been the basis for broad consensus when the second report was produced in 2011:

> The Coalition, with experts and advocates spanning the criminal justice system, is particularly troubled by the budget crises plaguing states and placing greater burdens on the federal government. To address this concern, the Coalition has expanded its membership since first convening in 2008 to publish the first edition of *Smart on Crime*, and has consulted a broad array of experts representing a diversity of philosophies and points of view. Our dedication to exploring all options means that *Smart on Crime* focuses on providing non-ideological, cost-effective, and evidence-based solutions to address the worst problems in our system.[51]

The introduction to the report states the principles according to which the Coalition operated in proposing solutions to criminal justice problems: each solution had to be fair, accurate, effective, proven, and cost-efficient. These principles appear to be a mix of humanitarian and pragmatic considerations; the fairness principle includes appeals to proportionality and equality, and the four other principles appear, on their face, to be value-neutral. The actual themes in the report, and the solutions proposed, while not a paragon of left radicalism, are clearly on the progressive, nonpunitive side of things. Overcriminalization and overenforcement are the first problems mentioned, and mass incarceration is a recurring theme in the report. The report remains shy of advocating for death penalty abolition but repeatedly states the strong human rights concerns that render the death penalty "broken beyond repair" and makes excessive pro-defendant recommendations for capital litigation reform. Prison overcrowding is mentioned as a serious problem, and the report strongly advocates for alternatives to incarceration. These considerations are combined with the pragmatic issues of cost. Virtually every chapter of the report makes the case for parsimony, even though it also contains plenty of less pragmatic, and more idealistic, drives for reform.[52]

Moving toward "smart" language has been the strategy of prudent progressive politicians appealing to a public they perceive as punitive. Kamala Harris, San Francisco district attorney running for state attorney general when her *Smart on Crime* was published, confronted a neopopulist, politically polarized state with four decades of punitive policies as heritage.[53] Harris's book uses the smart on crime language to legitimize her not traditionally tough notions of criminal justice policy. It opens with an examination of "myths about crime," deliberately crafted to situate the criminal justice debate outside partisan lines, urging readers to step out of the "tough/soft on crime" dichotomy. The power of the introduction lies in presenting innovative reentry programs as an alternative to current correctional techniques, with the novelty being that these programs are sponsored by law enforcement—prosecutor's offices and sheriff's offices.

Throughout the book, as in her campaign materials, Harris is intent on presenting herself as standing staunchly on the prosecutorial side. The book is rife with sympathetic references to the plight of crime victims. However, she relies on data to argue that violent and sensational crime constitutes a small percentage of the entire crime picture and that the much larger slice of nonviolent offenders will not be properly handled using lengthy prison sentences, which contribute to recidivism.

Harris suggests an expansion of the traditional prosecutor's role, arguing for including reentry projects and community involvement in the scope of prosecutorial responsibility. One issue in particular that she highlights is the need to address school truancy. As Harris explains in the book, she sees truancy as a major predictor of a criminal career and therefore believes that addressing education, and making sure children are not truants, will go a long way toward preventing crime in the long run. Her focus on truancy is interesting for various reasons: first, the "smartness" of her approach is highlighted by her reliance on the correlation between truancy and crime; and second, while innovative in focusing on behavior that precedes crime, it is an approach that criminalizes truants and sometimes their parents.[54]

Harris's book is meant for a popular readership, and much of the rhetoric (including examples of violent, dangerous offenders whom Harris has helped remove from the streets) is crafted to soothe readers who are concerned about violent crime and victimization. These sections read as genuinely prosecutorial rather than as an effort to deceive her constituents and hide a "real" soft on crime approach. Harris repeatedly affirms her commitment to law enforcement and her belief that some offenders do require lengthy incarceration. This genuine prosecutorial voice lends credibility to her smart on crime argument: she does not pity or coddle criminals but rather believes that her policies are likely to save money without compromising public safety. Her suggestions for reentry programs, like San Francisco's Back on Track, use deferred entry of judgment as a "test period," under the DA Office's supervision, combined with vocational skills and other types of support, and are presented as a method to reduce recidivism rates and thus save money rather than as a humanitarian way to offer hope to inmates.

Even organizations that are unmistakably "bleeding heart" progressive turn to costs and fiscal responsibility as a way to market antipunitive policies. One such example is CURB (Californians United for a Responsible Budget),[55] formed in 2003 as a coalition of individuals and more than forty inmates' rights organizations. CURB was convened when Sacramento policy makers were considering the possibility of closing a women's prison in response to budget cuts. During the Schwarzenegger administration, CURB issued an alternative report to the one by the gubernatorial commission, in which it recommended the closure of four state prisons. The CURB website proudly proclaims that is has "helped defeat over 140,000 new prison and jail beds proposed since 2004."[56] The CURB advisory board consists of people active in the inmate rights' movements, many of them formerly incarcerated themselves or with family members in prison. Despite the affiliation with inmates' rights, CURB relies on cost arguments in all its materials and campaigns. Its resources page contains links that provide a cost-benefit analysis of jail construction and maintenance, which activists can use to prevent the siting of a jail in their towns.[57] Its protests against Governor Brown's plan to comply with the Supreme Court mandate to reduce the prison population by building more private prisons referred to it as a "budget raid."[58]

Cost logic is not just a tool used by the left to eschew the "soft on crime" label. Right-wing lawmakers and politicians have managed to maintain integrity and public support by packaging their nonpunitive policies as fiscally prudent. An example of this strategy is Right on Crime, an initiative led by the Texas Public Policy Foundation and endorsed by prominent Republicans such as Jeb Bush, Newt Gingrich, George Kelling, and William Bennett. The Right on Crime initiative promotes less costly and more productive alternatives to incarceration, like drug treatment and community service for nonviolent offenders.[59] Rick Perry, governor of Texas, echoes this sentiment: "Let's focus more resources on rehabilitating [nonviolent] offenders so we can ultimately spend less money locking them up again."[60]

The initiative advocates that "criminal law should be reserved for conduct that is either blameworthy or threatens public safety."[61] It criticizes the growing amount of taxpayer dollars spent on correctional systems, which does not yield the best public safety return.[62] According to Gingrich, "There is an urgent need to address the astronomical growth in the prison population, with its huge costs in dollars and lost human potential. . . . The criminal justice system is broken, and conservatives must lead the way in fixing it."[63] Right on Crime calls for Americans to "ensure that government performs its public safety responsibilities effectively and efficiently."[64]

The feasibility of advocating for similar policies on the right and the left, relying on arguments that are palatable to constituents across the political spectrum, has made bipartisan efforts to reverse the punitive pendulum a plausible political tactic. Since the recession Senator Jim Webb (retired from the Senate in 2012) advocated for a bipartisan criminal justice commission to review various policies leading to budgetary waste and consider the possibility of nationally legalizing marijuana.[65] The proposal was defeated by the Republican Party.[66] More recently, Republican senator Rand Paul and Democratic senator Patrick Leahy came together to propose the Justice Safety Valve Act,[67] a measure to curb harsh sentencing and mass incarceration. In his speech before the Senate Judiciary Committee, Paul addressed the problematic nature of mandatory minimums: "Since mandatory sentencing began, America's prison population has exploded, quadrupled.

America now jails a higher percentage of citizens than any other country in the world, at the staggering cost of $80 billion a year."[68]

It is important to note that not all bipartisan criminal justice reform supporters are made of the same cloth, and the nuances that differentiate them matter. Progressive political figures, like Holder and Harris, often include fairness and the importance of reentry in their remarks while referring to cost. By contrast, Right on Crime politicians speak a language of flawed deterrence, arguing that excessively punitive policies have reached a point of diminishing returns. Another important difference involves emphasis on the state's role. Progressive politicians still speak of the importance of reentry and community rehabilitation (with the fiscal justification that recidivism reduction will save more in the long run), while conservative politicians emphasize the importance of a libertarian retreat from overcriminalization. Noting the differences in ideology makes the power of the cost argument in yielding bipartisan support even more impressive.

The debate over legalization of marijuana is an excellent example of new humonetarian coalitions in action. The failed campaign to legalize marijuana in California and the successful campaigns in Washington and Colorado are examples of smart on crime cost-centered messaging. The common thread of these examples, and of the federal rhetoric surrounding them, is the acknowledgment that marijuana enforcement should be a low governmental priority, as scant resources could be spent on more violent offenders and therefore yield more crime prevention. In addition, the campaigns feature the revenue-enhancement potential of legalizing and taxing marijuana as a luxury good.

LET'S TAX IT: HUMONETARIAN STATE
MARIJUANA REFORM

In California's 2010 midterm election, voters rejected Proposition 19, a state initiative to legalize marijuana possession and cultivation for personal use for those ages twenty-one and over in nonpublic places.[69] However, two years later, during the presidential election, Washington and Colorado voters approved initiatives to legalize marijuana for personal use by adults in their respective states.[70] All three campaigns focused heavily on economic arguments to sway voters.

California's Prop 19 was backed almost singlehandedly by the Oakland medical marijuana entrepreneur Richard Lee.[71] In addition to authorizing and regulating commercial marijuana-related activities, the measure sought to impose general, excise, and transfer taxes and fees on marijuana-related activity in order to raise revenue for state and local government as well as offset costs of marijuana regulation.[72] Materials containing information on Prop 19 emphasized the fiscal impact that this legislation could have, such as "potential increased tax and fee revenues in the hundreds of millions of dollars annually and potential correctional savings of several tens of millions of dollars annually."[73] A presentation on Prop 19 by the California Legislative Analyst's Office focused on the measure's potential positive impact on state and local expenditures and revenues, such as reduction in state and local correctional costs, sales and income taxes from marijuana sales and marijuana-related businesses, and other government-imposed taxes and fees.[74]

The campaign focused on the revenue-raising aspect of Prop 19, as well as its ability to free up police resources for more serious crimes. One television campaign ad featured former San Jose police chief Joseph McNamara making an economic argument for voting yes on Prop 19: "Proposition 19 will tax and control marijuana just like alcohol. It will generate billions of dollars for local communities, allow police to focus on violent crimes, and put drug cartels out of business."[75] The California ACLU also endorsed the legislation with a statement echoing a similar sentiment: "Arrests for possession of small amounts of marijuana divert scarce public safety dollars that could be used to address violent crime. . . . Enforcement of marijuana prohibition laws consumes California's police and court system resources."[76]

While supporters hoped that voters worried about the economy would embrace these economic arguments and approve Prop 19,[77] opposition undermined the fiscal arguments for Prop 19, contending that it would not generate much tax revenue.[78] According to Roger Salazar, spokesman for the "No on Prop 19" campaign, "Prop 19 cannot guarantee 'billions' in revenue to the state; it would make the job of law enforcement more difficult."[79]

Indeed, the presentation by the California Legislative Analyst's Office pointed out many of the fiscal argument's shortcomings. It said that savings in correctional costs and new revenues could be offset by filling jails with other criminals and by increased regulatory and enforcement costs, respectively, and that an increase in marijuana consumption could cause an increase in individuals seeking publicly funded substance abuse treatment.[80] It also noted that fiscal effects were subject to uncertainty because the federal government's prosecution of nonmedical marijuana activities could have the effect of impeding activities permitted by Prop 19.[81]

Even the *San Francisco Chronicle* urged voters to reject Prop 19, warning them that the initiative was flawed "with contradictions and complications that would invite legal chaos and, more than likely, fail to deliver its promised economic benefits."[82] It addressed many specific problems with the initiative, including issues with the taxation scheme.[83] According to the *Chronicle,* the measure "does nothing to help cure the state's budget deficit. . . . Prop. 19 allows the 58 counties and hundreds of cities to come up with their own taxation and regulatory schemes. In this critical element of legalization, Prop. 19 is more akin to the chaotic approach taken with medical marijuana than to the heavily taxed-and-regulated treatment of alcohol."[84]

In the end, it seems that the arguments undermining the economic benefits of Prop 19 won over voters, who rejected the measure with 54 percent of the vote. CNN speculated on the reasons that Prop 19 failed.

> Many advocates promised major benefits to California's budget because of reduced expenditure on marijuana prohibition and increased revenue from marijuana taxation. . . . [T]hese claims were overblown. The budgetary benefits, while not insignificant, would have been small compared with California's financial mess. . . . Many voters sensed that Prop 19 supporters were overreaching, and this made them suspicious of all the arguments in its favor. Common sense should have recognized that since marijuana was close to legal already, Prop 19 would not have had dramatic effects.[85]

Some blamed the timing of the election.[86] Generally, older, more conservative voters participate in midterm elections,[87] which meant a low turnout of young voters, who are more likely to support legalization.[88] According to a state exit poll, despite the public profile of Prop 19, voters under twenty-five did not turn out in unusually high numbers.[89] In fact, 13 percent of total voters were age eighteen to twenty-nine.[90] Yet two years later, in a presidential election year, Washington's and Colorado's economic arguments in support of legalizing marijuana fared much better.

In the 2012 presidential election, Washington voters approved Initiative 502 (I-502) with 55.7 percent of the vote,[91] legalizing possession of marijuana for adults twenty-one and over.[92] I-502 does not legalize personal cultivation of marijuana but requires Washington farmers and businesses to apply for licenses to grow and sell marijuana.[93] The measure also notably includes a marijuana DUI standard for active THC.[94] I-502 was summarized as follows on the ballot: "This measure would license and regulate marijuana production, distribution, and possession for persons over twenty-one; remove state-law criminal and civil penalties for activities that it authorizes; tax marijuana sales; and earmark marijuana-related revenues."[95]

New Approach Washington led the campaign for I-502. The organization is a "coalition of Washington citizens who believe that treating marijuana use as a crime has failed" and that "Washington should stop wasting law enforcement resources on adults who use marijuana, and instead create a tightly regulated system that takes money away from criminal organizations and generates tax revenue for our state and local governments."[96] Alison Holcomb, on loan from ACLU Washington, was the campaign manager.[97]

Similar to that of Prop 19, I-502's campaign heavily emphasized the economic impact that the measure would have. New Approach Washington's website states that the goal of I-502 is to "stop wasting law enforcement resources on adults who use marijuana . . . and generate[ ] tax revenue for our state and local governments."[98] However, unlike Prop 19's campaign, New Approach Washington put a new spin on the economic argument for marijuana, targeting parents and arguing that taxing and regulating marijuana could benefit children by funding schools, health care, and substance abuse prevention. I-502 earmarked 40 percent of new revenue for the state general fund and local budgets and 60 percent for substance abuse prevention, research, education, and health care.[99] I-502 was also carefully drafted with parent voters in mind, including provisions protecting youth such as a requirement that stores selling marijuana must be at least a thousand feet from schools, playgrounds, and parks; a ban on advertising in places frequented by youth; and the reiteration that selling marijuana to minors remains a felony.[100] The campaign even prepared a brochure explaining the dangers of smoking marijuana at a young age and offering advice on how parents can talk to their children about not smoking marijuana.[101]

In order to appeal to those who oppose using marijuana, particularly parents, New Approach Washington adopted a campaign strategy that made voters feel that they could approve legalization of marijuana purely on economic grounds while maintaining opposition to marijuana use. This strategy is evidenced by former regional FBI head Charles Mandigo's statement endorsing I-502: "I do not support or condone the use of marijuana. Rather, I think it is time for us to try a regulatory approach that frees criminal justice resources for more appropriate priorities."[102] The campaign commercial described at the beginning of this chapter went even further by featuring a character potentially sympathetic to conservative voters who proclaims "not to like" the idea of marijuana legalization.[103]

This campaign strategy drummed up high-profile support from the Children's Alliance, the state Labor Council, former U.S. attorneys John McKay and Kate Pflaumer, Seattle city attorney Pete Holmes, and King County sheriff Steve Strachan.[104] Even the *Seattle Times* endorsed the campaign.[105] It framed the issue as a cost-benefit analysis for voters: "The question for voters is not whether marijuana is good. It is whether prohibition is good. . . . The question is whether the war on marijuana is worth what it costs."[106] This supported the campaign's argument that voters can oppose the use of marijuana while still approving the initiative. This framing of the issue said to voters, this is not about drug use, this is about money.

The most notable endorsements came from high-profile Republicans, including Michael Baumgartner, a GOP candidate for the U.S. Senate and state senator from Spokane, and John McKay, a former Seattle U.S. attorney from a prominent Republican family.[107] Embracing the campaign's economic arguments, Baumgartner was quoted as saying that he "believes I-502 is a good step toward changing what he described as a wasteful policy of marijuana prohibition."[108]

It is significant that Washington's campaign emphasizing the economic benefits of legalizing marijuana, particularly for schools and health care, garnered Republican support. While it seems that the Great Recession left the ground ripe for legalizing marijuana on the basis of economic arguments for states in general, Washington took this opportunity a step further to hone in on the economic benefits to children.

This is not to say that I-502 faced no opposition. The Northwest High Intensity Drug Trafficking Area expressed concern about the effects on children if parents smoke marijuana openly in the home.[109] However, Baumgartner was quick to respond: "We have to be realistic about what's going on in people's homes today. Usage stays constant regardless of drug policy."[110] Some expressed concern for preemption by federal law,[111] while Washington attorney general Rob McKenna expressed concern for medical marijuana users: "Once we open the door to all kinds of marijuana, with use by all kinds of people, medical marijuana users will be swept up."[112] Overall, opposition to I-502 was minimal and did not focus on the economic arguments. Campaign manager Holcomb believes the lack of organized opposition stemmed from the way in which I-502 was drafted to have tough provisions for driving under the influence of marijuana and tough restrictions on who can sell to whom.[113]

Another victory for the marijuana legalization campaign was achieved the same night, when Colorado voters passed Amendment 64, legalizing marijuana for personal use, possession, and limited home growing for adults twenty-one and over.[114] Amendment 64, supported by the Campaign to Regulate Marijuana Like Alcohol (the Campaign), set forth a system to regulate and tax marijuana similar to alcohol.[115] The Campaign consisted of a broad coalition of organizations and activists,[116] and its website highlighted the positive fiscal impact Amendment 64 could have: generating millions of dollars for the state, job creation,[117] supporting schools, redirecting money from drug cartels to legitimate taxpaying businesses, and focusing law enforcement resources on violent and harmful crimes.[118]

Marijuana activists who were part of the Campaign worked for years prior to the election to reframe the debate "from one about getting high to one about law-enforcement and budgetary policy."[119] Brian Vicente, a Denver lawyer who helped write Amendment 64, sums up the campaign strategy: "What we figured out is that your average person doesn't necessarily like marijuana, but there's sort of this untapped desire by voters to end the drug war. If we can focus attention on the fact we can bring in revenue, redirect law enforcement resources and raise awareness instead of focusing on pot, that's a message that works."[120]

Similar to New Approach Washington, the Campaign specifically emphasized economic arguments that would appeal to parents. Amendment 64 earmarked the first $40 million in revenue raised annually for the state's struggling school construction program,[121] and the Campaign's website emphasized that regulating marijuana would allow the sale of marijuana to benefit schools as opposed to criminals.[122] A group of Colorado parents formed a coalition called Moms and Dads for Marijuana Regulation in order to endorse Amendment 64 and gain the support of more parents.[123] The Campaign also used ads to target parents. It launched a Mother's Day–themed television ad featuring a woman typing a letter to her mom saying she feels safer around people using marijuana as opposed to alcohol.[124] One campaign billboard featuring a father embracing his son read, "Please, card my son. Regulate the sale of marijuana and help me to keep it out of his hands."[125] Likely as a result of this campaigning to target parents, all age groups, with the exception of sixty-five and over, voted to approve Amendment 64.[126]

Parents were not the only hard-won supporters of Amendment 64. The Campaign also received support from the GOP. New Mexico's former Republican governor Gary Johnson endorsed the initiative.[127] And a majority (56 percent) of delegates at the Denver County Republican Assembly voted to support Amendment 64.[128] While the initiative did not receive the two-thirds vote necessary for the assembly to adopt it as a plank in the party's platform,[129] it is nonetheless significant that a political party that has historically taken a strong stance against marijuana legalization voted to support the measure.

Despite broad support, several groups and politicians voiced opposition, specifically attacking the economic arguments. Amendment 64 faced more, and more organized, opposition than I-502. Smart Colorado, an opposition group led by Ken Buck, former U.S. Senate candidate and Weld County DA, condemned the notion of an economic argument in general. Buck said that Amendment 64 puts "profits before people," essentially arguing that approving marijuana legalization based on the economic benefits reflects a prioritization of money over the safety and education of children.[130] Buck anticipated that "we're going to see proliferation . . . of young people using marijuana . . . and expulsion and dropout rates increase."[131]

Smart Colorado's tactic attempted to steer the argument away from law enforcement and budgetary policy and back to arguments reminiscent of *Reefer Madness* and Just Say No.[132] In response to this, the Campaign's spokeswoman, Betty Aldworth, countered that supporting the continuation of marijuana prohibition "makes unregulated marijuana widely available to teens on the streets" and noted that "teen use of cigarettes has dropped significantly in the U.S. since regulations on sales were enforced."[133]

While Smart Colorado condemned the economic argument in general, other opponents countered the Campaign's economic argument with specific reasons Amendment 64 would actually harm the economy. Denver mayor Michael Handcock, along with the heads of the Denver Metro Chamber of Commerce, the Downtown Denver Partnership, and Visit Denver, argued that "the measure would be bad for business in Colorado. They said it would discourage companies from moving to the state or tourists from visiting, both of which would hurt the state's economic recovery."[134] In response to this, United Food and Commercial Workers Union president Kim Cordova countered that Amendment 64 would create jobs in the marijuana industry and in businesses supporting it.[135] According to Cordova, "Removing marijuana from the underground market . . . will create living-wage jobs and bolster our state and local economies with tens of millions of dollars in new tax revenue and savings."[136]

The *Denver Post* opposed Amendment 64 while supporting the economic argu-ments behind the initiative.[137] It said that the nation's attempt to suppress mari-juana use has failed and "squandered valuable police and judicial resources."[138] Further, while possession and use of marijuana should be legal, a state constitu-tional amendment is not the way to go about legalization.[139] The op-ed expressed concern about "issues stemming from the federal-state conflict" and concluded that "the most appropriate venue for legalization remains the nation's capital."[140]

ON THE SIDELINES: FEDERAL REACTION TO MARIJUANA LEGALIZATION

Despite victories in Washington and Colorado, many expressed concern about the possibility of federal government prosecution in these states. The ACLU of Wash-ington, which is working to ensure that I-502 is fully and fairly implemented, said, "We hope federal officials will respect the will of our state's voters and not enforce federal laws against Washington residents who are obeying state law."[141] Prior to I-502's passage, then Washington governor Christine Gregoire wrote to the Justice Department, asking what the federal response to the law would be.[142] In reply, "Ormsby and the other U.S. attorney with jurisdiction in Washington sent back a fire-breathing letter threatening to prosecute anyone involved with the dispensa-ries, asserting . . . that the Ogden memo was strictly limited to 'seriously ill indi-viduals. . . . '"[143]

Colorado congressman Polis expressed similar concern when he asked Attor-ney General Holder about the recent federal crackdown on medical marijuana shops in California and whether Colorado could expect to get different treatment. Polis received a different response from Holder:, "Where a state has taken a posi-tion, has passed a law and people are acting in conformity with the law—not abus-ing the law—that would not be a priority with the limited resources of our Justice Department."[144] This response reiterated support for the oft-referenced Ogden memo, which essentially deprioritized federal prosecution of individuals whose use of medical marijuana is in compliance with state law.

The history of the Ogden memo is rife with "smart on crime" humonetarian discourse. On October 19, 2009, Deputy Attorney General David Ogden issued a memorandum to selected U.S. attorneys providing "clarification and guidance to federal prosecutors in States that have enacted laws authorizing the medical use of marijuana."[145] In an effort to make "efficient and rational use" of limited resources, the memo essentially deprioritized investigations and prosecutions of "individuals whose actions are in clear and unambiguous compliance with existing state laws providing for the medical use of marijuana."[146] In a statement accompanying the memo, Holder said, "It will not be a priority to use federal resources to prosecute patients with serious illnesses or their caregivers who are complying with state laws on medical marijuana."[147] Yet, the memo affirmed, "prosecution of significant traffickers of illegal drugs, including marijuana, remains a core priority."[148] The memo also made clear that it does not alter in any way the Justice Department's authority to enforce federal law," nor does it "'legalize' marijuana or provide a legal defense to a violation of federal law."[149]

Experts said that the memo "represent[s] an approach favored by President Obama and Vice President Biden to put new emphasis on violent crime and the sale of illicit drugs to children."[150] Marijuana legalization advocates saw the memo as a victory.[151] As a result, medical marijuana shops flooded many states.[152] One senior White House official, speaking anonymously, affirmed this causation: "Nobody can argue that the number of medical marijuana shops in California and Colorado didn't grow at an exponential rate directly because of this [the Ogden memo]."[153]

Despite the Ogden memo's deprioritization of medical marijuana prosecutions, the federal government continues to crack down hard on medical marijuana. Since the memo, the Justice Department has "raid[ed] hundreds of dispensaries, while the IRS and other federal law enforcement officials have gone after banks and landlords who do business with them. Fours years after promising not to make medical marijuana a priority, the government continues to target it aggressively."[154]

Take Richard Lee, for example. Lee is a paraplegic who uses marijuana for medical purposes. He also runs Oaksterdam University, a cannabis college, as well as a dispensary. In April 2012 federal agents raided his home and offices to confiscate plants.[155] This instance represents a wider trend in federal raids across the country. According to the *Economist*, "Dispensaries, and even landlords of dispensary-operators, all over California, Colorado and Montana have been getting menacing letters. Many have closed shop. Growers and users are by turns livid and scared."[156] Grim and Reilly report in their article, "In March 2011, agents swept through Montana, seizing property and arresting owners as part of a nationwide crackdown on medical marijuana. They timed the Montana raids to coincide with a legislative debate and votes in the state legislature over the future of medical marijuana. . . . The raids led to images on the evening news of guns, drugs, and men in handcuffs. It imbued medical marijuana with a sense of criminality—even though it was legal under state law—and soured the political climate against it."[157] In response to these raids, "Democratic and Republican legislators from five medical-marijuana states have written an open letter to Barack Obama to end the 'chaos' and leave this matter to the states."[158]

After Washington and Colorado legalized marijuana, the *Washington Post* published an op-ed advocating a "hands-off" approach for the federal government, urging it to refrain from staging an "aggressive intervention."[159] It said that enforcing marijuana prohibitions against users and small-time growers would require considerable resources and that filling jails with marijuana users is irrational, and therefore "the Justice Department should hold its fire on a lawsuit challenging Colorado and Washington's decision to behave more leniently. And state officials involved in good-faith efforts to regulate marijuana production and distribution according to state laws should be explicitly excused from federal targeting."

In addition to continuing medical marijuana raids, the federal government issued a "clarification" memo as a follow-up to the Ogden memo in June 2011. This memo, also known as the Cole Memo, was issued by Deputy Attorney General James Cole in response to state and local government inquiries seeking guidance about the DOJ's position on enforcement of the Controlled Substances Act in light of jurisdictions that at the time were considering approving the cultivation of large quantities of marijuana or broadening regulation and taxation of marijuana.[160]

According to the Cole Memo, the Ogden memo "was never intended to shield [people who commercially cultivate, sell, or distribute medical marijuana] from federal enforcement action and prosecution," even when those activities comply with state law.[161] According to White House officials, pro-marijuana groups and the media distorted the Ogden memo, which pro-marijuana groups dispute.[162] While on one side the federal government contends that the Ogden memo was limited to seriously ill individuals and their caregivers, others point out that the memo did refer to any individual who followed state law.

Steve DeAngelo, owner of Harborside Health Center, a medical cannabis shop, expressed concern about the negative effects the policy articulated in the Cole Memo could have on the economy, including lost jobs and tax revenue.[163] A recent report found that the legal marijuana business registered $1.7 billion in sales in 2010.[164] According to DeAngelo, the new policy would cost "tens of thousands of legal jobs, taking away hundreds of millions in tax revenue, giving 1.7 billion dollars to the cartels, and the patients go from a situation where they buy tested marijuana from people with a background check, to dealing with people on the street corner."[165]

Despite the Ogden memo, years later the federal government's position on prosecution of activities involving marijuana is unclear, as its actions have been wholly inconsistent with its words. The federal government's conflicting responses to Governor Gregoire of Washington and Congressman Polis of Colorado underscore the confusing and vague federal policy on state marijuana laws. The latest development is, however, somewhat encouraging to legalization activists. In a well-publicized call to the governors of Washington and Colorado, Attorney General Holder informed them that "the Department of Justice would allow the states to create a regime that would regulate and implement the ballot initiatives that legalized the use of marijuana for adults." Holder described the policy as a "trust but verify approach" to the state laws.[166] Subsequent to that call, Deputy Attorney General Cole also issued a three-and-a-half-page memo to U.S. attorneys nationwide, instructing them to stay away from marijuana enforcement, with the "expectation that states and local governments that have enacted laws authorizing marijuana-related conduct will implement strong and effective regulatory and enforcement systems that will address the threat those state laws could pose to public safety, public health and other law enforcement interests." Federal enforcement would be limited to sales to minors, diversion of marijuana to states in which the substance is illegal, and situations in which marijuana activity is a cover for, or related to, other illegal activity.[167]

The marijuana legalization example shows the strength of campaigns based on a genuine and thoughtful economic argument. The political "smart on crime" rhetoric, effectively bypassing the minefields of the tough/soft on crime dichotomy, was used in these campaigns to make two arguments: marijuana legalization would allow spending limited systemic resources on offenders whose crimes harm the community more and would also open the door to revenue raising through taxation. The success of the Washington and Colorado campaigns is the product of having raised these arguments in a thoughtful way, allaying concerns of vagueness or unsound policies, and convincing voters of the revenue enhancement calculus. The weakness of the California proposal, which also attempted to rely on "smart on crime" rhetoric, lay in the vagueness of its premise and the uncertain enforcement and implementation ahead.

It is also true, of course, that California differs from Washington and Colorado in its political culture. In *The Politics of Imprisonment,* Barker compares California, Washington, and New York, concluding that California's punitiveness, compared to Washington's parsimony, can be explained as a product of California's neopopulist, polarized, and shallow political system, compared to the deeper and less sensationalist public involvement in Washington politics.[168] It may well be that the difference between the political cultures allowed Washington (and perhaps Colorado) to present a more reasoned and thoughtful legalization plan, which appealed to voters beyond their party affiliations and worldviews.

The guarded optimism following Holder's announcement that the federal government will curb its enthusiasm about state-approved "marijuana activities" may suggest that humonetarian discourse is an overall salutary approach to the mass incarceration crisis. Indeed, the usage of bipartisan, economic logic by politicians and the success of political campaigns based on cost and revenue enhancement may suggest that such arguments always work to reduce the wasteful system of criminalization and incarceration. However, the crisis and the sense of austerity it fostered in public discourse have the potential to produce a range of policies and practices, some of which are immensely problematic from a human rights perspective. Moreover, on-the-ground incarceration practices still respond to the neoliberal logic of the market, and the changes produced by recession-era politics are best understood as the market behavior "doing less with less." The next chapter examines such practices and ties them to the market forces surrounding the carceral project.

6

THE NEW CARCERAL WHEELING
AND DEALING

From Incapacitation to the Inmate
Export Business

The death penalty abolition and marijuana legalization campaigns, using humonetarian discourse to bridge ideological chasms and reform the criminal justice system, presented the public with seemingly straightforward decisions about fiscal priorities. But things become more complicated when tackling more ambiguous, polycentric questions pertaining to incarceration policies. As many commentators have argued, it is very difficult to understand the monumental growth in incarceration without the context of neoliberalism, which includes, but is not limited to, the retreat of the state from its caretaking function, the despair of rehabilitative goals, and the focus on profitable and managerial goals. Although this chapter attempts to make sense of the salutary effect the past few years have had on incarceration rates—according to the Bureau of Justice Statistics, 2009 was the first time in thirty-seven years when the overall U.S. prison population declined, and the trend has continued through 2012[1]—it does not argue that this trend reversal indicates public or governmental renouncement of the neoliberal framework. Instead, following in the footsteps of public choice theorists, I locate the humonetarian decrease in incarceration in the context of a depressed financial market, showing all actors in the correctional field responding to real and perceived budgetary shortages through organizational experimentation: seeking other areas of profit-producing confinement, shipping inmates to alternative locations, making jurisdictional reform and juggling state and county responsibilities for incarceration, and bartering and repurposing prisons for closure. Far from a decisive swing of the pendulum away from the punitive trend of the forty years that preceded the crisis, these practices are an inconsistent stream of ill-directed emergency efforts. More important, privatization is not the be-all and end-all of the evils of mass incarceration, in times of either plenty or austerity. The financial crisis has produced a set of constraints that affect public and private actors alike, and the mechanisms surveyed here show that cost-benefit considerations operate among all actors in the correctional market.

INSIDE THE BELLY OF THE BEAST: PRIVATE PRISON PROVIDERS ADAPT TO THE RECESSION

No explanation of recession-era prison policies is complete without taking into account the complex interactions between state and local governments and private prison providers. The end of the twentieth century and first decade of the twenty-first saw a seismic shift in the privatization of state prisons across the United States. Unable to shoulder the burden placed on their taxpayers and treasuries, financially strapped states housing record numbers of prisoners have increasingly turned to privatizing their prison facilities as an ostensibly cost-saving measure. While the share of private prisons in the American carceral project is far from overwhelming—as of 2010, private prisons housed "128,195 of the 1.6 million state and federal prisoners in the United States"[2]—much of the for-profit incarceration industry, the prison industrial complex, reflects the overall mentality of·the many actors benefiting from the prison industry as well as its logical conclusion. Overall, the years between 1999 and 2010 marked an 80 percent increase in the number of prisoners held in private prisons, versus an 18 percent increase in prisoners overall; more specifically, the federal incarceration cost was $47,000 per inmate. The federal prison system has borne the brunt of this increase in prison privatization over the first decade of this century, with a rise in the number of federal prisoners in private prisons "from 3,828 to 33,830, an increase of 784%." By contrast, "the number of state prisoners incarcerated privately grew by 40% from 67,380 to 94, 365."[3]

Thirty states now employ private prisons to some degree to house inmates. Across the individual states, the number of inmates who have been placed in and removed from private prisons has fluctuated wildly. For example, between 1990 and 2010, Florida and Idaho saw an increase in the number of inmates in private facilities of 213 percent and 459 percent, respectively; Arkansas, Michigan, Minnesota, Maine, Utah, Washington, and Nevada, in contrast, each saw a 100 percent decrease as they removed all of their inmates from private prisons. Six states— Alaska, Montana, New Mexico, Hawaii, Vermont, and Idaho—currently hold at least 25 percent of their inmates in private prisons. As of 2010, Texas led in number of inmates incarcerated privately, with 19,155 in private prisons, followed by Florida, with 11,000.[4]

The biggest private prison provider in the United States is the Corrections Corporation of America,[5] a publicly traded company incorporated in the state of

TABLE 1. Per diem rates in CCA institutions

		06/12–09/12	06/11–09/11	01/12–09/12	01/11–09/11	FY 2011	FY 2010
Combined per diem averages, all facilities	Revenue	$59.19	$58.62	$59.16	$58.76	$58.48	$58.36
	Expenses	$41.34	$40.51	$41.83	$40.20	$40.15	$40.16
	Operating	$17.85	$18.11	$17.33	$18.56	$18.33	$18.20
	margin	(30.2%)	(30.9%)	(29.3%)	(31.6%)	(31.3%)	(31.2%)
Owned and managed facilities	Revenue	$67.25	$66.51	$67.22	$66.54	$66.68	$66.30
	Expenses	$44.06	$42.83	$33.91	$42.50	$42.47	$42.48
	Operating	$23.19	$23.68	$22.77	$24.04	$24.21	$23.82
	margin	(34.5%)	(35.6%)	(33.9%)	(36.1%)	(36.3%)	(35.9%)
Managed-only facilities	Revenue	$40.30	$40.70	$40.22	$40.93	$40.39	$39.60
	Expenses	$34.98	$35.22	$35.66	$34.93	$35.05	$34.69
	Operating	$5.32	$5.48	$4.56	$6.00	$5.34	$4.91
	margin	(13.2%)	(13.5%)	(11.3%)	(14.7%)	(13.2%)	(12.4%)

SOURCE: CCA 10Q, available at www.sec.gov/Archives/edgar/data/1070785/000119312512459397/d42078d10q .htm#toc420784_9; and 10K, available at www.sec.gov/Archives/edgar/data/1070985/000119312512081122/d231839d10k. htm.

Maryland.[6] As of September 30, 2012, CCA operated sixty-seven correctional facilities[7] and owned forty-nine[8] located in twenty states and the District of Columbia.[9] The CCA's fiscal year 2012 documents explain its business model, which is directly tied to prison occupancy rates.

> CCA is compensated for operating and managing facilities at an inmate per diem rate based upon actual or minimum guaranteed occupancy levels. Occupancy rates for a particular facility are typically low when first opened or immediately following an expansion. However, beyond the start-up period, which typically ranges from 90 to 180 days, the occupancy rate tends to stabilize. During 2011, the average compensated occupancy of its facilities, based on rated capacity, was 89.8% for all of the facilities it owned or managed, exclusive of facilities where operations have been discontinued. As of December 31, 2011, the Company had approximately 12,300 unoccupied beds at facilities that had availability of 100 or more beds.[10]

In order to understand how CCA and other private prison providers have adapted to the financial crisis, it is useful to explicate the private providers' business model. Because CCA is compensated based on a price per inmate per bed day, CCA monitors a number of per diem values. A distinction is made between the per diems for those facilities that CCA both owns and operates and those facilities that it only manages.[11] CCA's latest quarterly disclosure to the SEC, presented in table 1, compares per diems for June–September 2011 and 2012, as well as for the nine-month periods January–September 2011 and 2012. In addition, CCA's most recent annual disclosure compares these figures for the fiscal years ending in 2011 and 2012, respectively.[12]

TABLE 2. CCA's ten-year history of net income and facility composition

FY Ending Dec. 31	Net Income	No. Facilities Owned and Managed	No. Managed Only	No. Leased to Third Party Operators
2011	$162,510	46	20	2
2010	$157,193	45	21	2
2009	$154,954	44	21	2
2008	$150,941	43	20	3
2007	$133,373	41	24	3
2006	$105,239	40	24	3
2005	$50,122	39	24	3
2004	$61,081	39	25	3
2003	$126,521	38	21	3
2002	($28,875)	37	23	3
2001	$5,670	36	28	3

SOURCE: 10-K documentation for respective fiscal years, www.sec.gov/cgi-bin/browse-edgar?company=&match=&CIK=cxw&filenum=&State=&Country=&SIC=&owner=exclude&Find=Find+Companies&action=getcompany.

For the nine months ending September 2012, CCA's net income was $111.4 million, compared to $122 million for the nine months ending September 2011. For the entire year of 2011, CCA's net income was $162.5 million, compared to $157.2 million in 2010.[13] CCA explains this difference as follows: "Contributing to the increase in net income for 2011 compared to the previous year was an increase in operating income of $9.0 million, from $323.1 million during 2010 to $332.1 million during 2011 as a result of an increase in average daily inmate populations and new management contracts, partially offset by an increase in general and administrative expenses and depreciation and amortization."[14]

The private prison business, complete with construction, new contracts, and some changes to existing contracts, has continued to trudge along, to a considerable degree of success, deep into the recession. And CCA has been particularly fortunate. The quarterly data, presented in table 2 , reveal a continuing story of growth throughout the local government crisis.

CCA continues to do well in other ways. Compensation for its executives, in both basic compensation and stock options, is impressive,[15] and its stock is slightly less risky than the industry average.[16] This continuing success raises the question how CCA, and other prison providers, has adapted to the changes in incarceration nationwide.

A partial answer is found in CCA's quarterly and annual SEC filings, which go into a fair amount of detail about the development of new facilities, idling of vacant facilities, and changes in customer contracts. Table 3 offers a chronological list of recent major facilities changes, which reflects various modes of adaptation to a

TABLE 3. Recent changes in CCA facilities

Date	Development
February 2008– March 2009	Begin and suspend construction on Trousdale County, TN, facility "until there is greater clarity around the timing of future bed absorption by its customers" (10-K, F-16)
2009–2013	California accounted for 13% of CCA's management revenue in 2010 and 2011; however, the implementation of the Realignment program may affect an Intent to Award CCA a contract to house up to 3,256 additional inmates. (10-K, p. 52)
January 2010	Completion of removal of Washington and Minnesota inmates from Prairie facility due to low occupancy and in-state space. CCA in negotiations with California to fill beds. (10-K, p. 51)
March 2010	Completion of removal of Arizona inmates from Huerfano facility in Colorado due to budgetary concerns and subsequent idling of that facility (10-K, p. 51)
May 2010	Completion of removal of Arizona inmates from Diamondback facility in Oklahoma due to budgetary concerns and subsequent idling of that facility (10-K, p. 51)
May 2010	Increase in inmate populations at two expanded facilities in Georgia, Coffee and Wheeler (10-K, p. 47)
June–September 2010	CCA ceased managing the Gadsden and Hernando County, FL, facilities but commenced managing the Graceville and Moore Haven facilities in Florida, contributing to a management-only revenue increase of $28.3 million in 2011. (10-K, pp. 52, 54)
June–September 2010	Completion of Nevada Southern facility (10-K, p. 47)
June–September 2010	Decrease in FBOP population at California City facility (10-K, p. 47)
September 2011	Renegotiate Elizabeth, NJ, contract with ICE. New classification system for inmates, lower per diems, 95% occupancy guarantee (10-Q, p. 37)
October 2011	Contract with BOP to house federal inmates at McRae facility in Georgia; reduced margin but 90% occupancy guarantee and long-term contract up to 10 years (10-Q, p. 36)
November 2011	Closure of Delta 1,172-bed facility in Mississippi
December 2011	Purchase of Lake Erie facility from Ohio for $73 million (10-K, p. F-18)
December 2011	$44 million investment in property for construction of a facility in San Diego to house federal inmates to replace current San Diego facility, which will revert to County of San Diego in 2015 (10-K, p. F-18)
January–June 2012	New contract with Puerto Rico to manage up to 480 inmates at Cimarron facility in Oklahoma (10-Q, p. 34)
July 2012	Contract with Oklahoma expanded to house an additional 340 inmates at two CCA-owned facilities in the state (10-Q, p. 34)
July 2012	New contract with Idaho DOC to house 800 inmates at Kit Carson facility in Colorado (10-Q, p. 34)
June–September 2012	Renegotiation of lease of North Georgia Detention Center decreasing CCA's rent. Savings of $1.3 million annually. (10-Q p.34)
September 2012	New contract with Arizona DOC to house up to 1,000 inmates at Red Rock facility in the state. Ramping up to 90% guaranteed occupancy in 2015. (10-Q, p. 34)

SOURCE: CCA quarterly and annual SEC filings.

leaner correctional market: suspension of construction, renegotiation of contracts with states, and expansion to include other populations.

We now turn to a detailed discussion of these adaptation strategies.

Compromise

Several of the major steps taken by CCA have involved reaching compromises with old customers about occupancy rates. In some of these cases, CCA has amended its agreements to reduced margins while preserving occupancy guarantees and solidifying contract terms. In other cases, CCA has offered to settle for a slightly smaller occupancy rate. The report for the third quarter of 2012 regarding California's realignment program is a good example of the forgiving treatment CCA awards one of its best customers. As a response to a U.S. Supreme Court ruling that required the state of California to reduce the occupancy in its prisons from approximately 200 percent capacity to 137.5 percent, the state reallocated a considerable amount of its correctional resources to local jurisdictions, to which it started to transfer low-level offenders. The state's new five-year plan called for a continued decline in the total number of inmates. As a consequence, the report stated,

> in June 2012, we announced an agreement that modified our existing contract with the CDCR to reduce the total number of inmates we house for California [from a maximum of 9,588] to an average daily population of 9,038 for the State's fiscal year ending June 30, 2013. . . .
>
> It is unclear at this time how realignment or the five-year plan may impact the long-term utilization by the CDCR of our out of state beds. The return of the California inmates to the state of California would have a significant adverse impact on our financial position, results of operations, and cash flows. We housed approximately 8,700 inmates from the state of California as of September 30, 2012, compared with approximately 9,500 California inmates as of September 30, 2011. Approximately 12% and 13% of our management revenue for the nine months ended September 30, 2012 and 2011, respectively, was generated from the CDCR.[17]

It is notable that CCA is not shy, in the face of such compromises, to assert what its goal is and how it plans to profit from California's lack of foresight.

> We expect insufficient bed development by our partners to result in a return to the supply and demand imbalance that has benefited the private corrections industry.[18]

Diversification of the Investment Portfolio: From Inmates to Detainees

Even as CCA is compromising on its contract terms with some customers, it is on the prowl for new ones. As per its prospectus, CCA plans to incur capital expenditures "to expand the design capacity of certain of our facilities (in order to retain management contracts) and to increase our inmate bed capacity for anticipated demand from current and future customers." The potential to grow is mentioned as well: "We will also consider opportunities for growth, including potential acquisitions of businesses within our line of business and those that provide complementary services, provided we believe such opportunities will broaden our market share and/or increase the services we can provide to our customers."[19]

Indeed, in early 2012 the company sent a letter notifying state correctional officers that it had earmarked $250 million to purchase state prisons in good condition, specifying as one of the requirements "an assurance by the agency partner that the agency has sufficient inmate population to maintain a minimum 90 percent occupancy rate over the term of the contract."[20] States presented with this business opportunity responded that compliance with the required occupancy rate would mean reforming their sentencing laws to make them harsher. As the former Kansas secretary of corrections stated, "My concern would be that our state would be obligated to maintain these (occupancy) rates and subtle pressure would be applied to make sentencing laws more severe with a clear intent to drive up the population."[21]

The dwindling state prison market has increased CCA's interest in other opportunities. One such opportunity is Agecroft Prison Management, formerly owned by a subsidiary of CCA, which operates a correctional facility in England. In 2011 CCA extended a working capital loan to Agecroft.[22] CCA also fully owns and operates TransCor, which provides transportation services to governmental agencies, in particular, inmate transport. "During the years ended December 31, 2009, 2008, and 2007, TransCor generated total consolidated revenue of $4.0 million, $6.9 million, and $14.2 million, respectively, comprising 0.2%, 0.4%, and 1.0% of our total consolidated revenue in each respective year."[23] TransCor has been linked to various scandals and dysfunctions, including escape attempts and physical and sexual abuse of inmates by its drivers.[24]

CCA's reliance on collaborations with federal customers is particularly important, as the federal government's share in its profits has risen in recent years.[25] This market includes not only the Bureau of Prisons and the U.S. Marshals Service, but the increasing imprisonment needs of Immigration and Customs Enforcement (ICE). Detention services for undocumented immigrants are perceived as an emerging demand that could offset losses and setbacks resulting from the recession and the prison closures and decarcerations in state corrections. Immigration reform is perceived as a threaten to business,[26] which, according to CCA's annual report, "could affect the number of persons arrested, convicted, and sentenced, thereby potentially reducing demand for correctional facilities to house them."[27]

Indeed, a growing share of the private prison market consists of privatized detention centers. Nearly half of all detained undocumented immigrants are housed in private facilities.[28] CCA, the largest contractor with ICE, operates a total of fifteen ICE-contracted facilities with a total of 5,800 beds. GEO is not far behind, with seven facilities and 7,183 beds. Moreover, in December 2010, GEO purchased B.I. Incorporated, a company that has lucrative government contracts with ICE as the sole administrator of its alternatives to detention program.[29] How CCA and the private prison industry manage to not only find and exploit these opportunities but also actively create them is discussed below.

Political Influence

CCA exerts political influence by making donations independently and through its multiple political action committees: CCA, Corrections Corporation of America, and America's Leader in Partnership Corrections.[30] Between 2003 and 2012, CCA contributed $2,161,004 to political campaigns and ballot measures.[31] Of that amount, $1.3 million (60.4 percent) went to Republican candidates, $650,330 (30.1 percent) went to Democratic candidates, $1,500 went to third-party or "other" candidates, and $203,500 (9.4 percent) was donated to influence ballot measures.[32] By state, California received the greatest amount of those contributions, at $715,350, followed by Florida at $478,494, Georgia at $285,000, and CCA's home state of Tennessee at $126,500.[33] The $203,500 spent on ballot measures went to seven different ballot committees, including three in California.[34] The California contributions were $100,000 to Budget Reform Now, a committee that supported a slew of budgetary propositions in 2009; $50,000 in support of California's Proposition 30, the successful effort to raise taxes to fund public education in 2012; and $1,000 to the Yes on 6 Committee to Take Back Our Neighborhoods in 2008.[35]

CCA contributed to 239 separate lobbyists between 2003 and 2011, for a grand total of $1,858,094.[36] Again, California took the biggest slice of the pie, with the most lobbyists (sixteen) and the highest contribution total ($532,950).[37]

Given CCA's emerging interest in detention of undocumented immigrants, it is important to point out its role in shaping immigration policy. In April 2010 Arizona passed SB 1070, otherwise known as the Support Our Law Enforcement and Safe Neighborhoods Act, which would allow state law enforcement officials to profile possible undocumented immigrants during regular contact with community members and which made traveling without documentation a state offense.[38] Since then, in *Arizona v. United States*,[39] the Supreme Court invalidated portions of the law on federal preemption grounds while upholding the portion allowing Arizona state police to investigate the immigration status of an individual stopped, detained, or arrested if there is reasonable suspicion that that individual is in the country illegally.[40]

SB 1070 passed, in great part thanks to the lobbying efforts and monetary contributions of private prison providers.[41] CCA, along with other powerful corporate actors, is a member of ALEC, the American Legislative Exchange Council, which hoped to make SB 1070 into a model piece of legislation to be reproduced nationwide. As reported by NPR, when the bill was introduced on the floor, it received the unprecedented support of thirty-six cosponsors, two-thirds of whom either attended a preliminary planning meeting with ALEC or are ALEC members. That same week the *New York Times* reported that "the Corrections Corporation of America hired a powerful new lobbyist to work the capitol [and] . . . thirty of the 36 co-sponsors received donations over the next six months, from prison lobbyists or prison companies—Corrections Corporation of America, Management and Training Corporation and The GEO Group."[42]

The private prison industry's lobbying strategy is not dissimilar to the tactics employed by the California Corrections and Peace Officer Association (CCPOA), the powerful prison guard union that has played such a key role in creating California's punitive legal landscape.Clearly invested in the structure of mass incarceration, CCPOA has donated to Republican and Democrat candidates alike, targeting for special involvement legal propositions that advanced their interests. This method of hedging bets has allowed both CCA and CCPOA to remain afloat politically and continue to make a profit.[43]

These adaptation strategies have helped CCA remain profitable and successful throughout the recession, but have they changed prison conditions for inmates in these private institutions? It is by now a cliché in private prison scholarship to argue the obvious, namely, that the goal of economic profit is fundamentally at odds with any sort of rehabilitative focus. Several recession-era incidents show, in alarming ways, the ills stemming from the codependency between private prison companies and financially strained state governments.

In a telling microcosm of the standards pervasive in private prisons across the nation, the country's first privately owned prison, the Corrections Corporation of Ohio–run Ohio Correctional Facility, came under heat in early October 2012 after an audit report by the Ohio Department of Rehabilitation and Correction cited the institution for forty-seven violations of state prison standards.[44] The audit also found that CCA was in compliance with only "66.7 percent of the state's standards."

The history of abuse in Ohio's private prison begins in 1997, when Corrections Corporation of America opened a private prison in economically downtrodden Youngstown. CCA rushed to staff the prison "with inexperienced guards and then received 1,700 inmates—most charged with violent crimes—transferred from Washington, D.C., to the private prison. Within a year, 20 prisoners were stabbed and two were murdered. Six escaped."[45] Following a great public outcry and negative media coverage, CCA was forced to close the prison once it became clear that the standards it was expected uphold would not prove profitable.

In an act of collective amnesia, elected officials made a 2011 deal with CCA to "become the first state to sell a state-owned prison to a private company." Far from being hesitant to do business with the company responsible for the disastrous Youngstown incident, the Ohio legislature "proudly touted the sale for its potential taxpayer savings." The financial and legal implications of this Faustian bargain were atrocious. The benefit of using a private prison company was soon mitigated by the realization that the corporations did not want to hold high-risk inmates, who mean greater overhead costs for security and health care, and therefore had an incentive to overcrowd the institution with low-risk offenders.[46] The result was constant pressure on the state regarding sentencing policies and occupancy. And even with less serious offenders, "private prisons had a 50 percent higher incidence of inmate-on-staff assaults and two-thirds higher incidence of inmate-on-inmate assaults than state-run prisons." Furthermore, "the private prison industry's own statistics show[ed] that at private prisons the turn-over rate was 53 percent, while at public prisons it was a mere 16 percent."[47]

A variation on this theme is incarceration in Louisiana, which houses more inmates per capita than any other state in the United States.[48] Louisiana presents a particularly bleak case study of the devastating impact of prison privatization on the criminal justice system. Most of the state's inmates are housed in for-profit facilities.[49] While a number of states increasingly rely on private prisons to house their inmates, Louisiana's prison infrastructure is notable for the fact that "most prison entrepreneurs are rural sheriffs, who hold tremendous sway in remote parishes." The practical effect of this is that "if the inmate count dips, sheriffs bleed money. Their constituents lose jobs. The prison lobby ensures this does not happen by thwarting nearly every reform that could result in fewer people behind bars."[50] On the heels of pervasive reports of deplorable conditions in corporate-run prisons, there are signs that a backlash may be on the horizon.

The recent closure of a private prison in rural Kentucky highlights the tension between state economic needs and the lack of oversight and quality regulation in the private prison system. Otter Creek Correctional Center in Wheelwright had its state funding pulled in August 2012 after Hawaii removed all 168 female inmates it had housed at the facility due to allegations of sexual abuse by prison guards.[51] Despite the alleged abuses that led to Otter Creek being shut down, "because Eastern Kentucky is one of the poorest rural regions in the country, the prison was welcomed by local residents desperate for jobs."[52] A company town founded by a coal company in 1916, Wheelwright saw its economy grind to a halt as coal production slowed. Otter Creek "brought nearly 200 jobs to one of the poorest regions in the South when it opened in 1981. CCA paid employees $8.25 an hour—low pay by prison standards but welcome cash for the area." The relationship between CCA and Wheelwright highlights one of the dangers of private prisons operating in impoverished areas. Because the towns and counties in which private prisons are located are often reliant on the prisons for a much-needed economic boost, there tends to be a lack of rigor in oversight of their management and maintenance.[53]

In another egregious instance of private prisons run amok, GEO removed its presence entirely from Mississippi in April 2012, after federal judge Carlton Reeves wrote that the GEO-run Walnut Grove Youth Correctional Facility had "allowed a cesspool of unconstitutional and inhuman acts and conditions to germinate, the sum of which places the offenders at substantial and ongoing risk."[54] A scathing report by the Department of Justice found that, among other practices at the 1,450-bed prison housing "inmates ages 13 to 22 who are minors convicted as adults," prison staff routinely had sex with underage inmates, "poorly-trained guards brutally beat youth and used excessive pepper spray," prison guards turned a blind eye to inmates possessing homemade knives that were used in "gang fights and inmate rapes," and, perhaps most shocking, some guards themselves were members of gangs.

The corporate profit motive that is increasingly permeating the prison system affects more than the well-being of prisoners in privately run facilities. The emergence of private probation outfits has led to the allegation that probationary decision making has shifted from ostensibly neutral courts to for-profit corporations looking to reap financial gain by using probation as a tool to fine and fee cash-strapped individuals. A class action lawsuit pending in Alabama claims that the privately run Judicial Correction Services (JCS) uses for its own financial gain a probation system run amok.[55] Under the preexisting system in towns such as Childesburg, Alabama, people unable to pay fines imposed by the town for violations such as speeding are routinely placed on probation. Once placed on probation, JCS is tasked with aggressively collecting those fines from the individuals. Rather than charge public authorities for their services, companies like JCS work for municipalities at no charge and turn a profit by attaching fees to defendants' bills. This emerging paradigm "is about the mushrooming of fines and fees levied by money-starved towns across the country and for-profit businesses that administer the system. The result is that growing numbers of poor people . . . are ending up in jail and in debt for minor infractions."[56]

The risks of and cautionary tales about private prisons raise the question whether recession-era local governments benefit, on the bottom line, from privatizing their correctional systems. While the math is fairly clear on the private providers' side, it is more difficult to determine whether private institutions are truly more economically viable on the governments' side than their public counterparts. In a comparative study of prison assessment, Gerry Gaes found that different organizations came to different conclusions about the cost/performance equation of private and public prisons.[57] Specifically, he found differences between the way Abt Associates and the Bureau of Prisons assessed Taft, a private prison, in comparison to public institutions. The significant differences in assessing per diem costs per inmate were due to discrepancies in population sizes (private prisons with more inmates per year benefit from economies of scale, and any comparison between them and less-populated state prisons require adjusting the analysis to account for the difference) and in assessing overhead costs (governmental contribution may exceed the reported overhead).[58]

One more important consideration is that private and public prisons' performances are assessed in different ways: private prisons tend to be measured in terms of compliance with contract terms, whereas public prisons' performances are measured based on parameters established by auditors,[59] which becomes even more complicated considering that contract terms between private prisons and the government often differ on a contract-to-contract basis. The definitions of misconduct may differ from assessor to assessor; for example, while research groups included two escapes that had occurred at Taft, only the Bureau of Prisons noted a situation in which one thousand inmates had refused to return to their cells by curfew.

Another factor complicating the ability to compare private and public prisons is that their starting points, in terms of population type, are frequently different. A 2004 study found that "state-run prisons are generally left to take on a disproportionate number of expensive and high-risk inmates. For example, inmates with minimum or medium levels of security classification made up 90 percent of the private sector's population, compared with only 69 percent in the public sector."[60] The comparison is problematic under these conditions.

The adaptation strategies of private prison providers are a grim reminder that correctional developments motivated by financial prudence do not always lead away from punitivism, but they are not the only such development. We now turn to another marker of correctional austerity: charging inmates for their custodial experience.

PRISON CLOSURES: CROWDING, REPURPOSING, AND BEDS FOR SALE

Private prison companies are not the only site in which facilities have had to be adapted to leaner policies. States and providers have had to consider prison closures and repurposing. An article in the *Atlantic* lists states with very different political cultures resorting to similar measures.

> In 2011, 13 states were closing prisons or in the process of it. Michigan has now closed 22 facilities since 2002. New York State Governor Andrew Cuomo announced plans last year to close seven. And legislators in Texas—a state that had tripled its prison capacity since the late '80's—recently opted to close the 102-year-old Sugar Land prison.[61]

A 2011 report by the Sentencing Project elaborates on the recent incidences of prison closures, noting that those in Michigan prison closures are due predominantly to reform in the areas of sentencing and parole. A December 2012 follow-up report on the Sentencing Project's 2011 findings uncovered additional prison closures: "In 2012, at least six states have closed 20 prison institutions or are contemplating doing so, potentially reducing prison capacity by over 14,100 beds and resulting in an estimated $337 million in savings."[62] And especially notable: "during 2012,

Florida led the nation in prison closings with its closure of 10 correctional facilities; the state's estimated cost savings for prison closings totals over $65 million."[63]

One conundrum that states have faced over the past several years is that "while funds to manage expensive prison systems have lessened, so too have resources for services such as treatment for substance abuse and mental health."[64] At the same time, as of 2011, the National Conference of State Legislatures found that "corrections and public safety spending were above budgeted levels in seven states, including Alaska, where corrections spending exceed[s] the state's $258 million corrections budget by $9 million."[65] Compounding the problem of corrections overspending is the fact that many government jobs hinge on a robust corrections infrastructure. Michigan is a case in point: the prison population has significantly declined, but "state lawmakers are still continuing work to contain costs where one out of three state employees works in the criminal justice system and the corrections budget represents 23% of state general funds."[66]

But are prison closures merely a reflection of budget shortages, or do they represent a bigger ideological shift? In assessing potential causes of prison closures, Adam Gelb, director of the Public Safety Performance Project with the Pew Center on the States, dismisses the notion that the recent rash of prison closures is entirely driven by dwindling state budgets and economic concerns. Rather, Gelb suggests, there has been an ideological shift "by the public, politicians and public safety professionals, with the result that we may be entering a new phase of America's complex relationship to incarceration, one in which we now have to figure out what to do with all these empty, peculiar and often isolated buildings."[67] Gelb attributes this shift in thinking to public safety professionals knowing

> much more than they knew 35 years ago about how to keep people from re-offending, and they have better tools to manage offenders without using prison cells (better treatment programs, GPS tracking devices, alcohol detection ignition locks in cars). The public has also grown weary of the War on Drugs that helped fuel our prison boom. Last month, Colorado and Washington voted to legalize marijuana. And California voters passed a referendum de-fanging the state's "three strikes" law. Even political antipodes from Newt Gingrich to the ACLU have been jointly backing prison reform.[68]

In what appears to be an ideological shift, both the federal and state governments have refocused their efforts, away from keeping prisons full and toward reducing recidivism. A recent editorial in the *New York Times* suggests that this shift is partially attributable to the Second Chance Act of 2008, which aims to assist states in reducing recidivism.[69] By honing in on reducing recidivism rates, state governments aim to both decrease crime and cut prison costs. New York, in particular, now has "a glut of vacant correctional facilities because of lower crime rates, new programs that allow early release for nonviolent offenders, and the dismantling of its strict drug laws."[70] Following Governor David Paterson's lead in closing three prisons during his tenure, current New York Governor Andrew Cuomo announced that "prisons were 'not an employment program,' and proceeded to shut seven of the state's remaining 67 correctional facilities, removing 3,800 beds." This trend is a sharp departure from previous prison policy in the state. As with many recent prison reforms, the shift toward closing prisons can be largely attributed to a change in the state's view of drug sentencing. Thomas Kaplan, in a May 2012 article in the *New York Times,* stated that "after New York adopted mandatory drug sentences in 1973, the state's prison population soared from 13,437 to a peak of 71, 472 in 1999, prompting a boom in prison construction." However, he continued, "since then the number of inmates in state facilities has fallen nearly a quarter, to about 55,000, leaving thousands of empty beds."[71]

Part of the driving force behind the trend in prison closures is sentencing reform. In recent years,

> lawmakers in Kansas, Michigan, New Jersey, and New York enacted a mix of administrative and legislative policies that contributed to sustained prison population reductions of 5–20%. In each of these states a range of policy changes were adopted, including sentencing reforms, alternatives for "prison bound" people, reducing time served in prison, addressing parole release rates, and reducing revocations. The ability of these four states to control prison growth shows that policymakers and practitioners can collaborate to reduce the reliance on incarceration while maintaining public safety.[72]

As public safety and corrections officials have come to realize that keeping prisons full has been ineffective in deterring "drug market participation," steps have been taken to pursue policy changes that focus on rehabilitation and treatment in tandem with reducing the number of people in jails.

> In Missouri, for example, policymakers reduced the nation's most severe sentencing disparity for crack and powder cocaine when they changed the drug quantities that triggered a mandatory minimum prison sentence. Louisiana lawmakers authorized judges to depart from statutory penalties for certain persons who cooperate with law enforcement officials.[73]

Table 4 gives a breakdown of the projected prison closures in 2012. As the data show, many of the institutions that are being closed or under consideration are located in the South, which is typically regarded as more punitive.[74]

In light of prisons being closed to save vital resources, "at midyear for fiscal year 2012 states reported cutting correctional expenditures by $67.5 million." Furthermore, "an examination of projected budgets for fiscal year 2013 indicates that at least 12 states are planning to decrease correctional expenditures, with prison closures being one mechanism to do so." But beyond the obvious savings, have the closures had an impact on prison conditions?

TABLE 4. States closing or considering closing correctional facilities in 2012

State	Correctional Facility	Operational Capacity	Est. First-Year Savings
California	California Rehabilitation Center	3,900 beds	$160,000,000
Colorado	Colorado State Penitentiary II	316 beds	$4,500,000
Florida	Broward Correctional Institution	611 beds	$2,523,371
Florida	Caryville Work Camp	133 beds	$1,728,792
Florida	Demily Correctional Institution	342 beds	$6,068,260
Florida	Gainesville Correctional Institution	507 beds	$9,038,845
Florida	Hendry Work Camp	280 beds	$4,028,832
Florida	Hillsborough Correctional Institution	431 beds	$8,314,653
Florida	Indian River Correctional Institution	381 beds	$8,027,931
Florida	Levy Forestry Camp	292 beds	$3,866,263
Florida	New River Correctional Institution	1,363 beds	$17,644,740
Florida	River Junction Work Camp	736 beds	$4,268,454
Illinois	Dwight Correctional Center	1,212 beds	$36,900,000
Illinois	Joliet Renaissance Center—Youth Center	344 beds	$11, 700,000
Illinois	Murphysboro Youth Prison	156 beds	$6,000,000
Illinois	Tamms Super Maximum Security Correctional Center	700 beds	$25, 600,000
Kentucky	Otter Creek Correctional Center	656 beds	$9,450,000
Louisiana	C. Paul Phelps Correctional Center	942 beds	$12,000,000
Louisiana	Forcht-Wade Correctional Center	498 beds	$2,700,000
Louisiana	J. Levy Dabadie Correctional Center	300 beds	$3,000,000
Total Beds and Project Cost Savings		14,100 beds	$337, 380,141

SOURCE: Nicole D. Porter, *On the Chopping Block 2012: State Prison Closings* (December 2012), 5, http://sentencing-project.org/doc/publications/On%20the%20Chopping%20Block%202012.pdf.

Some of the reports have been encouraging, as some of the prison closures stem from actual sentencing reforms. But in some cases prison closures unaccompanied by a proportionate decrease in inmate numbers mean more overcrowding. In Illinois, Governor Quinn has had to defend his initiative to shut down prisons in court[75] and then battle the resulting overcrowding by filling gymnasiums with beds.[76] Similar concerns about overcrowding arose in Boston[77] and in New York.[78]

Another important question pertains to the ability to repurpose closing prisons. In some cases, states have been able to use closed men's prisons as women's prisons, repurpose juvenile institutions as adult institutions, and the like. Some institutions present special problems in that regard; maximum-security prisons with Security Housing Units (SHUs) in them, which are small and windowless, are difficult to repurpose. Nonetheless, the Vera Institute was able to implement its segregation reduction project in Ohio and Mississippi,[79] states that believed that, even with cells left empty and repurposed, considerable fiscal savings could be realized by emptying them.

But one of the most important ways in which states can repurpose their closed prisons can be offering the space to less prudent states. We now turn to a phenomenon that combines privatization, prison closures, and repurposing: incarcerating inmates out-of-state.

THE INMATE EXPORT BUSINESS: GEOGRAPHIC SHIFTS IN INCARCERATION

Chronic prison overcrowding has resulted in a trend toward exporting more and more prisoners across state lines, which is accomplished by enforceable legal contracts known as "interstate compacts."[80] Currently, there are three interstate compacts governing the transfer of inmates across state lines: "the National Interstate Compact for Corrections" (national) and "the Western Corrections Compact and New England Corrections Compact" (both regional). Forty states are currently signed on to the national agreement, although there are other mechanisms by which the interstate transfer of inmates may occur, including by statute or court order.[81]

As of July 1, 2005, corrections departments in at least forty-three states had inmates on transferred status in the custody of other public agencies. Approximately 4,900 inmates were on transferred status nationwide; of this number, 2,089 state-sentenced inmates were transferred between state prison systems, 345 were transferred to the Federal Bureau of Prisons, and 2,466 were transferred to private prisons in another state.[82]

The primary reason for interstate transfer of inmates was prison overcrowding, followed by inmate safety. Of the transfers due to overcrowding, 95 percent went to private prisons. The explosive growth of private prisons during the 1980s served a dual purpose: to accommodate the tough-on-crime ideology that was increasingly permeating the national consciousness and to provide economic opportunities for towns that suffered from a decline in manufacturing and other industries. Prisons began to pop up in rural and isolated areas that had suffered economically, the collateral effect of which was more and more prisoners shipped off to serve sentences far from their homes and families. The ramifications extended beyond the impact on the state's infrastucture: studies suggest that this separation from the familial structure can significantly hinder prisoners' rehabilitation, as well as increase the risk of recidivism. As Shelden and Teji note, "Interstate transfer virtually eliminates visitation by family members; exacerbated when private prisons are involved as they are not held to the same visitation and rehabilitation standards as the sending state."[83] This problem has come up in the context of Alaska, whic ships

30 percent of its inmates to other states, primarily Arizona. In 2000 an Alaskan court went so far as to rule that a prisoner who was moved to a CCA facility in Arizona had his constitutional rights jeopardized because the Alaska Constitution guarantees a prisoner's right to rehabilitation, and visitation was part and parcel of the rehabilitative process. By shipping the prisoner to Arizona, the state was effectively preventing any meaningful visitation rights that the prisoner might have.[84] Research has shown that visitation prevents prisoners from being "socialized to the life of an inmate [and helps transform them into] individuals who have the necessary skills and emotional stability to face up to their responsibilities as citizens, parents and spouses." Moreover, when prisoners are able to maintain contact with family members during incarceration, they are more likely to sustain the relationships after their release. Inmates who have families to support them on release are less likely to return to a life of crime.[85]

Bob Weier is a Hawaiian inmate who has served out his prison sentence in Minnesota, Oklahoma, and, most recently, a private prison in Arizona.[86] In 2007 fifty-three-year-old Weier told the *New York Times*, "You lose your family identity." Weier at the time had never met five of his grandchildren and had not seen his daughter in eleven years. He added, "And that's not good, because when we go back into society—and more than 95 percent of us will—the only ones who are going to take care of you are your family."[87] Compounding these difficulties, each time Weier was transferred to a different out-of-state prison "he had to reapply for phone privileges, a process that can take six months. Even when he was allowed to call home, he said, he could not always afford the long-distance bills."

Weier is not alone, and Hawaii is unique in the extent to which it is involved in the inmate export business. A special 2011 report by the University of Hawaii sociologist David Johnson[88] revealed that 54 percent of the state's prisoners are incarcerated on the mainland. The financial reasons for this policy are not as obvious as they may seem. As of the end of 2009, it cost approximately $118 per day to incarcerate an inmate on the islands as opposed to at least $62 per day to incarcerate him or her in a private institution on the mainland. However, after Hawaiian female inmates were sexually abused in a private institution in Kentucky,[89] suspicions on the Islands about cheaper incarceration were aroused, and the report found that the private prison cost assessment was far from inclusive. The report found no significant difference in recidivism rates between inmates incarcerated in Hawaii and on the mainland and recommended reassessing the benefits of out-of-state incarceration, with short-term costs being only one, but not the main, consideration.

Arizona is also an important state in the inmate export business, but on the importing side. Inmates from as far as Alaska and Vermont have been shipped to facilities run by Correctional Corporations of America in Arizona. Simultaneously, Arizona has found itself up against serious overcrowding issues. In an effort to alleviate this problem, Arizona initially looked to house some of its own inmates in private prisons out of state. In 2007 over two thousand Arizona inmates were being housed in prisons in Indiana and Oklahoma.[90]

Efforts to place yet more Arizona inmates outside the state were often thwarted in favor of private prison corporations, that is, putting the bottom line first. For example, Arizona found its overcrowding problem exacerbated when "two private prisons in Texas, now run by the GEO Group, canceled Arizona's contract and instead signed more lucrative deals with federal corrections agencies."[91]

Unreliability on the part of the private prison companies often led to Arizona officials scrambling to find a place to house its overflow of inmates. In 2010 Arizona announced plans to phase out-of-state beds out of its budget. This decision came on the heels of a 2005 finding that Arizona was paying private contractors "$11 per prisoner per day *more* than the average daily costs of state-operated prisons, totaling approximately $4.1 million in extra spending by the state per year.[92] In lieu of shipping inmates to private prisons in states such as Oklahoma and Colorado, Arizona has opted to contract with private prison companies to provide more beds in-state to house its prisoners, all the while continuing to take in prisoners from other states. Today, 16 percent of Arizona's inmates are housed in private prison facilities, and there are plans to build one thousand medium-security beds in private facilities.[93]

Curiously, this comes at a time when Arizona's prison population is actually in decline for the first time in decades. Recently, "corrections records show that in fiscal 2011 there were 296 fewer prisoners than the previous year, and this past fiscal year that ended June 30 [2012], there were 304 fewer inmates for a total of 38,977."[94] While State Corrections Director Charles Ryan attributed this decline to "fewer parole revocations, fewer illegal immigrants being placed in state custody and an overall downturn in crime," he nonetheless maintained that more beds were needed, because empty beds currently exist primarily in women's medium-security facilities at which other types of inmates cannot be housed. Opponents of the private prison expansion currently under way in Arizona also look to recent information showing that "the average daily cost per inmate in a state-run, medium-custody facility in 2010 was $48.42, while the average daily cost for an inmate in a similar private facility was $53.02. That translates into a 9.5% higher cost per inmate for a private prison."[95]

One particularly robust critique of private prison operations in Arizona stems from concern that there is a lack of oversight of the out-of-state prisoners housed by private prison contractors in Arizona facilities. While Arizona corrections officials maintain oversight of criminals convicted in Arizona and housed in private facilities, Arizona has no say in what kinds of inmates private prisons in Arizona accept from other states or from the federal government. Rather, "in those situations, private-prison operators work with their outside-government partners on training specifications and other operational details. They report to Arizona only the names, security classifications, and number of inmates housed at their facilities. State statutes do not require private operators to provide Arizona officials details about the crimes the prisoners committed or escape data."[96]

The lack of oversight by Arizona officials stirred controversy in 2007 when "two convicted killers sent from another state stole ladders from a maintenance building and climbed onto a roof at a private prison outside Florence. Brandishing a fake gun, they climbed over the prison walls and escaped to freedom. One was caught within hours, but it was almost a month before the other was caught— hundreds of miles away in his home state of Washington."[97]

Following this incident, a 2008 bill was drafted by then-Governor Janet Napolitano's office that would have required private prisons in Arizona to meet state construction standards. The bill also would have put an end to private prisons allowing murderers, rapists, and convicted felons into Arizona from out of state and sharing more out-of-state inmate information with Arizona officials. The bill ultimately died.[98]

If the number of overall inmates in Arizona is down and empirical evidence shows that housing inmates in private prisons is more expensive than housing them in state-run facilities, why the continued push for privatization? One answer may lie in the impact that private prisons have on local economies.

Despite the outcry that a for-profit prison system with questionable oversight is not what a state like Arizona needs, communities that stand to benefit from the presence of private prisons have been rallying around efforts to expand privatization. In Florence, Arizona, the state's unofficial "prison capital," a public hearing on the issue of private prisons reflected a nearly ubiquitous consensus that such prisons would be welcome. At the hearing, "Florence's mayor [Tom Rankin], town officials and the school superintendent all voiced support for more inmate beds, after they were told by GEO Group that the company's proposal to build a new 1,000 bed prison would create 2,000 construction jobs, 260 jobs at the facility and a $12 million annual payroll." Rankin added, "We are proud of our institutions, and proud to have a much-needed service to the state. . . . It will create more jobs, and more jobs mean that more people will shop here."[99] With a national economy in peril, it appears that the bottom-line appeal of private prisons has the power to extend beyond financial benefits to the corporations themselves and into the communities they affect.

PASSING THE BUCK: JURISDICTIONAL SHIFTS IN INCARCERATION

One way in which corrections officials are seeking to cut costs is by shifting inmate populations from state prisons to county jails. The idea is to eliminate the fiscal problem that Franklin Zimring and Gordon Hawkins referred to as the "correctional free lunch": charging and sentencing done on the county level, while the state picks up the tab for incarceration.[100] If, instead, prisons were run locally and states would allocate money to localities to make incarceration decisions as they saw fit, the costs involved in incarceration would at least be internalized and taken into account when designing policy.[101]

The main example of recession-driven jurisdictional shifts is, of course, the California Criminal Justice Realignment, which consists of several complex legislative changes.[102] First, the new legislation identifies hundreds of felonies that are eligible for jail sentences. Second, it shifts the sentencing rules governing nonviolent, nonsexual, nonserious offenders (the "non-non-nons"),[103] not only by transferring their incarceration locus from the state to the county, but also by providing judges with an array of sentencing tools, including "mandatory supervision"[104] and other programs.[105] And third, the Realignment fundamentally alters parole by shifting the responsibilities for many out-of-prison parolees from the state to the counties. In addition, the legislation has required counties to create alternatives to sentencing and reentry programs. Whether Governor Brown's push for the Realignment was a response to the fiscal crisis, the continuation of efforts to achieve jurisdictional shifts from the Schwarzenegger gubernatorial administration, or an answer to pressure from federal courts to comply with the Supreme Court mandate in *Brown v. Plata* depends on one's perspective; lawmakers, lawyers, judges, and other stakeholders offer a range of explanations, from a mere savings mechanism to a real change in policy.[106]

The jurisdictional shift raises two main problems: big variation among counties regarding incarceration and rehabilitation policies and a concern referred to by Margo Schlanger as "the hydra," that is, shifting dysfunction and abuse from state prisons to county jails. Both problems have already arisen in the context of the Realignment.

In 2012, shortly after the passage of Realignment legislation, the California Association of Counties attempted to undo its effects, raising financial concerns and practical problems of space for the prospective addition to their jail populations.[107] The opposition did not meet with success, and each of California's fifty-eight counties ended up adopting special policies to address the incoming inmates.[108] Research conducted by the Center on Juvenile and Criminal Justice since the Realignment's implementation reveals the variation in strategies adopted by the different counties. The average number of new prison admissions in 2012, per 1,000 felony arrests, was 90 statewide; Kings County was responsible for 237 admissions per 1,000 felony arrests, and San Francisco County for 25.[109] Thirty-two of the 58 counties, Los Angeles County among them, have opted to construct more jails using state funds. Other counties have strived to improve their existing facilities to better serve longer-term inmates.[110] And still other counties have aimed at reducing their reliance on incarceration altogether and finding alternative approaches to sentencing, such as relying more heavily on the mandatory supervision option.[111] The resulting disparities make it difficult to assess the success of the Realignment as an option, a problem compounded by the difficulty of obtaining data from all the counties.[112]

These varying county approaches are facilitated using subsidies from the state, which brings up the question of fund allocation to the counties. In the early stages of the Realignment, funding to the counties was based on the number of parolees returning to them from state prison. This created perverse economic incentives, because counties that were not successful in finding alternatives for incarceration were rewarded financially for their poor choices, allowing them to continue making said poor choices. W. David Ball has advocated a system that was adopted later on, which requires allocating funds based on county rates on violent crime, which arguably are a better representation of a given county's incarceration needs.[113]

The second concern has to do with the "hydra" problem. Shifting inmates from state prisons to county jails may reproduce the problematic incarceration conditions in the local settings. This becomes a serious issue when considering that jail conditions, in themselves, were not necessarily better than state prison conditions before the Realignment.[114] And, indeed, the fierce litigation over health care in prisons, which produced the Supreme Court decision in *Brown v. Plata,* is now echoed by emerging litigation against county jails with similarly abysmal health care. One such case is the Riverside Jail, which has adopted a new policy of charging its inmates $140 per night. The hotel-scale fee becomes even more absurd given current conditions: triple-stacked bunk beds to handle the flow of inmates, a months-long wait for the jail's four thousand inmates before seeing a doctor, cursory exams and inadequate follow-up.[115]

The Realignment may indeed be the biggest experiment in jurisdictional shifting, but it is far from the only one. In Florida, "a current proposal on the table could shift about 5,600 inmates from state prisons to county jails."[116] With 20 percent of county jails in Florida already over capacity, critics of the proposal suggest that instituting a realignment policy similar to that in California merely shifts the burden of improving the prison system from the state to the counties. Proponents of the proposal, however, counter that transferring inmates to county jails will save the state $47.7 million per year. While transferring inmates from the state to the counties entails financial incentives for the state, the move would likely cost the counties $100 million—over twice as much as the state would save.[117] The way that the proposed shift would be implemented is as follows: "Today, anyone sentenced to more than a year behind bars is sent to a state prison, with credit for 'time served' in a local jail while awaiting trial and sentencing. Under the proposal, if this 'time served' credit knocks the remainder of the sentence down to less than a year, the inmate would remain in the jail for the duration of the sentence."[118]

Privatization, geographic and jurisdictional shifts, and changes in numbers, locations, and population of prisons share several common features. Rather than being part of a concerted effort to curb prison spending, they are short-term emergency measures that can be revised and reversed. They are not part of a centralized policy; they are the product of negotiations between state governments, local authorities, and myriad private prison providers. Decisions and negotiations occur in administrative offices and corporate headquarters and are seldom advertised as conscious policies, with the exception of big-scale changes like the California Realignment. In that respect, these shifts differ substantially from the shifts explored in chapters 4 and 5. If the progressive political gains regarding the death penalty and the war on drugs can be said to be a new development after forty years of "tough on crime" political stances, these quiet but profound migrations of people, beds, and money are basically a continuation of the managerial, actuarial family of policies that Malcolm Feeley and Jonathan Simon referred to as "the new penology."[119] Rather than a profound change in priorities, they represent a continued commitment to the maintenance of the carceral universe, albeit with less resources, in the context of the market.

These changes also represent a growing awareness, not only among policy makers, but among prison administrators on the ground, of the costs and burdens associated with incarceration and an unwillingness to assume these costs as par for the course in crime control and punishment. The obligation to incarcerate no longer naturally assumes the accompanying obligation to provide the basic services that go hand in hand with incarceration. As the next chapter argues, these perspectives represent a shift in the image of the offender: from state ward to burden and consumer of services.

THE NEW INMATE AS
A FISCAL SUBJECT

From Ward to Consumer

In 1777 a horrified John Howard observed of conditions in English prisons:

> There are prisons, into which whoever looks will, at first sight of the people confined there, be convinced, that there is some great error in the management of them; the sallow meagre countenances declare, without words, that they are very miserable; many who went in healthy, are in a few months changed into emaciated dejected objects. Some are seen pining under diseases, "sick and in prison"; expiring on the floors, in loathsome cells, of pestilential fevers, and the confluent small-pox; victims, I must say not to the cruelty, but I will say to the inattention, of sheriffs, and gentlemen in the commission of the peace.
>
> The cause of this distress is, that many prisons are scantily supplied, and some almost totally unprovided with the necessaries of life.[1]

Underlying Howard's distress were his Enlightenment-era sensibilities, according to which inmates were at the mercy of the state and therefore prisons were obligated to provide basic living conditions. His critique is a grim reminder of an economic reality: while prison punishes, disciplines, and incapacitates, it also has to spend resources to clothe, feed, and house its inhabitants.

The perception of inmates as recipients of basic services is the fourth and last aspect of humonetarianism. This chapter examines how the advent of a neoliberal ethos has transformed our understanding of the inmate, from Howard's ward to a burden on the state's budget and a consumer of its services, and how perceiving the inmate as burden and consumer has led officials and prison administrators to question the extent of their obligation to provide for those in their custody. The view that inmates are an economic burden of course precedes the Great Recession;

and privatization and profit have shaped today's prison industrial complex. In that respect, the actions of Sheriff Greg Bartlett of Decatur, Alabama, will not surprise economists and public choice scholars. Between 2006 and 2009 Bartlett padded his wallet by feeding jail inmates on $1.75 per inmate per day, taking advantage of an old statute that allowed him to keep what he saved on their sustenance for himself.[2] While Bartlett's actions are an anomaly, they reflect the perverse implications of a neoliberal, supply-and-demand approach to incarceration. When the cost of holding people in custody exceeds the risk of releasing them, the state must either release more inmates or roll the costs of their confinement onto their own backs. New categories of inmates, whose incarceration is particularly cost-ineffective, become the focus of correctional regulations; new tiers of inmates, based on their financial capabilities to shoulder the burden of their own confinement, are created; and the inmates themselves participate in, and perpetuate, their own identities as burdens/consumers.

THE COST/RISK EQUATION: THE MONETARY SIDE OF THE "NEW PENOLOGY"

In their groundbreaking article, "The New Penology,"[3] Malcolm Feeley and Jonathan Simon identified an emerging model of corrections under which prisons have despaired of achieving traditional utilitarian aims of punishment, such as reducing recidivism deterrence and rehabilitation, and instead focused on internally achievable goals, such as incapacitation and warehousing in a continuum of institutions according to categories of risk. The great aspirations of the disciplinary era gave way to managerial, actuarial justice, which classifies inmates according to the risk they pose and places them in institutions appropriate to the classification.

Managerialism, however, has another aspect, which Feeley and Simon left largely unexamined: risk assessment, in an environment of limited resources, is always measured against cost. Given the public safety mentality of the past forty years, fueled by alliances between prison administrators and victim advocates,[4] a regime of incapacitation with unlimited means could potentially house all inmates in maximum-security facilities.

It is therefore more accurate to present the correctional regime not just via the concept of actuarial risk assessment, but as the outcome of a cost/risk equation. The decision whether to incarcerate an individual, and if so, where to place him or her, must take into account the resources necessary to maintain the appropriate facilities. During affluent times, the cost side of the equation remains relatively muted, and the concentration on the risk side leads to an increased focus on categories of perceived high-risk offenders that must be incarcerated for lengthy periods. A classic example is the sex offender category. As Chrysanthi Leon's survey demonstrates,[5] this unsympathetic group of offenders has been increasingly perceived as especially dangerous, resulting in less differentiation between differ-ent types of sex offenders and more monolithic, punitive legislation. Sex offender laws have come to apply broad, stigmatizing labels that fit only the worst offenders of the entire group; these legislative efforts have generated a large incarcerated population confronted with serious barriers to reentry on release, including regis-tration and notification laws, civil commitment, and strict residency limitations.

Similarly, habitual offenders—whose history indicates risk of reoffending—have been targeted by punitive legislation during eras in which such legislation was affordable. New York's Baumes Law, enacted in 1926 to make a 1907 statute more effective, imposed life imprisonment on three-time felons upon a fourth conviction; strong pressures from a Depression-era electorate led to the repeal of the Baumes Law, on grounds of injustice and administrative inapplicability, in 1932.[6] Nonetheless, in the late 1940s habitual offender laws existed in forty-three states,[7] and the combination of victim rights advocacy, conservative social mores,[8] and tough-on-crime policy brought about a newer generation of harsher laws, such as California's Three Strikes.[9]

But as the following examples show, the American punitive appetite to give offenders long prison sentences has been somewhat sated in the aftermath of the financial crisis. Categories of inmates that have received very little legislative energy, such as the old and the infirm, have become the focus of policy makers and administrators, yielding increased interest in geriatric and medical parole regimes. Also, while cost-saving was not the driving force behind the campaign to mitigate the effects of California's Three Strikes Law, it contributed to the passage of Propo-sition 36, which limited the law's application to violent offenders, effectively tilting the cost/risk balance to the cost side. These examples show a shifting attitude to those whose cost/risk profile raises questions about the profitability of their incar-ceration while retrenching opinions about those for whom perceived risk out-weighs cost.

THE NEW CATEGORIES: THE OLD AND THE INFIRM AS BURDENS

The idea that incarcerating old and infirm inmates may not be worthwhile from a cost/risk perspective is not new. Before the rise in crime rates and mass incarcera-tion in the 1960s, Republican lawmakers strongly argued for cost-saving measures, highlighting elderly inmates. At one point the National Council on Crime and Delinquency president, Milt Rector, a Utah Republican who had been a social worker, even argued for the abolition of prisons.[10] However, this perspective was soon forgotten, and the factors that brought about the cataclysmic increase in prison population since the 1970s contributed to the rise in age of inmates. While the aging prison population can be attributed in part to the aging baby boomer population, it is mostly attributable to the advent of tough sentencing laws that increased the length and likelihood of incarceration, as well as harsh parole revocation policies.[11] Twenty percent of prisoners between the ages of 61 and 70 are serving sentences of more than twenty years (not including life sentences), compared to 11.4 percent of prisoners age 31 to 40.[12] Age is, of course, an issue with inmates serving life sentences as well: state lifers' numbers between 1984 and 2008 ballooned from 34,000 to 140,610,[13] to the point that one in ten to eleven state inmates is serving a life sentence;[14] and in the federal system, the number of lifers grew from 410 in 1998 to 4,222.[15] Of federal prisoners age 51 or older, Human Rights Watch reports that 11 percent are serving sentences ranging from thirty years to life.[16]

While some of the inmates serving long sentences were convicted of nonviolent crime, increases in sentences for violent offenses and the requirement that violent offenders serve a greater portion of their sentences have also contributed to the growing older prison population. Violent offenders tend to serve longer sentences and thus grow old in prison; a higher percentage of older prisoners were serving state sentences for violent crimes than were younger offenders (65.3 percent vs. 49.6 percent), reflecting a "stacking" phenomenon: inmates enter the system but don't leave it at nearly the same rates.

Another contributor to the aging prison population is the fact that more inmates are entering prison at older ages. Between 1995 and 2009, the growth rate of people entering prison at an older age (109 percent) was significantly higher than that of younger people (9.7 percent) entering prison.[17] This is particularly notable given the fact that the percentage of aging prisoners who were first imprisoned after they turned 50 is declining. In 1979, 41 percent of aging prisoners were incarcerated at 50 or older, though this number is falling across the country. In Ohio only 25 percent of aging prisoners were first incarcerated after turning 50; likewise, in Florida, Texas, and New Hampshire, this number dropped to 4 to 8 percent in 2012.[18] The two data points are not inconsistent; despite the decline in older inmate prison entries, the inflated proportion of older prisoners incarcerated for the decade and a half between 1995 and 2009 continues to affect the increasing geriatric prison population due to the lengthy sentences that will likely keep them behind bars for most, if not all, of their lives.

As a result of these policies, the elderly prison population is the fastest growing subpopulation within the prison system, both at the state and federal levels. The Bureau of Justice Statistics reports that between 1999 and 2008 the number of men and women 55 and older increased by 76 percent (from 43,300 to 76,400), while the entire prison population increased by only 18 percent in that period.[19] In 1995 only 3 percent of sentenced state and federal prisoners were age 55 or older (32,600 inmates), but by 2010 that rate more than doubled, to 8 percent (124,400 inmates).[20] This trend continued throughout the recession. According to Human Rights Watch, "Between 2007 and 2010 . . . the number of sentenced state and federal prisoners age 65 or older . . . grew an astonishing 94 times faster than the total sentenced prisoner population . . . [and] increased by 63 percent, while the overall population of sentenced prisoners grew only 0.7 percent in the same period."[21] Moreover, the number of state and federal prisoners age 55 or older nearly quadrupled between 1995 and 2010, while the number of all prisoners grew by less than half.[22] At the end of 2011, 39 percent of sentenced state and federal prisoners were 40 or older.

The first indication of the focus on elderly inmates as an economically burdensome category is related to the definition of "elderly." Most studies and reports classify prisoners as "elderly" when they reach the age of 50; as discussed in further detail below, geriatric state parole policies vary but generally use around age 50 as a qualifier.[23] Experts have agreed that using this relatively low chronological age as a benchmark for defining inmates as "elderly" is appropriate since "an inmate's institutional age is much greater than his chronological age because of the stress of prison life."[24] The impact of institutional aging is significant: inmates who are chronologically 50 years old are physiologically closer to 60 and have the increased health problems associated with an older age, as well as the higher medical care costs associated with an older age.

In general, inmates of all ages are more likely than the general population to have physical or mental health problems because they are more likely to come from lower socioeconomic backgrounds, to have less education, to have a greater likelihood of substance abuse issues, and to have had less access to health care, particularly when they were young.[25] This pattern, in addition to the institutional age phenomenon, compounds the likelihood that elderly inmates will have physical or mental health problems. Anthony Sterns and colleagues find that "of noninstitutionalized people age 65 and older, 41 percent reported at least one disability in 2006, compared with 67 percent of those institutionalized."[26] While the calculus of expenses stemming from these health problems varies between different agencies, it is undisputed that older prisoners are far more expensive than their younger counterparts. Human Rights Watch recently reported on an effort to assess the impact of age on health care costs nationally, concluding that annual health care costs for prisoners aged 55 to 59 are approximately $11,000, with the figure steadily increasing with age and reaching upwards of $40,000 for prisoners age 80 or over, while the average annual cost for the general population was only $5,482.[27] An older report stated that elderly inmates cost $60,000 per year to maintain, compared to $20,000 for younger inmates,[28] while in 2010 the ACLU estimated that elderly prisoners cost about $72,000 per year compared to $24,000 for younger prisoners.[29] Experts tend to agree that elderly inmates cost three times more than younger inmates.[30] However, after gathering information that included annual medical expenditures and previously unpublished data, Human Rights Watch concluded that older state prisoners are three to eight times more expensive than others.[31] In California, for example, inmates 55 years old and above account for about 7 percent of the prison population but consume 38 percent of medical bed resources. In Florida, inmates 50 or older, who constitute 16 percent of the prison population, account for 40.1 percent of all episodes of care and 47.9 percent of all hospital days. The medical cost per year per 65-year-old and older inmates in Georgia is $8,565; the corresponding number for younger inmates is $961. Inmates younger than 50 in Texas cost $795 in average yearly medical expenses; an average older inmate costs $4,853.

The numbers become more meaningful when taking into consideration that the financial burden is shouldered by the states; federal health insurance programs do not cover medical care for inmates. In 2012 the ACLU conducted an analysis that concluded that states would save $66,294 per year per released aging prisoner, and even on the low end, states would save at least $28,362 per aging prisoner per year after accounting for "increased parole, housing, public benefits (including health-care), and emergency room costs to the state"; these figures also take into account any increased tax revenue.[32] The original version of Medicaid law excluded offenders from receiving any health benefits upon entering prison; however, a 1997 amendment allowed Medicaid reimbursement to states for inmates' hospital stays of more than twenty-four hours, excluding them from the category "inmates" for the duration of their hospitalization.[33] Unfortunately, this reimbursement is limited to Medicaid-eligible inmates, and most would not meet the requirements even if they were on the outside (low-income juveniles, pregnant women, adults with disabilities, and frail elderly people are among the eligible).[34] Despite the availability of state reimbursement of some inmates' hospital stays for over fifteen years, as of 2011 only six states had taken advantage of the Medicaid coverage due to confusion about the law and correction agencies' lack of knowledge about the law's existence.[35]

The upcoming expansion in health coverage to anyone with an income below 133 percent of the federal poverty line may favorably change this grim bottom line; virtually all of the nation's 1.4 million state inmates, who have no income while incarcerated, would qualify for Medicaid.[36] As pointed out by the ACLU,

> The potential savings for states will be significant, since not only will corrections agencies be able to get federal reimbursement for 50 to 84 percent of outside hospitalization costs for inmates, they will also benefit from the lower fees hospitals can charge for Medicaid patients. . . . As a bonus to state corrections agencies, most inmates would be considered new to Medicaid, making them eligible for 100 percent coverage by the federal government between 2014 and 2019. After that, states would be responsible for only 10 percent of their coverage. In addition, state health insurance exchanges—which are required to be functioning by 2014—would make it easier for corrections departments to sign inmates up for the program.[37]

Nonetheless, states will still bear some economic burden associated with inmates' health care. For instance, states will have a continued obligation to provide resources for transporting inmates to and from health care service providers and employing correctional officers to accompany inmates into the community to receive medical care.

These improvements notwithstanding, the history of prison health care litigation from *Estelle v. Gamble*[38] to *Brown v. Plata*[39] is a grim reminder of how state systems struggle with providing inmates with basic health care. Litigation on behalf of inmates has invoked not only constitutional standards but also the Americans with Disabilities Act (ADA).[40] In Colorado, for example, elderly inmates have benefited from a 1997 settlement that requires reasonable accommodations for prisoners with disabilities.[41] A federal case filed in Illinois alleges the state violated the ADA when it failed to provide assistance for hearing-impaired prisoners necessary to allow their effective communication and participation in prison programs. This case also aims to benefit elderly prisoners and includes two named plaintiffs over the age of fifty-five.[42] Some issues that are beyond the constitutional and ADA mandates but that would arguably prevent more serious health problems and associated expenses may be assignment to a lower bunk, permission to take shortcuts to walk to the chow hall, or the assignment of someone to help push an inmate's wheelchair. Inmates suffering from dementia or other mental weakening may need to be treated more leniently by staff.[43]

The expense involved in housing and caring for elderly inmates highlights the need to balance the cost/risk equation. Assessing this risk has become an extremely successful subdiscipline, life-course criminology, and the general view is that people tend to "age out of crime." A Justice Department statistician stated that "age is the strongest factor in the odds of whether a person will be arrested after release. . . . [A]ge is [a stronger predictor] than what a person was arrested for and the number of years spent in jail."[44] This argument is consistently supported by research finding that age is the most reliable predictor of recidivism, verifying that inmates over the age of forty-five are only 2.1 percent likely to reoffend;[45] recidivism drops sharply after thirty-five, while inmates in their forties and fifties have the lowest levels.[46] A federal study found a recidivist rate of 15 percent for inmates over fifty-five; and in Illinois, the recidivism rate for all inmates is 42 percent, while the rate of recidivism for inmates over the age of fifty-five drops to 17 percent.[47]

In fact, one of the pressing concerns with elderly inmates is not their own violence but rather their falling prey to younger inmates; a Human Rights Watch report found that older incarcerated individuals often reported a desire *not* to share cells or dormitories with "gangbangers" and "knuckleheads" who are still "wild."[48] Elderly inmates reported "the younger ones tend to be more defiant and engage in misconduct, which prompts a tougher attitude on the part of correctional staff, which can carry over into their treatment of the older inmates."[49] On the other hand, Human Rights Watch's research also suggested that older inmates do not want to spend all of their time solely among the geriatric population. They reported, "The older men and women we interviewed appreciated the stimulation, activities, and ability to 'stay young' that come from interacting with a mixed age group."[50] A recent study of older inmates in Rhode Island found that only 9 percent of interviewed older inmates suggested the geriatric population should be in a separate unit.[51]

These data, however, are nuanced with regard to type of offense. Older inmates are more likely to be incarcerated for a violent crime than other offenders, averaging 75 percent.[52] Slightly more than half of male inmates were convicted of a violent crime, and one-third of female inmates were convicted of a violent crime.[53] In comparison, *aging* inmates tend to be in prison for low-level, nonviolent crimes.[54] For example, in Texas 65 percent of aging prisoners are in prison for nonviolent offenses (e.g., drug or property crimes); in North Carolina 26 percent of prisoners over age fifty were incarcerated under habitual offender laws and for drug crimes, while 14 percent are incarcerated for fraud, larceny, burglary, breaking and entering, traffic violations, and public order violations.[55] An abundance of evidence suggests inmates over 50 are less likely to return to prison for new crimes than their younger cohorts. In New York only 7 percent of state prisoners released between the ages of 50 and 64 returned to prison for new convictions; this number decreased to 4 percent for prisoners released at age 65 and above; in Virginia, of prisoners age 55 and above, only 1.3 percent returned to prison for a new conviction.[56] Even for geriatric parole advocates, this means grouping inmates according to the risk they pose, making some releases more justifiable and more cost-effective than others.[57]

Elderly inmates were not at the forefront of criminal justice legislation for several years, even though some individuals and organizations were calling attention to the special needs of this population. Peter Turley, founder of the Project for Older Prisoners (POPS), which supports releasing low-risk elderly inmates, noted as early as 1992, "It's no longer a question today of whether or not somebody is going to be released, the question is who."[58] The two paths most frequently advocated for addressing elderly inmates have been implementing electronic detention or establishing early release policies. The Illinois Task Force on Crime and Corrections recommended the state implement both of these alternatives in a report as early as 1993. The Task Force concluded that older prisoners pose significant cost and space problems for the Department of Corrections, and after learning of the negative correlation between age and recidivism, it even recommended the state develop a relationship with POPS to determine which of these alternatives is most appropriate for a particular inmate.[59]

States have handled the special needs and expenses of incarcerating the elderly and infirm in two main ways: specialized housing and geriatric releases. Few geriatric programs are in place for prisoners, and those that exist allow "special treatment" that amounts to little more than offering elderly people a dollop of human dignity. For example, the Central California Women's Facility (CCWF) has a

Silver Fox program for women over the age of fifty-five that gives them certain privileges, "such as being able to take shortcuts when walking from one place to the next, extra pillows and blankets, and extra time for doing laundry."[60] Due to the self-advocacy and extensive organizing efforts of elderly women housed in the CCWF, the Silver Fox program was extended in August 2011 to include a senior living unit. Inmates must be at least fifty-five years old, have no history of elder abuse or victimization, and have no history of predatory behavior while in custody.[61] This special unit is merely an existing facility that allows "privileges" not otherwise available to inmates, including "additional mattresses upon request, unlimited access to the phone, designated space in the dayroom for small plants, and the ability to purchase a fan and not have it count towards the maximum number of appliances permitted."[62] While the unit has plans to include age-sensitive programs and support groups, some important procedures were not amended for this fragile population, including being placed in cuffs and shackles when taken offsite for medical care.[63]

A more common in-prison program for elderly inmates entails consolidating them in special institutions or units. Less exposed to critique on compromising public safety, these units have numerous benefits, including protecting elderly inmates from younger, more violent inmates; reducing security costs; centralizing multidiscipline health care services targeted for the elderly; creating open space in medium- and maximum-security facilities to house higher-risk, younger inmates; and creating "an environment wherein inmates may socially interact more appropriately and possibly improve both physically and emotionally."[64] But perhaps the most compelling argument for states is the cost-saving aspect of prison-run geriatric units. The Illinois Task Force on Crime and Corrections recommended establishing a special unit for older and chronically ill inmates, arguing that doing so would result in a more effective means of operational and fiscal management.[65] The biggest cost reduction would result from decreasing the number of correctional officers assigned to a unit. Turley argues, "More than 50% of the costs of maintaining prisoners are attributed to the salaries and packages of correctional officers. Decrease the number of guards, you decrease the per capita cost of inmates."[66] A reduction in the actual cost of confining prisoners should be achieved as well since eight feet of barbed wire over massive concrete walls is not necessary to detain the old and infirm. As Turley puts it, "Although a geriatric prisoner may still be a risk for a given category of crime, he is unlikely to toss his walker over a razor-wired fence or outrun perimeter guards."[67]

In addition, specialized geriatric units have the potential to significantly decrease health care costs because a smaller, specialized staff is more likely to catch the early onset of health issues, and inmates are more likely to receive the preventive care that their community counterparts receive. Specialized staff could identify the symptoms of chronic illnesses like heart disease, diabetes, and hepatitis;

and they would be better suited to identify sudden cognitive or physical changes such as confusion or changes in weight or appetite, which would signal that the older inmate must receive immediate medical attention. While the primary concern is the elderly prisoners' health condition, another concern is catching chronic conditions early so that they do not result in expensive long-term care.[68]

It is difficult to determine whether states have specific programs in place for elderly inmates, because most surveys do not include detailed questions and because there is no consistency among states in their responses to broad survey questions. For example, a 2001 survey by the Criminal Justice Institute asked state correctional systems whether they designated special housing areas or facilities for elderly inmates; in some states, like Texas, Louisiana, Idaho, Mississippi, and New York, placement in special units depends on medical condition.[69] A newer survey, conducted in 2008 and designed to include more detailed questions,[70] revealed that a majority of states have not created facilities specifically dedicated to managing older prisoners. Six states (15 percent) reported they had a dedicated prison for older offenders; thirteen states (32 percent) reported units dedicated to older prisoners; and nine states (22 percent) have dedicated medical facilities for the care of older prisoners. Only five state systems (11 percent) have a dedicated nursing home facility secured for older prisoners, and only eight states (20 percent) report having dedicated hospice facilities. This survey, too, should be regarded with caution, as different states have different definitions of "dedicated facility." Alabama, for example, considers all thirteen of its facilities infirmaries because it dedicates two hundred of its available beds to the "old and infirm." A closer look at the reporting states reveals that only a minority of thems housed elderly inmates in units in which staff were especially trained in medical and mental health concerns of the elderly and that while some states have what they refer to as "assisted living" facilities, others merely designate a number of beds to the elderly.

The other cost-effective solution to the incarceration of elderly inmates is releasing them into the community. One way of doing so is by using electronic detention, a policy whose efficiency stems from the ability to reduce the cost of human supervision and detention through technology. According to a 2006 assessment, placing a prisoner in an electronic detention program "can reduce the daily costs of incarceration from $65 a day to roughly $10."[71] Those inmates who are physically capable of working are ordered to obtain employment as a condition of their parole and must pay a percentage of their earnings to reimburse the state for their housing costs.[72]

The conditions of participating in an electronic detention program would likely mimic those recommended by the Illinois Task Force on Crime and Corrections. Elderly inmates must pass a stringent risk assessment analysis, and those serving time for sex crimes would be automatically excluded, based on the argument that sex offenders have high rates of recidivism.[73] The Task Force recommended that the state allow elderly inmates to participate in the electronic detention program for up to the last two years of their sentence, but other states could implement more liberal time restrictions to further reduce the cost of incarceration.[74] As suggested in Illinois, states could foster POPS programs at law schools, which would transfer the responsibility of risk assessment analysis to law students eager to gain real-life case experience. Law students assigned to elderly prisoners would have a significant amount of time to dedicate to their case to accurately assess whether an elderly inmate is a good candidate for an electronic detention program. The POPS program claims a 0 percent recidivism rate and includes helping inmates gain access to social programs like Social Security and disability or veterans' benefits.[75] Unfortunately, since many elderly inmates have lost contact with the outside world and do not have access to housing on the outside, about half of those who qualify for the program are ultimately rejected because they have no place to go for their detention.[76]

At the end of 2009, fifteen states and the District of Columbia had provisions for geriatric release, and in 2010, South Carolina joined the ranks by permitting parole for geriatric inmates in its Omnibus Crime Reduction and Sentencing Reform Act of 2010. These provisions, however, have not been used to the full extent in which they were intended.[77] An inmate release coordinator at a Nevada prison noted that while processing releases for parole based primarily on inmates' terminal illnesses, "only rarely was one of these inmates not severely incapacitated to the extent of confinement to a wheelchair or to total reliance on others for physical assistance. These inmates were close to death and their release to their families seemed to be one of common sense and moral justification."[78]

States vary in their geriatric and medical release policies.[79] Some states' statutes specifically target the elderly and define age as an eligibility requirement, while others focus on other criteria like medical incapacitation. There are thirty-nine states that have release policies specific to medical conditions that apply only to prisoners who are severely or terminally ill, regardless of their age.[80] Although all states have eligibility requirements for their geriatric parole program, some states define eligibility more broadly, which gives more discretion to releasing authorities such as parole boards. Other states have specific, narrower eligibility requirements that obligate releasing authorities to make affirmative findings before releasing an inmate. Most states require that inmates have some physical condition, chronic infirmity, illness, or disease related to their increased age or that inmates are completely incapacitated or in need of long-term care.[81]

Eligibility for geriatric release in some states—Maryland, Virginia, and Wisconsin, for example—does not require a medical condition. Instead, these states set thresholds for age and minimum length of sentence served. Tina Chiu writes in "Prison Culture," "In Maryland, eligible prisoners must be 65 and have served at least 15 years of their sentence. In Virginia and Wisconsin, people 65 and older must serve five years and those 60 to 64 must serve 10 years before applying for geriatric release."[82] On the other hand, some states do not specify age at all but instead make age-related physical or mental debilitation an eligibility requirement. For example, Missouri "requires that inmates be sufficiently 'advanced in age' that they are 'in need of long-term nursing home care.' Wyoming allows medical parole for inmates who are 'incapacitated by age to the extent that deteriorating physical or mental health substantially diminishes' their ability to take care of themselves in a prison setting."[83]

The procedures by which older prisoners may be released from prison vary across states as well. Some policies require specific conditions on release, like housing restrictions or periodic medical exams.[84] Other policies lay out automatic revocation policies in the event that an older former prisoner's health improves; and almost all policies identify the agency authorized to make release recommendations, like a corrections department official, the parole board, or a medical examiner.[85]

As mentioned above, states apply different definitions of "elderly" in their geriatric parole programs. Most experts agree that inmates' institutional age must be considered when drafting their policies to make them effective. There tends to be a rough consensus that considering inmates as young as 45 "elderly" is inappropriate because the rate of recidivism has not sufficiently fallen for this age group and 65 is too old because many inmates' health has already declined rapidly by this point. Age 50 to 60 seems to be the common middle ground that most states use to determine eligibility for early release programs.[86] There are outliers, though: Louisiana has set the age of eligibility at 45,[87] and South Carolina has defined age 70 as "geriatric."[88]

The U.S. Census Bureau does not consider institutional age, defining the "elderly" population as those 65 and older, but the National Commission on Health Care uses age 55 to define "elderly" inmates.[89] According to the 2008 survey that identified state prison facilities specifically dedicated to the elderly, at least twenty-seven states have a definition of "older prisoner." According to the survey, fifteen states used 50 years old; five states used age 55 as the cutoff; four states used 60; two states used 65; and one state used 70.[90] Although not included in the response to this survey, a 2010 Louisiana statute uses age 45 to define "geriatric."[91]

Early release policies have other eligibility requirements that exclude many otherwise qualified candidates. For example, many states make inmates with violent or sex offense convictions and those serving life sentences ineligible for geriatric parole. In some states, applicants are not eligible until they have served a minimum length or percentage of their sentence.

These exclusions are significant for a number of reasons. First they exclude the majority of geriatric parole policies' target population. Older prisoners are more likely to be serving time for violent or sex crimes and are also more likely to have life sentences. In fact, 75 percent of older offenders have been convicted of a violent crime and are therefore ineligible for most geriatric parole programs.[92] The Kansas, Maine, and Washington, DC, Departments of Corrections are among the only institutions that allow parole to inmates based solely on their medical condition.[93] Most other states' geriatric parole policies exclude the majority of the group it seeks to include, explaining their limited application. For example, a 2003 study of inmates 50 and older in Pennsylvania found that "older prisoners were more likely to have been incarcerated for serious offenses, including rape, murder, robber, aggravated assault, and burglary; 66% were serving maximum sentences of 10 years or more, with 21% serving life sentences."[94] A 2006 study in North Carolina reported that "almost 60% of inmates age 50 and older were serving sentences for violent or sex crimes . . . [and] [m]ost were serving a sentence of life or of 10 years to life."[95] The purpose of geriatric parole policies is to release low-risk, elderly offenders in an effort to reduce incarceration costs, but exclusions built into these policies indicate that considerations of punishment outweigh considerations of correctional cost savings or the negative correlation between age and recidivism.[96]

Second, states' geriatric parole policies that require "grave" physical conditions or terminal illness significantly limit the number of elderly inmates who qualify for early release. "Washington State, for instance, released only 22 prisoners in five years under its original 'extraordinary medical placement' statute, which sanctioned such placement only for those inmates who are physically incapacitated due to age or a medical condition."[97] This harsh restriction made the statute practically useless and prompted the legislature to amend it in 2009, modifying the eligibility criteria to include inmates who are not yet infirm but will likely be physically incapacitated at the time of their release.[98] These modifications can translate into huge cost savings for the state. Washington projected that under its new law forty-four elderly offenders would be released between 2009 and 2011, saving the state an estimated $1.5 million.[99]

The federal government also has a procedure for releasing old and infirm inmates, though the procedure is more controversial than the policy itself. In 1984 the Sentencing Reform Act (SRA) abolished parole and instituted determinate sentencing; however, the law includes "safety valves" that authorize federal courts to reduce sentences in a few specific situations.[100] One of these situations is compassionate release, whereby courts can reduce sentences for "extraordinary and compelling reasons."[101]

Congress established the United States Sentencing Commission (USSC) to create sentencing guidelines and determine what should be considered "extraordinary and compelling" reasons for a sentence reduction.[102] After receiving a strongly worded letter from the U.S. Department of Justice, warning against the adoption of a policy inconsistent with the Board of Parole's (BOP) narrow interpretation of compassionate release,[103] in 2007 the USSC issued guidelines[104] to the courts that essentially restate the statute and add that courts should not release prisoners if doing so would pose a threat to public safety.[105] However, the notes accompanying the USSC's guidelines recognize a range of medical and nonmedical situations that may constitute "extraordinary and compelling" reasons for release, including the following: if the offender is suffering from a terminal illness, a permanent physical or medical condition, deteriorating physical or mental health because of aging that substantially diminished the ability of the offender to provide self-care in prison and there is no promise of improvement.[106] Despite this directive, the BOP has never instructed its staff to use the USSC guidelines in determining whether an offender is eligible for compassionate release. When questioned by Human Rights Watch, BOP officials simply stated that the guidelines are not binding on them.[107]

The SRA gave federal courts the authority to determine whether an offender qualifies for a reduced sentence through compassionate release.[108] The act also directs courts to consider enumerated factors such as the purposes of punishment, the seriousness of the crime, and protection of the public.[109] Offenders play a surprisingly small role in this process because the law does not permit them to petition the courts for consideration of compassionate release directly. Instead, only the BOP has the authority to file motions with federal courts requesting judicial consideration of compassionate release. Human Rights Watch noted that the number of prisoners who have requested the BOP to make motions on their behalf is unknown because the BOP does not keep these records, but it is rare for the BOP to make such a request: "The federal prison system houses over 218,000 prisoners, yet in 2011, the BOP filed only 30 motions for early release, and between January 1 and November 15, 2012, it filed 37. Since 1992, the annual average number of prisoners who received compassionate release has been less than two dozen."[110] Not only is the number of motions very small, the percentage of motions over the past almost thirty years has not been consistent; that is, even though the federal prison population grew from 95,034 in 1994 to 218,170 in 2011, the number of motions for sentence reduction only increased from 23 to 30.[111] The lack of motions for sentence reductions based on compassionate release is not happenstance: the BOP insists that it has complete discretion in filing motions and has chosen to reject almost all requests.[112]

By refusing to submit motions to federal courts, the BOP is usurping the role of federal judges to make determinations of early release based on "extraordinary and compelling" reasons, as the SRA authorizes. The BOP should serve an administrative function to vet cases that do not fit within the act or the USSC's guidelines. The SRA instructed the *court* to consider the purpose of punishment, the seriousness of the crime, and the protection of the public. In practice, it is the BOP that is making these determinations, despite Congress's conflicting directive. For example, "BOP officials often conclude a dying prisoner should not be permitted to spend his final months with his family because he is still physically capable of committing a crime if released, however unlikely the prospect that he would do so."[113] The BOP's tainting of this process is much more than a procedural, technical error; rather, it strips offenders of basic human rights and due process, which requires that independent entities make criminal justice decisions and not law enforcement officers who are clearly partial. The BOP often consults the district attorney or attorney general before making a decision; it does not provide a hearing in which the offender can present his or her case or even inform the offender of information it has obtained, denying the offender an opportunity to defend himself or herself.[114] While an offender can appeal a warden's denial, practically any appeals up the BOP chain "are doomed; in 2011, for example, the BOP Central Office did not grant any administrative appeals in compassionate release cases."[115] Courts do not even review BOP decisions, as the Justice Department has successfully persuaded most courts that they lack the authority to do so.[116]

Fortunately, Human Rights Watch reports some promising signs of change: "the BOP has created an internal working group to look at its compassionate release program," and the new director of the BOP has claimed an interest in reforming the program.[117] With a new director in place, it is to be hoped that the number of motions for compassionate release will increase, along with the human rights of prisoners who are too infirm and frail to withstand prison life.

Tina Chiu of the Vera Institute of Justice identified four factors that explain the difference between the stated intent and the actual impact of geriatric release laws: political considerations and public opinion; narrow eligibility criteria; procedures that discourage inmates from applying for release; and complicated and lengthy referral and review processes.[118]

It is baffling that so many state policy makers push for geriatric parole policies to reduce incarceration costs but then do little to ensure that the policies are structured and implemented in a way that actually cuts spending. Some states have not released a single prisoner under its geriatric release law, for example, Oklahoma and Maryland (as of early 2009).[119] Other states have released fewer than a handful of prisoners under their policy: between 2001 and 2008, Colorado released just three prisoners; Oregon has not released more than two prisoners per year;[120] between 2001 and 2007, Virginia released only four inmates;[121] and between 1999 and 2008, New Mexico released thirty-five prisoners, a relatively higher number, but this was in combination with its medical program, and the number of elderly prisoners is not clear.[122] Missouri seems to have released the most prisoners under its policy, which applies to terminally ill inmates in addition to elderly inmates. Between 1998 and 2008, the state released 236 inmates, many of which were probably terminally ill, as at least 64 percent of these individuals have died since being released.[123]

A number of factors contribute to the relatively low impact geriatric release mechanisms have on states' elderly inmate populations. Many provisions of state geriatric parole policies make them less effective or efficient. For example, the statutes narrowly define eligibility and create broad exceptions, as noted earlier, or procedural issues may cause confusion or delays. Four contributing factors may be restricting the number of older inmates that states release: political considerations and public opinion, narrow eligibility requirements, application procedures, and referral and review processes.

Advocating for the early release of an inmate can be political suicide, even if doing so would result in considerable correctional cost savings. Despite evidence of older prisoners "aging out" of crime, the public may want to follow through with punishment even if they believe the inmate is no longer a threat to society. An inmate's poor health may not sway public opinion either. For example, "a Mansfield University survey of Pennsylvania residents in 2004 found that only 45% of respondents favored the early release to parole for chronically or terminally ill inmates, even if they posed no threat to society."[124]

Other opponents of geriatric release policies are concerned about whether correctional cost savings is actually *government* cost savings. In other words, they are concerned that only part of the fiscal picture is painted during geriatric parole policy debates, and much of the expense for caring for this population will simply shift to other state agencies, like Social Security and Medicare.[125] For other groups, like victim's rights groups, no amount of illness or money saved can tip the scale of justice. As Will Marling, executive director of the National Organization for Victim Assistance, said, "If a person is sentenced to life, we know they are naturally going to get old. A life sentence should mean life."[126]

As discussed above, narrow eligibility and broad exclusions, like older age restrictions and disqualifying violent felons and lifers, make the number of qualified candidates for geriatric release sharply decrease. Currently, there is a direct overlap in the group of people these policies target to offer early release and the group of people they make ineligible for release. If policy makers really want to see geriatric parole policies and their potential cost savings realized, these eligibility requirements must be given a critical reevaluation.

Some application procedures are so complicated they may discourage older prisoners from even seeking release. First, many of the eligibility requirements are too complex for some older prisoners to understand, so many likely do not know whether they are eligible. For example, in Virginia, offenders cannot be convicted of a Class 1 felony and must have served at least ten years of their sentence if they are sixty years old but must only serve five years if they are sixty-five.[127] Second, the application procedure for early release is often difficult to navigate. In Virginia applicants must apply to the Virginia Parole Board for consideration of geriatric release, but relatively few actually do so. In 2004 only about 10 percent of eligible inmates applied (39 of 375), and in 2007 about the same percentage of eligible inmates applied (52 of 500).[128] Part of the reluctance is likely because inmates are automatically considered for parole each year after they are eligible for discretionary parole release, but an inmate forfeits this automatic parole hearing if he seeks geriatric parole because the board refuses to hear both cases. Thus only inmates who are not eligible for discretionary parole have an incentive to apply for geriatric parole.[129]

The application procedure for consideration of the federal compassionate release program is problematic as well. There, a concern is mounting regarding prisoners' knowledge that such a program exists. To apply for consideration of compassionate release in the federal system, inmates must petition the warden to file a motion on their behalf in district court. Program Statement 5050.46, the BOP document that governs compassionate release, instructs prisoners to explain the circumstances he or she believes justifies compassionate release in their case but does not provide an explanation of what the BOP will consider as "extraordinary and compelling" reasons for compassionate release.[130] After interviewing numerous current and former prisoners, Human Rights Watch concluded that there is confusion as to the eligibility requirements for compassionate release.[131] The BOP claims that a copy of Program Statement 5050.46 is available to all prisoners via the Electronic Library, but it seems to be of little practical help. Further, prisoner handbooks seem to be useless in this area: in a random review of ten handbooks, Human Rights Watch did not even find a reference to compassionate release.[132]

The application procedure is yet another area policy makers should focus on to make geriatric and compassionate release policies serve their purpose to release low-risk prisoners and save the system a considerable amount of money. It is unlikely that these policies will reach their full potential unless practical barriers are removed and accurate information is disseminated to prisoners. The process of referral and review is often complex and difficult to understand. It usually includes identifying potentially eligible inmates, gathering information in support of an application for the parole board's (or another releasing authority) review, and developing a reentry plan that includes securing housing and medical care in the community.

According to the *Birmingham News,* several qualified inmates died while waiting for the Board of Pardons and Paroles to decide their parole applications. As a result, Alabama attempted to expedite release proceedings by specifying a time frame for the Board of Pardons and Paroles to decide whether qualified inmates would be granted medical or geriatric parole.[133] After several failed attempts to change the paroling process, in 2008 the legislature created a discretionary medical furlough program, administered by the Department of Corrections. Geriatric inmates are now eligible for medical furlough, but even under this program, releases can be time-consuming: as of August 2009, only three inmates had been released under the statute.[134]

In Texas a review of staffing and the referral process resulted in expanded use of geriatric or medical release and more efficient procedures. In 1991 the Texas legislature created the Medically Recommended Intensive Supervision (MRIS) program to allow for the early release of nonviolent offenders who are deemed not to be a risk to society because of their medical conditions. Under the program, the Texas Correctional Office for Offenders with Mental or Medical Impairments (TCOOMMI) identifies inmates who are "elderly, physically disabled, mentally ill, terminally ill, or mentally retarded" and recommends their cases to the Board of Pardons and Paroles (BPP). As a result of declining approval rates in 2002, a management audit was conducted that found that staff resources were insufficient to process referrals, complete interviews, compile relevant medical information, and coordinate case presentations to the parole board, which resulted in significant delays. In response to this problem, TCOOMMI contracted the Department of Aging and Disability Services (DADS) to provide case management services. The DADS staff conducts all prerelease interviews, handles federal entitlement applications, and coordinates postrelease services, including placement in nursing homes, hospices, or other facilities.[135] To ensure that staff make timely referrals for offenders with terminal illnesses or long-term care needs, TCOOMMI also made unit physicians responsible for initiating referrals.[136]

Chiu notes that only a few states regularly examine their use of parole for elderly offenders and modify procedures based on continual analysis, but those that do are in a better position to maximize their use of release mechanisms for older prisoners, resulting in increased cost savings.

The financial and moral dilemmas involved in caregiving for elderly inmates becomes even more complicated since medical release is not necessarily a path to humane and affordable care. Elderly people recently released from prison often lack access to other individuals to assist in daily routines, such as prison staff or other inmates, and need to learn how to navigate transportation to attend medical appointments.[137] Older prisoners may face difficulties obtaining support from friends and family. Nationwide, likely 63 percent to 88 percent of formerly incarcerated people of all ages live with a friend or family member upon their release,[138] but, as a 2006 study suggests, this figure may not represent the situation for elderly inmates, many of whom express concern about their postrelease housing situation and fear becoming homeless.[139] Older prisoners convicted of sexual offenses express concern for their personal safety once released from prison.[140] Long periods of confinement can strip people of their connections with the outside world. Familial relationships and friendships may cease to exist, either because of the nature of the offense that led to a lengthy sentence or because of the lengthy sentence itself. The lack of these relationships compounds the difficulty elderly former prisoners face when reintegrating into society.[141]

Finding stable housing may be one of the biggest obstacles, to the point that states considering geriatric parole are exploring the option of constructing special nursing homes for formerly incarcerated elderly people.[142] And finding employment, one of the major barriers to successful reentry,[143] is particularly difficult for elderly inmates, who may not have worked a steady job, acquired skills that would serve them in a changing market,[144] or maintained basic health that would enable them to work menial jobs.[145]

Formerly incarcerated elderly people are mentally and physically fragile; one report notes that "the risk of dying for former inmates is sharply increased in the [two] weeks immediately following release, with drug overdose, cardiovascular disease, homicide, and suicide as the leading causes of death."[146] Their fragility is compounded by institutional dependency, making it harder to adjust to life on the outside;[147] in interviews conducted with older inmates in England, researchers found that older inmates "doubted their ability to make independent decisions and, in many respects, viewed the prison as home."[148]

These abundant difficulties are hard to overcome for elderly inmates, many of whom prefer to remain in prison rather than be released into nursing homes or a strained family situation. One inmate, Chris Ballard, who had been in prison since 1993 and was seventy-seven at the time, stated that he is fine where he is: "I'd be a burden on my kids. I'd rather be a burden to these people."[149]

AGE, BURDEN, RISK, AND COST:
REFORMING THREE STRIKES

A more benign manifestation of the inmate-as-burden humonetarian discourse involves the 2012 amendment of California's Three Strikes Law, enacted by a significant majority of Californians in 1994.[150] Viscerally reacting to a heinous crime, voters approved the most extreme version of a habitual offender law, sentencing second strikers to a double sentence and Third Strikers to a minimum sentence of twenty-five years to life. Although crimes must be considered "serious or violent" felonies to qualify as a first or second strike, prior to the passage of Proposition 36, any subsequent felony qualified as a third strike. The Three Strikes Reform Act of 2012, or Prop. 36, states in Section I, Paragraph 4, that the "act will save hundreds of millions of taxpayer dollars every year for at least ten years. The state will no longer pay for housing or long-term health care for elderly, low-risk, non-violent inmates serving life sentences for minor crimes."[151] Proposition 36 was passed by a 69.3 percent majority vote, close to the majority that voted for the original law,[152] and amended the Three Strikes Law to require that a crime be "serious or violent" to qualify as a third strike.

As in the case of the marijuana legalization and death penalty abolition campaigns, the Committee for Three Strikes Reform, which spearheaded California's Proposition 36 initiative, was endorsed by dozens of law enforcement leaders and other groups, including Republican Los Angeles District Attorney Steve Cooley, elected officials, newspapers, civil rights organizations, municipals, law school deans, and community, state, and national leaders.[153] According to campaign manager Pedro

Rosado, the campaign sought to avoid the mistakes made during a previous reform attempt in 2004, which focused on abstract arguments about justice and fairness.[154] Instead, the campaign maintained tight focus on the three key points that yielded a positive response from voters in preelection polls:[155] the elimination of life sentences for nonviolent offenders; the restoration of the original intent and core purpose of the Three Strikes Law, namely, to keep dangerous and violent criminals behind bars; and the projected savings of $100 million per year to fund schools, prevent crime, and decrease the need for tax increases.[156]

The Prop 36 campaign is a particularly interesting example of a recession-era campaign that consciously chose not to focus on the humonetarian argument as the crux of reform. However, the campaign materials consistently addressed the cost/risk equation. The risk side of the equation was addressed by the Stanford Three Strikes Project, staffed by law students and devoted to addressing excessive sentences imposed under Three Strikes,[157] which publicly advocated for the proposition by highlighting its clients' "success stories."[158] These stories recrafted the public perception of Third Strikers, not as dangerous criminals in need of confinement, but as worthy objects of compassion and leniency, suffering from personal histories of child abuse, mental illness, drug addictions, and homelessness. In order to change the narrative in this fashion, "students track[ed] down clients' old files, ask[ed] about their childhoods and pr[ied] confirmation out of family members."[159] Using these factors, the Project has petitioned for the custodial release of nonviolent offenders by showing that punishment has been more than fulfilled for the petty offenses that made up these offenders' third strike—some so insignificant as stealing from a church's soup kitchen.[160] The director of the Stanford project, Michael Romano, has found a strong link between lengthy habitual offender and incarceration, commenting, "'In my experience, every person who has been sentenced to life in prison for a non-serious, non-violent crime like petty theft suffers from some kind of mental illness or impairment—from organic brain disorders, to schizophrenia, to mental retardation, to severe P.T.S.D.'"[161] The Committee for Three Strikes Reform openly collaborated with the Stanford Three Strikes Project. Well aware that concern about elderly and infirm inmates was "not a tipping point" for voters, many of whom were apathetic about the fate of inmates who were perceived to deserve their incarceration regardless of the price tag,[162] the Committee deferred to the Project's information about profiles of inmates wrongfully imprisoned under the Three Strikes Law[163] and relied on their recrafted perception of the offenders as lower-risk victims of their circumstances. The cost half of the cost/risk equation was addressed by the campaign committee in its materials, according to which the "average cost of a general population inmate [was] $41,849 per year," while the "average cost of a three strikes inmate [was] $50,105 per year, increase due to maximum security housing and increased medical needs."[164]

Proposition 36 received widespread media attention, primarily in the form of editorial support. Mirroring the Committee for Three Strikes Reform's campaign platform, the media typically characterized Proposition 36 in terms of the cost/risk equation, combining the waste of precious resources with the injustice of harshly punishing a lower-risk subset of the habitual offender population. Most newspaper articles supporting the proposition reprinted some variation of the Legislative Analyst's Report's prediction,[165] according to which "state correctional savings from [Prop. 36] would likely be around $70 million annually, with even higher savings—up to $90 million annually—over the next couple of decades."[166] Some periodicals pointed to more specific areas of reduced spending that Prop 36 would permit.

The nonpartisan California Legislative Analyst's Office estimates that Proposition 36 would save $70 million to $90 million a year. Most of the savings will result from the fact that some prisoners will no longer be incarcerated at the cost of $40,000 or more per year.[167]

Currently, untold numbers of inmates whose third strike was for non-violent drug possession are serving life sentences. This is a waste of money. Our priorities as a society are backward when we spend increasing amounts of money on incarceration and less and less on education.[168]

Prop. 36 doesn't let those third-strike criminals completely off the hook. A non-violent third strike would earn a sentence twice what such an offense would normally draw—while saving taxpayers an estimated $100 million over the next decade.[169]

Nor is the existing approach to three strikes always an effective use of public resources. Long terms for petty crimes adds to the crowding in state prisons which has bloated corrections costs and brought expensive court mandates.[170]

Locking up petty criminals who have no history of violent crimes for 25 years or more is . . . far too costly.[171]

If voters eventually approve the initiative, backers believe that about 3,000 of the 4,000 nonviolent third strikers currently serving time in state prisons could be eligible for resentencing, which could save taxpayers $150 million to $200 million a year.[172]

There was a problem with this state's version of three strikes that has led to . . . a huge waste of taxpayer money. Unlike in other states, the third felony conviction—or strike, triggering a sentence of 25 years to life—does not need to be a serious or violent offense.[173]

We choose to believe that voters who supported the original intention of three strikes realize locking up drug addicts for life because they are repeat offenders is both unfair and costly. . . . In the 18 years since three strikes became law, California also has faced prison overcrowding issues exacerbated by the 4,000 non-violent offenders locked up for third strikes at a cost of about $140 million a year.[174]

Some newspaper editorials made the inmate-as-burden argument more obvious, highlighting the age of Third Strikers and the medical expenses involved in incarcerating them.

Many prison-years are now served by inmates beyond the end of their criminal careers—of the 8,872 current third-strike inmates, about 4,300 are over 50 years old. The money we would save is desperately needed for other services in our state.[175]

Opponents say the Three Strikes law has led to the drop in the crime rate, and we agree that it is one of the many reasons for reduced crime. But this adjustment in the Three Strikes law makes sense.[176]

While no price should be put on justice, stopping wasteful government spending is another reason to support Prop. 36. When the U.S. Supreme Court in 2011 ordered the state to reduce its prison population by 30,000 inmates, it began releasing non-violent offenders. Unfortunately, those getting released are more violent than many third-strikers who are ineligible for release but are elderly, frail and ill, less of a public threat than many younger inmates being released. . . . It's unfortunate that any inmate must be released early. But as long as that's the order of the high court, it should be done fairly, sensibly and cost-effectively. That's not happening now. Make Three Strikes better and vote for Prop. 36.[177]

According to the Legislative Analyst's Office, of the approximately 9,000 third-strikers in California prisons, about 2,800 would be eligible to have their sentences reconsidered. Most of those men and women have been in prison for a very long time and are now into middle age and beyond, and some are quite infirm. Before they could be considered for release, they would have to petition their sentencing judge, who would have to determine that they no longer represent a threat to public safety. Several hundred aging ex-convicts judged not to be dangerous, spread across the state of California, seems an unlikely catalyst for a crime wave.[178]

Solutions to prison overcrowding include releasing elderly prisoners: Many studies show that people over the age of 50 rarely commit new crimes. We need sentencing reform, such as removing mandatory minimums from sentences, increasing good time credits and releasing the inmates who are eligible under Prop. 36, the three-strikes reform bill.[179]

Some campaign endorsements focused on mentally ill inmates as well, though these commentaries highlighted the injustice of lengthy incarceration and did not mention costs explicitly.

The resentencing process is shaping up as a kind of referendum on the state's barbaric treatment of mentally ill defendants, who make up a substantial number of those with life sentences under the three-strikes rule. It is likely that many were too mentally impaired to assist their lawyers at the time of trial. . . . Mentally ill inmates are nearly always jailed for behaviors related to their illness. Nationally, they account for about one-sixth of the prison population. The ratio appears to be higher among three-strike lifers in California. According to a 2011 analysis of state data by Stanford Law School's Three Strikes Project, nearly 40 percent of [three-strike lifers] qualify as mentally ill and are receiving psychiatric services behind bars. Nearly all had been abused as children, . . . had been homeless for extended periods, and many were illiterate. None [of the three strikers represented by the Stanford Clinic] had graduated from high school. In other words, these were discarded people who could be made to bear the brunt of this brutal law without risk of public backlash.[180]

22% of [the] general prison population inmates [are] designated as mentally ill, [while] 38% of Three Strikes prisoners [are] designated as mentally ill.[181]

But these statements were accompanied by more general statements pointing to the social injustices caused by the Three Strikes Law. Minor offenses such as stealing a "pair of socks or fall[ing] off the wagon of their 12-step program" resulted in a life sentence.[182] Beyond the general injustice identified, some effort was made to document the disproportionate impact of the Three Strikes Law on disadvantaged groups: racial minorities, the homeless, the mentally ill, and those suffering from abuse and trauma.

Under the law, judges must impose sentences of 25 years to life for people who are convicted of two violent or serious crimes and who then commit a third felony, regardless of what that third felony is. Serious and violent criminals deserve harsh sentences. But individuals who commit petty crimes on their third strike end up with sentences far in excess of what is fair.[183]

While Californians continue to support three strikes, which mandates a prison sentence of 25 years to life for offenders convicted of a third 'strike,' many who otherwise support the law are concerned that a non-serious, non-violent third conviction potentially can send an offender away for the rest of his life. Proposition 36, the Three-Strikes Reform Act, would address that concern.[184]

Arbitrarily harsh sentences for less serious, nonviolent crimes trample on American ideals of fair and objective justice. Matching punishment to the seriousness of the offense does not go soft on crime, but rather bolsters public confidence that the justice system operates without bias or malice.[185]

We are under no illusion that if voters approve Proposition 36, some felons who would face lesser sentences will commit other crimes. But locking up petty criminals who have no history of violent crimes for 25 years or more is fundamentally unfair.[186]

There was a problem with this state's version of three strikes that has led to gross injustices.[187]

Similar to the death penalty debate, a few statements highlighted the racial injustice of the Three Strikes Law.

Proposition 36 would also reduce racial disparities. African-Americans constitute only 6 percent of California's population, but among prison inmates, they made up

34 percent of second strikers and 44 percent of third-strikers. Even when offenses and criminal records are controlled, African Americans face 47 percent higher odds of third-strike sentences than whites. The greatest black-white differences in Three Strikes sentencing rates are observed for property and drug offenses. Amending Three Strikes to remove non-violent and non-serious crimes from the offenses that can trigger a third-strike sentence would not eliminate racial disparity, but would reduce it substantially. This would increase the legitimacy of our criminal justice system, particularly among minorities.[188]

Consider: Nearly 8,900 three-strikers are in prison in California, with 3,500 of them serving life sentences. A disproportionate 46 percent of three-strikers are African American.[189]

The California State Auditor's 2010 report on the fiscal impact of the Three Strikes Law found that "striker inmates . . . were sentenced on average to an additional nine years of incarceration due to the three strikes law,"[190] The report further concluded that "these additional years represent $19.2 billion in additional costs over the duration of the sentences of current striker inmates."[191] A subsequent report from 2010 estimated that $7.5 of the $19.2 billion in additional striker expenses are attributable to strikers who are currently imprisoned under felonies that are not strikes.[192]

The May 2010 report noted that health care is a significant contributor to the cost of housing inmates, and older inmates are generally more costly.[193] It found that $427 million of the $529 million spent on specialty health care is attributable to only 30 percent of the inmates receiving such care.[194] Further, of the inmates who incurred "more than $5,000 in specialty care costs," 63 percent were forty years of age or older, "even though this age group only represents 41 percent of all inmates."[195]

In addition to finding that health care costs increase with age and the oldest inmates were the most costly on average, the report found that striker inmates' health care costs were 13 percent more than the average nonstriker inmates' costs. Here, one should note that strikers are growing nine years older behind bars than their nonstriker counterparts due to Three Strikes' harsh sentencing requirements.[196]

The report recommended that the California Department of Corrections and Rehabilitation "explore methods of reducing the costs of medical care to the State, including those of inmates with high medical costs."[197] It further suggested that "[t]hese efforts could include proposing a review of the program that allows for the early release of terminally ill or medically incapacitated inmates."[198] The State Auditor noted that Corrections' Health Care Services concurred with the report's findings and recommendations but "also chose not to address them specifically."[199]

The Legislative Analyst's Office (LAO) estimated that Prop 36 could save California more than $100 million per year by reducing costs related to prison and parole operations.[200] The LAO noted, however, that Prop 36 could result in costs to local and state governments, including government-paid health care for released offenders who do not have private health insurance and other forms of government-funded medical care. Also, if a released offender were to reoffend, costs could arise from victim-related expenses. It is possible that any costs would be compensated by released offenders as they become taxpaying citizens.[201]

The campaign also benefited from the support of the California secretary of state, who, in the official voting brochure, raised savings issues in favor of Three Strikes reform.[202] These were, specifically, the benefits of diverting law enforcement resources spent on nonviolent offenders, as well as resources spent on their health care, to the prosecution and incarceration of violent and repeat offenders; projected savings of over $100 million every year to fund schools, fight crime, and reduce the state's budget deficit; and opening up prison space for truly violent and dangerous felons. These arguments notably framed nonviolent Third Strikers as the high-cost, low-risk category, distinguishing them from the potentially violent inmates whose confinement is worthy of the expenditure.

Like the humonetarian campaigns to abolish the death penalty and legalize marijuana examined in chapter 4, the advocacy for Proposition 36 did not make savings its sole focus. Nonetheless, the coverage and political debate surrounding the proposition show a retreat from the perception of Third Strikers as dangerous individuals who should be incapacitated at any price and a willingness to recalculate the cost/risk equation to resentence and release high-cost, low-risk Third Strikers.

THE NEW CLIENTS: "PAY TO STAY" AND THE BURDEN/CONSUMER

The previous examples addressed policies and campaigns that focused on specific categories of inmates as unnecessary financial burdens, effectively acting against the punitive trend. But cost-centered discourse has also operated in more sinister ways, by encouraging a perverse perception of inmates as customers, who can and should be made to internalize not only the cost of their crime (the pains of imprisonment) but also the cost of their punishment. This model manifests itself in the growth of pay-to-stay institutions, mostly local jails, in which some or all inmates foot the bill for their own incarceration, either during their sentence or after their release. Far from being a model that encourages free agency and accountability, it pits taxpayers against inmates, taking the state and the excesses of mass incarceration out of the cost/risk equation.

The idea of rolling costs onto the inmates themselves, a classic product of neoliberal thinking, was the brainchild of resource-stripped local jails long before the economic downturn. Kirsten Livingston's 2007 survey of such practices reveals that as early as the late 1980s the criminal justice system was already levying costs on inmates, including payments for victim compensation, court security. and probation fees.[203] The early 2000s saw the introduction of new fees, such as for electronic monitoring, sex offender registration, and, shockingly, room and board, as well as an increase in existing fees. In the early 2000s inmates were saddled with the costs of their diversion programs, and Livingston mentions cases of inmates doing time for debts incurred to the criminal justice system. These problematic aspects of "pay as you stay" have become worse in the recession: fueled by panic about the impact of the California Realignment on local jails, Riverside Jail and other county institutions are recurring to room-and-board fees to the tune of $140 per night to cover the expected costs from the addition to their population.[204]

Cost-rolling programs are ostensibly geared toward properly compensating victims, teaching inmates a moral lesson and fiscal responsibility, and avoiding the need to raise taxes, but, as Livingston points out, those goals have remained elusive. A recent New York State Bar survey found that 80 percent of all criminal defendants charged with a felony in the United States are indigent. Fifty-nine percent of inmates earned less than $1,000 a month before their arrest, and 29 percent were unemployed.[205] People of color are also overrepresented in the inmate population. The implication is that court-imposed debt adds a layer of disadvantage on the shoulders of already disadvantaged populations. Moreover, inmates who leave the correctional system with liens for jail room and board clearly face obstacles to rehabilitation that do not favorably affect their recidivism risks.

Beyond these utilitarian issues, pay-to-stay policies raise serious questions of fairness. Clearly, entering a correctional facility is not tantamount to voluntary consumption of products and services, and charging astronomical fees for the experience is akin to punishing an individual twice for the same offense. While taxpayers may feel that it is unfair for them to shoulder the costs of someone else's wrongdoing, it is just as unfair to levy those costs against people who are not incurring them voluntarily. Moreover, a population already disenfranchised, by class proxies and by felon status, does not have a real say in the costs being levied, which makes the "inmate as consumer" metaphor even more absurd.

The absurdity is compounded by the terminology accompanying the inmate-as-customer metaphor. Defending the City of Santa Ana's decision to move to a pay-to-stay system in the early 1990s, Police chief Paul Walters and jail administrator Russell Davis argued that the decision was precipitated by the combination of rising crime rates and a population reduction court order against the overcrowded Orange County jail. Santa Ana partnered with the police department to allow low-level offenders partial work-release while staying in general population. Their explanation of the plan is saturated in corporatespeak and business terminology, justifying the shift in revenue terms and explaining its financial logic as a business plan.[206] In a critical commentary about the same program, Robert Weisberg wryly observes that the brochure

> tells us that the jail "is pleased to host a full range of alternatives to traditional incar-
> ceration"; it reassures prospective "clients" seeking flexible work/jail schedules
> ("Work on Saturday or Sunday? No problem, your weekend days are our weekend
> days."); it guarantees "24-hour on-site medical staff"; it accommodates inmates near
> and far ("We have helped clients with sentences from other counties as well as other
> states."); and it generally brags that the jail "is the most modern and comfortable
> facility in the region," where, à la Cheers, "Each of our clients has a name . . . "
>
> Surely this manifestation of pay-to-stay is embarrassing. But, as so honestly rep-
> resented, pay-to-stay could prove salutary for the criminal justice system if recog-
> nized as part of our somewhat ritualized cycle of constructive self-embarrassment
> over the role of wealth in criminal justice. More specifically, pay-to-stay could
> become one of those occasional eruptions of transparency about the forms of cur-
> rency exchanged in the market for punishment.[207]

Unfortunately, Weisberg's hope that the absurdity will expose the embarrass-
ment seems misplaced. The serious concerns arising from pay-to-stay policies
regarding fairness, proportionality, and disenfranchisement have been lost in
translation when inmates have attempted to argue their unconstitutionality in
courts. A variety of constitutional challenges were raised in federal courts, and all
of them have been rejected.[208] Only recently, Tennessee commissioners have
approved pay-to-stay regimes in jails, finding no constitutional violation.[209]

One of the more problematic manifestations of the inmate-as-customer mind-
set is the creation of experiential tiers in jails, which allow charging wealthier
inmates more, explicitly, for comfort and safety. The Fremont Police Department
recently announced its intention to offer inmates a pay-to-stay option. For a one-
time fee of $45 and a "hotel payment" of $155 per night, "prisoners serving short
sentences on lesser charges can stay in a smaller facility while avoiding county
jails." "It's still a jail; there's no special treatment," Lt. Mark Devine, a Fremont
police official who oversees the program, told Chris De Benedetti of the *Argus*.
"They get the same cot, blanket and food as anybody in the county jail, except that
our jail is smaller, quieter and away from the county jail population."[210]

The notion of creating tiers of comfort in prison, and allowing inmates to
upgrade their prison experience as if they were airfare ticket purchasers, offends
not only the notion of state responsibility but also that of equality before the law.
Sheriffs, and other proponents of pay-to-stay, tend to be remarkably open about
conditions in jail, specifically, the risk of violence from other inmates, and sell the
tiered option as a way for select inmates who can afford it to avoid these additional
"pains of imprisonment."[211] It is a sad commentary on the system that a seasoned
defense attorney concluded that the costs were worth the peace of mind to the
inmates.[212] That some inmates' incarceration experience is "more pleasant" than

others' is inevitable, of course, but admission that violence is an obvious corollary of "free" incarceration, avoidable via "extra" payment for the select wealthier inmates who are, presumably, less deserving of having their safety threatened,[213] is one more example of the "inmate as consumer" perception run amok.

INMATES' SELF-PERCEPTION AS BURDENS/CONSUMERS

O. Henry's short story "The Cop and the Anthem" tells of Soapy, a former inmate at Rikers Island. When we meet Soapy, he is plotting various methods to commit crime and thus put himself back behind bars. O. Henry tells us of his motives:

> The hibernatorial ambitions of Soapy were not of the highest. In them there were no considerations of Mediterranean cruises, of soporific Southern skies drifting in the Vesuvian Bay. Three months on the Island was what his soul craved. Three months of assured board and bed and congenial company, safe from Boreas and bluecoats, seemed to Soapy the essence of things desirable.
>
> For years the hospitable Blackwell's had been his winter quarters. Just as his more fortunate fellow New Yorkers had bought their tickets to Palm Beach and the Riviera each winter, so Soapy had made his humble arrangements for his annual hegira to the Island. And now the time was come. On the previous night three Sabbath newspapers, distributed beneath his coat, about his ankles and over his lap, had failed to repulse the cold as he slept on his bench near the spurting fountain in the ancient square. So the Island loomed big and timely in Soapy's mind. He scorned the provisions made in the name of charity for the city's dependents. In Soapy's opinion the Law was more benign than Philanthropy. There was an endless round of institutions, municipal and eleemosynary, on which he might set out and receive lodging and food accordant with the simple life. But to one of Soapy's proud spirit the gifts of charity are encumbered. If not in coin you must pay in humiliation of spirit for every benefit received at the hands of philanthropy. As Caesar had his Brutus, every bed of charity must have its toll of a bath, every loaf of bread its compensation of a private and personal inquisition. Wherefore it is better to be a guest of the law, which though conducted by rules, does not meddle unduly with a gentleman's private affairs.[214]

In a cruel, recession-era echo of the O. Henry classic, a man was reported in December 2012 as seeking prison health care by committing shoplifting. As the blog reported, "The self-employed man told reporters that he makes too much to qualify for government programs, but not enough to afford his own health insurance or out-of-pocket care. . . . The health care Morrocco got in prison was free and would treat his cancer."[215]

As consumers in a neoliberal health care regime, inmates take control of their own health, litigating for service and coverage. In 2013 the Fourth Circuit Court of Appeals found that denying transgender inmates sex-reassignment surgery violated the Eighth Amendment.[216] The irony, of course, is that the "services" provided in prison are of a truly questionable nature. The realities of the quality of services notwithstanding, it is no wonder that inmates perceived as customers feel entitled to review and critique the conditions of their confinement. Yelp, a popular website featuring reviews of restaurants, businesses, and venues, also offers reviews of some less expected institutions. San Quentin State Prison, the recipient of three stars on Yelp, was reviewed thus:

> I really wanted to love this place.
>
> I heard that the kitchen used local farms and put great thought in to their seasonally changing menu and the service was not exactly friendly but "efficient."
>
> Boy was I wrong.
>
> It was pretty busy, but I was able to find a table. Again, I understand this is buffet style, but when I asked the gentleman by the front door near where I was sitting if I could sit further from the door he was SUPER RUDE about it. He just motioned for me to sit back down, but at least the front door led to a hallway and not the outside, so although it was raining, I figured I'd be fine.[217]

Similarly, the Los Angeles County Jail (which offered a tiered pay-to-stay option even before the recession)[218] received the following "endorsement."

> A Hotel for criminals and the like! Stay for free and enjoy complimentary breakfast, lunch AND dinner! While you are sharing space with other criminals, you can still enjoy your stay even more with indefinite alone time, reading material such as La Opinion, and if you are lucky, a 22in LCD TV might just be working that day!
>
> You also get complimentary alarm clock service, laundry (no dry clean), medical and psychological services, and 24 hour protection from correctional officers and sheriff deputies. Smiley faces all around =)[219]

Comical as these reviews are, they seem to be the logical conclusion of the shifting perceptions of inmates. Perceiving inmates as consumers does not permeate public knowledge and creates a lifeline for private contractors, as well as a convenient reduction in urgency to handle matters of incarceration conditions.[220]

The shift from viewing inmates as wards to seeing them as burdens or consumers may have resulted in fewer people behind bars and in more favorable conditions (for inmates who can afford it), but it also raises serious ethical and pragmatic problems. The new models of viewing inmates are far from empowering; rather than imbue inmates with a sense of personal responsibility for their rehabilitation, they blame them for consuming basic human necessities and imply that there is a financial conflict between inmates and taxpayers. This equation is far from likely to produce real change in public opinion and fails to accurately present the picture of mass incarceration: inmates would be lesser burdens on taxpayers' wallets if the state's punitive sentencing and correctional apparatus held fewer of them behind bars in the first place.

The other unsavory effect of these "new inmate" models is the inevitable classifications and distinctions between inmates who are and are not worth the cost of incarceration. Just as the attention to presumably high-risk violent and sex offenders diverted attention from the much larger number of low-risk offenders whose lengthy incarcerations were unnecessary from a public safety perspective, drawing attention to high-cost, low-risk inmates like the old and the infirm retrenches the notion that the inmates left behind bars are worth the cost of incarceration, in terms of public safety. These categories may include inmates for whom recession-era politics has not generated sympathy, such as sex offenders and violent offenders.

These factors, as well as other concerns discussed in the previous chapters, raise a number of important questions about cost-centered reforms: Can advocacy based primarily on humonetarian discourse be successful? Is it justifiable? And is it sustainable beyond years of economic downturn? Chapter 8 tackles these questions.

8

THE FUTURE OF HUMONETARIANISM

The previous chapters highlighted the complex and intricate ways in which the public conversation about American punishment was transformed by the introduction of emergency cost considerations. Speaking about financial prudence has freed politicians, administrators, and even law enforcement agents to advocate for policies that go against the grain of a four-decade-long project of mass incarceration. And while localities vary in their response to humonetarian discourse, political campaigns for change, such as death penalty abolition, scaling down of the war on drugs, and habitual offender law reform, have been successful in many states in which such reforms failed prior to the financial crisis. The causes for success and change were not solely related to the financial crisis; successful campaigns integrated arguments about cost-effectiveness with substantive arguments about innocence and injustice, but the emphasis on cost has made it possible to raise arguments that have long ago lost their public appeal. At the same time, some "tough 'n' cheap campaigns to streamline the criminal process have been launched, trying to capitalize on the cost argument to argue for traditionally punitive policies.

Concerns about the financial unsustainability of the correctional project affect other areas of policy making as well. State and local governments are shifting attention to certain categories of inmates, primarily the old and infirm, whose incarceration is deemed inefficient because of a combination of high cost and low risk. These inmates—classified and profiled according to their cost/risk profile— are the focus of savings policies that cast them as economic burdens or potential consumers, such as early releases, jurisdictional shifts, consolidation, and rolling costs. While some of these policies have resulted in overall shrinkage of the incarcerated population, they are not necessarily focused on the inmates' human rights and personal needs. In addition, these policies differentiate between inmates who are and are not worth the correctional expenditure, arguably improving the lot of the former at the expense of entrenching traditional punitive perspectives on the latter.

Governmental and private actors in the correctional market are adapting their behavior to an era of austerity. Private prison providers are amending their agreements with states and localities to allow for lower prison occupancy while at the same time devoting their energy to financing punitive reform and providing incarceration spaces for categories of inmates that do not benefit from the reduction in prison population, primarily undocumented immigrants. In this way, even within the framework of the market, a classification of inmates according to cost-effectiveness is made, while punitive energy is directed to new groups perceived as threats.

These developments suggest a complicated relationship between the two theoretical approaches presented at the beginning of the book—Rusche and Kirchheimer's theory of labor surplus and punitivism and Becker's economic approach to criminal justice. My survey of recession-era penal policies reveals a complex picture. On the one hand, the grim expectation that an economic downturn, indicated primarily by a rise in unemployment,[1] would lead to an increase in punitivism has not materialized, and in some cases, the opposite has occurred: prisons have closed, populations have been reduced, and significant strides have been made on drug legalization and death penalty abolition. On the other hand, it is difficult to say that the pendulum has fully swung away from punitive politics, and some trends—particularly the demonization of undocumented immigrants and the privatization of the correctional apparatus, with the expenses sometimes paid by the inmates themselves—are alive and well during recessions.

The explanation for this apparent contradiction relies on the economic literature on the costs of crime. As Becker and his followers argued, there is no criminal justice system on a national scale that can completely eradicate crime, and therefore the aspiration is to reach an equilibrium whereby the combined cost of a given rate of crime and enforcement—to society, to victims, and arguably to the offenders themselves—does not exceed the benefits of having the system in place. Rusche and Kirchheimer, as well as their followers, could not have foreseen the major characteristics of the American mass incarceration project: four decades of unprecedented expenditure on the project of criminal justice, incarceration rates of 1 of 100 nationwide, and a well-oiled private prison machine backed up by sophisticated financial instruments. Even if punitive animus is directed at lower-class populations in times of austerity, it is surely filtered and mitigated through the powers and rules of the market, as well as confined by their constraints.

As David Greenberg and Valerie West found in their regression model explaining trends in state imprisonment between 1971 and 1991,[2] periods of economic distress have had a more nuanced impact on the level of punitiveness. On the one hand, high rates of unemployment, which are a by-product of recession, yield higher rates of imprisonment, especially when they correlate with conservative governments; on the other, reduced revenues tend to produce reduced prison growth rates as economies slow down. These trends may explain the mixed effect of the recession on punitive practices. In other words, it is not that we have lost our taste for punishing offenders at the levels that have obtained for the past forty years; it is simply that we cannot afford to do so. Like Magritte's Castle of the Pyrenees, the giant correctional apparatus and the markets supporting it are floating unsupported in the air and cannot be sustained.

But while market forces contain the system's punitive capacities, they also function according to the logic of the market in a neoliberal era. The past four decades have seen the state retreat from the great promise to take care of the crime problem; private actors and profiteers have gradually stepped in to fill the correctional void created by governmental agencies. This logic of the market has not been changed by the recession. Indeed, humonetarian discourse has not contributed to the rise of serious human rights concerns or to a revival of the rehabilitative ideal; instead, it has operated like a lean version of the new penology, classifying inmates according to the cost-effectiveness of their incarceration, alleviating financial pressure by releasing some populations from correctional control while at the same time holding the fort with regard to other groups of inmates whose incarceration is reaffirmed as being cost-effective even in austere times. Actors and institutions in the punitive field, which have spent decades viewing the penal enterprise through the lens of managerial efficiency and profit, have retained that perspective; the difference is that in lean years they have to do "more with less."

The mixed success of humonetarianism in swinging back the punitive pendulum raises several important questions: How sensitive is cost-centered reform to a potential rise in crime rates? To what extent is it a function of public apathy to crime, fueled by lower crime rates? How durable and lasting is criminal justice reform based on an economic downturn? Which of the successful campaigns to reverse mass incarceration practices will endure when the economy improves? Does society, by focusing on cost arguments, pay a moral and discursive price in flattening public conversation and emptying it of human concern? And, finally, how can we infuse economic arguments with more substantive, reform-oriented content, which will powerfully steer the correctional conversation ship toward safer and saner shores?

PUNITIVE ANIMUS, CRIME RATES, AND FINANCIAL PRUDENCE

Given the persistence of the neoliberal profit- and efficiency-driven logic, one possible concern about recession-era reform is that the economic downturn may not have sated the public's appetite for punitive policies. "Get tough" control policies in the United States are often portrayed as the reflection of the public's will to lock up those whom they perceive to be a threat to public policy. Indeed, in a study of penal policies and public opinion since 1952, Peter Enns finds that public opinion has been a fundamental determinant of both congressional attention to criminal justice issues and the annual rate of new federal incarcerations, contributing, since the mid-1980s alone, to more than 160,000 federal incarcerations.[3] The public's presumed disappointment with rehabilitation, and growing perception that any success in recidivism reduction was illusory, sparked the movement for determinate sentencing.[4] Arguably, therefore, the public's appetite for punitive policies may return with a vengeance if and when crime rates rise, and the financial soundness of curbing incarceration and prison construction may not be enough to persuade politicians to resist the "tough on crime" trend. This may be particularly true if in the next elections the administration becomes more conservative; comparative research finds a strong correlation between conservative governments and punitive public opinion.[5]

However, a solid body of research on public punitiveness suggests that the simplistic notion that the public invariably demands and celebrates punitive policies is misguided and incomplete. It is true that the American public has, historically, supported a range of punitive policies, such as the death penalty and habitual offender laws. But support for get-tough policies is, as Francis Cullen and colleagues conclude, "mushy."[6] Citizens may be willing to substitute a sentence of life imprisonment without parole for the death penalty and have increasingly done so in various states since the onset of the recession. Especially when nonviolent offenders are involved, there is substantial support for intermediate sanctions and for restorative justice. Despite three decades of criticism, rehabilitation—particularly for juvenile offenders—remains an integral part of Americans' correctional philosophy. There is also widespread support for early intervention programs. In the end, the public seems to contain a multitude of opinions about criminal justice, both punitive and nonpunitive, wishing the correctional system to achieve the diverse missions of doing justice, protecting public safety, and reforming criminals.

Some specific examples of these complex public tendencies have been found in punitiveness surveys. Just as determinate sentencing guidelines were introduced in the federal system, William Samuel and Elizabeth Moulds asked respondents about recommended sentencing for six categories of crime.[7] Respondents supported nonincarceration sentences for petty theft and auto theft and incarceration for rape and homicide. Twenty-five percent of respondents did not support imprisonment for armed robbery. The researchers concluded that the community's views about appropriate punishments did not differ significantly from the newly introduced sentencing guidelines at the time, and when the public deviated from them, it was a downward deviation. Although opinions varied somewhat across demographic categories, the study revealed a strong amount of consensus.

Similar findings emerged from Douglas Thomson and Anthony Ragona's public opinion survey regarding punishment of residential burglars in Illinois. The survey responses revealed that respondents were significantly more willing to consider community options, albeit more severe than mere probation, when they were made aware of the consequences of incarceration, including fiscal consequences and costs. Only 7 percent of the respondents went as far as to suggest sentences as severe as the mandatory guidelines in effect at the time the study was conducted.[8]

In a telephone survey conducted in the District of Columbia,[9] respondents expressed a complex view of punishment, emphasizing that while it is important to punish people to protect society, it is also important to guarantee rehabilitation; 19 percent of respondents noted that rehabilitation "is" a goal of punishment, but 55 percent stated that it "should be." There was broad consensus about the need to rehabilitate, particularly with regard to women, juveniles, and first-time offenders.

Confirming these trends, Christopher Innes found that the public was able to contain ambivalent views about crime.[10] While studies have shown that the public is committed to public safety—in an ABC poll in 1982, 90 percent of respondents said they would approve constructing new prisons so that sentences could increase, even if it meant an increase in taxes[11]—they have also consistently shown that the public favors rehabilitative programs for inmates, possibly because it perceives them as less risky and ultimately contributing to public safety.

This complicated view of criminal justice is also supported by John Doble's review of attitudes to punishment in the United States.[12] Doble concludes that the public frequently and consistently endorses multiple aims of punishment. In 1995 politicians in Alabama, Delaware, and Pennsylvania who supported sentencing alternatives to incarceration and were concerned about prison overcrowding and costs thought that the public would endorse alternatives because of its perennial concern about government spending and taxation. However, the public in each of those states supported alternatives because other aims of punishment, such as restitution and rehabilitation, made sense to them on their own merits. Studies show that people's lack of support for mass incarceration stems from their perception of prison as a poor instrument for rehabilitation. Doble points out the strong commitment to rehabilitation in studies measuring willingness to pay, even including treatment for sex offenders.

One key variable that affects the public's level of punitiveness is the extent to which members of the public are informed about the criminal justice system. Jody Sundt reviewed several surveys conducted in the 1980s in Pennsylvania, Delaware, and Alabama that found that although a majority of survey participants initially preferred prison sentences for nonviolent offenders, when they were informed about alternatives to incarceration (e.g., strict probation, house arrest, boot camp, community service, and restitution) a clear majority in all three states favored community-based alternatives for nonviolent offenders.[13] Remarkably, in all these studies, the public's support for community corrections increased when they were provided with information about the content of these sanctions and informed about the costs of imprisonment. The problem is that these data are seldom presented to the public in the context of punitive litigation; instead, the public is presented with atypical examples of sensational and heinous crimes that evoke strong emotional responses. The passage of habitual offender laws in the 1990s is a classic example. In a survey conducted by Brandon Applegate, Francis Cullen, Michael Turner, and Jody Sundt in Cincinnati, respondents offered their general opinion about three strikes laws, with 88 percent of the sample offering support. However, when respondents were subsequently presented with a vignette describing a hypothetical offender who would qualify for a life sentence without the possibility of parole under the local version of three strikes and asked to select a sentence, only 7 percent favored life without parole, and an additional 10 percent favored life with the possibility of parole after twenty-five years. The largest proportion of respondents selected much milder sentences, ranging from five to fifteen years in prison.[14]

Julian Roberts's metaanalysis of public policies shows that public punitiveness is strongly and inversely correlated with knowledge about penal options.[15] In other words, the better informed the public is about the system, the less punitive opinions it espouses. Roberts's metaanalysis of public polls reveals a public no more punitive than the judiciary, when the studies are sensitive enough to account for knowledge and familiarity. When surveyed about the criminal justice system, respondents across studies tended to overestimate crime rates, the risks of property crime victimization, and recidivism rates.[16] Similarly, Catriona Mirrlees-Black's Britain-based study for the Home Office found that providing respondents with more evidence-based information about the criminal justice system changed attitudes away from punitiveness.[17]

Darrin Rogers's study of punitivism presented students and treatment professionals with vignettes describing a sexual offense ("fondling") and a violent, nonsexual offense ("hitting") committed by a male relative against a six-year-old female victim. The age of the offender was also controlled for and ranged between seven and twenty-seven.[18] The findings showed that punitivism increased with age, particularly for sexual offenses, and that white respondents endorsed lower punishment ratings than nonwhite participants. Gender was not a significant predictor of punitiveness. Treatment professionals were less punitive than community members. Younger offenders were perceived as less accountable for their actions, and all respondents tended to endorse lower punishment rates for younger offenders. While defining the offense as sexual had a statistically significant effect, it was not large enough to be of practical significance. Respondents who believed in the efficacy of rehabilitation tended to be less punitive and more supportive of treatment models.

There are also big differences in how the public responds to abstract questions and to specific scenarios. Jane Sprott, whose punitiveness survey combined general questions about penal policies with case-specific scenarios,[19] found that respondents reacted differently to the two. Research that presents questions about punitiveness in more nuanced ways tends to show less punitive results and more support for incarceration alternatives.[20]

Another barrier to the success of humonetarianism is the concern that individual experiences of economic anxiety may have an impact on public punitiveness to an extent that might counteract the cost-effectiveness argument. The macro-level analysis by Rusche and Kirchheimer[21] and the subsequent studies finding a connection between economic downturns and harsh punishment are explained by public opinion surveys via the intervening variable of public punitiveness. As David Garland has noted, "Shifts in the economic and social position of large sections of the middle and working classes" make citizens support "more aggressive controls for an 'underclass' that was perceived to be disorderly, drug-prone and dangerous."[22]

There are a number of explanations for this trend. David Greenberg argues that harsh punishment for others is a form of "compensatory satisfaction" for those who cannot derive satisfaction from other aspects of their lives.[23] Such a relationship has been variably described. Another possibility is that feelings of rage and frustration evoked by economic insecurity and job instability are soothed by attachment to convenient scapegoats—offenders, undocumented immigrants, and the like.[24] Another possibility is that punitivism is the manifestation of a sense of threat posed by large numbers of minorities to the economic and political well-being of the majority, triggering punitivism addressed to minorities.

Michael Hogan, Ted Chiricos, and Marc Gertz, favoring the latter explanation, have examined the extent to which punitive attitudes toward criminals are a function of economic insecurity, as well as a measure of blame for policies and phenomena perceived as affecting incomes, such as welfare, affirmative action, and immigration—namely, policies that benefit what some voters may perceive as the "undeserving poor."[25] Their survey of two thousand residents revealed that respondents who felt economically insecure and respondents who blamed progressive policies advancing racial equality for poor economic conditions tended to be more punitive than others. Moreover, the study identified that these attitudes—economic anxiety, resentment of what is perceived as privileges for minorities, and punitivism toward criminals—were significantly more prevalent among white males, who were far more likely to blame other segments of the population for their economic problems than were women and minorities.

A subsequent study by Costelloe, Chiricos, and Gertz examined two explanations for punitivism: crime salience and economic anxiety.[26] Crime salience is a function of crime rates, media reports, and references to crime by politicians. When operationalized as concern about crime and fear of crime, crime salience consistently and strongly predicted punitive attitudes. By contrast, actual experiences of victimization did not. Economic anxiety—measured as an expectation that one's financial circumstances will worsen in the near future—was a predictor of support for punitive measures among white males, particularly those white males who are less well educated and have relatively low income. Costelloe, Chiricos, and Gertz found these results consistent with some aspects of the "angry white male" phenomenon, especially to the extent that punitive sentiments and negative sentiments about criminals had a racial focus.

These notions of punitiveness and economic anxiety may have deeper cultural roots. In 1997 Tom Tyler and Robert Boeckmann conducted a telephone survey of California residents about the reasons for their support of the Three Strikes Law, which had been enacted a short time before.[27] Notably, respondents' support for the law was not correlated with experience of victimization; it was a more general expression of punitiveness and lack of regard for what was perceived as unnecessary procedural safeguards, stemming from broader political perspectives, primarily a sense that the fabric of traditional family values and morality was deteriorating.

Indeed, there are strong links between culture and ideology and opinions about crime; for example, the objection to gun control has been attributed to the heritage of frontier hunting culture.[28] As of 1980, fear of crime and the perception of crime as a major problem had increased, along with crime rates. But fear of crime in itself does not drive punitiveness; studies have found little or no correlation between a personal experience of victimization and punitivism. Groups that are disproportionately likely to be victimized, such as women and people of color, tend to be less punitive. Moreover, the perception of crime as a national problem has a direct impact on punitiveness, as does the degree to which the public is informed about the criminal justice system.

In light of the connection between punitiveness and cultural beliefs, it is valuable to examine how the public reacts to punitiveness surveys that include information about the cost of punishment and to measure the public's willingness to pay for various criminal justice policies. Mark Cohen, Ronald Rust, and Sara Steen's survey presented thirteen hundred respondents with realistic scenarios of crime, including bank robbery, identity theft, and counterfeiting and two illegal immigrant scenarios.[29] The survey controlled for eight types of offenses and for the offenders' criminal histories. The notable component of the survey is measuring respondents' willingness to pay for punishment: respondents were first asked about their willingness to forgo a tax rebate in exchange for programs that are designed to prevent or punish crime. Respondents were invited to put themselves in the shoes of the local mayor, who has just received a grant from the federal government equal to either $100 or $1,000 per household. Respondents were then asked to decide how to allocate that money among five different options: (1) prison construction, (2) more drug and alcohol treatment programs for nonviolent offenders, (3) increasing the police force, (4) increasing prevention programs geared at youth, or (5) returning all the money to local residents.

Responses from the public were varied across crime categories. The majority of respondents expressed the willingness to release offenders on time served when presented with scenarios in which people are typically sentenced for a year or two for street crimes. Their preferred incarceration rate for most street crimes was largely consistent with, but slightly less harsh than, current practice; the preferred incarceration rate for drug crimes was consistently lower than current practice. By contrast, there was much less willingness to parole offenders incarcerated for white-collar crimes. Even when offered imprisonment options, a significant number of respondents were willing to substitute the sentence for noncustodial alternatives. When addressing a scenario involving an undocumented immigrant with no criminal history, the vast majority of respondents, 75 percent, opted against a prison sentence, and 35.8 percent called for deportation. Respondents were notably much more willing to incarcerate repeat offenders, with a notable difference between drug offenders with and without criminal histories. Offenders without any prior criminal record who are convicted of crimes of identity theft and counterfeiting of currency were deemed worthy of prison, with about two-thirds of respondents calling for prison terms of an average length between four and five years. When allocating money to the different programs, the largest pro-portion of money (36.6 percent) was devoted to "programs to keep youth out of trouble." By comparison, drug treatment for nonviolent offenders received 22.1 percent of the budget, and increasing the police force received 21.1 percent, in con-trast to only 8.4 percent for additional prisons. The researchers converted these data into valuation, concluding that the average value of a taxpayer dollar was only about 71 cents when spent on prison but $3.07 when spent on prevention. That is, at the margin, respondents were indifferent when asked to select between a $1.00 tax rebate and $3.00 spent on prevention. Even respondents who made broad statements about the need to finance the police expressed a preference for drug treatment and prevention when allocating funds. In the aggregate, respondents' responses implied a willingness to pay to reduce crime at about $23,000 per bur-glary, $60,000 per serious assault, $213,000 per armed robbery, $225,000 per rape and sexual assault, and $9.1 million per murder. These figures, of course, represent average values across the United States and might not necessarily apply to the value that members of any one community might place on crime in their area.

Similarly, Peter Hart and Associates' punitivism survey incorporated questions to gauge public preferences for state government savings.[30] Notably, 23 percent of all adults answering the survey stated that they had been a victim of violent crime or had a family member who was a victim. Interestingly, victims of crime were found to be more supportive than the general public of crime prevention and reha-bilitation rather than of abundant and long prison sentences.

Vincent Schiraldi and Judith Greene documented research comparing crime-related attitudes before and after the September 11, 2001, attacks, which demonstrate a shift away from imprisonment and toward alternative sentencing approaches.[31] In these studies, more people supported noncustodial sentences when presented with a statement that doing so would "save millions of taxpayers' dollars."

It can be concluded, therefore, that pessimism about the public's punitive animus may be exaggerated. The public is capable of entertaining different notions of punishment, including deterrence and retribution as well as rehabilitation. The more informed voters are about the criminal justice system, including its related costs, the less they tend to support punitive policies. While crime rates matter, direct experiences of victimization are not significant contributors to punitivism. Strongly held ideological beliefs about one's position on the socioeconomic ladder make a difference, but the public is still capable of making a calculus of priorities when presented with the costs of its choices. These findings are largely encouraging in terms of the persuasive potential of humonetarian discourse.

THE DURABILITY OF HUMONETARIANISM

A serious concern about humonetarian policies pertains to their durability. If the main justification for policy changes is financial, how likely is it that these policies will be reversed when punishing more harshly becomes more financially sustainable? And is it possible to distinguish between different types of reform as to their reversibility?

This concern cannot be easily discounted. As the survey of social history literature in chapter 1 demonstrates, there is a strong correlation between how much a state can spend in general and how much it spends on corrections in particular, and as we saw in chapter 2, some of the major changes in law enforcement, sentencing, and corrections corresponded with cycles of the market. However, different policies may respond to an improved economy in different ways, and some reforms—like Prohibition after the recovery from the Great Depression—may be irreversible.

One example of a potentially irreversible transformation is abolition of the death penalty. Frank Zimring and David Johnson, who studied the death penalty in Asia,[32] found great variation among Asian countries in terms of their use of capital punishment. However, one important finding from their study was that death penalty abolition was consistently irreversible; once a country abolished the death penalty, it would be gone, never to return. A particularly interesting example is Hong Kong, which has the distinction of having been both a British colony until 1997 and the neighbor of China, a country where the death penalty is alive and well, including for nonhomicide offenses. The transition back to Chinese hands has not affected Hong Kong's repudiation of the death penalty in 1993.

Naturally, the applicability of these universal lessons is limited in the United States, whose adherence to the death penalty despite the four moratorium years between *Furman* and *Gregg* has been constantly regarded as the quintessential example of American exceptionalism. But it is important to take into account several factors. First of all, as argued in chapter 4, the moratorium imposed in *Furman* was not a repudiation of the death penalty as such but rather stemmed from concerns about procedural fairness. The death penalty's return in *Gregg* facilitated capital punishment state laws that complied with procedural requirements. By contrast, the trail of state abolitions since the eruption of the Great Recession is based on institutional constraints rather than on compliance with procedural requirements, and on more than a modicum of fatigue with efforts to "tinker with the machinery of death."[33] This is especially true in states in which abolition was the product of a combination of cost and innocence arguments. New abolitionism is a growing trend emerging from state governments themselves rather than federally imposed. Once a critical mass of states abolishes the death penalty, the transition to life without parole nationwide will likely be irreversible, especially if humonetarian logic leads states to repurpose death rows and restructure their array of prisons.

I expect that cost-based legalization of substances in general, and marijuana in particular, will also be an irreversible trend. Here it is possible to rely on a historical example. The repeal of Prohibition, largely possible because of arguments of enforcement costs, creation of an underground economy, and the potential of revenue enhancement via alcohol taxation in the aftermath of dramatic income tax decline, was not reversed once the American economy got back on track, despite the fact that liquor tax revenue never resumed its role as the main source of funding for the federal government. In the context of marijuana, as discussed in chapter 5, the push for legalization started with the introduction of state-sanctioned medical marijuana programs. Legalization of the drug will likely lead to fewer restrictions on clinical studies, which may, in turn, change the drug's classification and reframe its perception in terms of medical utility. It is also important to keep in mind that marijuana legalization follows a change in public opinion, which is largely a function of the aging out of legalization opponents.[34] It may well be that, in time, new substances may be criminalized, which could be the product of political backlash, moral panic, or xenophobia; after all, marijuana, opiates, and other substances became illegal and remained illegal despite the failure of alcohol prohibition. But a scientifically backed perception of marijuana as a relatively less harmful, and medically beneficial, substance in an era of legalization would make its criminalization less likely, especially given the now-universal prevalence and appeal of the harm principle as the main argument for criminalization.[35]

It is important to point out that some areas of reform will probably endure into the economic recovery precisely because the public conversation about them revolved around more than nickels and dimes. One such example is the campaign to reform Three Strikes in California. While cost arguments were mentioned during the campaign, the negative press associated with the lengthy incarcerations of nonviolent Third Strikers changed public opinion to the point that a large majority of Californians voted to do away with some provisions of the law. I expect that Californians will retain a bad taste in their mouths from years of lengthy, unnecessary incarceration of nonviolent, albeit habitual, offenders, and the relatively small numbers of beneficiaries from the policy change will also stand in the way of reversing these policies.

Another example of a successful campaign based on more than nickels and dimes is that to ameliorate the use of solitary confinement. Recent years have seen a humanitarian struggle against long-term segregation, supported by medical and psychological literature that consistently warns about its overwhelmingly negative and irreversible impact on inmates' health. The movement to limit the maximum time for solitary confinement, to reform conditions to allow some measure of human contact, and to abolish the practice of "gang validation" leading to preemptive segregation for indefinite terms is a classic human rights movement, and the struggle has featured primarily humanitarian arguments and traditional protest techniques, such as the three hunger strikes undertaken by California inmates between 2011 and 2013. But even here, the cost argument seems to make headway with lawmakers.

On October 9, 2013, the California legislature held legislative hearings regarding solitary confinement in the Security Housing Units.[36] The hearings followed a series of hunger strikes in California prisons against the process of segregation and the practice of sending suspected gang members to indefinite sentences in solitary confinement, sometimes on the basis of rumors and scant evidence. At the hearings, the legislature raised various issues concerning the conditions of confinement, asking officials from the California Department of Corrections and Rehabilitation (CDCR) to justify the necessity of confinement to a small cell for 22.5 hours a day and deprivation of human contact and nature. At some point during the hearing, Assembly member Nancy Skinner, member of the budget subcommittee, expressed interest in the cost of SHU housing. CDCR officials and other speakers before the committee estimated the costs as $20,000 per annum more than California's $49,000 figure for the yearly incarceration of an inmate in general population. It may well be that the cost argument will join other arguments raised in the struggle to end long-term solitary confinement and produce lasting change.

Abolishing, or ameliorating, the use of solitary confinement poses special types of problems for humonetarian reformers, as supermax institutions and cells, sturdy, windowless, and located in remote locations, are almost impossible to repurpose. Nonetheless, it seems that the costs of high security and special isolation procedures in themselves would decline with a decreased reliance on solitary confinement even if the cells stand empty. With the collaboration of the Vera Institute of Justice and the American Civil Liberties Union, states like Ohio and Mississippi have managed to keep down costs by significantly reducing their reliance on solitary confinement, with no adverse impact on public safety.[37]

One interesting wrinkle in the debate about solitary confinement involves the practice of double celling inmates in cells originally designed to hold only one inmate. As Keramet Reiter explains in *Parole, Snitch, or Die,* shortly after the completion of the supermax facility in Pelican Bay, and almost as an afterthought, a second bunk was added to every cell.[38] Currently, as revealed in the California legislative hearings, nearly half of the state's 4,054 segregated inmates are double-celled, ostensibly to alleviate overcrowding in the SHU. The use of double celling for efficiency reasons has historical precedent; Ashley Rubin's study of Eastern State Penitentiary reveals that the first-of-its-kind modern prison in the United States, which built its reputation on the reformative power of solitary confinement, frequently double-celled inmates, though it opted not to publicize this fact.[39] While one reason for this deviation from the correctional ideal was the need to prevent insanity among prisoners, others ostensibly stemmed from economic needs, namely, the need to send inmates to work outside the prison for revenue enhancement. Whether modern double-celling practices save or produce expenses is unclear, because very little exists in the way of statistics about prison violence and security. It is equally difficult to argue that double-celling policies in close quarters are necessarily better, or worse, than solitary confinement as it was originally intended. Regardless of the answer to these questions, it is quite clear that even in a struggle based on ideology, human rights, and dignity, there is room for cost-saving arguments, and these may help push the practice out of existence to the point that future generations will find it unacceptable.

With regard to prison closures, out-of-state incarcerations, and cost-rolling "pay to stay" mechanisms, the future is bleaker and the odds of reversal are higher. The myriad techniques and practices that states and localities have adopted to save money on corrections in a time of austerity—privatization, out-of-state incarceration, prison closures, bartering with other states, jurisdictional shifts—reveal a society that has not come to the conclusion that it is time for the punitive pendulum to swing in the other direction. States and localities are not quite ready to "exit Nixonland,"[40] policy-wise, but since sentencing and incarcerating at colossal rates have become financially unsustainable, these changes resemble emergency measures more than they resemble well-considered penal reform efforts.

It is also important to keep the overall decline in state prison populations in perspective. Despite the decline, twenty-five states, as well as the federal government, had stable or increasing prison populations as late as 2010.[41] This means there are many local considerations affecting change, not all of them necessarily in the direction of decreasing incarceration.

Why, then, has the financial crisis been successful in fueling the political struggle to abolish the death penalty and legalize marijuana and unsuccessful in creating long-lasting correctional policies? The answer may lie in part in two features that death penalty abolition and marijuana legalization share: monocentrism and a high political profile. The costs of informing the public about issues of high valance to which there is a yes/no answer (abolish? legalize?) are not as high as those involved in educating the public about complex polycentric problems, provided that the campaign is authentic and persuasive and that reform would not negatively affect public safety.[42] By contrast, issues of overcrowding, budgeting, and incarceration options tend to be polycentric questions with many moving parts,[43] and these are far less easy to present in a simplified way, whether in a polarized legislature or in a referendum in a neopopulist state.[44] Since resolving prison overcrowding is a complex task, which cannot be answered by a yes/no vote from the public, policy making in such matters typically takes place behind closed doors, in negotiations between prison administrators and private service providers.

Another important factor is the logic of the market. The existence of strong economic interests to preserve and increase mass incarceration acts as a counterweight to the need to create policies that better fit economically lean times. It is difficult for states to pare down their prisons when they are tied up in contractual obligations with private providers and with other states to provide space, inmates, or both. The Arizona example, discussed in depth in chapter 6, is particularly important; returning to the "tough 'n' cheap" days of early penal policies may not be a realistic expectation, but the strong partnership with CCA and other private elements is yielding a postmodern version of "tough 'n' efficient."

Of course, the question is whether overcrowding inmates in private institutions, shipping them away from their families, and shifting them out of state institutions and into county jails is "efficient" in terms of recidivism reduction. And that is a third important factor: austere times are not conducive to long-term planning that may require expenditures on prison rehabilitation programs and reentry schemes. The temptation to cut costs in the short term until the economy improves is understandable, but without a significant shift toward rehabilitation and true hope for recidivism reduction it is unlikely to yield results that will please us when the economy improves.

The lesson to be learned from these policies is that while costs are a powerful motivator of policy changes, they cannot achieve lasting positive reform without keeping the more fundamental arguments about human dignity, hope, and belief in change on the table. Which raises other concerns: the potential to use cost-related arguments to save money at the expense of inmates' conditions and human rights and the questionable price of crafting a public discourse that, while possessing broader appeal, is shallower and ideologically neutral.

TOUGH 'N' CHEAP

Another criticism of overreliance on cost-centered arguments is their potential for being used as a double-edged sword. One need not recur to the Dickensian examples of cost-saving at the expense of inmates, such as Sheriff Greg Bartlett of Morgan County, who starved Alabama inmates to line his own pockets, to see the great dangers of tough 'n' cheap justifications for punitiveness made in good faith.[45] The same criminal justice problems invoke punitive and nonpunitive solutions, both justified by the cost rationale. Perhaps one of the clearest examples of the common roots of humonetarianism and tough 'n' cheap policies is the contrast between death penalty abolition and the streamlining of capital litigation. As argued in chapter 4, much of the advocacy for recession-era death penalty abolition centered on the costs of postconviction legal proceedings, which in many states involve free legal representation not only for appeals but also for habeas corpus proceedings of death row inmates. In several states, punitive actors and institutions have responded by proposing streamlined appellate processes that would cut costs as well as inmates' judicial review options. The argument between abolitionists and proponents of the death penalty therefore centers on the problematic, and ideology-free, question of whether the death penalty, as administered currently, is broken beyond repair or merely defective to an extent that can be fixed by a less coddling postconviction process. Since the public is presented with two rival cost-saving proposals, extraneous arguments, such as the concern about wrongful convictions, have to be part of the debate.

Another example is the controversy over prison costs and savings in California. As discussed in chapter 6, the state has been embroiled in a series of moves and countermoves made by the state in an effort to comply with the letter, and circumvent the spirit, of *Plata v. Schwarzenegger*,[46] a 2009 order by a federal three-judge panel requiring that the state reduce its prison population to 137.5 percent capacity. This population reduction was mandated in order to improve the abysmal health care provided to inmates, which the panel found to be causally linked to prison overcrowding. The state vowed to appeal the order, but a five-to-four majority of Supreme Court Justices approved it in *Brown v. Plata*.[47]

Even before the Supreme Court decision, the Schwarzenegger administration (in which Governor Brown was attorney general) was hard at work trying to find solutions to prison overcrowding and its devastating budgetary impact.[48] In 2009, a year after the financial crisis hit private businesses and state and local government, the average yearly cost of incarceration was $47,000 per inmate.[49] Some ideas for mitigating these costs advocated by the Schwarzenegger administration, such as housing inmates in Mexico,[50] were the subject of downright mockery,[51] but some were more realistic, such as the idea to "downgrade" several offenses and try them as misdemeanors so that inmates would serve their time in county jails in lieu of state prisons.[52] The plan was submitted to the legislature,[53] approved by the senate,[54] and then gutted by the assembly;[55] but a later reincarnation of the plan, implemented during Governor Brown's tenure, became the Criminal Justice Realignment, an amalgam of legislative pieces shifting responsibility for tens of thousands of inmates from state prisons and parole offices to county jails and probation offices.[56] Realignment has been referred to as "the largest criminal justice experiment ever conducted in America."[57] The interplay between the federal judiciary and the state is an example of a situation in which a judicial order puts the agency under strict budgetary constraints and the agency resists.[58] An econometric analysis done on population reduction orders has revealed that when the court orders the state to de-crowd its prisons, the money to achieve the reform comes at the expense of welfare.[59]

The efforts to address the cost issue, as well as the Supreme Court mandate in *Brown*, led California to shift responsibility for incarcerating a substantial percentage of its inmates to the counties. And while some counties have chosen a humonetarian path, opting for community sanctions and reentry programs, others are addressing their new responsibilities via a frenzy of jail construction and expansions, pay-as-you-stay policies, and a push for further privatization of the prison industry. The newest development on the California overcrowding front is a sobering one to those concerned about the reversibility of humonetarian initiatives. On August 27, 2013, Governor Brown announced his new plan for solving the California prison crisis: the state would invest $315 million of its reserves in private prisons, on California soil and out of state.[60] This plan, promptly approved by the State Assembly,[61] would enable the state to avoid releasing ten thousand inmates, the remaining number of releases required by a federal court population reduction order. "Public safety is the priority, and we'll take care of it," the governor was quoted as saying. "The money is there." It was later made clear that Brown successfully used this threat of additional expenditures to extract a two-year extension from the federal courts to implement the Criminal Justice Realignment.[62]

Combating tough 'n' cheap policies and better economic times requires a combination of human rights arguments and financial acumen. The cost argument should not be abandoned, wholesale, to use by punitive legislators and mass incarceration advocates. Supplementing the cost argument with genuine care for the people caught in the correctional machine is important, but rather than abandon a line of rhetoric and policy making that has proved valuable and effective, I suggest reframing the cost argument to address the need for efficiency and sustainability in the long run, through comprehensive reentry policies and recidivism reduction.

MORALITY AND THE FLATTENING OF
PUBLIC DISCOURSE

The moral indignation and dismay expressed by many progressive advocates at the retreat from human rights discourse in corrections is understandable. A few months before the third hunger strike against solitary confinement in California prisons, Legal Services for Prisoners with Children, with UC Hastings students, organized a panel on conditions in the SHU, which I chaired. In addition to advocates, lawyers, and psychiatrists, the panel featured two current UC Berkeley students who served several years of incarceration in SHUs. As audience members raised the issue of potential savings if solitary confinement were to be minimized or abolished altogether, one of the formerly incarcerated students expressed indignation about the discourse. "I hear people say they are against prisons to save money," he said. "But it has to come from understanding that these are people like you and me and you can't do this."

This concern about the shallowness of humonetarianism has a strong symbolic component. It seems problematic to focus the public conversation on nickels and dimes when the intangible costs of dehumanization, desensitization, and social disengagement are on the line; a recent documentary by Eugene Jarecki, critically examining the war on drugs, raised serious humanitarian concerns about the ways in which mass incarceration has led American society to "give up" on the lowest rungs in its social ladder.[63] Such harms are left unaddressed in a cost-centered public conversation, and that is a heavy price to pay for a society that wants to value empathy and espouse ideas of hope and upward mobility. But the implications of flattening public discourse and narrowing it to market concerns are not merely symbolic. As demonstrated in earlier chapters, while the cost argument was a centerpiece of legal reform in various nonpunitive campaigns, it was often accompanied by deeper, more substantive arguments, such as the innocence issue in the context of the death penalty, disproportionate punishment in the context of Three Strikes, and racial disparities in the context of drug reform. These deeper arguments have not made headway in reform prior to the current recession, but they are still, arguably, an essential part of the conversation, because the cost argument does not carry enough moral force on its own to propel lasting change.

While the risk of tough 'n' cheap policies is real and disturbing, I find the moral concerns about the change in discourse understandable but less troubling, possibly because of my pessimism about the potential of making human rights, and dignity, the centerpiece of public conversation on correctional matters. In *Mass Incarceration on Trial,* Jonathan Simon analyzes the litigation on prison health services in California, culminating in the aforementioned Supreme Court decision in *Brown v. Plata.*[64] Simon finds encouragement in the opinion of Justice Kennedy, the Court's centrist, which he sees as providing significant support for a discourse of dignity regarding prison conditions. My take on *Plata* is less optimistic than Simon's. In the very same case, Justice Antonin Scalia expressed concern about the release of inmates, referring to them as "fine physical specimens who have developed intimidating muscles pumping iron in the prison gym." That such dehumanizing, Lombrosian terminology can be used with impunity and without shame by a Supreme Court justice is indication that this is not a court in which dignity has permeated and transformed the conversation. At best, it is a court in which some justices believe in dignity, and they do so in the face of truly abysmal conditions. My pessimism about the dignity conversation also stems from its failure to make headway in public discourse in other arenas, such as racial discrimination in applying the death penalty.[65] The strongest argument on behalf of centering criminal justice conversations on the humonetarian argument is simple practicality: it seems to succeed where other types of conversation have utterly failed.

I disagree, however, with the premise that the cost-benefit perspective on legal reform is necessarily shallow. Assessing priorities in terms of neoliberal cost-benefit analysis has long been a feature of American discourse. Kim Phillips Fine[66] and others have highlighted the role played by the conservative libertarian movement[67] and the ultra-rich[68] in reframing social issues and debates about funding and cost.[69] David Montgomery estimates that the shift toward market perspectives as an all-encompassing value occurred in the 1920s, after the labor movement lost much of its mobilization struggle and the left wing of the workers' movement was isolated from effective mass influence.[70] In *Prisoners of the American Dream*, Mike Davis argues that any last hope for change in the framework was lost after the fall of the social movements of the 1960s, leading right-wing thinkers to embrace a hypercapitalist approach to political and social issues and leaving left-wing voters without an alternative economic program to root for.[71] Alan Brinkley dates the shift to market perspectives to the second term of Franklin Delano Roosevelt, arguing that New Deal policies, which aimed to use the governmental apparatus to fight inequalities and curb modern industrial capitalism, were replaced by a Keynesian perspective that prioritized consumption and competition as a path for economic growth.[72]

Regardless of the historical origins of the logic of the market as the conceptual default for sociopolitical issues, cost-benefit analysis and public choice have become the default models for discussing social problems. Serious social issues that could generate conversations about tolerance, diversity, acceptance, and empathy are expressed in dollar values. The concern that one's tax money subsidizes activities by "others" is one that permeates every conversation about the "other," be it poverty programs, welfare, or homelessness. The racialized and genderized public discourse of "welfare queens" features disparagement of poor black women under the guise of concern about tax money paid for another person's presumed choice to have children without proper financial support.[73] San Francisco's transition to "care not cash" programs, which purported to offer services to the homeless while decreasing the amount of disposable cash they received, was framed as a way to ensure that public money was spent in acceptable ways.[74] Debates about sit-lie urban ordinances, effectively framed to exclude homeless people from urban sidewalks, have focused on concerns about the impact of the homeless population on economic activity and the need to improve the structure of public services for the homeless.[75] And debates about obesity as a public health issue have addressed public willingness to incur the costs of health care, presumably higher for the obese population, leading to controversial proposed measures such as a tax on sugar-sweetened beverages.[76]

All of these issues are fiercely battled in a "war of ideas" in an increasingly fragmented political world, and it may be that the effort to think about them in terms of nickels and dimes is a way to reach common ground in conversation and policy making. In *Age of Fracture*, Daniel Rodgers argues that the last quarter of the twentieth century was characterized by pushing aside monolithic Keynesian macroeconomics in favor of a plethora of think tanks, well-defined identities and interests, and political ideological platforms.[77] Rodgers does not directly address crime or criminal justice policy, but his analysis of the Reagan and Thatcher administrations shows a pattern of disaggregation and individualization and an increasingly divisive political world, accompanied by an uncritical acceptance of market mechanisms as the solution to public policy problems. It is not coincidental that this monumental cultural shift occurred at about the same time that symbolic, sensationalist notions of violent crime and threats to public safety were touted by ideology-motivated political figures. It is also not coincidental that the last push for common ground—the right-wing and left-wing critiques of indeterminate sentencing and the push for uniformity and equality in sentencing—gave way to a polarized debate, in which one side brings up just desserts, deterrence, and the need to wage war on drugs and the other side brings up racial inequalities, market critiques, and disenfranchisement.

It is worthwhile, therefore, to think about the cost argument as an idea that not only has the potential, but the proven ability, to bridge fractures in the conversation about crime and punishment.

Indeed, using dollar values and cost-benefit analyses can be a strong signal of public preferences. A good, albeit misguided, example is former California governor Arnold Schwarzenegger's well-intentioned effort to enact legislation that would prohibit the legislature from allocating more money for corrections than for public education in a given budget.[78] The idea, from an informed fiscal perspective, is highly problematic; as pointed out by the Legislative Analyst's Office, one cannot compare two budgetary items to each other and isolate them from all other budgetary items and the bigger fiscal context. But the importance of the proposal was not so much in the good it would perhaps do practically but in its symbolism. The message that Schwarzenegger wanted to send was that education should take priority over incarceration, and he chose to express it fiscally. In some ways, the simple fiscal comparison between expenditures on higher education (or, for that matter, K–12 education) and on imprisonment is much more effective than emotional pleas and protestations against the school-to-prison pipeline, and more important, it captures the same concern about priorities. Our tendency to examine social problems, values, and initiatives according to their costs is not only effective in creating common ground but also meaningful in the message it conveys.

TOWARD JUST AND EFFICIENT CORRECTIONS: REFRAMING HUMONETARIANISM

Humonetarianism is a mixed bag. Its successes and advances are highly dependent on the local political context and sensitive to changes in the economy, crime rates, and public animus. The risks of tough 'n' cheap policy suggestions, which would perpetuate mass incarceration and worsen its conditions, are ever present. How can its potential be fully harnessed to curb mass incarceration and bring proportion and sanity into the American prison system?

The way to counter cynical tough 'n' cheap arguments, as well as emergency policies with little forethought, is to frame the cost conversation, in a genuine and deep way, to address costs in the long term. While cuts to programs and rolling expenses onto inmates in pay-to-stay jails may prove cost-effective in the short term, the resulting recidivism rates may not make them worthwhile. The tendency in a crisis-prompted discourse is to resolve the immediate problem, but the fact that the investment has to be permanent and thorough to yield results has to be part of the advocacy effort against punitivism.

One possible example pertains to felon reentry through enfranchisement. The California Criminal Justice Realignment brought up the possibility that California, which denies the right to vote to people "in prison or on parole for conviction of a felony," would now have to award voting rights to inmates who are doing time in jails in lieu of prisons for "non-non-non" felonies.[79] This was not, of course, the interpretation the secretary of state gave Realignment before the 2012 election. When several civil rights organizations sued for an original writ demanding that the constitutional ambiguity be resolved in favor of the fundamental right to vote, the Court of Appeals, and subsequently the California supreme court, rejected the argument without even providing reasons. Very few studies have systematically explored the logical hypothesis that civic engagement in the form of voting rights and decline in recidivism may be correlated, and those that have involved fairly limited local settings. The argument "allowing inmates to vote saves money" is possibly true, but to date it remains largely unproven and is unconvincing without an accompanying text about the importance of voting rights to civic engagement, racial and class integration, and the revival of communities and neighborhoods beyond the disenfranchised individuals.

In other cases, however, the connection is more immediate. Some lawmakers arguing from a "smart on crime" stance emphasize strong rehabilitation programming, arguing that the ultimate savings in recidivism reduction may be worth the initial expenditure involved in providing programming.[80] The success of framing the cost argument in a broad way depends, as the account in this book demonstrates, on several factors. The political process needs to be sufficiently committed to economic recovery to move beyond partisan positions and accept prudence—a condition existing in some local governments and not in others. The cost argument itself needs to be genuine and irrefutable, with demonstrated savings extolled by nonpartisan fiscal analysts. The argument needs to be incremental in nature and appeal to conservative segments of the public as well, accessing the libertarian logic of small government. And the argument needs to properly address the issues of risk to public safety, which would become the obvious emotional resistance to it.

Framing the conversation about cost as one that encompasses long-term investment in reintegrating more than two million Americans into their communities and accepts long-term recidivism reduction as long-term savings is not a fanciful dream. Lawmakers, policy makers, criminal justice institutions, and taxpayers are embracing a new way of understanding corrections, which has bridged decades-long political gaps and can bring people together in an era of warring ideals and values. Making cost language inclusive is valuable not only in drawing attention to pressing issues that could otherwise be framed as externalities or intangible costs. It is through this opportunity that real, lasting change can be brought to the American correctional project. Here's hoping that, paraphrasing Rahm Emanuel, we will not allow a serious crisis to go to waste.[81]

NOTES

INTRODUCTION

1. J. Campbell Bruce, *Escape from Alcatraz: The True Crime Classic* (Berkeley: Ten Speed Press, [1963] 2005).

2. China Mieville, *The City and the City* (New York: Random House, 2010).

CHAPTER 1

1. Katherine Beckett, *Making Crime Pay: Law and Order in Contemporary American Politics* (New York: Oxford University Press, 1997).

2. Marie Gottschalk, *The Prison and the Gallows: The Politics of Mass Incarceration in America* (Cambridge: Cambridge University Press, 2006).

3. Vanessa Barker, *The Politics of Imprisonment: How the Democratic Process Shapes the Way America Punishes Offenders* (New York: Oxford University Press, 2009).

4. Mona Lynch, *Sunbelt Justice: Arizona and the Transformation of American Punishment* (Stanford, CA: Stanford University Press, 2009).

5. Robert Perkinson, *Texas Tough: The Rise of America's Prison Empire* (New York: Metropolitan Books, 2010).

6. Michelle Alexander, *The New Jim Crow: Mass Incarceration in the Age of Colorblindness* (New York: New Press, 2010).

7. Ruth Wilson Gilmore, *Golden Gulag: Prisons, Surplus, Crisis, and Opposition in Globalizing California* (Berkeley: University of California Press, 2007). Gilmore provides an extensive analysis of the bond process and of the private profiteering and private prison companies' dealings with California.

8. David Garland, *The Culture of Control: Crime and Social Order in Contemporary Society* (Chicago: University of Chicago Press, 2001).

9. Jonathan Simon, *Governing through Crime: How the War on Crime Transformed American Democracy and Created a Culture of Fear,* Studies in Crime and Public Policy (New York: Oxford University Press, 2007).

10. Loïc Wacquant, *Punishing the Poor: The Neoliberal Government of Social Insecurity* (Durham: Duke University Press, 2009).

11. Joe Soss, Richard C. Fording, and Sanford F. Schram, *Disciplining the Poor: Neoliberal Paternalism and the Persistent Power of Race* (Chicago: University of Chicago Press, 2011).

12. Mona Lynch, "Theorizing Punishment: Reflections on Wacquant's *Punishing the Poor,*" *Critical Sociology* 37(2): 237–44 (2011).

13. See Angela Davis, "Masked Racism: Reflections on the Prison Industrial Complex," *Colorlines,* September 10, 1998, http://colorlines.com/archives/1998/09/masked_racism_ reflections_on_the_prison_industrial_complex.html; Alexander, *The New Jim Crow.*

14. Joshua Page, *The Toughest Beat: Politics, Punishment, and the Prison Officers Union in California* (New York: Oxford University Press, 2011); Tara Herivel and Paul Wright, eds., *Prison Profiteers: Who Makes Money from Mass Incarceration* (New York: New Press, 2009).

15. The Obama administration's diminishing of the gap between crack and powder cocaine and changes to mandatory minimums for drug offenders, reviewed in chapter 5, can be attributed partly to its commitment to racial justice.

16. The death penalty moratorium in Illinois, reviewed in chapter 4, has been explained as a reaction to the alarming number of exonerations; recently introduced policies to record police investigations stem from the same rationales and concerns.

17. Gallup polls in Washington and Colorado, whose recent decisions to legalize recreational marijuana are extensively reviewed in chapter 5, showed strong public support for legalization and low levels of stigma associated with users.

18. The term is borrowed from David Garland's *The Culture of Control,* chapter 2.

19. Georg Rusche and Otto Kirchheimer, *Punishment and Social Structure* (Edison, NJ: Transaction Publishers, 2003). As Dario Melossi explains in his introduction to the 2003 edition of the book, the book expanded upon ideas first presented in Rusche's 1931 article "Labour Market and Penal Sanction," which was written and presented before both Rusche and Kirchheimer fled Nazi Germany. The article provoked the interest of leading sociologists in the United States, such as Thorsten Sellin and Edwin Sutherland, who hoped that its thesis would be expanded beyond the framework of the article. In the late 1930s, Kirchheimer reworked Rusche's ideas; the latter was mysteriously "not available" to assist in that process, and the book, while appearing under both names, is largely the product of Kirchheimer's expansion and reediting of Rusche's original work. Dario Melossi, Introduction to Rusche and Kirchheimer, *Punishment and Social Structure,* xiii–xx.

20. See, e.g., Dario Melossi and Massimo Pavarini, *The Prison and the Factory: Origins of the Penitentiary System* (London: Macmillan, 1981); Ivan Jankovic, "Labor Market and Imprisonment," *Crime and Social Justice* 8 (Fall–Winter 1977): 17–31.

21. William J. Chambliss, "A Sociological Analysis of the Law of Vagrancy," *Social Problems: Journal of the Society for the Study of Social Problems* 12 (1964): 67–77.

22. E. P. Thompson, *Whigs and Hunters* (London: Breviary Stuff Publications, 2013).

23. Douglas Hay, "Property, Authority and the Criminal Law," in Douglas Hay et al., *Albion's Fatal Tree: Crime and Society in Eighteenth-Century England* (New York, 1975), 17–63.

24. Troy Duster, *The Legislation of Morality: Law, Drugs, and Moral Judgment* (New York: Free Press, 1972).

25. Anthony Platt, "The Triumph of Benevolence: The Origins of the Juvenile Justice System in the United States," in *Criminal Justice in America: A Critical Understanding*, ed. Richard Quinney (Boston: Little, Brown, 1974), 356–89.

26. Jonathan Simon, *Poor Discipline: Parole and the Social Control of the Underclass, 1890–1990* (Chicago: University of Chicago Press, 1993).

27. Stanley Cohen, *Visions of Social Control: Crime, Punishment and Classification* (Hoboken, NJ: Wiley, 1985).

28. David J. Rothman, *Conscience and Convenience: The Asylum and Its Alternatives in Progressive America* (Hoboken, NJ: Aldine Transaction, 2002).

29. Michel Foucault, *Discipline and Punish*, trans. Alan Sheridan (New York: Random House, 1977).

30. David Garland, *Punishment and Modern Society: A Study in Social Theory* (Chicago: University of Chicago Press, 1990).

31. Theorists writing about Marxist criminology often distinguish between instrumental and structural Marxism, which differ in their approach to the role of law. The former framework sees law as an instrument of the elites, whereas the latter regards it as a semiautonomous mechanism. Alan Stone, "The Place of Law in the Marxian Structure-Superstructure Archetype," *Law and Society Review* 19 (January 1985): 39–67; Isaac Balbus, "Commodity Form and Legal Form: An Essay on the 'Relative Autonomy' of the Law," Law and Society Review 11 (1977): 571–88; Steven Spitzer, "Toward a Marxian Theory of Deviance," *Social Problems* 22, no. 5 (1975): 638–51.

32. See, e.g., Dario Melossi, "Georg Rusche and Otto Kirchheimer: Punishment and Social Structure," *Crime and Social Justice* 9 (1978): 73–85; Melossi and Pavarini, *The Prison and the Factory*; Jankovic, "Labor Market and Imprisonment."

33. For a thorough historical critique, see John M. Beattie, *Crime and the Courts in England, 1660–1800* (Oxford: Clarendon Press, 1986). An example of a particular critique is Gil Gardner's analysis of the emergence of prisons in New York: Gil Gardner, "The Emergence of the New York State Prison System: A Critique of The Rusche-Kirchheimer Model," Crime and Social Justice 29 (1987): 88–109.

34. Jeffrey Adler, "A Historical Analysis of the Law of Vagrancy," *Criminology* 27 (1987): 209–29, which uses the example of Saint Louis to show that many factors came together to create vagrancy laws.

35. Theodore Chiricos and Miriam Delone, "Labor Surplus and Punishment: A Review and Assessment of Theory and Evidence," *Social Problems* 39 (1992): 421–46.

36. Also see David Greenberg, *Crime and Capitalism: Readings in Marxist Criminology* (Philadelphia: Temple University Press, 1993), 648.

37. Greenberg, *Crime and Capitalism*.

38. Steven Box and Chris Hale, "Economic Crisis and the Rising Prisoner Population in England and Wales, 1949–1979," *Crime and Social Justice* 16 (1982): 20–35.

39. Dario Melossi, "Punishment and Social Action: Changing Vocabularies of Punitive Motive within a Political Business Cycle," *Current Perspectives in Social Theory* 6 (1985): 169–97, 183.

40. Raymond Michalowski and Susan Carlson, "Unemployment, Imprisonment, and Social Structures of Accumulation: Historical Contingency in the Rusche-Kirchheimer Hypothesis," *Criminology* 37 (2006): 217–50.

41. David E. Barlow, Melissa Hickman Barlow, and Theodore G. Chiricos, "Long Economic Cycles and the Criminal Justice System in the U.S.," *Crime, Law and Social Change* 19 (March 1993): 143–69.

42. Richard Freeman, "Crime and the Labour Market," in *The Economic Dimensions of Crime*, ed. Nigel Fielding, Alan Clarke, and Robert Witt (New York: St. Martin's Press, 2000), 150–76.

43. James Inverarity and Daniel McCarthy, "Punishment and Social Structure Revisited: Unemployment and Imprisonment in the United States, 1948–1984," *Sociological Quarterly* 29 (June 1988): 263–79.

44. Alessandro de Giorgi, *Rethinking the Political Economy of Punishment* (Surrey, UK: Aldershot Ashgate, 2006).

45. Don Weatherburn, "Economic Adversity and Crime," *Trends and Issues in Criminal Justice* 40 (1992): 1–9, http://aic.gov.au/documents/6/4/E/%7B64EB228A-70C9-4D5C-91A7-81118F819423%7Dti40.pdf.

46. United Nations Office of Drugs and Crime, "Monitoring the Impact of the Economic Crisis on Crime," 2010, www.unodc.org/documents/data-and-analysis/statistics/crime/GIVAS_Final_Report.pdf.

47. "U.K. Crime Falls Despite Hard Times," *Wall Street Journal,* July 18, 2013, http://online.wsj.com/article/SB10001424127887323993804578613670285006836.html.

48. Ross Colvin, "U.S. Recession Fuels Crime Rise, Police Chiefs Say," Reuters, January 27, 2009, www.reuters.com/article/2009/01/27/us-usa-economy-crime-idUSTRE50Q6FR20090127.

49. "FBI Releases Preliminary Annual Crime Statistics for 2010," FBI National Press Office, May 23, 2011, www.fbi.gov/news/pressrel/press-releases/fbi-releases-preliminary-annual-crime-statistics-for-2010.

50. Andrew Karmen, *New York Murder Mystery: The True Story behind the Crime Crash of the 1990s* (New York: New York University Press, 2006).

51. Anthony Amatrudo, *Criminology and Political Theory* (New York: Sage, 2009).

52. Clifford R. Shaw and Henry D. McKay, *Juvenile Delinquency and Urban Areas* (Chicago: University of Chicago Press, 1942).

53. Robert K. Merton, "Social Structure and Anomie," *American Sociological Review* 3 (October 1938): 672–82.

54. Box and Hale, "Economic Crisis and the Rising Prisoner Population."

55. Beckett, *Making Crime Pay.*

56. Simon, *Governing through Crime.*

57. Barker, *The Politics of Imprisonment.*

58. "FBI: Crime Falls, but Small Town Violence Rises," *Huffington Post,* June 1, 2009, www.huffingtonpost.com/huff-wires/20090601/crime/.

59. Freeman, "Crime and the Labour Market."

60. Bruce Western, *Punishment and Inequality in America* (New York: Russell Sage Foundation, 2007).

61. Franklin E. Zimring and Gordon Hawkins, *The Scale of Imprisonment* (Chicago: University of Chicago Press, 1991); Franklin E. Zimring, *The Great American Crime Decline* (New York: Oxford University Press, 2008).

62. Emile Durkheim, *The Division of Labor in Society* (New York: Macmillan, [1897] 1933; New York: Free Press, 1964).

63. Kai Erikson, *Wayward Puritans: A Study in the Sociology of Deviance* (Upper Saddle River, NJ: Prentice Hall, 2004), 196.

64. Martin Killias, "Power Concentration, Legitimation Crisis and Penal Severity: A Comparative Perspective," *International Annals of Criminology* 24 (1986): 184–211.

65. De Giorgi, "Rethinking the Political Economy of Punishment."

66. Gary Becker, "Crime and Punishment: An Economic Approach," *Journal of Political Economy* 76 (March–April 1968): 169–217.

67. Ibid., 176.

68. One notable example is Isaac Ehrlich's study of the deterrent effect of capital punishment, concluding that each execution prevented eight murders: Isaac Ehrlich, "The Deterrent Effect of Capital Punishment: A Question of Life and Death," *American Economic Review* 65 (1975): 397–417. Ehrlich's work and its effect on death penalty litigation are discussed at length in chapter 4. Also see Mark A. Cohen, *The Costs of Crime and Justice* (London: Routledge, 2005).

69. Becker, "Crime and Punishment," 193.

70. George W. Wickersham, *Enforcement of the Prohibition Laws: Official Records of the National Commission on Law Observance and Enforcement Pertaining to Its Investigation of the Facts as to the Enforcement, the Benefits and the Abuses under the Prohibition Laws, Both Before and Since the Adoption of the Eighteenth Amendment to the Constitution,* 5 vols. (Washington, DC: U.S. Government Printing Office, 1931).

71. Samuel Walker, ed., *Records of the Wickersham Commission on Law Observance and Enforcement* (Bethesda, MD: University Publications of America, 1997), www.lexisnexis .com/documents/academic/upa_cis/1965_wickershamcommpt1.pdf. The report on Prohibition was titled *The Enforcement of the Prohibition Laws of the United States.*

72. Charles M. Gray, *The Costs of Crime* (Thousand Oaks, CA: Sage, 1979), 13–39.

73. Maxwell L. Stearns and Todd J. Zywicki, *Public Choice Concepts and Applications in Law* (New York: West, 2009.)

74. Task Force on Assessment, the President's Commission on Law Enforcement and Administration of Justice, *Task Force Report: Crime and Its Impact—An Assessment* (Washington, DC: US Government Printing Office, 1967), 42.

75. Cohen, *The Costs of Crime and Justice.* Also see Mark Cohen, "Measuring the Costs and Benefits of Crime and Justice," *Criminal Justice* 4 (2000): 263–315.

76. Allen K. Lynch, Todd Clear, and David W. Rasmussen, "Modeling the Cost of Crime," in Fielding, Clarke and Witt, *The Economic Dimensions of Crime,* 226–39.

77. Ted Miller, Mark Cohen, and Brian Wiersema, "Victim Costs and Consequences: A New Look," National Institute of Justice Research Report, 1996, www.ncjrs.gov/pdffiles /victcost.pdf.

78. Fox Butterfield, "Survey Finds That Crimes Cost $450 Billion a Year," *New York Times,* April 22, 1996.

79. David Anderson, "The Aggregate Burden of Crime," *Journal of Law and Economics* 42 (1999): 611–43.

80. For more of the difficulties of bounding data and deciding on the pertinent items, see Janna Shapland, "Auditing Criminal Justice," in Fielding, Clarke, and Witt, *The Economic Dimensions of Crime*, 239–50.

81. For example, health care expenses of guards and other officers. Christian Hendrichson and Ruth Delaney, "The Price of Prisons: What Incarceration Costs Taxpayers," Vera Institute of Justice, 2012, www.pewstates.org/uploadedFiles/PCS_Assets/2012/http_www .vera.org_download_file = 3495_the-price-of-prisons-updated.pdf.

82. Cohen, *The Costs of Crime and Justice*, 85.

83. Sara Wakefield, "Invisible Inequality, Million Dollar Blocks, and Extra-Legal Punishment: A Review of Recent Contributions to Mass Incarceration Scholarship," *Punishment and Society* 12 (2010): 209–15.

84. Raymond B. Swaray, Roger Bowls, and Rimaway Pradiptyo, "The Application of Economic Analysis to Criminal Justice Interventions: A Review of the Literature," *Criminal Justice Policy* 16 (2005): 141–63.

85. Cynthia McDougall, Mark Cohen, Raymond Swaray, and Amanda Perr, "The Costs and Benefits of Sentencing: A Systematic Review," *Annals of the American Academy of Political and Social Science* 587 (2003): 160–77.

86. James Austin, "Using Early Release to Relieve Prison Crowding: A Dilemma in Public Policy," *Crime and Delinquency* 32 (1986): 404–502.

87. Mark Cohen, "Pain, Suffering, and Jury Awards: A Study of the Cost of Crime to Victims," *Law and Society Review* 22 (1988): 537–55.

88. Andrew S. Rajkumar and Michael T. French, "Drug Abuse, Crime Costs, and the Economic Benefits of Treatment," *Journal of Quantitative Criminology* 13 (1997): 291–324.

89. U.S. Department of Health and Human Services, "National Treatment Improvement Evaluation Study," 1997, www.icpsr.umich.edu/icpsrweb/SAMHDA/studies/2884.

90. Michael K. Block and Thomas S. Ulen, "Cost Functions for Correctional Institutions," in Gray, *The Costs of Crime*, 187–212.

91. Amos Tversky and Daniel Kahneman, "Judgment under Uncertainty: Heuristics and Biases," *Science* 185 (1974): 1124–31.

92. Daniel Nagin and Greg Pogarsky, "Integrating Celerity, Impulsivity, and Extralegal Sanction Threats into a Model of General Deterrence: Theory and Evidence," *Criminology* 39 (2000): 865–92; Daniel S. Nagin and Raymond Paternoster, "Enduring Individual Differences and Rational Choice Theories of Crime," *Law and Society Review* 27 (1993): 467–96; Valerie Wright, "Deterrence in Criminal Justice: Evaluating Certainty vs. Severity of Punishment," Sentencing Project, 2010, www.sentencingproject.org/doc/deterrence%20briefing%20.pdf.

93. Yael Hassin, "Two Models for Predicting Recidivism, Clinical versus Statistical— Another View," *British Journal of Criminology* 26 (1986): 270–86.

CHAPTER 2

1. Jonathan Simon, *Governing through Crime: How the War on Crime Transformed American Democracy and Created a Culture of Fear*, Studies in Crime and Public Policy (New York: Oxford University Press, 2007).

2. Katherine Beckett, *Making Crime Pay: Law and Order in Contemporary American Politics* (New York: Oxford University Press, 1999). See also Marie Gottschalk, *The Prison and the Gallows: The Politics of Mass Incarceration in America* (Cambridge: Cambridge University Press, 2006).

3. Malcolm M. Feeley and Jonathan Simon, "The New Penology: Notes on the Emerging Strategy of Corrections and Its Implications," *Criminology* 30, no. 4 (November 1992): 449–74, doi:10.1111/j.1745-9125.1992.tb01112.x. See also Jonathan Simon, "From the Big House to the Warehouse: Rethinking Prisons and State Government in the 20th Century," *Punishment and Society* 2, no. 2 (April 2000): 213–34, doi:10.1177/14624740022227962.

4. Loïc Wacquant, *Punishing the Poor: The Neoliberal Government of Social Insecurity* (Durham: Duke University Press, 2009); and David Garland, *The Culture of Control: Crime and Social Order in Contemporary Society* (Chicago: University of Chicago Press, 2002).

5. Mona Lynch, *Sunbelt Justice: Arizona and the Transformation of American Punishment* (Redwood City, CA: Stanford Law Books, 2009).

6. Robert Perkinson, *Texas Tough: The Rise of America's Prison Empire* (New York: Picador, 2010).

7. Franklin E. Zimring, *The City That Became Safe: New York's Lessons for Urban Crime and Its Control* (New York: Oxford University Press, 2011).

8. Vanessa Barker, *The Politics of Imprisonment: How the Democratic Process Shapes the Way America Punishes Offenders* (New York: Oxford University Press, 2009).

9. Lisa L. Miller, *The Perils of Federalism: Race, Poverty, and the Politics of Crime Control* (New York: Oxford University Press, 2008).

10. Daniel Okrent, *Last Call: The Rise and Fall of Prohibition* (New York: Scribner, 2011).

11. David E. Kyvig, *Repealing National Prohibition* (Chicago: University of Chicago Press, 1979), 9, citing Charles Stelzle, *Why Prohibition!* (New York: George H. Doran, 1918).

12. Donald J. Boudreaux and A. C. Pritchard, "The Price of Prohibition," *Arizona Law Review* 36 (1994): 1–11.

13. National Commission on Law Observance and Enforcement, "Wickersham Report on Police," *American Journal of Police Science* 2, no. 4 (July–August 1931): 337–48, www.jstor.org/stable/1147362, excerpted from United States National Commission on Law Observance and Enforcement, *Report on Police*, no. 14 (Washington, DC: Government Printing Office, 1931).

14. Henry W. Anderson, "Report on the Enforcement of the Prohibition Laws of the United States," report 2, in National Commission on Law Observance and Enforcement, *The Wickersham Commission Report on Alcohol Prohibition* (Washington, DC: Government Printing Office, 1931), 1:97–98 (separate report, January 7, 1931).

15. Boudreaux and Pritchard, "The Price of Prohibition." See also Kyvig, *Repealing National Prohibition*.

16. Fletcher Dobyns, *The Amazing Story of Repeal: An Exposé on the Power of Propaganda* (Chicago: Willett, Clark & Co.,1940).

17. V. F. Nourse, "Rethinking Crime Legislation: History and Harshness," *Tulsa Law Review* 39 (2004): 925–39, http://scholarship.law.georgetown.edu/facpub/1124.

18. Daniel Katkin, "Habitual Offender Laws: A Reconsideration," *Buffalo Law Review* 21 (1971): 99–120.

19. "Repeal of Baumes Law Asked in Bill," *St. Petersburg Times,* April 21, 1929; "A Sensible Repeal," *Milwaukee Sentinel,* March 23, 1929.

20. Daniel T. Rodgers, *Age of Fracture* (Cambridge, MA: Belknap Press, 2011).

21. Lynch, *Sunbelt Justice.*

22. This is why Michelle Alexander's book refers to incarceration as "the new Jim Crow." Michelle Alexander, *The New Jim Crow: Mass Incarceration in the Age of Colorblindness* (New York: New Press, 2010).

23. Malcolm M. Feeley and Edward L. Rubin, *Judicial Policy Making and the Modern State: How the Courts Reformed America's Prisons* (Cambridge: Cambridge University Press, 1998).

24. This era is soberly depicted in Stephen King's "Rita Hayworth and the Shawshank Redemption," later made into the motion picture *The Shawshank Redemption.* Stephen King, "Rita Hayworth and Shawshank Redemption: Hope Springs Eternal," in *Different Seasons* (New York: Viking Press, 1982); *The Shawshank Redemption,* dir. Frank Darabont (1994; Castle Rock Entertainment, Beverly Hills, CA, 2007), DVD.

25. Feeley and Rubin, *Judicial Policy Making and the Modern State.*

26. Dagoberto Gilb, "Writ Writer: One Man's Journey for Justice," *Independent Lens,* season 9, episode 23, dir. Susanne Mason, aired June 3, 2008 (New Day Films, Harriman, NY, 2008), DVD.

27. Ruiz v. Estelle, 503 F. Supp. 1265 (S.D. Tex. 1980), *aff'd in part, rev'd in part,* 679 F.2d 1115 (5th Cir. 1982) *amended in part, vacated in part,* 688 F.2d 266 (5th Cir. 1982).

28. Mapp v. Ohio, 367 U.S. 643 (1961).

29. Gideon v. Wainwright, 372 U.S. 335 (1963).

30. Duncan v. Louisiana, 391 U.S. 145 (1968).

31. Miranda v. Arizona, 384 U.S. 436 (1966).

32. Terry v. Ohio, 392 U.S. 1 (1968).

33. Tracey Maclin, "*Terry v. Ohio*'s Fourth Amendment Legacy: Black Men and Police Discretion," *St. John's Law Review* 72, no. 3 (Summer–Fall 1998): 1271–1322, http://scholarship.law.stjohns.edu/lawreview/vol72/iss3/25; Akhil Reed Amar, "Terry and Fourth Amendment First Principles," *St. John's Law Review* 72, no. 3 (Summer–Fall 1998): 1097–1132, http://scholarship.law.stjohns.edu/lawreview/vol72/iss3/15.

34. Hadar Aviram, "Packer in Context: Formalism and Fairness in the Due Process Model," *Law and Social Inquiry* 36, no.1 (Winter 2011): 237–61, doi:10.1111/j.1747–4469.2010.01230.x.

35. For more about the financial concerns behind Gideon, see Anthony Lewis, *Gideon's Trumpet* (New York: Knopf Doubleday, 1989).

36. Abraham S. Blumberg, "The Limits of the Criminal Sanction by Herbert L. Packer," *University of Pennsylvania Law Review* 117, no. 5 (March 1969): 790–94.

37. Abraham S. Blumberg, "The Practice of Law as a Confidence Game: Organizational Cooptation of a Profession," *Law and Society Review* 1 (1967): 15–39; David Sudnow, "Normal Crimes: Sociological Features of the Penal Code in the Public Defender's Office," *Social Problems* 12 (1965): 255–77; and Lisa J. McIntyre, *The Public Defender: The Practice of Law in the Shadow of Repute* (Chicago: University of Chicago Press, 1987).

38. *The Challenge of Crime in a Free Society: A Report by the President's Commission on Law Enforcement and Administration of Justice* (Washington, DC: Government Printing Office, 1967), www.ncjrs.gov/pdffiles1/nij/42.pdf.

39. Ibid., 31–35.

40. Jeffrey A. Roth and Paul B. Wice, *Pretrial Release and Misconduct in the District Of Columbia,* Promis Research Project, Pub. 16 (Washington, DC: Institute for Law and Social Research, 1978). See also Jeffrey A. Roth, "Financial Release and Pretrial Misconduct Risk in the District of Columbia," in *The Costs of Crime,* ed. Charles M. Gray (Beverly Hills, CA: Sage, 1979), 99–120.

41. Beckett, *Making Crime Pay.*

42. See also John F. Pfaff, "The Micro and Macro Causes of Prison Growth," *Georgia State University Law Review* 28, no. 4 (Summer 2012): 1239–73, http://digitalarchive.gsu .edu/gsulr/vol28/iss4/9.

43. Joseph L. Hoffmann and Nancy J. King, "Rethinking the Federal Role in State Criminal Justice" *New York University Law Review* 84, no. 2 (June 2009): 791.

44. Omnibus Crime Control and Safe Streets Act of 1968 (OCCSSA), Pub. L. No. 90–351, 82 Stat. 197 (1968) (codified as amended at 42 U.S.C. § 3711 *et seq.* and in scattered sections of 42 U.S.C. and 18 U.S.C.), http://transition.fcc.gov/Bureaus/OSEC/library /legislative_histories/1615.pdf. The provision at issue was codified at 18 U.S.C. § 3501.

45. This law, never repealed but never actually relied on, would later become the subject of a constitutional debate in *Dickerson,* which declared *Miranda* neither constitutional nor a mere prophylactic but a "constitutional prophylactic." Dickerson v. United States, 530 U.S. 428 (2000).

46. Packer and his cohorts refer to this kind of thinking as the "due process revolution." See, e.g., Herbert L. Packer, "Two Models of the Criminal Process," *University of Pennsylvania Law Review* 113, no. 1 (1964): 1–68, www.jstor.org/stable/3310562; and Herbert L. Packer, "Criminal Code Revision," *University of Toronto Law Journal* 23 (1973): 1, 13.

47. Pamela Irving Jackson and Leo Carroll, "Race and the War on Crime: The Sociopolitical Determinants of Municipal Police Expenditures in 90 Non-Southern U.S. Cities," *American Sociological Review* 46, no. 3 (June 1981): 290–305, www.jstor.org/stable/2095061.

48. Erving Goffman, *Asylums: Essays on the Social Situation of Mental Patients and Other Inmates* (New York: Anchor Books, 1961).

49. Norman Bruce Johnston, Leonard Savitz, and Marvin E. Wolfgang, eds., *The Sociology of Punishment and Correction* (New York: Wiley, 1962).

50. Donald Clemmer, *The Prison Community* (Boston: Christopher Publishing House, 1940).

51. Gresham M. Sykes, "The Pains of Imprisonment," in *The Society of Captives: A Study of a Maximum Security Prison* (Princeton: Princeton University Press, 1958), 63–83.

52. John D. Lofton Jr., "How Do You Fight Crime? Mandatory Prison Sentences Proposed" (editorial, based on an interview with James Q. Wilson), *Victoria Advocate,* April 11, 1975; John D. Lofton Jr., "The Case for Jailing Crooks," *Telegraph-Herald,* April 14, 1975.

53. Douglas Lipton, Robert Martinson, and Judith Wilks, *The Effectiveness of Correctional Treatment: A Survey of Treatment Evaluation Studies* (New York: Praeger, 1975).

54. Robert Martinson, "What Works? Questions and Answers about Prison Reform," *Public Interest* 35 (Spring 1974): 22–54. See also Rick Sarre, "Beyond 'What Works?': A 25-Year Jubilee Retrospective of Robert Martinson" (paper presented at the History of Crime, Policing and Punishment Conference, Australian Institute of Criminology and Charles Sturt University, Canberra, Australia, December 9–10 1999).

55. Martinson, "What Works?," 25.

56. Ibid., 49.

57. Robert Martinson, Ted Palmer, Stuart Adams, *Rehabilitation, Recidivism, and Research* (Oakland, CA: National Council on Crime and Delinquency, 1976).

58. Paul Gendreau and Robert R. Ross, "Effective Correctional Treatment: Bibliotherapy for Cynics," *Crime and Delinquency* 25, no. 4 (October 1979): 463–89; Paul Gendreau, "Treatment in Corrections: Martinson Was Wrong," *Canadian Psychology/Psychologie Canadienne* 22, no. 4 (October 1981): 332–38, doi:10.1037/h0081224; and Paul Gendreau and Robert R. Ross, "Revivification of Rehabilitation: Evidence from the 1980s," *Justice Quarterly* 4, no. 3 (1987): 349–407, doi:10.1080/07418828700089411. See also the later reframing of these works in Francis T. Cullen and Karen E. Gilbert, *Reaffirming Rehabilitation* (Cincinnati: Anderson Publishing Co., 1982).

59. Robert Martinson, "New Findings, New Views: A Note of Caution Regarding Sentencing Reform," *Hofstra Law Review* 7, no. 2 (Winter 1978): 243–58, 244.

60. Marvin E. Frankel, *Criminal Sentences: Law without Order* (New York: Hill and Wang, 1973).

61. National Council on Crime and Delinquency, *National Assessment of Structured Sentencing,* Bureau of Justice Assistance Monograph (Washington, DC: Bureau of Justice Assistance, 1996), www.ncjrs.gov/pdffiles/strsent.pdf.

62. "This Week's Citation Classic: Frankel M. E. Criminal Sentences: Law without Order," *Institute for Scientific Information Current Contents / Social & Behavioral Sciences,* no. 25, sec. 2A-6, June 23, 1986, www.garfield.library.upenn.edu/classics1986/A1986C697400001.pdf.

63. American Friends Service Committee, *Struggle for Justice: A Report on Crime and Punishment in America* (New York: Hill and Wang, 1971). See also David F. Greenberg and Drew Humphries, "The Co-optation of Fixed Sentencing Reform," *Crime and Delinquency* 26, no. 2 (April 1980): 206–25.

64. Norman Bruce Johnston, Kenneth Finkel, and Jeffrey A. Cohen, *Eastern State Penitentiary: Crucible of Good Intentions* (Philadelphia: Philadelphia Museum of Art for the Eastern State Penitentiary Task Force of the Preservation Coalition of Greater Philadelphia, 1994).

65. Alan M. Dershowitz, *Fair and Certain Punishment: Report of the Twentieth Century Fund Task Force on Criminal Sentencing* (New York: McGraw-Hill, 1976).

66. Andrew Von Hirsch, *Doing Justice—The Choice of Punishments,* Final Report of the Committee for the Study of Incarceration (New York: Farrar, Straus and Giroux, 1976).

67. James M. Anderson, Jeffrey R. Kling, and Kate Stith, "Measuring Interjudge Sentencing Disparity: Before and after the Federal Sentencing Guidelines," *Journal of Law and Economics* 42, no. S1 (April 1999): 271–308, www.jstor.org/stable/10.1086/467426.

68. For an account that places the prosecutor's power to bargain in the context of the guidelines, see Stephanos Bibas, "Incompetent Plea Bargaining and Extrajudicial Reforms," *Harvard Law Review* 126 (2012): 150–74. See also Stephanos Bibas, Max M. Schanzenbach, and Emerson H. Tiller, "Policing Politics at Sentencing," *Northwestern University Law Review* 103, no. 3 (Summer 2009): 1371–98, www.law.northwestern.edu/journals/lawreview/v103/n3/1371/LR103n3Bibas&Schanzenbach&Tiller.pdf.

69. David Sudnow, "Normal Crimes: Sociological Features of the Penal Code in a Public Defender Office," *Social Problems* 12, no. 3 (Winter 1965): 255–76, www.jstor.org/stable/798932.

70. Federal sentencing guidelines have yielded much more research than state schemes, not only because the federal data is more accessible, but also because states do not generally have the funds to collect and report such data.

71. William H. Pryor Jr., "Federalism and Sentencing Reform in the Post-Blakely /Booker Era," *Ohio State Journal of Criminal Law* 8 (2011): 515–31, http://moritzlaw.osu.edu /osjcl/Articles/Volume8_2/Pryor.pdf.

72. Franklin E. Zimring, Gordon Hawkins, and Sam Kamin, *Punishment and Democracy: Three Strikes and You're Out in California* (New York: Oxford University Press, 2001); and Tom R. Tyler and Robert J. Boeckmann, "Three Strikes and You Are Out, but Why? The Psychology of Public Support for Punishing Rule Breakers," *Law and Society Review* 31, no. 2 (1997): 237–66, www.jstor.org/stable/3053926.

73. Joshua Page, *The Toughest Beat: Politics, Punishment, and the Prison Officers Union in California* (New York: Oxford University Press, 2011).

74. Charles K. Coe and Deborah Lamm Wiesel, "Police Budgeting: Winning Strategies," *Public Administration Review* 61, no. 6 (November–December 2001): 718–27, doi:10.1111 /0033–3352.00142.

75. SEARCH, National Consortium for Justice Information and Statistics, *Report of the National Task Force on Federal Legislation Imposing Reporting Requirements and Expectations on the Criminal Justice System, Findings and Recommendations,* Criminal Justice Information Policy Series (Washington, DC: US Bureau of Justice Statistics, 2000), http://bjs.ojp .usdoj.gov/content/pub/pdf/rntffl.pdf.

76. Chrysanthi S. Leon, *Sex Fiends, Perverts, and Pedophiles: Understanding Sex Crime Policy in America* (New York: New York University Press, 2011).

77. Tamara Rice Lave, "Throwing Away the Key: Has the Adam Walsh Act Lowered the Threshold for Sexually Violent Predator Commitments Too Far?," *University of Pennsylvania Journal of Constitutional Law* 14, no. 2 (December 2011): 391–429.

78. Prosecutorial Remedies and Other Tools to End the Exploitation of Children Today ("PROTECT") Act of 2003, Pub. L. No. 108–21, 117 Stat. 650, (2003) (codified as amended in scattered sections of 5, 18, 21, 28, 42, and 47 U.S.C.). See, e.g., "Megan's Law: Keeping Children Safe from Sexual Offenders," Kids Live Safe, LLC, accessed October 21, 2013, www .meganslaw.com.

79. Adam Walsh Child Protection and Safety Act of 2006, Pub. L. No. 109–248, 120 Stat. 587 (2006), codified as amended at 42 U.S.C. § 16901 *et seq.* and in scattered sections of 5, 8, 10, 18, 20, 21, 28, 42, and 47 U.S.C.

80. Coe and Wiesel, "Police Budgeting," 718–27.

81. Public Safety Performance Project, "One in 100: Behind Bars in America 2008," report issued February 28, 2008 (Pew Center on the States, Washington, DC).

82. See "Prisoners under Jurisdiction of Federal or State Correctional Authorities— Summary by State," Pub. 347; and "Adults under Correctional Supervision," Pub. 348, in "Law Enforcement, Courts, & Prisons: Correctional Facilities, Prisoners," sec. 5 in *The National Data Book: The 2012 Statistical Abstract,* Bureau of the Census (Washington, DC, 2012), www.census.gov/compendia/statab/cats/law_enforcement_courts_prisons /correctional_facilities_prisoners.html.

83. Public Safety Performance Project, "One in 31: The Long Reach of American Corrections," report issued March 2, 2009 (Pew Center on the States, Washington, DC).

84. James J. Stephan, *Census of State and Federal Correctional Facilities, 2005,* October 2008 Report of the National Prisoner Statistics Program (Washington, DC: Bureau of Justice Statistics, 2008), http://bjs.ojp.usdoj.gov/content/pub/pdf/csfcf05.pdf.

85. Kristen A. Hughes, *Justice Expenditure and Employment in the United States, 2003,* April 2006 Bulletin of the Bureau of Justice Statistics, rev. May 10, 2006 (Washington, DC: Bureau of Justice Statistics, 2006), www.bjs.gov/index.cfm?ty=pbdetail&iid=1017.

86. Frank E. Zimring and Gordon Hawkins, *The Scale of Imprisonment* (Chicago: University of Chicago Press, 1991).

87. Alan Carlson, Kate Harrison, and John K. Hudzik, *Adequate, Stable, Equitable, and Responsible Trial Court Funding: Reframing the State v. Local Debate* (Denver: Justice Management Institute, 2008).

88. W. David Ball, "Tough on Crime (on the State's Dime): How Violent Crime Does Not Drive California Counties' Incarceration Rates—And Why It Should," *Georgia State University Law Review* 28 (Summer 2012): 987–1083, http://dx.doi.org/10.2139/ssrn.1871427.

89. Phillip J. Cooper, "Between the Legal Rock and the Political Hard Place: Interactions of the Federal District Court Judges and State and Local Officials" (paper presented at the 79th Annual Meeting of the American Political Science Association, Chicago, IL, September 1–4, 1983).

90. For a full explanation of the bond mechanism, see Judith A. Greene, "Entrepreneurial Corrections: Incarceration as a Business Opportunity," in *Invisible Punishment: The Collateral Consequences of Mass Incarceration,* ed. Marc Maurer and Meda Chesney-Lind (New York: New Press, 2002), 200–220, www.justicestrategies.org/sites/default/files/Judy/EntrepreneurialCorrections.pdf. An underwriter, usually an investment bank or a syndicate, acts as an intermediary to issue bonds. Investors trade bonds in the secondary market, through a network of independent dealers. Dealers usually sell the bonds in denominations of $5,000. Direct owners of bonds tend to be affluent investors, primarily pension funds, insurance companies, banks, and mutual funds. Today a larger population of investors owns bonds through bond mutual funds. The bond's "coupon" refers to the interest rate of the bond. Not all bonds have traditional coupons; some bonds do not pay interest until maturity. The value of a bond is its value at maturity; when it sells at less than its value at maturity, it is a discounted bond, and when it sells for more, it is a premium bond. Dealers and investors quote bond prices in two parts: bid and ask. The difference between bid and ask is referred to as the "market spread." The size of the spread reflects the bond's liquidity. Bond prices fluctuate to account for changes in the market: for example, if the interest goes up, the bond price will likely go up as well. Most bonds have "call provisions," which allow the issuer to repurchase and retire all or a portion of the bond before its maturity date at a set price, usually above par, even though the bond has not yet paid out its full interest.

91. Jeffrey I. Chapman, "The Fiscalization of Land Use: The Increasing Role of Innovative Revenue Raising Instruments to Finance Public Infrastructure," *Public Works Management and Policy* 12, no. 4 (April 2008): 551–67, doi:10.1177/1087724X08316159.

92. For a comparison of the two bonds, see Shama Gamkhar and Mona Koerner, "Capital Financing of Schools: A Comparison of Lease Purchase Revenue Bonds and General Obligation Bonds in Texas," *Public Budgeting and Finance* 22, no. 2 (June 2002): 21–39.

93. Peter Schrag, *Paradise Lost: California's Experience, America's Future* (New York: New Press, 1998).

94. D. Roderick Kiewiet and Kristin Szakaty, "Constitutional Limitations on Borrowing: An Analysis of State Bonded Indebtedness," *Journal of Law, Economics, and Organization* 12, no. 1(1996): 62–97.

95. Philip A. Ethridge and James W. Marquart, "Private Prisons in Texas: The New Penology for Profit," *Justice Quarterly* 10, no. 1(March 1993): 29–48.

96. For the story of one such California institution's failure due to objections from the California Correctional Peace Officers Association (CCPOA), see Page, *The Toughest Beat.*

97. Ruth Wilson Gilmore, *Golden Gulag: Prisons, Surplus, Crisis, and Opposition in Globalizing California* (Berkeley: University of California Press, 2007). In "California's Response to Its Prison Overcrowding Crisis," *McGeorge Law Review* 39, no. 1 (2008): 482–502, Muradyan describes a similar use of the bond mechanism shortly before the financial crisis.

98. Muradyan, "California's Response to Its Prison Overcrowding Crisis."

99. Christian Henrichson and Ruth Delaney, *The Price of Prisons: What Incarceration Costs Taxpayers,* Report of the Vera Institute of Justice, the Center on Sentencing and Corrections, and the Public Safety Performance Project, issued January 2012, updated July 20, 2012 (Washington, DC: Pew Center on the States, 2012), www.pewstates.org/uploadedFiles/PCS_Assets/2012/http_www.vera.org_download_file=3495_the-price-of-prisons-updated.pdf.

CHAPTER 3

1. Henry K Lee, "Many Contra Costa Crooks Won't Be Prosecuted," *San Francisco Chronicle,* April 22, 2009, www.sfgate.com/crime/article/Many-Contra-Costa-crooks-won-t-be-prosecuted-3243986.php.

2. Andrew W. Lo, "Reading about the Financial Crisis: A Twenty-One-Book Review," *Journal of Economic Literature* 50 (March 2012): 151–78, doi: 10.1257/jel.50.1.151. http://hdl.handle.net/1721.1/75360.

3. Carmen M. Reinhart and Kenneth Rogoff, *This Time Is Different: Eight Centuries of Financial Folly* (Princeton: Princeton University Press, 2009).

4. Federal Reserve Chairman Ben S. Bernanke, "Reflections on a Year of Crisis" (Remarks presented at the Federal Reserve Bank of Kansas City's Annual Economic Symposium, Jackson Hole, WY, August 21, 2009), www.federalreserve.gov/newsevents/speech/bernanke20090821a.htm. Chairman Bernanke delivered the same remarks at the Brookings Institution, on September 15, 2009.

5. *Causes of the Recent Financial and Economic Crisis: Testimony before the Financial Crisis Inquiry Commission, Washington, DC* (September 2, 2010) (statement of Ben S. Bernanke, Chairman of the Federal Reserve), www.federalreserve.gov/newsevents/testimony/bernanke20100902a.htm.

6. Federal Reserve Chairman Ben S. Bernanke, "Some Reflections on the Crisis and the Policy Response" (Speech presented at the Russell Sage Foundation and the Century Foundation conference "Rethinking Finance: New Perspectives on the Crisis," New York, April 13, 2012, www.federalreserve.gov/newsevents/speech/bernanke20120413a.htm.

7. Gary B. Gorton, *Slapped by the Invisible Hand: The Panic of 2007,* Financial Management Association Survey and Synthesis (New York: Oxford University Press, 2010).

8. Christopher L. Foote, Kristopher S. Gerardi, and Paul S. Willen, "Why Did So Many People Make So Many Ex Post Bad Decisions? The Causes of the Foreclosure Crisis" (Paper presented at the Russell Sage and Century Foundation conference, "Rethinking Finance: New Perspectives on the Crisis," New York, April 13, 2012). Reprinted in *Rethinking the Financial Crisis*, ed. Alan S. Blinder, Andrew W. Lo, and Robert M. Solow (New York: Russell Sage, 2012), 136–86, 165.

9. Robert Shiller, *The Subprime Solution: How Today's Global Financial Crisis Happened, and What to Do about It*(Princeton: Princeton University Press, 2008).

10. Vitaly M. Bord and João A. C. Santos, "The Rise of the Originate-to-Distribute Model and the Role of Banks in Financial Intermediation," *FRBNY Economic Policy Review* 18, no. 2 (July 2012): 21–34, www.newyorkfed.org/research/epr/12v18n2/1207bord.pdf.

11. Lo, "Reading about the Financial Crisis."

12. John Crawford, "CDO Ratings and Systemic Instability: Causes and Cure," *New York University Journal of Law and Business* 7, no. 1 (Fall 2010): 1–45, http://ssrn.com/abstract=2203100.

13. Gary B. Gorton and Andrew Metrick, "The Federal Reserve and Financial Regulation: The First Hundred Years," NBER Working Paper No. 19292, National Bureau of Economic Research, July 1, 2013, www.nber.org/federalreserve_SI2013/Gorton-Metrick.pdf.

14. Nouriel Roubini and Stephen Mihm, *Crisis Economics: A Crash Course in the Future of Finance* (New York: Penguin Press, 2010).

15. Joseph E. Stiglitz, *Freefall: America, Free Markets, and the Sinking of the World Economy* (London: Allen Lane, 2010).

16. Simon Johnson and James Kwak, *13 Bankers: The Wall Street Takeover and the Next Financial Meltdown* (New York: Pantheon, 2010).

17. Bethany McLean and Joe Nocera, *All the Devils Are Here: The Hidden History of the Financial Crisis* (New York: Penguin Press, 2010).

18. George A. Akerlof and Robert J. Shiller, *Animal Spirits: How Human Psychology Drives the Economy, and Why It Matters for Global Capitalism* (Princeton: Princeton University Press, 2010).

19. Ross Garnaut and David Llewellyn-Smith, *The Great Crash of 2008* (Carlton, Australia: Melbourne University Publishing, 2009).

20. Roger C. Altman, "The Great Crash, 2008: A Geopolitical Setback for the West," *Foreign Affairs* 88, no. 1 (January–February 2009), www.foreignaffairs.com/articles/63714/roger-c-altman/the-great-crash-2008.

21. Simon Cox, "The Long Climb," *Economist*, October 1, 2009, www.economist.com/node/14530093.

22. Ibid.

23. Ron Martin, "The Local Geographies of the Financial Crisis: From the Housing Bubble to Economic Recession and Beyond," *Journal of Economic Geography* 11 (2011): 587–618.

24. Jake Grovum, "2008 Financial Crisis Impact Still Hurting States," *USA Today*, September 15, 2013, www.usatoday.com/story/money/business/2013/09/14/impact-on-states-of-2008-financial-crisis/2812691/.

25. Betsy Donald, Amy Glas Meier, Mia Gray, and Linda Lobao, "Austerity in the City: Economic Crisis and Urban Service Decline?" *Cambridge Journal of Regions, Economy and Society* 7 (2014): 3–15.

26. Meredith Whitney, *Fate of the States: The New Geography of American Prosperity* (New York: Penguin, 2013).

27. Michael Lewis, "California *and* Bust," *Vanity Fair,* November 2011, www.vanityfair.com/business/features/2011/11/michael-lewis-201111.

28. Darien Shanske, "What Would the Delegates Talk About? A Rough Agenda for a Constitutional Convention," *Hastings Constitutional Law Quarterly* 37, no. 4 (March 4, 2010): 641–60, http://ssrn.com/abstract=1565050.

29. Peter Schrag, *Paradise Lost: California's Experience, America's Future* (Berkeley: University of California Press, [1998] 2004).

30. Shawn Tully, "Meredith Whitney's New Target: The States," *CNN Money,* September 28, 2010, http://finance.fortune.cnn.com/2010/09/28/meredith-whitneys-new-target-the-states/.

31. National Association of State Budget Officers, *The Fiscal Survey of States,* Report by the National Governors Association and the National Association of State Budget Officers, Washington, DC, Spring 2013, www.nasbo.org/sites/default/files/Spring%202013%20Fiscal%20Survey%20of%20States.pdf.

32. Public Safety Performance Project, *Public Safety, Public Spending: Forecasting America's Prison Population, 2007–2011* (Washington, DC, rev. June 2007), www.pewstates.org/uploadedFiles/PCS_Assets/2007/Public%20Safety%20Public%20Spending.pdf. Reprinted in "Information-Based Sentencing Analysis," *Federal Sentencing Reporter* 19, no. 4 (April 2007): 234–52, www.jstor.org/stable/10.1525/fsr.2007.19.4.234.

33. Public Safety Performance Project, *Public Safety, Public Spending,* iv.

34. Public Safety Performance Project, "One in 100: Behind Bars in America 2008," Report by the Pew Center on the States, Washington, DC, February 2008, www.pewstates.org/uploadedFiles/PCS_Assets/2008/one%20in%20100.pdf.

35. John Gramlich, "Study Finds Disparity in Corrections Spending," *Stateline,* March 2, 2009, www.pewstates.org/projects/stateline/headlines/study-finds-disparity-in-corrections-spending-85899384728.

36. Pew Center on the States, "Public Safety, Public Spending: Forecasting America's Prison Population 2007–2011," Report, available online at www.pewstates.org/research/reports/public-safety-public-spending-85899378514 (last accessed April 5, 2014.)

37. Tracey Kyckelhahn, "Local Government Corrections Expenditures, FY 2005–2011," U.S. Department of Justice, Bureau of Justice Statistics (2013), available at www.bjs.gov/content/pub/pdf/lgcefy0511.pdf (last accessed April 5, 2014.)

38. John Pfaff, "The Micro and Macro Causes of Prison Growth," *Georgia State University Law Review* 28, no. 4 (Summer 2012): 1237–72, http://scholarworks.gsu.edu/cgi/viewcontent.cgi?article = 2700&context = gsulr.

39. Ibid., 1256.

40. William Spelman, "Crime, Cash, and Limited Options: Explaining the *Prison Boom,*" *Criminology and Public Policy* 8, no. 1 (February 2009): 29–77, doi: 10.1111/j.1745-9133.2009.00546.x.

41. Ibid, 40–41.

42. Pfaff, "The Micro and Macro Causes of Prison Growth," 1257.

43. Public Safety Performance Project, *Changing Direction: A Bipartisan Team Paves a New Path for Sentencing and Corrections in Texas,* Expert Q&A No. 4 with Whitmire File &

Madden File, prepared by the Pew Center on the States, Washington, DC, January 2008, www.pewstates.org/uploadedFiles/PCS_Assets/2008/changing%20direction.pdf.

44. Public Safety Performance Project, *Maximum Impact: Targeting Supervision on Higher-Risk People, Places and Times,* Public Safety Policy Brief No. 9, prepared by the Pew Center on the States, Washington, DC, July 2009, www.pewstates.org/uploadedFiles/PCS_ Assets/2009/Maximum_Impact_web.pdf.

45. Public Safety Performance Project, *Arkansas: Improving Public Safety and Containing Corrections Costs,* Issue Brief, prepared by the Pew Center on the States, Washington, DC, June 2010, www.pewstates.org/uploadedFiles/PCS_Assets/2010/PSPP_Arkansas_ Brief_web.pdf.

46. Public Safety Performance Project, *South Carolina's Public Safety Reform: Legislation Enacts Research-Based Strategies to Cut Prison Growth and Costs,* Issue Brief, prepared by the Pew Center on the States, Washington, DC, June 2010, www.pewstates.org /uploadedFiles/PCS_Assets/2010/South_Carolina's_Public_Safety_Reform.pdf.

47. Public Safety Performance Project, *2011 Kentucky Reforms Cut Recidivism, Costs,* Issue Brief, prepared by Pew State and Consumer Initiatives, Washington, DC, July 1, 2011, www .pewstates.org/research/analysis/2011-kentucky-reforms-cut-recidivism-costs-85899380803.

48. Public Safety Performance Project, *Right-Sizing Prisons: Business Leaders Make the Case for Corrections Reform,* Issue Brief, prepared by the Pew Center on the States, Washington, DC, January 2010, www.pewstates.org/uploadedFiles/PCS_Assets/2010/Right-Sizing%20Prisons.pdf.

49. Public Safety Performance Project, *South Dakota's 2013 Criminal Justice Initiative: Legislation to Improve Public Safety, Hold Offenders More Accountable, and Reduce Corrections Spending,* Report prepared by Pew State and Consumer Initiatives, Washington, DC, June 24, 2013, www.pewstates.org/research/reports/south-dakotas-2013-criminal-justice-initiative-85899485948.

50. Public Safety Performance Project, *Right-Sizing Prisons.*

51. Public Safety Performance Project, *U.S. Prison Population Drops for Third Year as States Adopt New Policy Strategies,* Project Update, prepared by Pew State and Consumer Initiatives, Washington, DC: August 8, 2013, www.pewstates.org/news-room/press-releases /us-prison-population-drops-for-third-year-as-states-adopt-new-policy-strategies-85899496150.

52. Public Safety Performance Project, *Leading on Public Safety: 4 Governors Share Lessons Learned from Sentencing and Corrections Reform,* Issue Brief, prepared by Pew State and Consumer Initiatives, Washington, DC, August 2013, www.pewstates.org/uploaded-Files/PCS_Assets/2013/Pew_PSPP_Governors_QA.pdf.

53. Ibid., 4–5. Also see chap. 5 here.

CHAPTER 4

1. Jonathan Simon, *Governing through Crime: How the War on Crime Transformed American Democracy and Created a Culture of Fear,* Studies in Crime and Public Policy (New York: Oxford University Press, 2007).

2. David Garland, *Peculiar Institution: America's Death Penalty in an Age of Abolition* (New York: Belknap Press, 2012); Franklin E. Zimring, *The Contradictions of American*

Capital Punishment (New York: Oxford University Press, 2004); Carol Steiker, "Capital Punishment and American Exceptionalism," *Oregon Law Review* 81 (2002): 97.

3. David Greenberg and Valerie West, "Siting the Death Penalty Internationally," *Law and Social Inquiry* 33 (June 2008): 295–343. The only European country to have retained the death penalty is Belarus.

4. David T. Johnson and Franklin E. Zimring, *The Next Frontier: National Development, Political Change, and the Death Penalty in Asia* (New York: Oxford University Press, 2009).

5. In 1972 the Supreme Court placed a moratorium on death penalty proceedings in Furman v. Georgia, 408 U.S. 238 (1972); it removed those hurdles in Gregg v. Georgia, 428 U.S. 153 (1976). More on the doctrine and social realities behind this change below.

6. Gallup Historical Polls, accessed October 4, 2013, www.gallup.com/poll/1606/death-penalty.aspx.

7. Neil Vidmar and Phoebe Ellsworth, "Public Opinion and the Death Penalty," *Stanford Law Review* 26 (June 1974): 1245–70. Justice Thurgood Marshall theorized in *Gregg* that more knowledge about the operation of the death penalty in practice would reduce public support of it. For one effort to test this hypothesis, see Austin Sarat and Neil Vidmar, "Public Opinion, the Death Penalty, and the Eighth Amendment: Testing the Marshall Hypothesis," *Wisconsin Law Review* 1 (1976): 171–207.

8. Gregg, 428 U.S. 153.

9. Austin Sarat, "The 'New Abolitionism' and the Possibilities of Legislative Action: The New Hampshire Experience," *Ohio State Law Journal* 63 (2002): 343, 364.

10. Bob Egelko, "Lawmakers Team Up to Oppose New Death Row," *San Francisco Chronicle,* December 17, 2008.

11. Cesare Beccaria, *On Crimes and Punishments,* trans. Edward D. Ingraham (Huntington, WV: Empire Books, 2013).

12. Marcello Maestro, *Cesare Beccaria and the Origins of Penal Reform* (Philadelphia: Temple University Press, 1973).

13. Stuart Banner, *The Death Penalty: An American History* (Cambridge, MA: Harvard University Press, 2003).

14. For more on the origins of the Black Code and why its ideological roots would be reprehensible to colonists seeking to disengage from the British heritage, see E. P. Thompson, *Whigs and Hunters* (London: Breviary Stuff Publications, 2013).

15. Louis P. Masur, *Rites of Execution: Capital Punishment and the Transformation of American Culture, 1776–1865* (New York: Oxford University Press, 1989), 64.

16. David Garland, *Peculiar Institution.*

17. Furman, 408 U.S. 238.

18. Gregg, 428 U.S. 153.

19. Isaac Ehrlich, "The Deterrent Effect of Capital Punishment: A Question of Life and Death," *American Economic Review* 65 (June 1975): 397–417.

20. Notably, *Fowler v. North Carolina:* Brian E. Forst, "The Deterrent Effect of Capital Punishment: A Cross-State Analysis of the 1960's," *Minnesota law Review* 61 (1976–77): 743.

21. Jon K. Peck, "The Deterrent Effect of Capital Punishment: Ehrlich and His Critics," *Yale Law Journal* 85 (January 1976): 359–67.

22. Peter Passell, "The Deterrent Effect of the Death Penalty: A Statistical Test," *Stanford Law Review* 28 (1975–76): 61; Hans Zeisel, "The Deterrent Effect of the Death Penalty: Facts v. Faiths," *Supreme Court Review* 1976 (1976): 317–43.

23. David Garland, Commentary on Franklin Zimring and David Johnson's *The Next Frontier* (Author Meets Reader Panel, American Society of Criminology, Washington, DC, November 16–19, 2011).

24. Daniel S. Nagin and John V. Pepper, "Deterrence and the Death Penalty," National Research Council, 2012.

25. Hashem Dezhbakhsh, Paul Rubin, and Joanna Sheppard, "Does Capital Punishment Have a Deterrent Effect? New Evidence from Postmoratorium Panel Data, "*American Law and Economics Review* 5 (2003): 344–76; "Study: Death Penalty Deters Scores of Killings," *Atlanta Journal-Constitution,* March 14, 2002.

26. John Donohue and Justin Wolfers, "Uses and Abuses of Empirical Evidence in the Death Penalty Debate," *Stanford Law Review* 58 (2006): 971.

27. Cornell Law School, Third Conference on Empirical Legal Studies, September 12–13, 2008, www.lawschool.cornell.edu/cels2008/index.cfm.

28. This may be one of the interesting side effects of the hype surrounding the crack epidemic: Jeffrey Fagan, "Deterrence and the Death Penalty: A Critical Review of New Evidence," testimony to the New York State Assembly Standing Committee on Codes, Assembly Standing Committee on Judiciary, and Assembly Standing Committee on Correction Hearings on the Future of Capital Punishment in the State of New York, January 21, 2005, http://66.39.33.150/FaganTestimony.pdf.

29. David C. Baldus, *Statistical Proof of Discrimination* (New York: Shepherd's /McGraw-Hill, 1980).

30. For some thoughts on the application of conflict theory to this apparent leniency to black defendants, see Darnell Hawkins, "Beyond Anomalies: Rethinking the Conflict Perspective on Race and Criminal Punishment," *Social Forces* 65 (1987): 719–45.

31. McClesky v. Kemp, 481 U.S. 279 (1987).

32. Ibid., 279.

33. Randall L. Kennedy, "*McCleskey v. Kemp:* Race, Capital Punishment, and the Supreme Court," *Harvard Law Review* 101 (1988): 1388–1443.

34. John Blume, Theodore Eisenberg, and Sheri Lynn Johnson, "Post-McCleskey Racial Discrimination Claims in Capital Cases," *Cornell Law Review* 83 (1997–98): 1771.

35. Michelle Alexander, *The New Jim Crow: Mass Incarceration in the Age of Colorblindness* (New York: New Press: 2010).

36. These data, in themselves, do not undo the need for a racialized analysis, but they create problems for the overrepresentation argument. James Forman, "Racial Critiques of Mass Incarceration: Beyond the New Jim Crow," *New York University Law Review* 87 (February 2012): 101–46.

37. Sabrina Hodges and Heather Larrabee, "Mumia Abu-Jamal: A Call for Economic Militancy," *Radical Philosophy Review* 3 (2000): 46–59.

38. Sam Sommers, "On Race, te Death Penalty, and Troy Davis," *HuffPost Politics Blog,* September 23, 2011, www.huffingtonpost.com/sam-sommers/troy-davis-execution-_b_977219.html.

39. Keith Findley, "The Pedagogy of Innocence: Reflection on the Role of Innocence Projects in Clinical Legal Education," *Clinical Law Review* 13, no. 1 (2006): 111–46.

40. Jay D. Aronson and Simon A. Cole, "Science and the Death Penalty: DNA, Innocence, and the Debate over Capital Punishment in the United States," *Law and Social Inquiry* 34 (Summer 2009): 603–33.

41. James D. Unnever and Francis T. Cullen, "Executing the Innocent and Support for Capital Punishment: Implications For Public Policy," *Criminology and Public Policy* 4 (February 2005): 3–38.

42. Carol S. Steiker and Jordan M. Steiker, "The Seduction of Innocence: The Attraction and Limitations of the Focus on Innocence in Capital Punishment Law and Advocacy," *Journal of Criminal Law and Criminology* 95 (2005): 587–624.

43. The average time spent in prison prior to exoneration is fourteen years: Brandon Garrett, *Convicting the Innocent: Where Prosecutions Go Wrong* (Cambridge, MA: Harvard University Press, 2011).

44. B. S. Ledewitz, "Procedural Default in Death Penalty Cases: Fundamental Miscarriage of Justice and Actual Innocence," *Criminal Law Bulletin* 24 (1988): 379–423.

45. Limin Zheng, "Actual Innocence as a Gateway through the Statute-of-Limitations Bar on the Filing of Federal Habeas Corpus Petitions," *California Law Review* 90 (December 2002): 2101–41.

46. Jodi Wilgoren, "Citing Issue of Fairness, Governor Clears Out Death Row in Illinois," *New York Times*, January 12, 2003, www.nytimes.com/2003/01/12/us/citing-issue-of-fairness-governor-clears-out-death-row-in-illinois.html.

47. Lawrence C. Marshall, "The Innocence Revolution and the Death Penalty," *Ohio State Law Journal* 1 (2004): 573.

48. Northwestern University Law School Center on Wrongful Convictions, "Updates," www.law.northwestern.edu/cwc/ (accessed October 4, 2013).

49. Callins v. Collins, 510 U.S. 1141 (1994) (Blackmun, J. dissenting).

50. Richard Moran, *Executioner's Current: Thomas Edison, George Westinghouse, and the Invention of the Electric Chair* (New York: Vintage Books, 2003).

51. Baze v. Rees, 553 U.S. 35, 35 (2008).

52. Brewer v. Landrigan, 131 S.Ct. 445 (2010).

53. Landrigan v. Brewer (2010), Order Granting Motion for a Temporary Restraining Order, no. CV-10-02246-PHX-ROS, p. 2. Original emphasis.

54. Baze, 553 U.S. 35.

55. Dickens v. Brewer, 631 F.3d 1139 (9th Cir. 2011).

56. Landrigan, 131 S. Ct. 445, 451.

57. Landrigan, 131 S. Ct. 445, 452.

58. Landrigan, 131 S.Ct. 445, 453.

59. Brewer v. Landrigan, Order in Pending Case (2010), available at www.supremecourt.gov/orders/courtorders/102610zr.pdf. Original emphasis.

60. Naimah Jabal-Nash, "Romell Broom Survived Ohio Execution Try, Ordered to Remain on Death Row," *CBS News*, December 3, 2010, /www.cbsnews.com/8301-504083_162-20024577-504083.html.

61. Bruce Japsen, "Hospira Ceases Production of Anesthetic Used in Executions," *Chicago Tribune,* January 21, 2011, http://articles.chicagotribune.com/2011–01–21/business/ct-biz-0122-execution-drug-20110121_1_hospira-executions-capital-punishment.

62. Erik Eckholm and Katie Zezima, "States Face Shortage of Key Lethal Injection Drug," *New York Times,* January 22, 2011, www.nytimes.com/2011/01/22/us/22lethal.html?_r=0.

63. AMA Code of Medical Ethics, "Opinion 2.06, Capital Punishment," July 1980, www .ama-assn.org//ama/pub/physician-resources/medical-ethics/code-medical-ethics /opinion206.page.

64. "PAs and NPs May Now Sign Death Certificates," *North Carolina Medical Board Newsletter,* Fall 2011, www.ncmedboard.org/articles/detail/pas_and_nps_may_now_sign_ death_certificates.

65. North Carolina Dept. of Corr. v. North Carolina Med. Bd. 675 S.E.2d 641, 643 (N.C. 2009).

66. Second Bush-Dukakis Presidential Debate, October 13, 1988, transcript, University of California, Los Angeles, www.debates.org/index.php?page=october-13-1988-debate-transcript.

67. "New Hampshire Veto Saves Death Penalty," *New York Times,* May 20, 2000, www .nytimes.com/2000/05/20/us/new-hampshire-veto-saves-death-penalty.html.

68. Wilgoren, "Citing Issue of Fairness, Governor Clears Out Death Row in Illinois."

69. Michael Powell, "In N.Y., Lawmakers Vote Not to Reinstate Capital Punishment," *Washington Post,* April 13, 2005, www.washingtonpost.com/wp-dyn/articles/A47871– 2005Apr12.html.

70. Jeremy W. Peters, "Death Penalty Repealed in New Jersey," *New York Times,* December 17, 2007, www.nytimes.com/2007/12/17/nyregion/17cnd-jersey.html?_r=0.

71. "New Mexico Abolishes Death Penalty," *CBS News,* March 18, 2009, www.cbsnews .com/2100–201_162–4874296.html.

72. Christopher Wills, "Illinois Gov. Pat Quinn Abolishes Death Penalty, Clears Death Row," *Washington Post,* March 9, 2011, www.washingtonpost.com/wp-dyn/content /article/2011/03/09/AR2011030900319.html.

73. David Ariosto, "Connecticut Becomes 17th State to Abolish Death Penalty," CNN, April 25, 2012, www.cnn.com/2012/04/25/justice/connecticut-death-penalty-law-repealed /index.html.

74. Katie Sanders, "House Democrat Wants Repeal Of Death Penalty (Again)," *Tampa Bay Times,* September 27, 2011, www.tampabay.com/blogs/the-buzz-florida-politics /content/house-democrat-wants-repeal-death-penalty-again.

75. Jeanne Koranda, "Repeal of Death Penalty Fails in Kansas Senate," Wichita Eagle, February 19 2010, www.kansas.com/2010/02/19/1189624/senate-advances-repeal-of-death. html.

76. Brian Witte, "Governor Signs Repeal of Death Penalty in Md.," *USA Today,* May 2, 2013, www.usatoday.com/story/news/nation/2013/05/02/maryland-death-penalty/2130327/.

77. Alan Johnson, "Blair Takes Lead in Fight against Death Penalty," *Springfield News-Sun* (Springfield, OH), August 21, 2011, www.springfieldnewssun.com/news/news/state-regional/blair-takes-lead-in-fight-against-death-penalty-1/nMtX3/.

78. Joseph A. Slobodzian, "Rarely Used, Pennsylvania's Death Penalty Remains a Headache on Both Sides of the Debate," *Philadelphia Inquirer,* May 15, 2011, http://articles.philly

.com/2011–05–15/news/29545856_1_death-penalty-capital-punishment-first-degree-murder-cases.

79. Texas Moratorium Network, "Bills Filed in Texas Legislature to Abolish Death Penalty," January 26, 2011, www.texasmoratorium.org/archives/1476.

80. Howard Mintz, "Defeat of Proposition 34: California's Death Penalty Battle Will Continue," *San Jose Mercury News* (San Jose, CA), November 7, 2012, www.mercurynews.com/ci_21951068/defeat-proposition-34-californias-death-penalty-battle-will.

81. "Delaware Senate Approves Repeal of Death Penalty," *Politico*, March 26, 2013, www.politico.com/story/2013/03/death-penalty-repeal-delaware-89363.html.

82. Adam Liptak, "Citing Cost, Judge Rejects Death Penalty," *New York Times*, August 18, 2002, www.nytimes.com/2002/08/18/us/citing-cost-judge-rejects-death-penalty.html.

83. American Civil Liberties Union, "The Case against the Death Penalty," December 11, 2012, www.aclu.org/capital-punishment/case-against-death-penalty.

84. Furman, 408 U.S. 238, 309.

85. "In Ryan's Words: 'I Must Act': Complete Text," *New York Times*, January 11, 2003, www.nytimes.com/2003/01/11/national/11CND-RTEX.html.

86. Richard C. Dieter, "The 2% Death Penalty: How a Minority of Counties Produce Most Death Cases at Enormous Cost to All," Report from the Death Penalty Information Center, October 2013, http://deathpenaltyinfo.org/documents/TwoPercentReport.pdf.

87. Phil Willon, "Kamala Harris Is a Different Kind of Prosecutor," *Los Angeles Times*, October 20, 2010, http://articles.latimes.com/2010/oct/20/local/la-me-harris-20101015.

88. Kat Anderson, "Gascón Won't Seek Death Penalty, nor Prosecute Eliana Lopez," *Fog City Journal*, February 17, 2012, www.fogcityjournal.com/wordpress/3407/gascon-wont-seek-death-penalty-nor-prosecute-eliana-lopez/; George Gascón, "SF's District Attorney on the Death Penalty," *SFGate*, April 30, 2011, www.sfgate.com/opinion/article/S-F-s-district-attorney-on-the-death-penalty-2373226.php.

89. Austin Sarat, "The 'New Abolitionism' and the Possibilities of Legislative Action: The New Hampshire Experience," *Ohio State Law Journal* 63 (2002): 343.

90. "N.H. House Votes to End Death Penalty," *Boston Globe*, March 26, 2009, www.boston.com/news/local/new_hampshire/articles/2009/03/26/nh_house_votes_to_end_death_penalty/.

91. Robert Perkinson, *Texas Tough: The Rise of America's Prison Empire* (New York: Metropolitan Books, 2010).

92. David G. Savage, "Los Angeles County Leads the U.S. in Imposing the Death Penalty," *Los Angeles Times*, October 1, 2013, www.latimes.com/nation/la-na-california-death-penalty-20131002,0,1736185.story.

93. Keith B. Richburg, "N.J. Approves Abolition of Death Penalty; Corzine to Sign," *Washington Post*, December 14, 2007, www.washingtonpost.com/wp-dyn/content/article/2007/12/13/AR2007121301302.html; Lincoln Caplan, "End the Death Penalty in New Hampshire," *New York Times*, November 14, 2012, http://takingnote.blogs.nytimes.com/2012/11/14/end-the-death-penalty-in-new-hampshire/?_r=0.

94. New Hampshire Coalition to Abolish the Death Penalty, "How Much Does the Death Penalty Cost New Hampshire?," accessed October 5, 2013, http://nodeathpenaltynh.org/wp-content/uploads/2013/10/NH-Cost-Fact-Sheet-2013.pdf.

95. Joseph Lentol, Helen Weinstein, and Jeffrion Aubrey, "The Death Penalty in New York," Report prepared for the New York State Assembly, April 3, 2005, http://assembly .state.ny.us/comm/Codes/20050403/deathpenalty.pdf.

96. Ian Simpson, "Maryland Becomes Latest U.S. State to Abolish Death Penalty," Reuters, May 2, 2013, www.reuters.com/article/2013/05/02/us-usa-maryland-deathpenalty-idUSBRE9410TQ20130502

97. Floridians for Alternatives to the Death Penalty, "Florida's Execution Costs Rekindle Death Penalty Debate," video, 1:40, accessed October 4, 2013, www.fadp.org/.

98. Indiana Abolition Coalition, "Seven Myths about the Death Penalty," video, 3:35, accessed October 4, 2013, www.indianaabolition.org/index.php/learn-more-one-pagers /2-uncategorised/18-myths.

99. Kansas Coalition Against the Death Penalty, "2013 Abolition Conference," accessed October 4, 2013, www.ksabolition.org/events/2013-abolition-conference.

100. Ohioans to Stop Executions, "Former Supreme Court Justice Evelyn Stratton: 'Personally I am now against the death penalty,'" June 13, 2013, www.otse.org/.

101. Rob Warden, "How and Why Illinois Abolished the Death Penalty," *Law and Inequality* 30 (May 2012): 245–86, www.deathpenaltyinfo.org/documents/RWardenIL.pdf.

102. "New Mexico Governor Repeals Death Penalty in State," CNN, March 18, 2009, www.cnn.com/2009/CRIME/03/18/new.mexico.death.penalty/.

103. SAFE California, "Costs & Savings," accessed October 4, 2013, www.safecalifornia .org/facts/savings.

104. Carol J. Williams, "California Death Penalty Foes to Try for Ballot Initiative," *Los Angeles Times,* August 26, 2011, http://articles.latimes.com/2011/aug/26/local/la-me-death-penalty-20110826 (last accessed April 6, 2014).

105. Death Penalty Information Center, "Death Penalty Repeal Initiative Qualifies for Ballot in California," April 23, 2012, www.deathpenaltyinfo.org/death-penalty-repeal-initiative-qualifies-ballot-california (last accessed April 6, 2014).

106. Howard Mintz, "Defeat of Proposition 34: California's Death Penalty Battle Will Continue," *San Jose Mercury News* (San Jose, CA), November 7, 2012, www.mercurynews. com/ci_21951068/defeat-proposition-34-californias-death-penalty-battle-will.

107. Howard Mintz, "California's Dormant Death Penalty System Faces Another Legal Test," *San Jose Mercury News* (San Jose, CA), April 14, 2013, www.mercurynews.com /ci_23016479/californias-dormant-death-penalty-system-faces-another-legal.

108. Richard Duboc, "The Uncertain Future of San Quentin's New Death Row," *Pioneer Online* (California State University, East Bay), January 8, 2011, http://thepioneeronline.com /news/2011/01/the-uncertain-future-of-san-quentin%E2%80%99s-new-death-row/.

109. Most recently, Ramirez, "the Night Stalker." "Even Richard Ramirez Dodged California's Death Penalty: Opinion," *Los Angeles Daily News,* June 6, 2013, www.dailynews .com/general-news/20130607/even-richard-ramirez-dodged-californias-death-penalty-opinion.

110. Bob Egelko, "Judge Signs Off on San Quentin Improvements," *SFGate,* April 17, 2009, www.sfgate.com/bayarea/article/Judge-signs-off-on-San-Quentin-improvements-3164975.php.

111. SAFE California, "About the Coalition," accessed October 14, 2013, www.safecalifornia .org/about/coalition.

112. California Legislative Analyst's Office, "Death Penalty Repeal. Initiative Statute," July 18, 2012, www.lao.ca.gov/ballot/2012/34_11_2012.aspx. For a more detailed analysis of the costs at the county level, based on panel data from Los Angeles County, see Nicolas Peterson and Mona Lynch, "Prosecutorial Discretion, Hidden Costs, and the Death Penalty: The Case of Los Angeles County," *Journal of Criminal Law and Criminology* 102 (2012): 101–44, http://papers.ssrn.com/sol3/papers.cfm?abstract_id = 2166018.

113. SAFE California, "Proposition 34 Volunteer Instructions," 2012 (on file with author).

114. Mark Leno, Keynote Address, World Coalition Against the Death Penalty 2010 Gathering, June 13, 2010, University of California, Hastings College of the Law, available at www.worldcoalition.org/World-Coalition-AGM-encourages-US-to-join-the-abolitionist-majority.html.

115. Adam Nagourney, "Seeking an End to an Execution Law They Once Championed," *New York Times*, April 6, 2012, www.nytimes.com/2012/04/07/us/fighting-to-repeal-california-execution-law-they-championed.html?_r=1.

116. Judy Kerr, "California's Death Penalty and Public Safety," *San Gabriel Valley Tribune*, August 4, 2011, www.sgvtribune.com/opinion/20110805/californias-death-penalty-and-public-safety.

117. Richard C. Dieter, "On the Front Line: Law Enforcement Views on the Death Penalty," Report, Death Penalty Information Center, February 1995, www.deathpenaltyinfo.org/front-line-law-enforcement-views-death-penalty.

118. Carol J. Williams, "Former California Prisons Leader Joins Fight against Death Penalty," *Los Angeles Times*, May 12, 2011, http://articles.latimes.com/2011/may/12/local/la-me-0512-warden-anti-death-penalty-20110512.

119. "Yes on 34: Justice That Works for Everyone," YouTube video, 2:38, posted by "SafeCalifornia," October 3, 2012, www.youtube.com/watch?v=kTXTZ3x2JjY.

120. Bob Egelko, "Death Row Inmates Oppose Prop. 34," *SFGate*, September 24, 2012, www.sfgate.com/news/article/Death-Row-inmates-oppose-Prop-34-3891122.php.

121. SAFE California, conference call for campaign volunteers with SAFE headquarters, November 10, 2012 (on file with author.)

122. Carol J. Williams, "Californians' Support for Death Penalty Waning," *Los Angeles Times*, September 2, 2009, http://articles.latimes.com/2009/sep/02/local/me-death-penalty2.

123. Jennifer McNulty, "New Poll by UCSC Professor Reveals Declining Support for the Death Penalty," *University of California Santa Cruz Newscenter*, September 1, 2009, http://news.ucsc.edu/2009/09/3168.html.

124. Bob Egelko, "Measure's Support Jumps," *SFGate*, November 1, 2012, www.sfgate.com/news/article/Death-penalty-measure-s-support-jumps-4002211.php.

125. Tom Harman, "Legal Stalling Is Packing Death Row," *SFGate*, June 15, 2009, www.sfgate.com/opinion/article/Legal-stalling-is-packing-Death-Row-3295575.php.

126. Mary Ellen Klas, "Gov. Rick Scott Signs Bill to Speed Up Executions in Florida," *Tampa Bay Times*, June 14, 2013, www.tampabay.com/news/publicsafety/crime/gov-rick-scott-signs-bill-to-speed-up-executions-in-florida/2126764.

127. Bob Egelko, "Death Penalty Changes Rejected," *SFGate*, May 1, 2013, www.sfgate.com/crime/article/Death-penalty-changes-rejected-4480847.php.

128. Ben Adler, "Govs. Davis, Wilson, Deukmejian Back Death Penalty Initiative," Capital Public Radio, February 13, 2014, available at www.capradio.org/articles/2014/02/13 /govs-davis,-wilson,-deukmejian-back-death-penalty-initiative/ (last accessed April 6, 2014).

129. Ernest DeWayne Jones v. Kevin Chappell, Docket No. 2:09-cv-02158 (C.D. Cal., July 16, 2014).

130. Ibid., 28–29.

131. Judge Carney's order does not bind other district courts, and, in the absence of an affirmative Ninth Circuit decision, other inmates looking to benefit from the decision would have to appeal to Judge Carney's discretion and ask that he hear their cases as "related" to Jones's case. Applying the decision to other California districts and other inmates would require several legal and political steps. On the other hand, while a Ninth Circuit court decision would govern the fate of all inmates in California, there is no guarantee that the higher court will affirm the decision. Moreover, even a favorable decision could be appealed to the United States Supreme Court, where it is likely to be reversed. Hadar Aviram, "The Road to Abolishing the Death Penalty," *Daily Journal*, August 12, 2014.

132. Johnson and Zimring, *The Next Frontier*.

CHAPTER 5

1. Nick Wing, "'New Approach Washington' Launches Pro-Marijuana Legalization Ad in Evergreen State," Associated Press via Huffington Post, August 7, 2012, www.huffingtonpost .com/2012/08/07/new-approach-washington-marijuana-ad_n_1751291.html.

2. "Washington's 1st Legalize Marijuana Commercial," YouTube video, 0:31, posted by "Nicolas WeedMaps," August 7, 2012, www.youtube.com/watch?v = T8A_Kglz1IQ.

3. Jonathan Simon, *Governing through Crime: How the War on Crime Transformed American Democracy and Created a Culture of Fear*, Studies in Crime and Public Policy (New York: Oxford University Press, 2007); Katherine Beckett, *Making Crime Pay: Law and Order in Contemporary American Politics* (New York: Oxford University Press, 1997).

4. Joshua Page, *The Toughest Beat: Politics, Punishment, and the Prison Officers Union in California* (New York: Oxford University Press, 2011).

5. Gerald Ford, *A Time to Heal: The Autobiography of Gerald Ford* (New York: Harper & Row, 1979).

6. H.R. 6028, 93rd Cong. (1973).

7. Jimmy Carter, Campaign speech, Detroit, October 15, 1976, reprinted in *A Government as Good as Its People*, 2nd ed. (Little Rock: University of Arkansas Press, 1996), 220–21.

8. Carter, *A Government as Good as Its People*, 220.

9. Lou Cannon, *President Reagan: The Role of a Lifetime* (New York: Public Affairs, 1991), 813.

10. Reagan oversaw an execution as governor of California; see Cannon, *Role of a Lifetime*, 504, 803. See also John Ashcroft, *Lessons from a Father to His Son* (Nashville: Thomas Nelson, 1998), 138–39.

11. Rosemary Gartner, Anthony N. Doob, and Franklin Zimring, "The Past as Prologue? Decarceration in California Then and Now," *Criminology & Public Policy* 10 (April 2011): 291–325, 302, doi: 10.1111/j.1745-9133.2011.00709.x.

12. Cannon, *Role of a Lifetime,* 153.

13. Doro Koch Bush, *My Father, My President* (New York: Warner Books, 2006), 247.

14. George H. W. Bush, Inaugural Address, January 20, 1989, transcript and video, West Front, U.S. Capitol, Washington, DC, www.inaugural.senate.gov/swearing-in/address /address-by-george-h-w-bush-1989.

15. Steve Daley, "Clinton Shows Democrats Tough Crime Talk Wins Political Points," *Chicago Tribune,* April 17, 1994, http://articles.chicagotribune.com/1994–04-17 /news/9404170204_1_crime-bill-crime-prevention-violent-crime.

16. Clinton ingeniously linked the Republican initiative to cut federal funding from the COPS program and their gun rights advocacy: "Our policy was to put more police on the street and to take assault weapons off the street. And it gave you eight years of declining crime and eight years of declining violence. Their policy is the reverse. They're taking police off the streets while they put assault weapons back on the street." Bill Clinton, Speech to the Democratic National Convention, July 29, 2004, transcript and video, FleetCenter, Boston, www.cnn.com/2004/ALLPOLITICS/07/26/dems.clinton.transcript/.

17. Joe Klein, *The Natural: The Misunderstood Presidency of Bill Clinton* (New York: Broadway Books, 2003), 37.

18. Second Gore-Bush Presidential Debate, October 11, 2000, transcript, Wake Forest University, www.debates.org/index.php?page = october-11–2000-debate-transcript.

19. James Dao, "The 2000 Campaign: The Crime Issue; A Get-Tough Gore Focuses on Drug Tests," *New York Times,* May 3, 2000, www.nytimes.com/2000/05/03/us/the-2000-campaign-the-crime-issue-a-get-tough-gore-focuses-on-drug-tests.html.

20. Anne E. Kornblut and Glen Johnson, "Candidates Cheer Running Mates, Woo Undecideds," *Boston Globe,* October 7, 2000.

21. Third Bush-Kerry Presidential Debate, October 13, 2004, transcript, Arizona State University, http://en.wikisource.org/wiki/2004_U.S._Presidential_Debate_-_October_13.

22. "How to Stop the Drug Wars," *The Economist,* March 5, 2009, www.economist.com /node/13237193.

23. Robert Kuttner, *Obama's Challenge: America's Economic Crisis and the Power of a Transformative Presidency* (White River Junction, VT: Chelsea Green, 2008), 190; John K. Wilson, *Barack Obama: This Improbable Quest* (Boulder, CO: Paradigm, 2007), 145.

24. Barack Obama, Campaign speech, 99th NAACP Convention, Cincinnati, July 12, 2008, http://2008election.procon.org/sourcefiles/Obama20080714.pdf; John McCain, Campaign speech, 99th NAACP Convention, Cincinnati, July 12, 2008, http://2008election .procon.org/sourcefiles/McCain20080716.pdf; Obama for America, "Blueprint for Change: Barack Obama's Plan for America," Campaign booklet, February 2, 2008, www.miafscme .org/PDF%20Files/ObamaBlueprintForChange.pdf, 42.

25. Barack Obama, Chicago church campaign speech, March 18, 2008, in *Change We Can Believe In* (New York: Three Rivers Press, 2008), 235.

26. Third Democratic Primary Debate, June 28, 2007, transcript, Howard University, www.nytimes.com/2007/06/28/us/politics/29transcript.html?pagewanted=all&_r=0.

27. Obama, "Blueprint for Change," 48–49.

28. Congressional Black Caucus Democratic Debate, January 21, 2008, transcript, South Carolina, www.nytimes.com/2008/01/21/us/politics/21demdebate-transcript .html?pagewanted=all.

29. David Mendell, *Obama: From Promise to Power* (New York: HarperCollins, 2007), 202.

30. First Obama-Romney Presidential Debate, October 3, 2012, transcript, University of Denver, CO, http://debates.org/index.php?page=october-3-2012-debate-transcript. Foreign policy did not address drug trafficking. Biden-Ryan Vice Presidential Debate, October 11, 2012, transcript, Danville, KY, www.debates.org/index.php?page = october-11-2012-the-biden-romney-vice-presidential-debate. No one raised these topics at the Town Hall meetings either: Second Obama-Romney Presidential Debate, October 16, 2012, transcript, Hofstra University, www.debates.org/index.php?page = october-1-2012-the-second-obama-romney-presidential-debate; Third Obama-Romney Presidential Debate, October 23, 2012, transcript, Lynn University, Boca Raton, FL, http://abcnews.go.com/Politics/OTUS/presidential-debate-full-transcript/story?id=17538888#.UIYNgortQtE.

31. See Radley Balko, "Criminal Justice, Civil Liberties Issues Missing from 2012 Campaign," *Huffington Post,* October 15, 2012, www.huffingtonpost.com/2012/10/15/criminal-justice-civil-liberties-2012-campaign_n_1966791.html, ascribing the lack of focus on crime to declining crime rates.

32. Alex Kreit, "Beyond the Prohibition Debate: Thoughts on Federal Drug Laws in an Age of State Reforms," *Chapman Law Review* 13 (2013): 555–82.

33. Daniel Klaidman, "How Eric Holder Got His Chance to Overhaul Broken Sentencing System," *Daily Beast,* August 16, 2013, www.thedailybeast.com/articles/2013/08/16/how-eric-holder-got-his-chance-to-overhaul-broken-sentencing-system.html (last accessed April 6, 2014).

34. Drug Sentencing Reform and Kingpin Trafficking Act, S.1711, 110th Cong. (2007).

35. CNN Wire Staff, "Obama Signs Bill Reducing Cocaine Sentencing Gap," *CNN Politics,* August 3, 2010, www.cnn.com/2010/POLITICS/08/03/fair.sentencing/ (last accessed April 6, 2014).

36. Alfred Blumstein "The Notorious 100:1 Crack: Powder Disparity—The Data Tells Us That It Is Time to Restore the Balance," *Federal Sentencing Reporter* 16 (2003): 87–93; Matthew F. Leitman, "A Proposed Standard of Equal Protection Review for Classifications within the Criminal Justice System That Have a Racially-Disparate Impact—A Cast Study of the Federal Sentencing Guidelines' Classification between Crack and Powder Cocaine," *University of Toledo Law Review* 25 (1994): 215–53.

37. Federal Crack Cocaine Sentencing, the Sentencing Project, available at www.sentencingproject.org (last accessed April 6, 2014).

38. Congressional Budget Office Cost Estimate, Fair Sentencing Act of 2010, March 19, 2010, www.cbo.gov/sites/default/files/cbofiles/ftpdocs/114xx/doc11413/s1789.pdf (last accessed April 6, 2014).

39. Liz Goodwin, "Obama Not Waiting for Congress on Clemency for Crack Offenders," *Yahoo News,* January 31, 2014, http://news.yahoo.com/obama-not-waiting-for-congress-on-clemency-for-crack-offenders-223234501.html (last accessed April 6, 2014).

40. Remarks as Prepared for Delivery by Deputy Attorney General James Cole at the New York State Bar Association Annual Meeting, Jaunary 30, 2014, available at www.justice.gov/iso/opa/dag/speeches/2014/dag-speech-140130.html (last accessed April 6, 2014).

41. Department of Justice Office of Public Affairs official press release, "Attorney General Eric Holder Urges Congress to Pass Bipartisan 'Smarter Sentencing Act' to Reform

Mandatory Minimum Sentences," January 23, 2014, available at www.justice.gov/opa/pr/2014/January/14-ag-068.html (last accessed April 6, 2014).

42. Remarks as Prepared for Delivery by Deputy Attorney General James M. Cole at the Press Conference Announcing the Clemency Initiative, April 23, 2014, available at www.justice.gov/iso/opa/dag/speeches/2014/dag-speech-140423.html (last accessed April 28, 2014).

43. In the British context: Ian Brownlee, "New Labour—New Penology? Punitive Rhetoric and the Limits of Managerialism in Criminal Justice Policy," *Journal of Law and Society* 25 (December 2002): 313–35, doi: 10.1111/1467–6478.00094. In the Swedish context: Henrik Tham, "Law and Order as a Leftist Project? The Case of Sweden," *Punishment & Society* 3 (July 2001): 409–26, doi: 10.1177/1462474501003003004.

44. Marc Mauer, "Why Are Tough on Crime Policies So Popular?," *Stanford Law and Policy Review* 11 (1999–2000): 9.

45. Kevin Stenson, "The New Politics of Crime Control," in *Crime, Risk, and Justice: The Politics of Crime Control in Liberal Democracies,* ed. Kevin Stenson and Robert R. Sullivan (Collumpton, UK: Willan Press, 2001), 15–28.

46. Simon, *Governing through Crime.*

47. Francis T. Cullen, Gregory A. Clark, and John F. Wozniak, "Explaining the Get Tough Movement—Can the Public Be Blamed?" *Federal Probation* 49 (1985): 16–24.

48. Beckett, *Making Crime Pay.*

49. Smart on Crime Coalition, "Smart on Crime: Recommendations for the Administration and Congress," 2011, www.besmartoncrime.org/pdf/Complete.pdf.

50. Kamala Harris, *Smart on Crime* (San Francisco: Chronicle Books, 2009).

51. Smart on Crime Coalition, 2011, www.besmartoncrime.org/about.php.

52. "Cost-Efficient—State and federal governments annually spend billions of dollars on the criminal justice system. In the current economic climate, the country literally cannot afford to maintain a status quo that fails too many. While justice cannot be reduced to dollars and cents on a balance sheet, any changes to the system must be considered with concern for cost efficiency." Smart on Crime Coalition, "Recommendations for the Administration and Congress."

53. For more on this, see Vanessa Barker, *The Politics of Imprisonment: How the Democratic Process Shapes the Way America Punishes Offenders* (New York: Oxford University Press, 2009).

54. Bob Egelko, "Court OKs Lockups for Severe Truants," *SFGate,* October 3, 2012, www.sfgate.com/education/article/Court-OKs-lockups-for-severe-truants-3917825.php.

55. Californians United for a Responsible Budget, home page, accessed April 21, 2013, http://curbprisonspending.org.

56. Californians United for a Responsible Budget, "Who We Are: History," accessed April 21, 2013, http://curbprisonspending.org/?page_id=107.

57. Californians United for a Responsible Budget, "How to Stop a Jail in Your Town: A Compilation of Resources from Fights against Jail Expansion," accessed April 21, 2013, http://curbprisonspending.org/?page_id=2990.

58. Californians United for a Responsible Budget,"#StoptheCABudgetRaid Twitter Bomb all @AssemblyDems #NoPrisonExpansion" accessed April 21, 2013, http://curbprisonspending.org/?p=2789.

59. Right on Crime, "Statement of Principles," accessed April 21, 2013, www.rightoncrime .com/wp-content/uploads/2012/11/RightOnCrime-Statement-of-Principles.pdf; Right on Crime, "The Case for Reform," accessed April 21, 2013, www.rightoncrime.com/the-conservative-case-for-reform/.

60. Right on Crime, "What Conservatives are Saying," accessed April 21, 2013, www .rightoncrime.com/the-conservative-case-for-reform/what-conservatives-are-saying/.

61. Right on Crime, "Statement of Principles."

62. Right on Crime, "Cost to the Taxpayer," accessed April 21, 2013, www.rightoncrime. com/the-criminal-justice-challenge/cost-to-the-taxpayer/.

63. Right on Crime, "What Conservatives Are Saying."

64. Right on Crime, "The Case for Reform."

65. Senator Jim Webb, "Why We Must Reform Our Criminal Justice System," *Huffington Post,* June 11, 2009, http://www.huffingtonpost.com/sen-jim-webb/why-we-must-reform-our-cr_b_214130.html.

66. Mike Sacks, "Jim Webb's Criminal Justice Overhaul Commission Blocked Again in Senate," *Huffington Post,* October 20, 2011, www.huffingtonpost.com/2011/10/20/jim-webb-criminal-justice-commission-blocked-senate_n_1022722.html.

67. Justice Safety Valve Act of 2013, H.R. 1695, 113th Cong. (2013), www.govtrack.us /congress/bills/113/s619.

68. Jacob Sullum, "Rand Paul: 'I Am Here to Ask That We Begin the End of Mandatory Minimum Sentencing,'" *Hit & Run Blog,* September 18, 2013, http://reason.com/blog/2013/09/18 /rand-paul-i-am-here-to-ask-that-we-begin; Ray Sanchez, *California's Proposition 19 Rejected by Voters,* ABC News video, 2:31, November 3, 2010, http://abcnews.go.com/Politics /proposition-19-results-california-votes-reject-marijuana-measure/story?id=12037727&single Page=true#.UWj3T7_mMaU.

69. While the California and Colorado measures sought to legalize personal cultivation of marijuana, Washington's did not, limiting the law to possession for personal use.

70. Legislative Analyst's Office, Presentation on Proposition 19, September 21, 2010, www.lao.ca.gov/handouts/crimjust/2010/Prop_19_09_27_10.pdf.

71. Legislative Analyst's Office, Presentation on Proposition 19.

72. Ibid.

73. Legislative Analyst's Office, "Summary of Legislative Analyst's Estimate of Net State and Local Government Fiscal Impact," July 15, 2010, www.lao.ca.gov/ballot/2010/19_11_2010 .aspx.

74. Legislative Analyst's Office, Presentation on Proposition 19.

75. Paul Armentano, "Yes on Prop. 19 Campaign Releases TV Advertisement," *NORML* (blog), October 25, 2010, http://blog.norml.org/2010/10/25/yes-on-prop-19-campaign-releases-tv-advertisement%C2%A0.

76. Kelli M. Evans, "Moving towards Rational Marijuana Policy: California ACLU Affiliates Endorse Prop 19," ACLU of Northern California, August 30, 2010, www.aclunc.org /blog/moving-towards-rational-marijuana-policy-california-aclu-affiliates-endorse-prop-19.

77. John Hoeffel, "Youth Vote Falters; Prop. 19 Falls Short," *Los Angeles Times,* November 3, 2010, http://articles.latimes.com/2010/nov/03/local/la-me-pot-20101103–1.

78. Sanchez, *California's Proposition 19 Rejected.*

79. Dennis Romero, "No on Prop. 19 Campaign Already Practically Claiming Victory in Its Battle against California Marijuana Legalization," *LA Weekly,* November 2, 2010, http://blogs.laweekly.com/informer/2010/11/opponents_marijuana_victory.php.

80. Legislative Analyst's Office, Presentation on Proposition 19.

81. Ibid.

82. "Proposition 19: Vote No," *San Francisco Chronicle,* September 16, 2010, www.sfgate.com/opinion/editorials/article/Proposition-19-Vote-no-3174435.php.

83. Ibid.

84. Ibid.

85. Jeffrey A. Miron, "Why Did California Vote Down Legal Pot?," CNN, November 3, 2010, www.cnn.com/2010/OPINION/11/03/miron.pot.vote/index.html.

86. "Proposition 19: California Rejects Marijuana Legalization Measure," *Washington Post,* November 3, 2010, www.washingtonpost.com/wp-dyn/content/article/2010/11/03/AR2010110304231.html.

87. Ibid.

88. Ibid.

89. Hoeffel, "Youth Vote Falters."

90. CNN *Politics,* "Exit Polls," accessed September 26, 2013, www.cnn.com/ELECTION/2010/results/polls/#CAI01p1.

91. "New Law Is Historic Step in Reforming Marijuana Policies," ACLU Washington, December 5, 2012, www.aclu-wa.org/news/new-law-historic-step-reforming-marijuana-policies.

92. New Approach Washington, "About the Initiative," accessed April 13, 2013, www.newapproachwa.org/content/about-initiative.

93. Ibid.

94. Ibid.

95. Ibid.

96. Ibid.

97. Doug Honig, "Support for I-502 Is Busting Out All Over," ACLU Washington, October 4, 2012, http://aclu-wa.org/blog/support-i-502-busting-out-all-over-0.

98. New Approach Washington, "About the Initiative."

99. Ibid., "About the Initiative"; Gene Johnson, "Marijuana Legalization: How Strategy and Timing Translated into Lawful Pot Possession," Associated Press via *Huffington Post,* December 2, 2012, www.huffingtonpost.com/2012/12/02/marijuana-legalization-ho_n_2228104.html.

100. New Approach Washington, "About the Initiative."

101. Jim Camden, "Opposition to I-502 Low on Funds, Outreach Efforts," *Spokesman-Review* (Spokane, WA), October 30, 2012.

102. Ballot Pedia, "Washington Marijuana Legalization and Regulation, Initiative 502 (2012)," accessed September 26, 2013, http://ballotpedia.org/wiki/index.php/Washington_Marijuana_Legalization_and_Regulation,_Initiative_502_(2012) .

103. Wing, "'New Approach Washington' Launches Pro-Marijuana Legalization Ad."

104. "New Law Is Historic Step in Reforming Marijuana Policies," ACLU Washington, December 5, 2012, www.aclu-wa.org/news/new-law-historic-step-reforming-marijuana-policies; Gene Johnson, "Campaign to Legalize Pot Gets High-Profile GOP Support," *Komo*

News, October 3, 2012, http://www.komonews.com/news/local/Campaign-to-legalize-pot-gets-high-profile-GOP-support-172545801.html.

105. "Editorial: Approve Initiative 502—It's Time to Legalize, Regulate and Tax Marijuana," *Seattle Times,* September 22, 2012, http://seattletimes.com/html/editorials/2019226555_editmarijuanainitiative502xml.html.

106. Ibid.

107. Honig, "Support for I-502 Is Busting Out."

108. Ibid.

109. Johnson, "Campaign to Legalize Pot."

110. Ibid.

111. Ballot Pedia, Initiative 502.

112. Ibid.

113. Camden, "Opposition to I-502."

114. Campaign to Regulate Marijuana Like Alcohol, "About," accessed April 21, 2013, www.regulatemarijuana.org/about.

115. Ibid.

116. Campaign to Regulate Marijuana Like Alcohol, "Colorado Group Launches Campaign to Place Statewide Marijuana Initiative on 2012 Ballot," July 7, 2011, www.regulatemarijuana.org/s/colorado-group-launches-campaign-place-statewide-marijuana-initiative-2012-ballot; see Campaign to Regulate Marijuana Like Alcohol, "Endorsements," accessed April 21, 2013, www.regulatemarijuana.org/endorsements, for a comprehensive list of individuals and organizations supporting the passage of Amendment 64.

117. According to the Colorado Center on Law and Policy, Amendment 64 could create more than 350 new jobs, primarily in the construction industry, as a result of more funding for the school construction program. Christopher Stiffler, "Amendment 64 Would Produce $60 million in New Revenue and Savings for Colorado," Colorado Center on Law and Policy, August 16, 2012, www.cclponline.org/postfiles/amendment_64_analysis_final.pdf.

118. Campaign to Regulate Marijuana Like Alcohol, "About"; Campaign to Regulate Marijuana Like Alcohol, "Bolster Colorado's Economy," accessed April 21, 2013, www.regulatemarijuana.org/economic-impact.

119. John Ingold, "The Inside Story of How Marijuana Became Legal in Colorado," *Denver Post,* December 28, 2012, http://blogs.denverpost.com/thespot/2012/12/28/story-marijuana-legal-colorado/87640/.

120. Gene Johnson, "Marijuana Legalization: How Strategy and Timing Translated into Lawful Pot Possession," Associated Press via *Huffington Post,* December 2, 2012, www.huffingtonpost.com/2012/12/02/marijuana-legalization-ho_n_2228104.html.

121. Campaign to Regulate Marijuana Like Alcohol, "About"; Campaign to Regulate Marijuana Like Alcohol, "Bolster Colorado's Economy."

122. Campaign to Regulate Marijuana Like Alcohol, "Regulating Marijuana Works," accessed April 21, 2013, www.regulatemarijuana.org/regulation-works.

123. Patrick Svitek, "Marijuana Legalization Campaign Targets Parents," *Huffington Post,* July 2, 2012, www.huffingtonpost.com/2012/07/01/marijuana-legalization-colorado_n_1638818.html.

124. Lucia Graves, "Colorado Marijuana Legalization Campaign Launches Mother's Day–Themed TV Ad," *Huffington Post,* May 11, 2012, www.huffingtonpost.com/2012/05/11/colorado-marijuana-legalization-mothers-day-tv-ad_n_1509564.html.

125. Svitek, "Marijuana Legalization Campaign Targets Parents."

126. Fox News, "2012 Exit Polls," accessed April 21, 2013, www.foxnews.com/politics/elections/2012-exit-poll/CO/Issue1#.

127. "Former Republican Gov. Gary Johnson Endorses Initiative to Regulate Marijuana Like Alcohol as Campaign Submits Additional Signatures to Qualify for the November Ballot," Campaign to Regulate Marijuana Like Alcohol, February 17, 2012, www.regulatemarijuana.org/s/former-republican-gov-gary-johnson-endorses-initiative-regulate-marijuana-alcohol-campaign-submits.

128. Lucia Graves, "Majority of Denver Republicans Vote to Legalize Marijuana," *Huffington Post,* March 15, 2012, www.huffingtonpost.com/2012/03/15/denver-assembly-marijuana-laws-gop_n_1348765.html.

129. Ibid.

130. Michael Roberts, "Marijuana: Ken Buck Says Amendment 64 Backers Care More about Profit than People," *Denver Westword Blogs,* June 12, 2012, http://blogs.westword.com/latestword/2012/06/marijuana_ken_buck_amendment_64_women.php.

131. Ibid.

132. Gene Johnson, "The Time Nancy Reagan Invented 'Just Say No' and Other Great Moments in Pot History," *Business Insider,* December 9, 2012, http://www.businessinsider.com/the-history-of-marijuana-2012–12#ixzz2g2MHpdAD.

133. Roberts, "Ken Buck Says Amendment 64 Backers Care More about Profit."

134. John Ingold, "Colorado Business, Labor Leaders Differ over Marijuana Legalization," *Denver Post,* October 16, 2012, www.denverpost.com/news/marijuana/ci_21780082/colorado-business-labor-leaders-differ-over-marijuana-legalization.

135. Ibid.

136. Ibid.

137. "Editorial: Amendment 64 Is the Wrong Way to Legalize Marijuana," *Denver Post,* October 14, 2012, www.denverpost.com/opinion/ci_21760094/editorial-amendment-64-is-wrong-way-legalize-marijuana.

138. Ibid.

139. Ibid.

140. Ibid.

141. "I-502—Washington's New Marijuana Regulation Law Frequently Asked Questions," ACLU Washington, December 3, 2012, www.aclu-wa.org/sites/default/files/attachments/Marijuana%20I-502%20FAQs%20-%20120312.pdf.

142. Ryan Grim and Ryan J. Reilly, "Obama's Drug War: After Medical Marijuana Mess, Feds Face Big Decision on Pot," *Huffington Post,* February 8, 2012, www.huffingtonpost.com/2013/01/26/obamas-drug-war-medical-marijuana_n_2546178.html.

143. Ibid.

144. Lucia Graves, "Federal Interference in State Medical Marijuana Laws Is a Low Priority, Attorney General Affirms," *Huffington Post,* December 8, 2011, www.huffingtonpost.com/2011/12/08/medical-marijuana-federal-interference_n_1137745.html.

145. David W. Ogden, "Memorandum for Selected United States Attorneys," Memorandum prepared for the Department of Justice, October 19, 2009, http://blogs.justice.gov/main/archives/192.

146. Ibid.

147. David Stout and Solomon Moore, "U.S. Won't Prosecute in States That Allow Medical Marijuana," *New York Times,* October 19, 2009, www.nytimes.com/2009/10/20/us/20cannabis.html?_r=0.

148. James M. Cole, "Guidance Regarding Marijuana Enforcement," Memorandum prepared for the Department of Justice, August 29, 2013, www.justice.gov/iso/opa/resources/3052013829132756857467.pdf (discussing the Ogden memo).

149. Ogden, "Memorandum."

150. Carrie Johnson, "U.S. Eases Stance on Medical Marijuana," *Washington Post,* October 20, 2009, www.washingtonpost.com/wp-dyn/content/article/2009/10/19/AR2009101903638.html.

151. Grim and Reilly, "Obama's Drug War." (Steph Sherer, head of American for Safe Access, a California-based medical marijuana group, was thrilled and put out a press release touting the memo. "We were so beside ourselves in so many ways that we were finally recognized by a government agency," said Sherer.)

152. Ibid.

153. Ibid.

154. Ibid.

155. "Up in Smoke," *Economist,* April 14, 2012, www.economist.com/node/21552609.

156. Ibid.

157. Grim and Reilly, "Obama's Drug War."

158. "Up in Smoke."

159. "Marijuana's Foot in the Door," *Washington Post,* November 25, 2012, http://articles.washingtonpost.com/2012-11-25/opinions/35509121_1_possession-of-small-amounts-marijuana-federal-government.

160. Cole, "Guidance Regarding Marijuana Enforcement."

161. Ibid.

162. Grim and Reilly, "Obama's Drug War."

163. DeAngelo, quoted in Ryan Grim, "Medical Marijuana Memo: DOJ Cracks Down on Pot Shops," *Huffington Post,* August 31, 2011, www.huffingtonpost.com/2011/07/01/medical-marijuana-memo-doj_n_888995.html.

164. Ibid.

165. Ibid.

166. Ryan Grim and Ryan J. Reilly, "Eric Holder Says DOJ Will Let Washington, Colorado Marijuana Laws Go into Effect," *Huffington Post,* August 29, 2013, www.huffingtonpost.com/2013/08/29/eric-holder-marijuana-washington-colorado-doj_n_3837034.html.

167. Alex Kreit, "The Federal Response to State Marijuana Legalization: Room for Compromise?," *Oregon Law Review* 91 (2013): 1029–40.

168. Barker, *Politics of Imprisonment.*

CHAPTER 6

1. Bureau of Justice Statistics, "U.S. Prison Population Declined for Third Consecutive Year in 2012," July 25, 2013, www.bjs.gov/content/pub/press/p12acpr.cfm.

2. Cody Mason, "Too Good to Be True: Private Prisons in America," Sentencing Project, January 2012, http://sentencingproject.org/doc/publications/inc_Too_Good_to_be_True .pdf.

3. Ibid.

4. Ibid.

5. "Financial Tear Sheet: Corporate Profile," Corrections Corporation of America, Investor Relations, accessed September 26, 2013, http://ir.correctionscorp.com/Tearsheet .ashx?c=117983. CCA had its initial public offering in October 1986, issuing two million shares at $9.00 per share. "FAQs," Corrections Corporation of America, Investor Relations, accessed September 26, 2013, http://ir.correctionscorp.com/phoenix.zhtml?c=117983&p=irol-faq. In 1999 CCA's Tennessee predecessor merged with Prison Realty Trust, a Maryland Real Estate Investment Trust, to form the current iteration of CCA. The company initially sought to retain REIT status to take advantage of tax benefits, but in October 2000 it reorganized into a traditional C-corporation. Prison Realty Trust Inc., FY99 Form 10-K for the Period Ending December 31, 1999 (filed March 30, 2000), Securities and Exchange Commission archive, www.sec.gov/Archives/edgar/data/1070985/0000950144-00-004324.txt.

As of September 2012 CCA was investigating options to convert back to a REIT, and its board of directors approved the conversion on February 2013 following a favorable IRS ruling. Karin Demler and Steven Owen, Press Release: "CCA Board of Directors Authorizes REIT Conversion," *Wall Street Journal*, February 7, 2013, available at http://online.wsj.com /article/PR-CO-20130207–915211.html.

6. Corrections Corporation of America, FY12-Q3 Form 10-Q for the Period Ending September 30, 2012 (filed November 8, 2012), Securities and Exchange Commission archive, www .sec.gov/Archives/edgar/data/1070985/000119312512459397/d420784d10q.htm#toc420784_9. CCA projects that the switch would reduce their cost of capital, facilitate expansion, and attract more shareholders (for more on the consequences of the shift, see Alex Planes, "Are For-Profit Prisons Ready to Break Out After Reaching New Highs?," *Motley Fool*, September 7, 2012, www.fool.com/investing/general/2012/09/07/are-for-profit-prisons-ready-to-break-out-after-r.aspx).

7. There are 20 facilities that CCA operates but does not own: Bartlett State Jail, Bay Correctional Facility, Bradshaw State Jail, Citrus County Detention Facility, Dawson State Jail, Elizabeth Detention Center, Graceville Correctional Facility, Hardeman County Correctional Center, Idaho Correctional Center, Lake City Correctional Facility, Lindsey State Jail, Marion County Jail II, Metro-Davidson County Detention Facility, Moore Haven Correctional Facility, North Georgia Detention Center, Silverdale Detention Facilities, South Central Correctional Center, Wilkinson County Correctional Facility, Willacy County State Jail, and Winn Correctional Center. See Mason, "Too Good to Be True."

8. There are 41 facilities for which CCA is the owner and the operator: Adams County Correctional Center, Bent County Correctional Facility, Bridgeport Pre-Parole Transfer Facility, California City Correctional Center, Central Arizona Detention Center, Cibola County Correctional Center, Cimarron Correctional Facility, Coffee Correctional Facility,

Correctional Treatment Facility, Crossroads Correctional Facility, Crowley County Correctional Facility, Davis Correctional Facility, Eden Detention Center, Eloy Detention Center, Florence Correctional Center, Houston Processing Center, Jenkins Correctional Center, Kit Carson Correctional Center, La Palma Correctional Center, Lake Erie Correctional Institution, Laredo Processing Center, Leavenworth Detention Center, Lee Adjustment Center, Marion Adjustment Center, McRae Correctional Facility, Mineral-Wells Pre-Parole Transfer Facility, Nevada Southern Detention Center, New Mexico Women's Correctional Facility, North Fork Correctional Facility, Northeast Ohio Correctional Center, Red Rock Correctional Facility, Saguaro Correctional Center, San Diego Correctional Facility, Stewart Detention Center, T. Don Hutto Residential Center, Tallahatchie County Correctional Facility, Torrance County Detention Facility, Webb County Detention Center, West Tennessee Detention Facility, Wheeler Correctional Facility, and Whiteville Correctional Facility. See Mason, "Too Good to Be True."

9. CCA FY12-Q3 Form 10-Q, p. 23. In addition, CCA owns the Leo Chesney Correctional Center, which it leases to another operator, and the Community Education Partners, which it did lease but which is currently idle. Diamondback Correctional Facility, Huerfano County Correctional Center, Otter Creek Correctional Center, Prairie Correctional Facility, Queensgate Correctional Facility, and Shelby Training Center are all also owned by CCA and currently idle. This brings the total number of owned, managed, and leased facilities to 69.

10. Reuters, "Profile: Corrections Corporation of America (CXW)," modified September 23, 2013, accessed September 26, 2013, www.reuters.com/finance/stocks/companyProfile?rpc=66&symbol=CXW.

11. As the quarterly report explains, per diems are generally higher for owned and managed facilities because CCA incurs the cost of investment in the facility, repairs, real estate taxes, and insurance and assumes the risk of continuing to pay these costs even if the management contract is terminated and the facility sits vacant. CCA FY12-Q3 Form 10-Q, pp. 32–33.

12. The data in the table are taken from both the 10Q, previously cited, and the 10K: Corrections Corporation of America, FY11, Form 10-K for the Period Ending December 31, 2011 (filed February 24, 2012), Securities and Exchange Commission archive, www.sec.gov/Archives/edgar/data/1070985/000119312512081122/d231839d10k.htm.

13. CCA FY11 Form 10-K, p. 46.

14. CCA FY12–Q3 Form 10-Q, p. 28.

15. Publicly traded companies are required to disclose the amount and type of compensation paid to the CEO, the CFO, and the three other highest-compensated officers. For the fiscal year ending December 31, 2011, CCA's CEO and president, Damon T. Hininger, was paid $3,696,798 in basic compensation. Special assistant to the CEO, Richard P. Seiter, received the second highest basic compensation package at $1,845,566. CFO Todd J. Mullenger was paid $1,835,048 in basic compensation, plus $58,201 in stock options. John D. Ferguson, chairman of the board and former CEO, was paid $1,734,793 in basic compensation and $1,242,172 in stock options. Anthony L. Grande, executive vice president and chief development officer, received $1,735,039 in basic compensation and $31,550 in stock options. Brian Collins, executive vice president and chief human resources officer, received $1,505,146 in basic compensation and $1,000 in stock options. In sum, the executive compensation (exclusive of stock options) of all the above-listed executive officers totaled $12,352,390 in

2011. This is compared to the fiscal year ending December 31, 2010, when the same officials received total basic compensation of $10,861,830, 2011 saw a 13.72 percent increase in executive compensation. Morningstar, "Corrections Corporation of America (CXW), accessed April 5, 2014: http://quotes.morningstar.com/stock/cxw/s?t=CXW; http://insiders.morningstar.com/trading/executive-compensation.action?t=CXW; also see Reuters, "People: Corrections Corporation of America (CXW)," modified September 23, 2013, accessed September 26, 2013, www.reuters.com/finance/stocks/companyOfficers?symbol=CXW.

16. As of the close of the market on November 9, 2012, CCA stock (trading on the NYSE under ticker symbol CXW) was trading at $33.67/share. Google Finance, "Corrections Corp Of America (NYSE:CXW)," accessed November 10, 2012, www.google.com/finance?cid = 143893. With 100.05 million shares outstanding, the market cap of CCA (its number of shares outstanding multiplied by price of share) sits at $3.37 billion. CCA pays a quarterly dividend of $0.20/share: CCA, "Investor FAQs." CCA's beta, which is a measure of the volatility of the stock relative to a market average, is .94. A beta of 1 means that the stock has average risk, so CCA's stock is considered very slightly less risky than market but more risky than the "industry average" beta of .74. Reuters, "Financials: Corrections Corporation of America (CXW)," modified September 23, 2013, accessed September 26, 2013, www.reuters.com/finance/stocks/financialHighlights?symbol=CXW.

17. Of CCA's state customers, California is a major contributor, with 13 percent of management revenue for the years ended December 31, 2011 and 2010, coming from the California Department of Corrections and Rehabilitation. CCA FY12–Q3 Form 10-Q, p. 35.

18. CCA FY12–Q3 Form 10-Q, p. 30.

19. CCA FY11 Form 10-K, p. 63.

20. Chris Kirkham, "Private Prison Corporation Offers Cash in Exchange for State Prisons," *HuffPost Business*, February 14, 2012, www.huffingtonpost.com/2012/02/14/private-prisons-buying-state-prisons_n_1272143.html. The text of the letter is obtainable at http://big.assets.huffingtonpost.com/ccaletter.pdf. Also see Dana Rasor, "America's Top Prison Corporation: A Study in Predatory Capitalism and Cronyism," *Truthout*, May 3, 2012, http://truth-out.org/news/item/8875-corrections-corporation-of-america-a-study-in-predatory-capitalism-and-cronyism.

21. Kevin Johnson, "Private Purchasing of Prisons Locks Occupancy Rates," *USA Today*, August 3, 2012, http://usatoday30.usatoday.com/news/nation/story/2012-03-01/buying-prisons-require-high-occupancy/53402894/1.

22. See CCA FY11 Form 10-K, p. F-19, for more.

23. CCA FY11 Form 10-K, p. 7.

24. Alex Friedmann, "For-Profit Transportation Companies: Taking the Prisoners and the Public for a Ride," in *Prison Profiteers: Who Makes Money from Mass Incarceration*, ed. Tara Herivel and Paul Wright (New York: New Press, 2009).

25. Federal revenues increased $31.5 million, or 4.4 percent, from $717.8 million in 2010 to $749.3 million in 2011, comprising 43 percent of CCA's total revenue for both of the years ended December 31, 2011 and 2010. CCA FY11 Form 10-K, p. 48. Federal customers also generated approximately 42 percent of CCA's total revenue for the three months ended September 30, 2012, and 44 percent for the same period in 2011, increasing $0.4 million, from $188.4 million during the three months ended September 30, 2011, to $188.9 million during the three months ended September 30, 2012. CCA FY12-Q3 Form 10-Q, p. 30.

26. Angelo Young, "Top Private Prison Operators Geo, Corrections Corp of America Worry about Fewer Illegal Immigrants to Jail Because It's Good for Business," *International Business Times*, March 21, 2013, www.ibtimes.com/top-private-prison-operators-geo-corrections-corp-america-worry-about-fewer-illegal-immigrants-jail.

27. Corrections Corporation of America, 2012 Annual Report, accessed August 29, 2013, http://ir.correctionscorp.com/phoenix.zhtml?c=117983&p=irol-reportsannual. Similar statements can be found in GEO's annual report, indicating that this is an industry trend: The Geo Group, Inc., FY10 Form 10-K for the Period Ending January 2, 2011 (filed March 2, 2011), http://yahoo.brand.edgar-online.com/displayfilinginfo.aspx?filingid=7767347&tabindex=2&type=html.

28. Laura Wides-Munoz and Garance Burke, "Immigrants Prove Big Business for Prison Companies," Associated Press–Miami, August 2, 2012, http://news.yahoo.com/immigrants-prove-big-business-prison-companies-084353195.html.

29. National Immigration Forum, "The Math of Immigration Detention: Runaway Costs for Immigration Detention Do Not Add Up to Sensible Policies," August 2013, www.immigrationforum.org/images/uploads/mathofimmigrationdetention.pdf.

30. Follow the Money, "Noteworthy Contributor Summary: Corrections Corp of America," accessed September 26, 2013, www.followthemoney.org/database/topcontributor.phtml?u=695&y=0.

31. Ibid.

32. Ibid.

33. Ibid.

34. Ibid.

35. Ibid.

36. Follow the Money, "Client Summary: Corrections Corp of America," accessed September 26, 2013, www.followthemoney.org/database/lobbyistclient.phtml?lc=100552&y=0&s=CA#CA. It appeared to me that the $1.8 million in lobbying contributions was separate from the $2.1 million in political contributions, but that issue warrants a second look.

37. Ibid.

38. S.B. 1070, Arizona Senate, 49th Leg. (2010).

39. Arizona v. United States, 567 U.S. (2012).

40. Adam Liptak, "Blocking Parts of Arizona Law, Justices Allow Its Centerpiece," *New York Times*, June 25, 2012, www.nytimes.com/2012/06/26/us/supreme-count-rejects-part-of-arizona-immigration-law.html?_r=2&hp&.

41. Laura Sullivan, "Prison Economics Help Drive Ariz. Immigration Law," NPR, October 28, 2010, www.npr.org/2010/10/28/130833741/prison-economics-help-drive-ariz-immigration-law?sc=fb&cc=fp.

42. Ibid.

43. Joshua Page, *The Toughest Beat: Politics, Punishment, and the Prison Officers Union in California* (New York: Oxford University Press, 2011).

44. Leigh Owens, "Private Prison in Violation of Ohio State Law," *Huffington Post*, October 10, 2012, www.huffingtonpost.com/2012/10/09/private-prison-violates-state-law_n_1951917.htm.

45. German Lopez, "Liberty for Sale," *City Beat*, September 19, 2012, www.citybeat.com/cincinnati/article-26206-liberty_for_sale.html.

46. Mike Brickner, "Prisons for Profit: A Look at Prison Privatization," ACLUOhio.org, April 2011, www.acluohio.org/issues/CriminalJustice/PrisonsForProfit2011_04.pdf.

47. A higher turnover rate implies a less knowledgeable staff and decreased stability.

48. One in every 86 Louisiana adults is in prison, twice the national average. Cindy Chang, "Louisiana Is the World's Prison Capital," *Times-Picayune*, May 13, 2012, www.nola .com/crime/index.ssf/2012/05/louisiana_is_the_worlds_prison.html. In addition, Louisiana has the highest percentage of inmates serving life without parole and spends more on local inmates than any other state, and two-thirds of its inmates are nonviolent offenders. Charles M. Blow, "Plantations, Prisons and Profits," *New York Times*, May 25, 2012, www .nytimes.com/2012/05/26/opinion/blow-plantations-prisons-and-profits.html?_r=1&.

49. Chang, "Louisiana Is the World's Prison Capital."

50. Ibid.

51. Brett Barroquere, "Rural Ky. Town Readies For Private Prison Closure," Associated Press, April 24, 2012, www.foxnews.com/us/2012/04/24/rural-ky-town-readies-for-private-prison-closure/. Other aspects of Hawaii's choice to house its inmates out of state are discussed below.

52. Ian Urbina, "Hawaii to Remove Inmates over Abuse Charges," *New York Times*, August 25, 2009, www.nytimes.com/2009/08/26/us/26kentucky.html?_r=0.

53. For more on private prison providers' promises to improve the economy of prospective prison towns, see Ruth Wilson Gilmore, *Golden Gulag: Prisons, Surplus, Crisis, and Opposition in Globalizing California* (Berkeley: University of California Press, 2007). An economic analysis of before-and-after economic conditions suggests that such towns end up not benefiting from the prison industry as promised, because locals are seldom hired to work in the prisons and staff choose to live elsewhere. Clayton Mosher, Gregory Hooks, and Peter B. Hood, "Don't Build It Here: The Hype versus the Reality of Prisons and Local Employment," in Herivel and Wright, *Prison Profiteers*, 90–98.

54. John Burnett, "Miss. Prison Operator Out; Facility Called a 'Cesspool,'" NPR, April 24, 2012, www.npr.org/2012/04/24/151276620/firm-leaves-miss-after-its-prison-is-called-cesspool.

55. Mike Oliver, "Private Probation Outfits Raise Eyebrows Over Profit Seeking," *Alabama Live*, September 16, 2012, http://blog.al.com/spotnews/2012/09/private_probation_ outfits_rais.html.

56. Ethan Bronner, "Poor Land in Jail as Companies Add Huge Fees for Probation," *New York Times*, July 2, 2012, www.nytimes.com/2012/07/03/us/probation-fees-multiply-as-companies-profit.html?pagewanted=all.

57. Gerry Gaes, "Cost Performance Studies Look at Prison Privatization," *National Institute of Justice Journal* 259 (March 2008): 32–36, www.ncjrs.gov/pdffiles1/nij/221507.pdf.

58. Ibid., 33.

59. Ibid., 35. This "internal yardstick" is reminiscent of Feeley and Simon's comment, in "The New Penology," about how actuarial justice is based on internal measures, such as number of escapes, rather than on external, utilitarian goals like recidivism reduction. Malcolm M. Feeley and Jonathan Simon, "The New Penology: Notes on the Emerging Strategy of Corrections and Its Implications," *Criminology* 30 (November 1992): 449–74.

60. Mason, "Too Good to Be True," citing C. R. Blakely and V. W. Bumphus, "Private and Public Sector Prisons—A Comparison of Select Characteristics," *Federal Probation* 68 (2004): 27–31.

61. Emily Badger, "America Is Finally Closing Down Prisons, Now What Do We Do With Them?," *Atlantic,* December 6, 2012, www.theatlanticcities.com/design/2012/12 /america-finally-closing-prisons-now-what-do-them/4083/#.

62. Nicole D. Porter, "On the Chopping Block 2012: State Prison Closings," Sentencing Project 1, December 2012, http://sentencingproject.org/doc/publications/On%20the%20 Chopping%20Block%202012.pdf.

63. Ibid.

64. Ibid.

65. Ibid.

66. Ibid.

67. Badger, "America Is Finally Closing Down Prisons."

68. Ibid.

69. Editorial, "How to Cut Prison Costs," *New York Times,* November 11, 2012, www .nytimes.com/2012/11/11/opinion/sunday/how-to-cut-prison-costs.html.

70. Thomas Kaplan, "New York Has Some Prisons to Sell You," *New York Times,* May 27, 2012, www.nytimes.com/2012/05/28/nyregion/closed-new-york-prisons-prove-hard-to-sell.html.

71. Ibid.

72. Nicole Porter, "On the Chopping Block."

73. Ibid., 5.

74. For more on the heritage of punitiveness in the South, see Robert Perkinson, *Texas Tough: The Rise of America's Prison Empire* (New York: Metropolitan Books, 2010); Mona Lynch, *Sunbelt Justice: Arizona and the Transformation of American Punishment* (Stanford, CA: Stanford University Press, 2009).

75. Kurt Erickson, "Court Lifts Prison Closures Injunction; Quinn Pledges Action within Weeks," *Herald Review,* February 20, 2012, http://herald-review.com/news /state-and-regional/court-lifts-prison-closures-injunction-quinn-pledges-action-within-weeks/article_4d70ccca-4a6d-11e2-bc63-0019bb2963f4.html.

76. Monique Garcia and Rafael Guerrero, "Quinn Stands by Decision to Close 2 Prisons, Despite Inmate Crowding," *Chicago Tribune,* February 18, 2013, http://articles .chicagotribune.com/2013-02-18/news/ct-met-quinn-prison-closures-0219-20130219_1_ three-transitional-centers-inmate-population-tamms; Aaron Cynic, "Quinn Defends Prison Closures amid Overcrowding Complaints," *Chicagoist,* February 22, 2013, http:// chicagoist.com/2013/02/22/despite_overcrowding_quinn_defends.php.

77. Johanna Kaiser, "Officials on Prison-Closure Plan: They're Already Overcrowded," *Lowell Sun* (Lowell, MA), January 28, 2011, www.lowellsun.com/todaysheadlines/ci_17226167.

78. Cara Matthews, "Union: Prisons Overcrowded; State Shouldn't Close More," *Politics on the Hudson,* March 23, 2011, http://polhudson.lohudblogs.com/2011/03/23/union-prisons-are-overcrowded-state-shouldnt-close-more/.

79. Vera Institute of Justice, "Segregation Reduction Project," accessed September 27, 2013, www.vera.org/project/segregation-reduction-project.

80. Randall G. Shelden and Selena Teji, "Collateral Consequences of Interstate Transfers of Prisoners," Center on Juvenile and Criminal Justice, July 2012, www.cjcj.org/uploads /cjcj/documents/Out_of_state_transfers.pdf.

81. Ibid.

82. Ibid., 1, citing Morris L. Thigpen, George Keiser, and Kermit Humphries, "Interstate Transfer of Prison Inmates in the United States," National Institute of Corrections, February 2006, http://static.nicic.gov/Library/021242.pdf.

83. Sheldon and Teji, *Collateral Consequences,* 4.

84. Ibid.

85. Shymeka L. Hunter, "More than Just a Private Affair: Is the Practice of Incarcerating Alaska Prisoners in Private Out-of-State Prisons Unconstitutional?," *Alaska Law Review* 17 (2000): 319–42, citing Justin Brooks and Kimberly Bahna, "It's a Family Affair—The Incarceration of the American Family: Confronting Legal and Social Issues," *University of San Francisco Law Review* 28 (1994): 271, 277.

86. Solomon Moore, "States Export Their Inmates as Prisons Fill," *New York Times,* July 31, 2007, www.nytimes.com/2007/07/31/us/31prisons.html?pagewanted=all.

87. Ibid.

88. David T. Johnson, Janet T. Davidson, and Paul Perone, "Hawaii's Imprisonment Policy and the Performance of Parolees Who Were Incarcerated In-State and on the Mainland," Department of Sociology, University of Hawaii at Manoa, and Department of the Attorney General, State of Hawaii, January 2011, http://ag.hawaii.gov/cpja/files/2013/01/AH-UH-Mainland-Prison-Study-2011.pdf.

89. Ibid., 25.

90. Ibid., 111; see also Moore, "States Export Their Inmates."

91. Moore, "States Export Their Inmates."

92. Lucas Anderson, "Kicking the National Habit: The Legal and Policy Arguments for Abolishing Private Prison Contracts," *Public Contract Law Journal* 39 (Fall 2009): 113, 130. Emphasis in the original.

93. Craig Harris, "Arizona Prison Contract Will Go to Private Firm," *Arizona Republic,* August 26, 2012, www.azcentral.com/news/articles/20120820arizona-prison-expansion-private-firm.html.

94. Ibid.

95. Ibid.

96. Casey Newton, Ginger Rough, and J. J. Hensley, "Arizona Inmate Escape Puts Spotlight on State Private Prisons," *Arizona Republic,* August 22, 2010, www.azcentral.com/news/articles/2010/08/22/20100822arizona-private-prisons.html.

97. Ibid.

98. Ibid.

99. Harris, "Arizona Prison Contract will Go to Private Firm,"

100. Franklin E. Zimring and Gordon Hawkins, *The Scale of Imprisonment* (Chicago: University of Chicago Press, 1991): "The parable of the free lunch is relevant to the discussion of prison population because prisons in the United States are . . . paid for at the state level of government out of state correctional budgets, but prison populations are determined by the number of prisoners referred by local officials and the length of sentences imposed at the local level. Since localities do not contribute to central state correctional budgets, the marginal cost of an extra prisoner may be zero at the local level of government, where the decision to confine is made."

101. W. David Ball, "Defunding State Prisons," *Criminal Law Bulletin* 50 (2013), available at SSRN: http://ssrn.com/abstract=2220028 or doi.org/10.2139/ssrn.2220028..

102. For a concise summary of these, see Aaron Rappaport, "Realigning California Corrections," *Federal Sentencing Reporter* 25 (2013): 207–16.

103. California Penal Code 1170(h) amends hundreds of felonies so as to make them punishable by a term in county jail. As opposed to "wobblers," offenses that can be tried as felonies or misdemeanors, these would be felonies, and the only difference is in the physical place of confinement. The Department of State, and the California courts, treats the "non-non-nons" as felons for all other purposes, including felon disenfranchisement. Hadar Aviram and Jessica Willis, "Reintegrating Citizens: Felon Disenfranchisement, Realignment, and the California Constitution," *Journal of Civil Rights and Economic Development* (forthcoming).

104. Cal. Penal Code § 1203.1.

105. Such as electronic monitoring (Cal. Penal Code §§ 1203.017, 1203.018) and programs for women with a history of substance abuse (Cal. Penal Code § 1174.4).

106. Margo Schlanger, "*Plata v. Brown* and Realignment: Jails, Prisons, Courts, and Politics," *Harvard Civil Rights–Civil Liberties Law Review* 48, no. 1 (2013): 165–216.

107. Kathleen Haughney, "Counties Fear $100M Cost of State Cost-Cutting Proposal," *Sun-Sentinel* (South Florida), December 3, 2012, http://articles.sun-sentinel.com/2012-12-03/news/fl-state-puts-pressure-county-jails-20121202-26_1_county-jails-stockade-facility-extra-inmates.

108. Kathryn Jett and Joan Hancock, "Realignment in the Counties," *Federal Sentencing Reporter* 25 (2013): 236–40.

109. Mike Males and Lizzie Buchen, "Beyond Realignment: Counties' Large Disparities in Imprisonment Underlie Ongoing Prison Crisis," Center on Juvenile and Criminal Justice, March 21, 2013, www.cjcj.org/uploads/cjcj/documents/beyond_realignment_march_2013 .pdf.

110. Leroy D. Baca and Gerald K. Cooper, "Can AB 109 Work in Los Angeles County?," *Federal Sentencing Reporter* 25 (2013): 241.

111. Callie Shanafelt, "Alameda Probation Chief Sees Opportunity in Prison Reform," *California Health Report,* August 30, 2011, www.healthycal.org/archives/5559.

112. Mona Lynch, "Realigning Research: A Proposed (Partial) Agenda for Sociolegal Scholars," *Federal Sentencing Reporter* 25 (2013): 254.

113. W. David Ball, "Tough on Crime (on the State's Dime): How Violent Crime Does Not Drive California Counties' Incarceration Rates—And Why It Should," *Georgia State Law Review* 28 (2012): 987.

114. Indeed, some of the more atrocious conditions that yielded federal litigation existed in county jails. Malcolm Feeley and Edward Rubin, *Judicial Policy Making and the Modern State: How the Courts Reformed America's Prisons* (Cambridge: Cambridge University Press, 2000).

115. "Riverside among California Counties Facing Inmate Lawsuits after State Prison Realignment," KPCC, Southern California Public Radio, March 19, 2013, www.scpr.org /news/2013/03/19/36435/ca-counties-now-facing-inmate-lawsuits-after-state/. For more on pay-to-stay jail schemes, see chapter 7 below.

116. "Will Florida Follow in California's Path?," *Correctional News,* December 12, 2012, www.correctionalnews.com/articles/2012/12/12/will-florida-follow-in-california-s-path.

117. Ibid.

118. Ibid.

119. Feeley and Simon, "The New Penology."

CHAPTER 7

1. John Howard, *The State of the Prisons in England and Wales, with an Account of Some Foreign Prisons* (Cambridge: Cambridge University Press, [1777] 2013).

2. Adam Nossiter, "While His Inmates Grew Thinner, a Sheriff's Wallet Grew Fatter," *New York Times*, January 8, 2009, www.nytimes.com/2009/01/09/us/09sheriff.html?emc = eta1&_r = 0.

3. Malcolm M. Feeley and Jonathan Simon, "The New Penology: Notes on the Emerging Strategy of Corrections and Its Implications," *Criminology* 30 (November 1992): 449–74.

4. Joshua Page, *The Toughest Beat: Politics, Punishment, and the Prison Officers Union in California* (New York: Oxford University Press, 2011).

5. Chrysanthi Leon, *Sex Fiends, Perverts, and Pedophiles: Understanding Sex Crime Policy in America* (New York: New York University Press, 2011).

6. Khalil Muhammad, "Vindictive Justice: New York State's Four Strikes Law of 1926" (Paper presented at the Annual Meeting of the Midwest Political Science Association, Chicago, IL, April 15, 2004).

7. Paul Tappan, "Habitual Offender Laws in the United States," *Federal Probation* 13 (1949): 28–32.

8. Tom Tyler and Robert J. Boeckmann, "Three Strikes and You Are Out, but Why? The Psychology of Public Support for Punishing Rule Breakers," *Law and Society Review* 31, no. 2 (1997): 237–66.

9. Franklin Zimring, Gordon Hawkins and Sam Kamin, *Punishment and Democracy: Three Strikes and You're Out in California* (New York: Oxford University Press, 2001).

10. Russ Immarigeon, "Advocacy, Elderly Prisoners, and Mass Imprisonment," in *Aging Prisoners: A Crisis in Need of Intervention*, ed. Tina Maschi, May Beth Morrissey, Russ Immarigeon, and Samantha L. Sutfin (New York: Fordham University Be the Evidence Project, 2012), 117–22, https://docs.google.com/viewer?a=v&pid=sites&srcid=ZGVmYXVs dGRvbWFpbnxiZXRoZWV2aWRlbmNlHJvamVjdHxneDpiNmMxNTgwZ-TNkYmQ3YzA.

11. Ronald H. Aday, *Aging Prisoners: Crisis in American Corrections* (Westport, CT: Praeger, 2003).

12. Human Rights Watch, "Old Behind Bars: The Aging Prison Population in the United States," accessed April 4, 2014, www.hrw.org/sites/default/files/reports/usprisons0112webw-cover_0.pdf.

13. Ashley Nellis and Ryan S. King, "No Exit: The Expanding Use of Life Sentences in America," *The Sentencing Project* (July 2009): 7, www.sentencingproject.org/doc /publications/publications/inc_noexitseptember2009.pdf.

14. Adam Liptak, "To More Inmates, Life Term Means Dying Behind Bars," *New York Times*, October 2, 2005, www.nytimes.com/2005/10/02/national/02life.web.html?pagewanted = all&_r = 0; American Civil Liberties Union (ACLU), "At America's Expense: The Mass Incarceration of the Elderly," Report, June 2012: vii, www.aclu.org/files/assets /elderlyprisonreport_20120613_1.pdf; Human Rights Watch, "Old Behind Bars," 26, 33–34.

15. Human Rights Watch, "Old Behind Bars," citing data obtained from the Bureau of Justice Statistics Federal Justice Statistics Program, http://bjs.ojp.usdoj.fjsrc (accessed July 7, 2011). This online statistical tool provides public access to data regarding federal prisoners sorted according to a number of variables, including year, age, and offense.

16. Human Rights Watch, "Old Behind Bars," 6.

17. Ibid., 39.

18. ACLU, "Mass Incarceration of the Elderly," vi.

19. "Aging in Prison: States Figure Out How to Address a Prison Population That's Growing Old," *Columbia Daily Tribune* (Columbia, MI), August 22, 2010, www.columbiatribune.com/news/2010/aug/22/aging-in-prison/. See also W. J. Sabol and H. Couture, "Prison Inmates at Midyear 2007," *Bureau of Justice Statistics Bulletin*, NCJ Publication No. 221944 (June 2008): 1–24 (noting that the population of prisoners aged 50 and above in 2008 was five times as large as it was in 1990, representing about 12 percent of the 2.3 million prisoners).

20. Sabol and Couture, "Inmates at Midyear," 19.

21. Human Rights Watch, "Old Behind Bars," 6.

22. The age distribution varied among racial groups. Almost half (48 percent) of white male prisoners were age 40 or older, compared to 37 percent of black and 32 percent of Hispanic male prisoners. About 60 percent of both white and black female prisoners were age 39 or younger, compared to 67 percent of Hispanic female prisoners. E. Ann Carson and William J. Sabol, "Prisoners in 2011," Bureau of Justice Statistics (accessed January 30, 2012), 1, http://bjs.ojp.usdoj.gov/index.cfm?ty=pbdetail&iid=4559. Nonetheless, because of over-representation of people of color among inmates, minority prisoners were still the majority among older prisoners. In 2011 Hispanic and black male prisoners age 65 or older were imprisoned at rates between three and five times those of white males, and among persons age 60 to 64, the black male imprisonment rate was five times that of the white male imprisonment rate. Human Rights Watch, "Old Behind Bars," 8. The majority of older prisoners are men (93 percent); women made up only 7 percent of the older prisoner population in 2006. W. J. Sabol, H. Couture, and P. M. Hamilton, "Prisoners in 2006," Bureau of Justice Statistics (2007). According to Human Rights Watch, there were about twenty-one times more men age 55 and older than women of that age in prisons in 2009, even though men outnumbered women by only 13 to 1.3 in the total state prison population in 2010. Human Rights Watch, "Old Behind Bars," 21. States vary considerably in terms of the relative size of their population of older inmates. Among states reporting prison population data to the National Corrections Report Program in 2009, the proportion of prisoners age 55 or over ranged from 4.2 percent to 9.9 percent. However, much higher percentages were posted in a 2010 prison culture blog, "Top 10 States with Prisoners over 55 Years Old," citing the 2010 Directory of Adult and Juvenile Correctional Departments, Institutions, Agencies and Probation and Parole Authorities (a directory available exclusively to American Correctional Association members). This "Top 10" list named the state of New Hampshire #1, with 15.2 percent of its prison population over age 55, and Idaho was listed #10, with 10.4 percent. Tina Chiu, "Prison Culture: How the PIC Structures Our World, Top 10 States with Prisoners over 55 Years Old," *Prison Culture* (blog), August 2, 2010, www.vera.org/sites/default/files/resources/downloads/Its-about-time-aging-prisoners-increasing-costs-and-geriatric-release.pdf, citing 2010 Directory of Adult and Juvenile Correctional Departments, Institutions, Agencies and Probation and Parole Authorities.

23. Correctional Health Care: Addressing the Needs of Elderly, Chronically Ill, and Terminally Ill Inmates,U.S. Department of Justice National Institute of Corrections (2004), available at http://static.nicic.gov/Library/018735.pdf.

24. Susan Lundstorm, "Dying to Get Out: A Study on the Necessity, Importance, and Effectiveness of Prison Early Release Programs for Elderly Inmates Suffering from HIV Disease and other Terminal-Centered Illnesses," *BYU Journal of Public Law* 9 (1994–95): 155. Figures somewhat vary; federal figures indicate a chronological-institutional age difference of seven to eight years, while other studies show a difference of up to ten years. Jonathan Turley, "POPS: Project for Older Prisoners—Release Elderly Inmates, Older, Lower-Risk Prisoners Should Be Removed from the State's Perilously Overcrowded Jails," *Los Angeles Times,* October 7, 2006, www.latimes.com/news/la-oe-turley7oct07,0,7405392.story.

25. Anthony A. Sterns, Greta Lax, Chad Sed, Patrick Keohane, and Ronni S. Sterns, "The Growing Wave of Older Prisoners: A National Survey of Older Prisoner Health, Mental Health and Programming," *Corrections Today,* August 1, 2008, www.aca.org /fileupload/177/ahaidar/stern_keohame.pdf.

26. Ibid., citing U.S. Census Bureau, "The Older Population in the United States: 2006," U.S. Census Bureau, Population Division, Washington, DC, accessed January 7, 2008, www .census.gov/population/www/socdemo/age/age_2006.html.

27. Human Rights Watch, "Old Behind Bars," 75.

28. David Holmstrom, "Using Older Convicts as Safety Valve," *Christian Science Monitor,* May 11, 1992, www.csmonitor.com/1992/0511/11012.html (quoting Jonathan Turley).

29. Human Rights Watch, "Old Behind Bars."

30. Ibid.; Tina Chiu, "It's about Time: Aging Prisoners, Increasing Costs, and Geriatric Release," Vera Institute of Justice, 2010, www.vera.org/sites/default/files/resources /downloads/Its-about-time-aging-prisoners-increasing-costs-and-geriatric-release.pdf; Chad Kinsella, "Correctional Health Care Costs," Council of State Governments, 2004, www.csg.org/knowledgecenter/docs/TA0401CorrHealth.pdf.

31. Human Rights Watch, "Old Behind Bars."

32. ACLU, "Mass Incarceration of the Elderly," 26.

33. Human Rights Watch, "Old Behind Bars," 78.

34. Christine Vestal, "Medicaid Expansion Seen Covering Nearly All State Prisoners," *Governing,* October 18, 2011, www.governing.com/blogs/politics/Medicaid-Expansion-Covering-Nearly-All-State-Prisoners.html.

35. Ibid. Louisiana, Mississippi, Nebraska, North Carolina, Oklahoma, and Washington have taken advantage of the ruling. California launched a program in 2014: Barnini Chakraborty, "Inmates Getting Coverage under ObamaCare, As States Shift Cost to Feds", Fox News, April 6, 2014, available at:http://www.foxnews.com/politics/2014/04/06 /states-sign-up-inmates-for-obamacare-shift-costs-to-federal-government/. Alabama, Michigan, New Jersey, and Utah are studying the idea.

36. Human Rights Watch, "Old Behind Bars."

37. Ibid., 79.

38. Estelle v. Gamble, 429 U.S. 97 (1976).

39. Brown v. Plata, 131 S.Ct. 1910 (2011).

40. Human Rights Watch, "Old Behind Bars," 78.

41. Marquiz v. Romer, 92-k-1470 (D. Colorado), unreported.

42. Human Rights Watch, "Old Behind Bars," 78.

43. Ibid., 10.

44. Tyler Bridges, "Angola Pays Big Tab for Its Elderly Inmates," *New Orleans Times-Picayune,* August 20, 1989.

45. Sam Negri, "'Scandal' of Aging Convicts," *Arizona Republic,* June 10, 1990.

46. Matt Neufeld, "Release for Older Inmates Sought," *Washington Times,* July 28, 1992 (paraphrasing Jonathan Turley).

47. Holstrom, "Using Older Convicts as Safety Valve," 163, citing Jonathan Turley, "Solving Prison Overcrowding—Prisons Aren't Nursing Homes," *New York Times,* October 9, 1989, A17.

48. Human Rights Watch, "Old Behind Bars," 55.

49. Ibid.

50. Ibid.

51. Ibid.

52. Ibid.

53. Ibid.

54. ACLU, "Mass Incarceration of the Elderly," 17.

55. Ibid.

56. Ibid., 24.

57. Holstrom, "Using Older Convicts as Safety Valve," 1 (quoting Turley).

58. Holmstrom, "Using Older Convicts as Safety Valve."

59. Human Rights Watch, "Old Behind Bars," 9–10.

60. Human Rights Watch, "Old Behind Bars."

61. Central California Women's Facility Housing Division, "Operational Procedure P-054," August 2011, on file at Human Rights Watch.

62. Feeley and Simon, "The New Penology."

63. Ibid.

64. Lundstorm, "Dying to Get Out," 169.

65. Anton R. Valukas, "Final Report," Illinois Task Force on Crime and Corrections, March 1993, www.ncjrs.gov/pdffiles1/Digitization/142786NCJRS.pdf.

66. Turley, "POPS: Project for Older Prisoners."

67. Ibid.

68. Zimring, Hawkins, and Kamin, *Punishment and Democracy.*

69. B. Jaye Anno, Camelia Graham, James E. Lawrence, and Ronald Shansky, "Correctional Healthcare: Addressing the Needs of Elderly, Chronically Ill, and Terminally Ill Inmates, Appendix A: Criminal Justice Institute Survey," National Institute of Corrections, February 2004, 66–69, http://static.nicic.gov/Library/018735.pdf.

70. Sterns et al., "The Growing Wave of Older Prisoners."

71. Marquiz v. Romer, 92-k-1470 (D. Colorado).

72. Turley, "Preliminary Report to the State of Illinois," 24, 22.

73. Human Rights Watch, "Old Behind Bars," 80.

74. Ibid.

75. Zimring, Hawkins, and Kamin, *Punishment and Democracy.*

76. Neufeld, "Release for Older Inmates Sought," 28.

77. Maschi et al., "A Crisis in Need of Intervention," Fordham University Be the Evidence Project. Also see Tina Chiu, "CHAPTER 15: It's Still about Time: Aging Prisoners,

Increasing Costs, and Geriatric Release," https://docs.google.com/viewer?a=v&pid=sites-&srcid=ZGVmYXVsdGRvbWFpbnxiZXRoZWV2aWRlbmNlHJvamVjdHxneDpiNmMx NTgwZTNkYmQ3YzA (accessed January 30, 2012).

78. Human Rights Watch, "Old Behind Bars"; Brown v. Plata, 131 S.Ct. 1910 (2011).

79. Chiu, "Prison Culture."

80. Bren Gorman, "With Soaring Prison Costs, States Turn to Early Release of Aged, Infirm Inmates," *State Health Notes* 29 (September 2008): 4–5, www.ncsl.org/Portals/1 /documents/health/shn/shn522.pdf.

81. Chiu, "Prison Culture."

82. Ibid.

83. Ibid.

84. Ibid.

85. Ibid.

86. Robert H. Aday and Jenifer J. Krabill, *Women Aging in Prison: A Neglected Population in the Correctional System* (Boulder, CO: Lynne Reiner, 2011); see also Susan J. Loeb, Darrell Steffensmeier, and Frank Lawrence, "Comparing Incarcerated and Community-Dwelling Older Men's Health," *Western Journal of Nursing Research* (2008): 30.

87. La. Rev. Stat. Ann. § 15:574.4(A)(2), www.legis.state.la.us/lss/lss.asp?doc= 79239&showback=.

88. S.C. Code Ann. § 55-7-21-24 (1976), www.scstatehouse.gov/sess118_2009-2010 /bills/1154.htm.

89. Anno et al., "Correctional Healthcare."

90. Forty-one states responded to the survey.

91. La. Rev. Stat. Ann. § 15:574.4(A)(2), www.legis.state.la.us/lss/lss.asp?doc= 79239&showback=.

92. Carson and Sabol, "Prisoners in 2011."

93. Ibid.

94. Pennsylvania Department of Corrections, "Elderly Inmate Profile," accessed October 18, 2009, www.portal.state.pa.us/portal/server.pt/gateway/ PTARGS_0_482992_0_0_18 /elderlyinmateprofile.pdf.

95. Charlotte A. Price, "Aging Inmate Population Study," North Carolina Department of Corrections, Division of Prisons, May 2006, www.ncdps.gov/div/adultcorrection /AgingStudyReport.pdf.

96. Lundstorm, "Dying to Get Out," 9.

97. Washington State Engrossed House Bill Report, HB 2194, An act relating to extraordinary medical placement for offenders (as reported by House Committee on Human Services and Ways & Means: requested by the Department of Corrections, 2009), http://apps.leg.wa .gov/documents/billdocs/2009–10/Pdf/Bill%20Reports/House/2194.E%20HBR%20PL%2009 .pdf (accessed December 28, 2009).

98. Ibid.

99. Multiple agency fiscal note summary, HB 2194, Washington State, March 11, 2009, https://fortress.wa.gov/ofm/fnspublic/ legsearch.asp?BillNumber=2194&SessionNumber=61.

100. Human Rights Watch and Families Against Mandatory Minimums, "The Answer Is No: Too Little Compassionate Release in US Federal Prisons" (2012), 16, www.hrw.org /sites/default/files/reports/us1112ForUploadSm.pdf.

101. 18 U.S.C. section 3582 (c)(1)(A)(i).

102. Chiu, "Prison Culture," 16.

103. Letter from Michael J. Elston, Senior Counsel to the Assistant Attorney General, Department of Justice, to Ricardo H. Hinojosa, Chair, U.S. Sentencing Commission (Elston Letter), July 14, 2006, 4. See appendix in Human Rights Watch and Families Against Mandatory Minimums, "The Answer Is No," for full text of letter.

104. U.S. Sentencing Commission, "Guidelines Manual," Section 1B1.13, November 1, 2006, www.ussc.gov/Guidelines/2006_guidelines/Manual/CHAP1.pdf (accessed March 19, 2013), 42. Section 1B1.13, subdivision (2), states that the court should only reduce a term of imprisonment if "the defendant is not a danger to the safety of any other person or to the community."

105. La. Rev. Stat. Ann. § 15:574.4(A)(2), 25.

106. U.S. Sentencing Commission, "2011 Federal Sentencing Guidelines Manual," Section 1B1.13, Application Note no. 1, www.ussc.gov/Guidelines/2011_Guidelines/Manual_HTML/1b1_13.htm (accessed March 19, 2013).

107. Chiu, "Prison Culture," 16.

108. Ibid., 19.

109. The pertinent part of 18 U.S.C. section 3553(a) reads:

Factors to Be Considered in Imposing a Sentence.—consider—

(1) the nature and circumstances of the offense and the history and characteristics of the defendant;

(2) the **need** for the sentence imposed—

- (A) to reflect the **seriousness** of the offense, to **promote respect** for the law, and to provide **just punishment** for the offense;

- (B) to afford adequate **deterrence** to criminal conduct;

- (C) to **protect the public** from further crimes of the defendant; and

- (D) to provide the defendant with needed educational or vocational training, medical care, or other **correctional treatment** in the most effective manner;

(3) the kinds of sentences available;

(4) the kinds of sentence and the sentencing range established for—(A) the applicable category of offense committed by the applicable category of defendant as set forth in the guidelines—

(5) any pertinent policy statement—

(6) the need to **avoid unwarranted sentence disparities** among defendants with similar records who have been found guilty of similar conduct; and

(7) the need to **provide restitution** to any victims of the offense.

110. Chiu, "Prison Culture," 2.

111. Ibid., 35.

112. Ibid., 2.

113. Ibid., 3.

114. La. Rev. Stat. Ann. § 15:574.4(A)(2), 4.

115. Ibid.

116. Ibid., 3.

117. Ibid., 8.

118. Ibid., 52.

119. Ibid., 6.

120. Ibid.

121. Ibid., citing Virginia Criminal Sentencing Commission, Virginia's Geriatric Release Provision (Virginia: VCSC 2008).

122. Ibid., citing Sherry Stevens, Deputy Director of the New Mexico Adult Parole Board, phone interview by Adrienne Austin, New York, NY, February 18, 2009.

123. Ibid., citing David Oldfield, Director of Research and Evaluation for the Missouri Department of Corrections, phone interview by Adrienne Austin, New York, NY, February 19, 2009.

124. "Report of the Advisory Committee on Geriatric and Seriously Ill Inmates," General Assembly of the Commonwealth of Pennsylvania, Joint State Government Commission, June 22, 2005, http://jsg.legis.state.pa.us/resources/documents/ftp/publications /2005-40-INMATES%20REPORT.pdf.

125. Lundstorm, "Dying to Get Out," 8.

126. Stephanie Chen, "Prison Health-Care Costs Rise as Inmates Grow Older and Sicker," CNN, November 13, 2009, www.cnn.com/2009/CRIME/11/13/aging.inmates/.

127. Va. Code Ann. § 53.1-40.01.

128. Lundstorm, "Dying to Get Out," 9, citing Dr. Rick Kern, Presentation to the Commonwealth of Virginia Senate Finance Committee, Virginia Criminal Sentencing Commission, Richmond.

129. Lundstorm, "Dying to Get Out," 10.

130. Ibid., 28.

131. Ibid.

132. La. Rev. Stat. Ann. § 15:574.4(A)(2), 29.

133. Carla Crowder, "Medical, Geriatric Paroles Weighed," *Birmingham News* (Birmingham, AL), January 10, 2004.

134. Markeshia Ricks, "It's Tough for Terminally Ill Inmates to Receive Medical Furloughs in Alabama," *Montgomery Adviser* (Montgomery, AL), August 23, 2009.

135. Lundstorm, "Dying to Get Out," citing Dee Wilson, Director of the Texas Correctional Office on Offenders with Medical or Mental Impairments, February 20, 2009, personal e-mail.

136. Lundstrom, "Dying to Get Out," citing Texas Board of Criminal Justice, Biennial Report of the Texas Correctional Office of Offenders with Medical and Mental Impairments (2007).

137. Elaine Crawley and Richard Sparks, "Is There Life after Imprisonment? How Elderly Men Talk about Imprisonment and Release," *Criminology and Criminal Justice* 6 (2006): 63–82, www.sagepub.com/prccj3/overviews/pdfs/Crawley.pdf.

138. Urban Institute, "Housing and Reentry", available at www.urban.org/projects /reentry-portfolio/housing.cfm.

139. Ibid.

140. Ibid.

141. Chiu, "Prison Culture"; see also Rosenberg, "Aging Inmates: A Convergence of Trends in the American Criminal Justice System," *Journal of Correctional Health Care* 13, no. 3 (2007): 150–62.

142. Muhammad, "Vindictive Justice," 80–81.

143. Steven J. Bahr, Lish Harris, James K. Fisher, and Anita Harker Armstrong, "Successful Reentry: What Differentiates Successful and Unsuccessful Parolees?," *International Journal of Offender Therapy and Comparative Criminology* 54 (October 2010): 667–92; see also Richard P. Seiter and Karen R. Kadela, "Prisoner Reentry: What Works, What Does Not, and What Is Promising," *Crime & Delinquency* 49 (2003): 360–88, www.caction.org /rrt_new/professionals/articles/SEITER-WHAT%20WORKS.pdf.

144. Sterns et al., "The Growing Wave of Older Prisoners," 112.

145. Heidi Strupp and Donna Willmott, "Dignity Denied: The Price of Imprisoning Older Women in California," Report, Legal Services for Prisoners with Children (2005), www.prisonerswithchildren.org/pubs/dignity.pdf.

146. Sarah E. Wakeman, Margaret E. McKinney, and Josiah D. Rich, "Filling the Gap: The Importance of Medicaid Continuity for Former Inmates," *Journal of General Internal Medicine* 24 (2009): 861, www.ncbi.nlm.nih.gov/pmc/articles/PMC2695526/.

147. John Kerbs, "The Older Prisoner: Social, Psychological, and Medical Considerations," in *Elders, Crime, and the Criminal Justice System: Myth, Perceptions, and Reality in the 21st Century*, ed. Max B. Rothman, Burton David Dunlop, and Pamela Entzel (New York: Springer, 2000), 207–28.

148. ACLU, "Mass Incarceration of the Elderly," 71.

149. Associated Press, "Aging Inmates Straining Prison Systems," *Daily Caller*, August 16, 2010, online at http://dailycaller.com/2010/08/16/aging-inmates-straining-prison-systems/.

150. Franklin Zimring, *Three Strikes and You're Out in California* (New York: Oxford University Press, 2001).

151. State of California Office of the Attorney General record, online at http://ag.ca.gov /cms_attachments/initiatives/pdfs/i1000_11–0057_(three_strikes).pdf (accessed January 9, 2013).

152. California Secretary of State records, online at www.sos.ca.gov/elections/sov /2012-general/06-sov-summary.pdf (accessed January 16, 2013).

153. An extensive list of endorsers of Proposition 36 can be found at www.fixthreestrikes. com/endorsements (accessed January 16, 2013).

154. California Secretary of State Official Voter Guide, at http://vote2004.sos.ca.gov /voterguide/propositions/prop66-title.htm (accessed January 17, 2013). An archived copy of the "Yes on 66" campaign is available at http://digital.library.ucla.edu/websites/2004_ 996_015/index.htm (accessed January 17, 2013).

155. Telephone interview with Pedro Rosado, Campaign Manager, January 16, 2013.

156. The Committee for Three Strikes Reform's platform can be found at www.fixthree-strikes.com/ (accessed January 16, 2013).

157. Stanford Law School Three Strikes Project, "Three Strikes Basics," accessed October 8, 2013, www.law.stanford.edu/node/149642.

158. Stanford Law School Three Strikes Project, "Success Stories," accessed October 8, 2013, www.law.stanford.edu/organizations/programs-and-centers/stanford-three-strikes-project/success-stories.

159. Emily Bazelon, "Arguing Three Strikes," *New York Times*, May 21, 2010, www .nytimes.com/2010/05/23/magazine/23strikes-t.html?hp=&pagewanted= print&_r=0.

160. Stanford Law School, Three Strikes Project, profile of Gregory Taylor (among others), accessed October 8, 2013, www.law.stanford.edu/organizations/programs-and-centers/stanford-three-strikes-project/success-stories.

161. Brent Staples, "California Horror Stories and the 3-Strikes Law," *New York Times*, November 24, 2012, www.nytimes.com/2012/11/25/opinion/sunday/california-horror-stories-and-the-3-strikes-law.html?ref=brentstaples&_r=0.

162. Interview with Pedro Rosado, Campaign Manager, "Yes on 36."

163. Ibid.

164. Committee for Three Strikes Reform, "Why We Won," accessed January 16, 2013, www.fixthreestrikes.com/.

165. Elsa Y. Chen, Editorial, "Prop. 36 Will Save Money and Increase Fairness," *Mercury News* (San Jose, CA), November 1, 2011, www.mercurynews.com/opinion/ci_21905517 /elsa-y-chen-prop-36-will-save-money. See also "Fair Penalties with Prop. 36," *Merced Sun-Star* (Merced, CA), October 12, 2012, www.mercedsunstar.com/2012/10/12/2587857/fair-penalties-with-prop-36.html; "Election: Yes on 36," *Press-Enterprise* (Riverside, CA), October 4, 2012, www.pe.com/opinion/editorials-headlines/20121004-election-yes-on-36.ece; Staff Writers, "Endorsements 2012: State Ballot Measures," *San Francisco Bay Guardian*, October 3, 2012, www.sfbg.com/2012/10/03/endorsements-2012-state-ballot-measures?page=0,3.

166. Legislative Analyst's Report, "Proposition 36: Three Strikes Law, Sentencing for Repeat Felony Offenders, Initiative Statute," July 18, 2012, www.lao.ca.gov/ballot/2012/36_11_2012.pdf.

167. Chen, "Prop. 36 Will Save Money and Increase Fairness."

168. "Editorial: State Ballot Measures," *Bay Area Reporter* (San Francisco), September 20, 2012, www.ebar.com/news/article.php?sec=news&article=68060.

169. "Big Changes for Crime, Punishment," *Lompoc Record* (Lompoc, CA), October 12, 2012, www.lompocrecord.com/news/opinion/editorial/big-changes-for-crime-punishment /article_1fe53398–1432–11e2-b8e3–0019bb2963f4.html.

170. "Election: Yes on 36," *Press-Enterprise* (Riverside, CA), October 4, 2012, www.pe .com/opinion/editorials-headlines/20121004-election-yes-on-36.ece.

171. "Endorsements: Yes on Prop. 36, a Modest Fix for Three-Strikes Law," *Sacramento Bee*, October 4, 2012, www.sacbee.com/2012/10/04/4880076/endorsements-yes-on-prop-36-a.html#storylink=misearch.

172. Marisa Lagos, "'3 Strikes': Proposed Law Tries to Restore Intent," *San Francisco Chronicle*, November 28, 2011, www.sfgate.com/politics/article/3-strikes-Proposed-law-tries-to-restore-intent-2296566.php#ixzz2Aivrdfrx.

173. "Editorial: Chronicle Recommends," *San Francisco Chronicle*, October 8, 2012, www.sfgate.com/default/article/Editorial-Chronicle-recommends-3923462.php.

174. Santa Cruz Sentinel Editorial Board, "Editorial: Yes on 36: Measure Would Modify Three Strikes Law While Still Protecting Public Safety," *Santa Cruz Sentinel*, October 2, 2012, www.santacruzsentinel.com/opinion/ci_21684514/editorial-yes-36-measure-would-modify-three-strikes.

175. Chen, "Prop. 36 Will Save Money and Increase Fairness."

176. "Editorial: Three Strikes Changes under Prop. 36 Needed," *Fresno Bee,* October 8, 2012, www.fresnobee.com/2012/10/07/3018954/editorial-prop-36-changes-needed.html.

177. Editorial, "Endorsement: Yes on Prop. 36—Make Three Strikes Better and Streets Safer with this Sensible Measure," *Los Angeles Daily News,* October 4, 2012, www.dailynews.com /opinions/ci_21701507/endorsement-yes-prop-36-make-three-strikes-better?IADID=Search-www.dailynews.com-www.dailynews.com; also published in *Long Beach Press-Telegram,* October 4, 2012, www.presstelegram.com/opinions/ci_21701507/endorsement-yes-prop-36-make-three-strikes-better.

178. "Endorsement: Yes on Proposition 36: In Reserving Harsh Penalties Only for Dangerous Felons, It Would Help Fix Flaws in the Three-Strikes Law," *Los Angeles Times,* | September 26, 2012, www.latimes.com/news/opinion/endorsements/la-ed-end-prop36–20120926,0,3913799.story.

179. Lisa E. Overton, Letter to the Editor, "Education Reform, Class Sizes, GOP and More," *San Diego Union-Tribune,* January 12, 2013, www.utsandiego.com/news/2013/jan/12 /education-reform/?page=2#article-copy.

180. *New York Times,* www.nytimes.com/2012/11/25/opinion/sunday/california-horror-stories-and-the-3-strikes-law.html?_r=0.

181. Editorial, "Endorsement: Yes on Prop. 36, an Improvement to Three Strikes," *San Bernardino Sun,* October 4, 2012, www.sbsun.com/editorial/ci_21701495/prop-36-is-an-improvement-three-strikes.

182. "Endorsement: Yes on Prop. 36—Make Three Strikes Better and Streets Safer with This Sensible Measure." *Los Angeles Daily News,* October 3, 2012, www.dailynews.com /opinion/20121004/endorsement-yes-on-prop-36-make-three-strikes-better-and-streets-safer-with-this-sensible-measure.

183. Editorial, "Endorsements: Yes on Prop 36, a Modest Fix for Three Strikes Law," *Sacramento Bee,* October 4, 2012, www.sacbee.com/2012/10/04/4880076/endorsements-yes-on-prop-36-a.html.

184. Editorial, "Editorial: Yes on Prop. 36, Revising '3 Strikes,'" *Orange County Register,* October 4, 2012, www.ocregister.com/opinion/prop-373656-strikes-third.html.

185. Editorial, "Endorsements," *Sacramento Bee.*

186. Lundstrom, "Dying to Get Out."

187. Sterns et al., "The Growing Wave of Older Prisoners."

188. Editorial, "Endorsements," *Sacramento Bee.*

189. Ibid.

190. As of April 2009, inmates sentenced under the Three Strikes Law totaled 43,500, or approximately 25 percent of the total inmate population in California institutions. California State Auditor, "California Department of Corrections and Rehabilitation: Inmates Sentenced under the Three Strikes Law and a Small Number of Inmates Receiving Specialty Health Care Represent Significant Costs," Report, May 2010, 2009–107.1, p. 2.

191. Ibid.

192. Ibid., fig. 3.

193. Ibid., 37.

194. Ibid., 38; also see fig. 5, p. 39.

195. Ibid., 38.

196. The largest age group of striker inmates ranges between the ages of 40 and 44, while the range for the largest age group of nonstrikers is 25 to 29. Ibid., 39.

197. Ibid., 4.

198. Ibid.

199. Ibid., 5.

200. Legislative Analyst's Office, "Proposition 36, Three Strikes Law. Sentencing for Repeat Felony Offenders. Initiative Statute," online at www.lao.ca.gov/ballot/2012/36_11_2012.aspx.

201. Ibid.

202. Secretary of State, Official Voter Information Guide, "Proposition 36 Arguments and Rebuttals," http://vig.cdn.sos.ca.gov/2012/general/pdf/36-arg-rebuttals.pdf; see also "Official Summary," http://vig.cdn.sos.ca.gov/2012/general/pdf/36-title-summ-analysis.pdf.

203. Kirsten Livingston, "Making the Bad Guy Pay: Growing Use of Cost Shifting as an Economic Sanction," in *Prison Profiteers: Who Makes Money from Mass Incarceration*, ed. Tara Herivel and Paul Wright (New York: New Press, 2009).

204. Jennifer Medina, "In California, a Plan to Charge Inmates for Their Stay," *New York Times*, December 11, 2011, www.nytimes.com/2011/12/12/us/in-riverside-california-a-plan-to-charge-inmates.html?_r=1&adxnnl=1&src=ISMR_AP_LI_LST_FB&adxnnlx=1378062950-u2fNHQbzYxIpZoxQyE/nfA.

205. Laurie L. Levenson and Mary Gordon, "The Dirty Little Secrets about Pay-to-Stay," *Michigan Law Review First Impressions* 106 (2007): 67–70.

206. Paul Walters and Russell Davis, "Government Entrepreneurship: How COP, Direct Supervision, and a Business Plan Helped Solve Santa Ana's Crime Problems," *Michigan Law Review First Impressions* 106 (2007): 71–75.

207. Robert Weisberg, "Pay-to-Stay in California Jails and the Value of Systemic Self-Embarrassment, First Impressions," *Michigan Law Review* 106 (2007): 55–59, www.michiganlawreview.org/articles/pay-to-stay-in-california-jails-and-the-value-of-systemic-self-embarassment.

208. Tillman v. Lebanon Correctional Facility, 221 F.3d 410 (3d Cir. 2000) (arguing excessive fines, cruel and unusual punishment, and even equal protection, as another inmate was not saddled with his incarceration costs). Among the advocates using an ex post facto argument, which was not raised in Tillman, is Joshua Michtom, "Making Inmates Pay for Their Stay: How a Popular Correctional Program Violates the Ex Post Facto Clause," *Public Interest Law Journal* 13 (2004): 187, www.bu.edu/law/central/jd/organizations/journals/pilj/vol13no2/documents/13-2MichtomNote.pdf.

209. Lauren Brooke-Eisen, "Tennessee Inmates Must Pay to Stay," *Brennan Center for Justice Blog*, August 28, 2013, www.brennancenter.org/blog/tennessee-inmates-pay-stay.

210. "California Prison's 'Pay-To-Stay' Option Offers 'Quieter' Rooms for $155 a Day," *Huffington Post*, July 28, 2013, www.huffingtonpost.com/2013/07/28/california-prison-pay-to-stay_n_3667573.html.

211. Kim Buchanan, "It Could Happen to 'You': Pay-to-Stay Jail Upgrades," *Michigan Law Review First Impressions* 106 (2007): 60–66.

212. Shawn Chapman Holley, "Why the County Jail Is Often a Better Choice," *Michigan Law Review First Impressions* 106 (2007): 76–78.

213. Buchanan, "It Could Happen to 'You.'"

214. O. Henry, "The Cop and the Anthem," in *The Gift of the Magi and Other Short Stories* (New York: Dover Thrift Editions, 1992), 5–10.

215. Deanne Katz, "Ex-Con Shoplifts to Get Free Health Care in Prison," *Legally Weird* (blog), *FindLaw,* December 12, 2012, http://blogs.findlaw.com/legally_weird/2012/12 /ex-con-shoplifts-to-get-free-health-care-in-prison.html?DCMP=NWL-pro_top.

216. www.reuters.com/article/2013/01/29/us-usa-crime-sexchange-idUSBRE90S03X 20130129.

217. Review by Dylan D., February 13, 2013, www.yelp.com/biz/san-quentin-state-prison-san-quentin.

218. Buchanan, "It Could Happen to 'You.'"

219. Review by Long T., August 22, 2012, www.yelp.com/biz/l-a-county-jail-los-angeles-2?hrid=uJAUUPp_G5q6it3CCXD5MA.

220. Levenson and Gordon, "Dirty Little Secrets about Pay-to-Stay."

CHAPTER 8

1. Linda Levine, Cong. Research Serv., 7–5700, Economic Growth and the Unemployment Rate (January 7, 2013), www.fas.org/sgp/crs/misc/R42063.pdf. The correlation between unemployment and economic downturn is strong, albeit not perfect. In most postwar recessions, it takes at least eight months for the unemployment rate to fall by one full percentage point. The 2007–9 recession was no different: the speed of economic improvement was more typical of the so-called jobless recoveries in prior recessions.

2. David F. Greenberg and Valerie West, "State Prison Populations and Their Growth, 1971–1991," *Criminology* 39, no. 3 (August 2001): 615–54.

3. Peter K. Enns, "The Public's Increasing Punitiveness and Its Influence on Mass Incarceration in the United States" (Paper presented at the Annual Meeting of the American Political Science Association, Washington, DC, September 2–5, 2010), http://ssrn.com /abstract=1642977.

4. Andrew Von Hirsch, Committee for the Study of Incarceration, *Doing Justice: The Choice of Punishments* (New York: Hill and Wang, 1976).

5. Helmut Kury and Theodore Ferdinand, "Public Opinion and Punitivity," *International Journal of Law and Psychiatry* 22, nos. 3–4 (May–August 1999): 373–92, 379, doi:10.1016/S0160-2527(99)00016-3.

6. Francis T. Cullen, Bonnie S. Fisher, and Brandon K. Applegate, "Public Opinion about Punishment and Corrections," *Crime and Justice* 27 (2000): 1–79, http://scholarcommons.sc.edu/cgi/viewcontent.cgi?article=1011&context=crim_facpub.

7. William Samuel and Elizabeth Moulds, "The Effect of Crime Severity on Perceptions of Fair Punishment: A California Case Study," *Journal of Criminal Law and Criminology* 77, no. 3 (Autumn 1986): 931–48, www.jstor.org/stable/1143444.

8. Douglas R. Thomson and Anthony J. Ragona, "Popular Moderation versus Government Authoritarianism: An Interactionist View of Public Sentiments toward Crime Sanctions," *Crime and Delinquency* 33, no. 3 (July 1987): 337–57, doi:10.1177/0011128787033003002.

9. Francis T. Cullen, Jennifer A. Pealer, Bonnie S. Fisher, Brandon K. Applegate, and Shannon A. Santana, "Public Support for Correctional Rehabilitation in America:

Change or Consistency?," in *Changing Attitudes to Punishment: Public Opinion, Crime and Justice,* ed. Julian V. Roberts and J. Michael Hough (Portland, OR: Willan Publishing, 2002), 128–47.

10. Christopher A. Innes, "Recent Public Opinion in the United States toward Punishment and Corrections," *Prison Journal* 73, no. 2 (June 1993): 220–36, doi:10.1177/0032855593073002006.

11. Ibid., 227.

12. John Doble, "Attitudes to Punishment in the US—Punitive and Liberal Opinions," in Roberts and Hough, *Changing Attitudes to Punishment,* 148–62.

13. Jody L. Sundt, "Is There Room for Change? A Review of Public Attitudes toward Crime Control and Alternatives to Incarceration," *Southern Illinois University Law Journal* 23, no. 4 (Winter 1989): 519–37.

14. Brandon K. Applegate, Francis T. Cullen, Michael G. Turner, and Jody L.Sundt, "Assessing Public Support for Three-Strikes-and-You're-Out Laws: Global vs. Specific Attitudes," *Crime & Delinquency* 42, no. 4 (October 1996) 517–34.

15. Julian V. Roberts, "Public Opinion, Crime, and Criminal Justice," *Crime and Justice* 16 (1992): 99–180, www.jstor.org/stable/1147562.

16. Ibid., 110.

17. Catriona Mirrlees-Black, "Improving Public Knowledge about Crime and Punishment," in Roberts and Hough, *Changing Attitudes to Punishment,* 184–97.

18. Darrin L. Rogers, "Structural Analysis of Treatment and Punishment Attitudes toward Offenders" (PhD diss., Ohio State University, 2005), http://rave.ohiolink.edu/etdc/view?acc_num=osu1121749945.

19. Jane B. Sprott, "Are Members of the Public Tough on Crime? The Dimensions of Public 'Punitiveness,'" *Journal of Criminal Justice* 27, no. 5 (September–October 1999): 467–74, http://dx.doi.org/10.1016/S0047-2352(99)00017-3.

20. Michael Tonry and Kathleen Hatlestad, eds., *Sentencing Reform in Overcrowded Times: A Comparative Perspective* (New York: Oxford University Press, 1997).

21. Georg Rusche and Otto Kirchheimer, *Punishment and Social Structure* (New York: Columbia University Press, 1939).

22. David Garland, *The Culture of Control: Crime and Social Order in Contemporary Society,* paperback ed. (2001; repr., Chicago: University of Chicago Press, 2002), 148.

23. David F. Greenberg, "Punishment, Division of Labor, and Social Solidarity," in *The Criminology of Criminal Law: Advances in Criminological Theory,* vol. 8, ed. William S. Laufer and Freda Adler (New Brunswick, NJ: Transaction Press, 1999), 283–362, 334.

24. Lynn Chancer and Pamela Donovan, "A Mass Psychology of Punishment: Crime and the Futility of Rationally Based Approaches," *Social Justice* 21 (1996): 50–72.

25. Michael J. Hogan, Ted Chiricos, and Marc Gertz, "Economic Insecurity, Blame, and Punitive Attitudes," *Justice Quarterly* 22, no. 3 (2005): 392–412, doi:10.1080/07418820500219144.

26. Michael T. Costelloe, Ted Chiricos, and Marc Gertz, "Punitive Attitudes toward Criminals: Exploring the Relevance of Crime Salience and Economic Insecurity," *Punishment and Society* 11, no. 1 (January 2009): 25–49, doi:10.1177/1462474508098131.

27. Tom R. Tyler and Robert J. Boeckmann, "Three Strikes and You Are Out, but Why? The Psychology of Public Support for Punishing Rule Breakers," *Law and Society Review* 31, no. 2 (1997): 237–66, www.jstor.org/stable/3053926.

28. Arthur L. Stinchcombe et al., *Crime and Punishment—Changing Attitudes in America* (San Francisco: Jossey-Bass, 1980).

29. Mark A. Cohen, Roland T. Rust, and Sara Steen, *Measuring Public Perceptions of Appropriate Prison Sentences, Final Report, Document No. 199365*, Report submitted to the National Institute of Justice, April 2003, www.nicic.org/Library/020047.

30. Peter D. Hart Research Associates, Inc., *Changing Public Attitudes toward the Criminal Justice System: Summary of Findings*, Report prepared for the Open Society Institute, submitted February 2002 (New York: Open Society Foundations, 2002), www.opensocietyfoundations.org/reports/changing-public-attitudes-toward-criminal-justice-system.

31. Vincent Schiraldi and Judith Greene, "Reducing Correctional Costs in an Era of Tightening Budgets and Shifting Public Opinion," in *Federal Sentencing Reporter* 14, no. 6, *Recent State Reforms I: Developments in Sentencing Drug Offenders* (May–June 2002): 332–36, www.jstor.org/stable/10.1525/fsr.2002.14.6.332.

32. David T. Johnson and Franklin E. Zimring, *The Next Frontier: National Development, Political Change, and the Death Penalty in Asia* (New York: Oxford University Press, 2009), doi:10.1093/acprof:oso/9780195337402.001.0001.

33. The original phrase was used by Justice Harry Blackmun in Callins v. Collins, 510 U.S. 1141 (1994). A good example is U.S. District Court Judge Cormac Carney's recent decision, according to which the death penalty in California is unconstitutional due to the delays and uncertainty in inflicting it, which according to Judge Carney cannot be cured by streamlining the process. Jones v. Chappell (2014), Dist. Court, CD California.

34. Frank Newport, "Record-High 50% of Americans Favor Legalizing Marijuana Use: Liberals and Those 18 to 29 Most in Favor; Americans 65 and Older Most Opposed," *Gallup News*, October 17, 2011, www.gallup.com/poll/150149/record-high-americans-favor-legalizing-marijuana.aspx.

35. Bernard E. Harcourt, "The Collapse of the Harm Principle," *Journal of Criminal Law and Criminology* 90, no. 1 (Autumn 1999): 109–94, www.jstor.org/stable/1144164.

36. Paige St. John, "Lawmakers Schedule One-Day Hearing on Solitary Confinement," *Los Angeles Times*, October 7, 2013, www.latimes.com/local/political/la-me-ff-solitary-20131007,0,7499923.story.

37. Stop Solitary Advocacy Campaign, *Recent State Reforms to Limit the Use of Solitary Confinement* (New York: American Civil Liberties Union, June 6, 2013), www.aclu.org/files/assets/state_reforms_to_limit_the_use_of_solitary_confinement.pdf.

38. Keramet A. Reiter, " Parole, Snitch, or Die: California's Supermax Prisons and Prisoners, 1997–2007," *Punishment and Society* 14, no. 5 (December 2012): 530–63, doi:10.1177/1462474512464007.

39. Ashley T. Rubin, "Violating the Pennsylvania System: An Organizational Framework" (Paper presented at the Conference for the American Society of Criminology, Chicago, IL, November 2012, and at the Conference for the Western Society of Criminology, Berkeley, CA, February 2013).

40. Jonathan Simon, "Fear of Crime," review of *Nixonland: The Rise of a President and the Fracturing of America,* by Rick Perlstein (New York: Scribner, 2008), *Governing through Crime* (blog), August 25, 2008, http://governingthroughcrime.blogspot.com/2008/08/fear-of-crime.html.

41. Nicole D. Porter, *On the Chopping Block 2012: State Prison Closings* (Washington, DC: Sentencing Project, December 2012), 5, http://sentencingproject.org/doc/publications /On%20the%20Chopping%20Block%202012.pdf.

42. Granted, the legalization of various substances and the abolition of various penalties are not simply "yes or no" questions. Any such policy change would require considerable regulation to take effect. However, discussion of these policy changes would flow better from a "yes or no" determination of whether the current policy should stay in place.

43. Lon L. Fuller and Kenneth I. Winston, "The Forms and Limits of Adjudication," *Harvard Law Review* 92, no. 2 (December 1978): 353–409, www.jstor.org/stable/1340368.

44. For the effects of neopopulism on decision making in matters of punitiveness, see Vanessa Barker, *The Politics of Imprisonment: How the Democratic Process Shapes the Way America Punishes Offenders* (New York: Oxford University Press, 2009), doi:10.1093 /acprof:oso/9780195370027.001.0001.

45. Adam Nossiter, "As His Inmates Grew Thinner, a Sheriff's Wallet Grew Fatter," *New York Times,* January 8, 2009, www.nytimes.com/2009/01/09/us/09sheriff.html?emc= eta1&_r=0.

46. See Brown v. Plata, 131 S. Ct. 1910 (2011). *Plata v. Schwarzenegger* was a class action civil rights lawsuit filed on April 5, 2001, docket no. 3:01-cv-01351-TEH (N.D. Cal.), alleging that the California Department of Corrections and Rehabilitation provided such inadequate medical care that the conditions of confinement constituted cruel and unusual punishment under the Eighth Amendment. The parties stipulated to injunctive relief, which the United States Court for the Northern District of California ordered on June 13, 2002, requiring defendants to provide "only the minimum level of medical care required under the Eighth Amendment." On October 3, 2005, the District Court issued an order appointing a federal receiver to oversee the California Department of Corrections and Rehabilitation's medical care program and enforce its compliance with the stipulated order. After the federal receiver ordered California to reduce prison overcrowding, the state appealed. The court consolidated *Plata* with Coleman v. Schwarzenegger, docket no. 2:90-cv-00520-LKK-JFM (E.D. Cal.), on July 26, 2007, a class action lawsuit alleging unconstitutionally deficient mental health care in California's prisons. The Ninth Circuit Court of Appeals upheld the federal receiver's order in Plata v. Schwarzenegger, 603 F. 3d 1088 (9th Cir. 2010), *affirmed by* Brown v. Plata, 131 S. Ct. 1910 (2011).

47. Brown v. Plata, 131 S. Ct. 1910 (2011).

48. Margo Schlanger, "*Plata v. Brown* and Realignment: Jails, Prisons, Courts, and Politics," *Harvard Civil Rights–Civil Liberties Law Review* 48, no. 1 (2013): 165–215, http:// harvardcrcl.org/wp-content/uploads/2013/04/Schlanger_165–215.pdf.

49. "California Criminal Justice FAQ: How Much Does It Cost to Incarcerate An Inmate? California's Annual Costs to Incarcerate an Inmate in Prison, 2008–2009," California Legislative Analyst's Office, accessed October 22, 2013, www.lao.ca.gov/laoapp /laomenus/sections/crim_justice/6_cj_inmatecost.aspx?catid=3.

50. Wyatt Buchanan, "Governor Looks South of the Border for Prisons," *San Francisco Chronicle,* January 26, 2010, www.sfgate.com/news/article/Governor-looks-south-of-the-border-for-prisons-3274745.php.

51. John Diaz, "Have the Governor's Senses Headed South?," *San Francisco Chronicle,* January 27, 2010, www.sfgate.com/opinion/article/Have-the-governor-s-senses-headed-south-3274710.php.

52. Molly Hennessy-Fiske and Richard Winton, "Bid to Divert California Prisoners to County Jails Denounced," *Los Angeles Times,* May 23, 2009, http://articles.latimes .com/2009/may/23/local/me-jails23.

53. Michael Rothfeld, "Vote on Prison Plan in California Budget Is Delayed," *Los Angeles Times,* July 23, 2009, www.latimes.com/news/local/la-me-budget23–2009jul23,0,7093912. story.

54. Matthew Yi and Wyatt Buchanan, "Plan to Free State Prison Inmates Moves Ahead," *San Francisco Chronicle,* August 21, 2009, www.sfgate.com/news/article/Plan-to-free-state-prison-inmates-moves-ahead-3219630.php.

55. Matthew Yi, "Prison Bill Gutted by State Assembly," *San Francisco Chronicle,* August 28, 2009, www.sfgate.com/bayarea/article/Prison-bill-gutted-by-state-Assembly-3288123 .php.

56. Schlanger, "*Plata v. Brown* and Realignment," 165–215.

57. Tim Stelloh, "California's Great Prison Experiment," *The Nation,* June 5, 2013 (June 24–July 1, 2013), www.thenation.com/article/174680/californias-great-prison-experiment# axzz2dH8EZ69x.

58. Jeffrey D. Straussman, "Courts and Public Purse Strings: Have Portraits of Budgeting Missed Something?," *Public Administration Review* 46, no. 4 (July–August 1986): 345–51.

59. Richard T. Boylan and Naci H. Mocan, "Intended and Unintended Consequences of Prison Reform" (Working Paper No. 15535, National Bureau of Economic Research, Cambridge, MA, November 2009, presented at the Fourth Annual Conference on Empirical Legal Studies, University of Southern California, Los Angeles, November 20–21, 2009), www.nber.org/papers/w15535.

60. Don Thompson, Associated Press, "California Governor Proposes $315M Prison Fix," *Yahoo News,* August 27, 2013, http://news.yahoo.com/california-governor-proposes-315m-prison-fix-212715959.html.

61. Patrick McGreevy, "Gov. Jerry Brown's Prison Plan Clears Assembly Committee," *Los Angeles Times,* August 29, 2013.

62. Sam Stanton and Denny Walsh, "California Wins Two-Year Extension in Fight over Inmate Releases," *Sacramento Bee,* February 10, 2014, www.sacbee.com/2014/02/10/6144537 /california-wins-two-year-extension.html.

63. *The House I Live In,* documentary film, directed by Eugene Jarecki (Charlotte Street Films, New York, 2012), www.thehouseilivein.org/.

64. Jonathan Simon, *Mass Incarceration on Trial: A Remarkable Court Decision and the Future of Prisons in America* (New York: New Press, 2014).

65. Stephen B. Bright, "Discrimination, Death, and Denial: The Tolerance of Racial Discrimination in Infliction of the Death Penalty," *Santa Clara Law Review* 35, no. 2 (1994–95): 433–84, http://digitalcommons.law.scu.edu/lawreview/vol35/iss2/3/.

66. Kim Phillips-Fein, *Invisible Hands: The Businessmen's Crusade against the New Deal* (New York: Norton, 2009).

67. Jennifer Burns, "Godless Capitalism: Ayn Rand and the Conservative Movement," in *American Capitalism: Social Thought and Political Economy in the Twentieth Century,* ed. Nelson Lichtenstein (Philadelphia: University of Pennsylvania Press, 2006), 271–89; also published in *Modern Intellectual History* 1, no. 3 (November 2004): 359–85, doi:10.1017 /S1479244304000216.

68. Alice O'Connor, "The Politics of Rich and Rich: Postwar Investigations of Foundations and the Rise of the Philanthropic Right," in Lichtenstein, *American Capitalism*, 228–48.

69. For a discussion of this political influence on public discourse within the legal community, see Steven M. Teles, *The Rise of the Conservative Legal Movement: The Battle for Control of the Law* (Princeton: Princeton University Press, 2008).

70. David Montgomery, *The Fall of the House of Labor* (Cambridge: Cambridge University Press, 1987).

71. Mike Davis, *Prisoners of the American Dream: Politics and Economy in the History of the US Working Class*, ill. repr. ed. (London: Verso, 1986).

72. Alan Brinkley, *The End of Reform: New Deal Liberalism in Recession and War* (New York: Knopf, 1995). See also Ira Katznelson, *Fear Itself: The New Deal and the Origins of Our Time* (New York: Norton, Liveright Imprint, 2013).

73. Catherine R. Albiston and Laura Beth Nielsen, "Welfare Queens and Other Fairy Tales: Welfare Reform and Unconstitutional Reproductive Controls," *Howard Law Journal* 38 no. 3 (1994–95): 473–520, http://scholarship.law.berkeley.edu/facpubs/892.

74. Teddy Ky-Nam Miller, "The Unmet Promises of Care not Cash," *Hastings Race and Poverty Law Journal* 5, no. 1 (Winter 2008): 171–94.

75. Jeffrey Selbin et al., "Does Sit-Lie Work: Will Berkeley's 'Measure S' Increase Economic Activity and Improve Services to Homeless People?" (Working Paper, Policy Advocacy Clinic, University of California, Berkeley, School of Law, October 22, 2012), http://dx.doi.org/10.2139/ssrn.2165490.

76. Kelly D. Brownell et al., "The Public Health and Economic Benefits of Taxing Sugar-Sweetened Beverages," *New England Journal of Medicine* 361 (October 15, 2009): 1599–1605, doi:10.1056/NEJMhpr0905723.

77. Daniel T. Rodgers, *Age of Fracture* (Cambridge, MA: Belknap Press, 2011).

78. Jennifer Steinhauer, "Schwarzenegger Seeks Shift from Prisons to Schools," *New York Times*, January 6, 2010, www.nytimes.com/2010/01/07/us/07calif.html.

79. Garrick Byers, *Realignment*, rev. ed. (Oakland: Continuing Education of the Bar, California, December 3, 2011), 11. "Non-Non-Non" refers to nonserious, nonviolent offenses that do not require registration as sex offenses.

80. Kamala D. Harris, *Smart on Crime* (San Francisco: Chronicle Books, 2009).

81. Gerald F. Seib, "In Crisis, Opportunity for Obama," *Wall Street Journal Capital Journal*, November 20, 2008 (updated November 21, 2008), http://online.wsj.com/article/SB122721278056345271.html.

INDEX

The letter f *following a page number denotes a figure. The letter* t *following a page number denotes a table.*

ABC poll, 154

Abt Associates, 108

Abu Jamal, Mumia, 64

ACLU (American Civil Liberties Union), 89–90, 94, 110, 162; in California, 89; and elderly /infirm prisoners, 124–25; in Washington State, 90, 94

activism, political, 34–35, 36; drug war protesters, 56; inmates' rights organizations, 12, 31, 85, 86–87, 128, 161; and marijuana legalization, 85, 86–87, 92, 96; and solitary confinement, 161. *See also* death penalty abolition campaigns

actuarial justice, 57, 119, 121. *See also* risk management

Adam Walsh Child Protection and Safety Act (2006), 42

Addison, Michael, 71

affirmative action, 156

African Americans: and cocaine, 16; and death penalty, 61, 63–64; elderly/infirm prisoners as, 142–43, 212n22; and financial crisis (2008), 51; Holder as, 82; incarceration rate of, 43, 212n22; political activism of, 34–35; poor black women, 167; and prison labor, 31, 178n22, 178n24; in San Francisco, 51; young men, 43. *See also* people of color; racial justice/injustice

Agecroft Prison Management, 104

Age of Fracture (Rodgers), 168

Alabama, 108, 121, 154; Board of Pardons and Paroles, 136; Department of Corrections, 136; and elderly/infirm prisoners, 121, 129, 136, 164; Judicial Correction Services (JCS), 108

Alaska, 99, 110, 113–14; constitution of, 114

Alcatraz Prison, 1–3, 9; escapes from, 2

alcohol: and detection ignition locks in cars, 110; manufacturing/sales of, 28–29; marijuana legalization compared to, 89, 92–93, 160; taxes on, 28–29, 160; treatment programs for, 157. *See also* Prohibition

Aldworth, Betty, 93

ALEC. *See* American Legislative Exchange Council (ALEC)

Alexander, Michelle, 12, 178n22

Amatrudo, Anthony, 19–20

Amendment 64 (Colo.), 92–94, 200n117

America for Safe Access (Calif.), 202n151

American dream, 19

American Friends Service Committee, 37–38

American Legislative Exchange Council (ALEC), 105

American Medical Association, 68

American Recovery and Reinvestment Act (ARRA, 2009), 53

American Revolution, 60, 187n14

Lee, Richard, 88, 95
Lee, Sheila Jackson, 82
leftist politicians, 84–85, 87, 167–68. *See also*
  progressives
Legal Services for Prisoners with Children
  (Calif.), 166
legislatures/legislators. *See* politics/politicians
Leno, Mark, 74
Leon, Chrysanthi, 42, 121–22
lethal injection practices, 61, 66–69; and sodium
  thiopental, 66–68
Lewis, Michael, 52
libertarians, 6, 12, 22, 85, 88; and humonetarianism, 56, 167, 170
Lipton, Doug, 36
liquor. *See* alcohol
Livingston, Kirsten, 144–45
lobbying/lobbyists, 49, 79, 105–7, 206n36
local correctional policies, 3, 6, 7, 25, 26–27,
  30–33; and elderly/infirm prisoners, 144; and
  humonetarianism, 56, 150–51, 157–58, 162,
  164–65, 169–170; and jurisdictional shifts in
  incarceration, 116–19, 164–65; and jury trials,
  32; and Kennedy administration, 33; and
  marijuana legalization, 88–91, 93, 96–97; and
  pay-to-stay policies, 144–48, 165, 221n208;
  and prison construction, 12, 44–46, 54; and
  prisoners as consumers, 144–48, 221n208;
  and prison labor, 30–31; and private prison
  industries, 7, 86, 91, 101, 107–8, 151; and
  Prohibition, 28; and punitivism, 12, 20, 27,
  44, 150–51, 157–58; and work-release, 145–46.
  See also county correctional policies;
  municipalities
local governments: and bonds, 45–47, 52; and
  budgets, 3, 6, 33, 43–45, 49, 54–55, 157–58;
  and federal funding, 27, 43, 157–58; and
  financial crisis (2008), 6, 48–55. *See also* local
  correctional policies
Lochner, 30
Los Angeles County (Calif.), 117, 148
Louisiana: and elderly/infirm prisoners, 129, 131,
  213n35; and prison closures, 111, 112t; and
  private prison industries, 107, 207n48
lower classes. *See* underclass
low-level offenders. *See* nonviolent offenders
Lynch, Mona, 12, 27, 30
lynchings, 64

Magritte, René, 152
Maine, 132; Department of Corrections, 132
Making Crime Pay (Beckett), 12, 20, 33

Management and Training Corporation, 106
managerialism, 121
Mandigo, Charles, 91
Mansfield University survey, 135
Mapp v. Ohio, 31
marijuana legalization, 4, 7, 16, 56, 78–79, 87,
  88–97; ads for, 78–79, 91, 92–93; in California,
  88–90, 94–95, 97, 138, 202n151; and Cole
  memo, 96; in Colorado, 7, 88, 90, 92–97, 110,
  172n17, 200n117; costs of, 78–79, 85, 88–94,
  96–97, 160; and DUI standard for active
  THC, 90, 92; and federal drug laws, 79, 89,
  92, 94–97; and humonetarianism, 7, 79,
  88–94, 97, 98, 151, 163; irreversibility of, 160;
  and job creation, 92–93, 96, 200n117; and
  licenses, 90; and medical marijuana, 88–89,
  92, 94–96, 160, 202n151; and minors, 78,
  90–93, 95, 97; and Obama administration, 7,
  79, 81–84, 94–97, 172n15, 202n151; and Ogden
  memo, 94–96, 202n151; and parents/children,
  78, 90–93, 95; public opinion concerning, 14,
  78, 160, 172n17; and recreational use, 4,
  172n17; and regulation, 78, 88–93, 96–97; and
  substance abuse treatment, 89, 91; and taxes/
  fees, 78, 88–90; underground market in, 93,
  96; in Washington State, 7, 78–79, 88, 90–92,
  93, 94–97, 110, 172n17
markets, financial, 7; and corporate profit
  motive, 108; "doing less with less," 97; doing
  "more with less," 152; emerging markets, 50;
  and financial crisis (2008), 49–50, 52; and
  free market ideology, 5, 6, 12–14; and humonetarianism, 151–52, 159, 163, 166–68; and logic
  of market, 7, 97, 152, 163, 167; market crash,
  51–52; and market share, 104; and monopoly,
  22; and prison construction, 45; and private
  prison industries, 101, 104, 108, 151, 204n15,
  205n16; and Prohibition, 29
Marling, Will, 135
Marshall, Thurgood, 187n7
Marshals Service (U.S.), 104
Martinez, Susana, 72
Martinson, Robert, 36–37
Marxism, 11, 15, 17, 173n31. *See also* sociohistori-
  cal studies
Maryland, 69, 72, 100, 130, 134, 203n5
Massachusetts, 69, 112
Mass Incarceration on Trial (Simon), 166
McCain, John, 82
McCarthy, Daniel, 18
McClesky v. Kemp, 63
McKay, John, 91